W9-CIC-096

FAMOUS AMERICAN CRIMES AND TRIALS

FAMOUS AMERICAN CRIMES AND TRIALS

Volume 5: 1981–2000

Edited by Frankie Y. Bailey
and Steven Chermak

Praeger Perspectives

Crime, Media, and Popular Culture

Westport, Connecticut
London

Library of Congress Cataloging-in-Publication Data

Bailey, Frankie Y.
 Famous American crimes and trials / Frankie Y. Bailey and Steven Chermak.
  p. cm.—(Crime, media, and popular culture, ISSN 1549-196X)
 Includes bibliographical references and index.
 Contents: Vol. 1. 1607–1859—v. 2. 1860–1912—v. 3. 1913–1959—v. 4. 1960–1980—
v. 5. 1981–2000.
 ISBN 0-275-98333-1 (set : alk. paper)—ISBN 0-275-98334-X (vol. 1 : alk. paper)—
ISBN 0-275-98335-8 (vol. 2 : alk. paper)—ISBN 0-275-98336-6 (vol. 3 : alk. paper)—
ISBN 0-275-98337-4 (vol. 4 : alk. paper)—ISBN 0-275-98338-2 (vol. 5 : alk. paper)
 1. Criminal justice, Administration of—United States—Case studies. 2. Criminal
justice, Administration of—United States—History. I. Chermak, Steven M. II. Title.
III. Series.
HV9950.B3 2004
364.973—dc22   2004050548

British Library Cataloguing in Publication Data is available.

Library of Congress Catalog Card Number: 2004050548
ISBN: 0-275-98333-1 (set)
      0-275-98334-X (vol. I)
      0-275-98335-8 (vol. II)
      0-275-98336-6 (vol. III)
      0-275-98337-4 (vol. IV)
      0-275-98338-2 (vol. V)
ISSN: 1549-196X

First published in 2004

Praeger Publishers, 88 Post Road West, Westport, CT 06881
An imprint of Greenwood Publishing Group, Inc.
www.praeger.com

Printed in the United States of America

The paper used in this book complies with the
Permanent Paper Standard issued by the National
Information Standards Organization (Z39.48-1984).

10 9 8 7 6 5 4 3 2 1

Contents

Set Foreword

Famous American Crimes and Trials covers over four centuries, from the colonial era to the end of the twentieth century, in five volumes. In each volume, we introduce the social and historical contexts in which the cases appearing in the volume occurred. We discuss the evolution of the criminal justice system and the legal issues that were dominant during that time period. We also provide an overview of the popular culture and mass media, examining in brief the nexus between news/entertainment and the criminal justice system. In each introduction, we also identify the common threads weaving through the cases in the volume.

Many of the cases featured in these five volumes provide examples of what Robert Hariman (1990) describes as "popular trials," or "trials that have provided the impetus and the forum for major public debates" (p. 1). As we note elsewhere, cases generally achieve celebrity status because they somehow encapsulate the tensions and the anxieties present in our society; or, at least, this has been the case until the recent past. In the last half-century, the increasing importance of television (and more recently the internet) in delivering the news to the public, and the voracious appetite of the media for news stories to feed the twenty-four-hour news cycle, has meant that stories—particularly crime stories—move quickly into, and sometimes as quickly out of, the public eye. So, as we address in volume 5, we now have a proliferation of crime stories that vie for the status of "famous." It remains to be seen whether these cases will have true "staying power" in the same sense as the cases that are still remembered today after many decades or centuries.

Oddly enough, some cases that were celebrated, though attracting a great deal of public attention when they occurred, have now disappeared from

American collective memory. Perhaps some of these cases for one reason or another only touched a public nerve at the time because they resonated with some passing interest or concern, or fit some media theme. Occasionally, such forgotten cases are rescued from the dustbins by a journalist, a true-crime writer, or a historian and undergo a new wave of public attention. That has happened with several of the cases that appear in these volumes. Perhaps the rediscovery of such cases reflects their relevance to current social issues; or perhaps these cases are interesting to modern readers because they are not only enthralling stories but because they occurred in the past and are now entertaining "period" pieces.

We think that the reader will agree that the cases included in these volumes are among the most important of each era. Since space was limited, many famous cases had to be excluded, but many of these have been covered in other books or media. The cases that are included cover each crime, the setting, and the participants; the actions taken by law enforcement and the criminal legal system; the actions of the media covering the case; the trial (if there was one); the final resolution of the case; the relevant social, political, and legal issues; and, finally, the significance of the case and its impact on legal and popular culture.

REFERENCE

Hariman, R. (1990). *Popular trials: Rhetoric, mass media, and the law*. Tuscaloosa, AL: University of Alabama Press.

Series Foreword

The pervasiveness of media in our lives and the salience of crime and criminal justice issues make it especially important to provide a home for scholars who are engaged in innovative and thoughtful research on important crime and mass media issues.

This series will focus on process issues (such as the social construction of crime and moral panics), presentation issues (such as images of victims, offenders, and criminal justice figures in news and popular culture), and effects (such as the influence of the media on criminal behavior and criminal justice administration).

With regard to this latter issue—effects of media/popular culture—as this foreword was being written the *Los Angeles Times* and other media outlets reported that two young half-brothers (ages 20 and 15) in Riverside, California, had confessed to strangling their mother and disposing of her body in a ravine. The story was attracting particular attention because the brothers told police they had gotten the idea of cutting off her head and hands to prevent identification from a recent episode of the award-winning HBO series, *The Sopranos*. As the *Los Angeles Times* noted, this again brought into the spotlight the debate about the influence of violent media such as *The Sopranos*, about New Jersey mobsters, on susceptible consumers.

In this series, scholars engaged in research on issues that examine the complex nature of our relationship with media. Peter Berger and Thomas Luckman coined the phrase the "social construction of reality" to describe the process by which we acquire knowledge about our environment. They and others have argued that reality is a mediated experience. We acquire what Emile Durkheim described as "social facts" through a several-prolonged process of personal experience, interaction with others, academic education, and, yes, the mass media. With regard to crime and the criminal justice system, many people acquire much of their information from the news and from entertainment media. The issue raised by the report above and other anecdotal stories of "copy cat" crime is how what we consume—read, watch, see, play, hear—affects us.

What we do know is that we experience this mediated reality as individuals. We are all not affected in the same way by our interactions with mass media. Each of us engages in interactions with mass media/popular culture that are shaped by factors such as social environment, interests, needs, and opportunities for exposure. We do not come to the experience of mass media/popular culture as blank slates waiting to be written upon or voids waiting to be filled. It is the pervasiveness of mass media/popular culture and the varied backgrounds (including differences in age, gender, race/ethnicity, religion, etc.) that we bring to our interactions with media that make this a particularly intriguing area of research.

Moreover, it is the role of mass media in creating the much discussed "global village" of the twenty-first century that is also fertile ground for research. We exist not only in our communities, our cities, and states, but in a world that spreads beyond national boundaries. Technology has made us a part of an ongoing global discourse about issues not only of criminal justice but of social justice. Technology takes us to events around the world "as they happen." It was technology that allowed Americans around the world to witness the collapse of the World Trade Center's Twin Towers on September 11, 2001. In the aftermath of this "crime against humanity," we have been witnesses to and participants in an ongoing discussion about the nature of terrorism and the appropriate response to such violence.

Frankie Y. Bailey and Steven Chermak
Series Editors

Acknowledgments

We would like to thank the contributors who worked so hard on the individual chapters. The contributors are a very diverse group, but they all share a passion for the cases they tackled. We appreciate their hard work and their willingness to quickly respond to our suggestions for revision. Many of the contributors have published frequently about a case, but they took the approach we requested in these chapters to offer fresh insights into their work. Other contributors had not written specifically about a case but answered our solicitation because they were curious about it. Our thanks to all of them for producing very insightful and entertaining accounts of the most important cases and trials that have occurred throughout the history of the United States.

The staff at Greenwood Publishing contributed significantly to bringing this project to publication. We are especially grateful to Suzanne Staszak-Silva, Senior Editor at Greenwood, for encouraging us to work on this five-volume set. We considered several different ways to approach the organization of the five volumes, and we appreciate her insights and suggestions for organizing the work by historical era. We were both skeptical about being able to cover so many different cases in such a short amount of time, but her energy was contagious and she was able to convince us of the great potential for such a large project. Mariah Krok was the Developmental Editor for the volumes, and we would like to thank her for being such an effective liaison between the contributors and us. We were able to avoid the many problems that can arise from a project with so many different contributors because of her ability to keep us organized. Thanks to Dan Harmon for tackling the very arduous task of tracking down illustrations and seeking permissions.

The staff at Capital City Press was terrific to work with: special thanks to Bridget Wiedl.

Steve's wife was incredibly supportive and interested in the work of this project. Alisha and I welcomed Mitchell into our family during this project. Thanks to him for deciding to sleep through the night on occasion—this is when most of the work got done.

Frankie Y. Bailey and Steven Chermak

Introduction

Steven Chermak and Frankie Y. Bailey

Less than two months after the shooting spree that occurred in Littleton, Colorado, construction workers began renovating Columbine High School. One goal of the renovation was to erase the memory of the events of April 20, 1999—the day Eric Harris and Dylan Klebold entered the school with a large arsenal of weapons and homemade bombs and systematically set out to kill as many of their classmates and teachers as possible. Harris and Klebold were, unfortunately, successful; they killed twelve students and one teacher and wounded twenty-three other students.

The impact that the shooting at Columbine High School had on the United States was substantial. There was a general outpouring of support, prayers, letters, and donations to the people of Littleton. For example, over $2 million was donated to assist the victims and surviving family members. The public feared that the incident at Columbine was not an isolated event—schools would now be considered dangerous places, and administrators and legislators had to take quick action. They responded in different ways. Many school districts had symposiums, and national experts on violence and violence prevention were invited to discuss school safety issues. Some schools locked down their hallways: students could only enter and leave from a secure door that was manned by security guards and metal detectors. The punishment for brandishing any type of weapon increased substantially. Students practiced drop-and-roll drills, and administrators made changes to dress codes and advised students to carry their books in bags with the contents clearly visible.

The construction workers had a difficult job. They had to repair nearly 25,000 square feet that was damaged in the attack, and they had to cover, fill, or remove over 1,000 bullet holes left at the crime scene (CNN, 1999a; CNN, 1999b). Rooms were remodeled, new carpet was installed, the walls were given a fresh coat of paint, and the school purchased new furniture. School administrators were quick to note that the school was adding surveillance cameras and adopting a wide range of other security devices. The school also installed fire alarms that would emit a calmer tone to minimize the "psychological impact" on the students (CNN, 1999a). The construction efforts signified an important step toward overcoming the pain and suffering caused by this tragedy.

The shooting at Columbine was an extraordinary media event. The event itself was tragic, but reporters emphasized that it was not isolated. In the eighteen months before the shooting at least six other school incidents had received national media attention, including the killing of three students in West Paducah, Kentucky; five in Jonesboro, Arkansas; and two killed and twenty-two other students wounded by Kip Kinkel in Springfield, Oregon. Reporters presented Columbine as part of a recurring theme: school violence was getting out of control and needed to be stopped. Columbine was particularly important, however, because of the larger number of actual and potential victims. Columbine also captivated the public because the video footage of the immediate aftermath of the shooting was breathtaking. Television cameras quickly arrived at the scene; they recorded panicked students exiting the school with their hands in the air, and others were shown dropping to safety from windows.

The final volume in this series focuses on the famous cases and trials that occurred between 1980 and 2000. The Columbine shooting is not included. Although an important case, the number of entries that could be included in each volume was limited; author interest, previous investigations of the case, the length of time a case was in the news, and whether the critical issues of that particular case were covered in other chapters determined the final contents of each volume. In short, we wanted to provide broad coverage of the celebrated cases of an era. As another example, there is also no chapter examining the Unabomber case. The case is a sensational case for several reasons. First, Kaczynski's reign of terror lasted over twenty years, and a large number of victims were murdered or injured. Second, the case challenged law enforcement because separate incidents were linked together, but a suspect could not be identified. Third, it was the publication of his "Manifesto" in the mainstream media that brought Kaczynski's brother to provide a lead to law enforcement that broke the case. Finally, although Kaczynski plead guilty to the crimes and is currently serving a life sentence in a "supermax" prison facility in Colorado, the case often generates media publicity, as when recently some of his journals and other writing materials were to be donated to a university library collection. Although an important case, we decided to focus on two other celebrated cases of terrorism from this era: the 1993 bombing of the World Trade Center and the 1995 bombing of the Murrah Building in Oklahoma City by Timothy McVeigh.

Volume 5 was particularly challenging because the number of cases that could have been included was remarkable. Of particular interest was how quickly cases had become celebrated in the modern era. It is true that important cases had to be excluded from each of the volumes, but the quantity of cases was by far the densest during the past twenty years. It seemed as though one high-profile trial would barely conclude before another would immediately replace it and fill the void of public interest. Other famous cases not presented in volume 5 include: John Gotti, John Hinkley, Megan Kanka, Ruby Ridge, Waco, Jeffrey Dahmer, JonBenet Ramsey, the Olympic Park bombing, Louise Woodward, scandals in the White House, Andrew Cunanan, Bernard Goetz, Manuel Noriega, the murders of Tupac Shukar and "Biggie" Smalls, Hedda Nussbaum-Joel Steinberg, the murder of John Lennon, Ivan Boesky and Michael Milken, the McMartin Preschool Trial, and Michael Jackson.

It was, of course, impossible to present all of the cases, and the cases that have been included engage a similar set of issues and concerns that are highlighted within these cases that have been excluded. First, volume 5 discusses the changing media environment, highlighting the technological and economic shifts that occurred in the media industry. The changing media environment is relevant to explain the large number of celebrated cases. Second, volume 5 highlights one particular shift in criminal justice case processing: the prison building boom and then a discussion on two cases relevant to this issue follows. Third, volume 5 discusses serial murder, child abduction, and white-collar crime events as representative of the celebrated themes of this era. Fourth, volume 5 addresses the cases that directly engaged the racial concerns of this era. Finally, the volume concludes with two events that have helped build a foundation for understanding terrorism, which was employed on September 11, 2001.

THE CHANGING MEDIA BUSINESS

The introduction of new media into the marketplace has directly impacted the cases that have become famous, as well as the strategies used by reporters to tell these stories. The introduction of radio into the marketplace was significant, as it highlighted the importance of storytelling. Television added a completely new dimension because consumers could view famous cases in more experiential ways. The beating of Rodney King, the destruction of wildlife after the oil spill from the *Exxon Valdez* in Alaska, and the damage to the Murrah building in Oklahoma City provide examples of how television has impacted public consumption of famous cases. Another new medium was popularized during the era that volume 5 covers: the internet. The internet has provided opportunities for other major media (television, newspaper, and radio) to explore new ways to communicate with their audience. There are three ways that the internet has directly altered the consumption of famous case materials. First, the immediate availability of information on the internet rivals television's ability to reach a broad audience. When the airplanes struck the towers of the World Trade Center on September 11, for example, people were either glued to a television or attempted to gain access to a news organization's website. Second, the internet has become a repository of information on famous cases. Authors who had contributed to these volumes had benefited from the amount of primary source materials available on the internet about these cases.[1] Third, the internet has provided expanded opportunities for the worldwide audience to experience the famous cases and trials occurring in the United States. For example, the trial of Louise Woodward (the nanny who had been convicted of second-degree murder by a jury, but the judge reduced the verdict to manslaughter and sentenced her to time served) demonstrated the potential of the internet— the defendant had her own website, supporters designed hundreds of "Free Louise" websites, thousands of online petitions were signed and given to the judge, video and audio clips and trial documents were made immediately available, and chat rooms were flooded with people from all over the world with an opinion about the case (Kennedy, 1997). The judge had planned to release his verdict online to share it with the trial's worldwide audience (Lee, 1997). However, this plan had failed because of a power outage just before the reading of the decision, but reporters noted that the internet quickly rebounded: "By then, the internet was doing what it does best: Enabling people all from over the world to communicate. Chat rooms buzzed with debate from residents of the United States and the United Kingdom. Support sites for the au pair, such as the Louise Woodward Campaign for Justice, spread the word. News sites had posted much more extensive stories. Some, such as CNN, pared down their sites to accommodate more visitors. The CNN website had about half a million page views between 10 a.m. and 11 a.m., and slightly more starting at 3 p.m. for Woodward's sentencing hearing" (Lee, 1997, p. 11).

There were also significant structural changes in the media industry. David Croteau and William Hoynes (2001, pp. 73–74) highlight four major trends: growth, integration, globalization, and the concentration of media ownership.

The number of media outlets and the size of media companies expanded dramatically. Fewer corporations were controlling more of the media marketplace, attempting to cross-market products in a variety of different formats. The impact of these structural trends on the presentation of famous cases is both direct and indirect. The growth and expansion into new media forms gives the impression that any national crime story has the potential to be considered famous. A story that is immediately picked up by any wire service will appear in thousands of newspapers, on nightly news broadcasts, and on the internet. The changes also increased the profitability of these famous cases.

The O. J. Simpson case provides an opportunity to explore many critical issues, but certainly the financial exploitation of justice is a crucial element. Everybody involved in the O. J. Simpson case, including the news media, attempted to make a financial profit from the case: the defendant, the victims' families, the attorneys, witnesses, and jurors. Books have been written about the affairs, participants have become television analysts, and the major players have gone on speaking tours. National and local television stations provided gavel-to-gavel coverage that received high ratings, and media organizations battled viciously for the exclusive rights to tell and then sell some aspect of the O. J. Simpson trial.

THE PRISON BUILDING BOOM

In the 1970s, the political climate leaned toward reducing the number of people sent to prison (Mauer, 2001). The incarceration rate remained very stable over the course of the 1970s. However, between 1980 and 2000 in the United States, the number of people incarcerated increased dramatically (Beckett and Sasson, 2000). For example, jail populations tripled and prison populations more than quadrupled. There were just fewer than 200,000 inmates in jails and just over 300,000 inmates in prison in 1980. The number of inmates in jail jumped to 600,000 and inmates in prison soared to over 1.3 million by 2000 (Bureau of Justice Statistics, 2004). The incarceration rate is nearly 500 prisoners for every 100,000 residents (Harrison and Beck, 2003). This general rate masks disparities in sentencing—the imprisonment rate for blacks increased far greater than it did for whites. This growth has resulted in a prison construction boom. Over 1,000 jails and prisons have been constructed since 1980 (Beckett and Sasson, 2000). Scholars have offered a variety of explanations for this growth, including the U.S. criminal justice system's crackdown on drug offenses, mandatory minimum sentences for a variety of crimes, and the perception that the public was fed up with crime and supported such growth.

Two cases presented in volume 5 illustrate the changing attitudes toward imprisonment quite effectively. In chapter 1, Lee Bernstein describes the incarceration, the release, and the reincarceration of Jack Henry Abbott. Abbott's book *In the Belly of the Beast*, which describes his experiences behind bars, was a critically acclaimed work. Writers and intellectuals supported his release from prison in 1981 and campaigned strongly for him so he would not be incarcerated on other charges. His release from prison was brief because Abbott soon committed another murder. Critics used this murder to declare that inmates can only be dangerous to society and that there is no promise for reform. As Bernstein suggests, critics "used the killing . . . as an opportunity to call for the further marginalization of incarcerated people." In chapter 4, Heidi Ahl-Quanbeck discusses the pickax murders committed by Karla Faye Tucker. The Tucker case is interesting because the investigation and trial received very little national media attention. The media did not take notice until she was scheduled to be executed in 1998. The media were interested because Tucker would become the first women executed in Texas in over one hundred years. It was also important because Tucker had been a model inmate and dramatically changed her life while she was incarcerated. The public struggled with understanding how such a petite, well-spoken young woman could have committed such a horrible crime. Despite pleas for clemency, Karla Faye Tucker was executed as planned.

LINKING CRIMES TO BROADER THEMES

The importance of a famous case can be exacerbated when several events with similar features are tied to a broader issue. Famous cases often serve as the best example of some social problem that needs to be remedied. They can also ignite a significant social control response. Legislation is often passed, police strategies are enacted, new organizations are formed, and resources are expended to respond to the concerns caused by the tragic act. Consider the impact of the abduction and murder of Polly Klaas (as discussed in chapter 10) and other high-profile child cases that had occurred in the 1990s. Get-tough-on-crime strategies, including the three-strikes-and-you're-out law, were supported, and legislation was passed that toughened sentences for child abductors. Resources were allocated to organizations that worked to prevent such abductions and find abductees. A new process, Amber Alert, was put in place so law enforcement, in conjunction with the media, can disseminate any descriptions of victims or abductors to increase the likelihood of capture.

Another theme emphasized in the last twenty years was serial murder. Serial murderers have been a recurring category of cases in volume 5. Phil Jenkins (1994) described why serial murder is such an appealing news topic.

The serial murderer is our ultimate vision of evil: A great, dangerous villain able to avoid detection from the authorities usually for a long period of time. They prey on innocent victims and attack in savage and even cannibalistic ways. Jeffrey Dahmer murdered at least seventeen people who he had lured to his apartment. After drugging his victim, he would murder him, have sex with the corpse, and then dismember him. He would boil the skulls of his victims and save them as trophies. Jenkins (1994) concluded that "serial murder can in fact be presented as a remarkably rich system of contemporary mythology in which the killers fulfill the symbolic roles that would in earlier societies have been taken by a wide variety of imaginary villains and folk-devils" (p. 101). He also concluded that serial murder became even more notorious in the 1980s and 1990s. It is interesting that the increased significance of serial murder was not because there was a sudden increase in the actual number of serial murderers identified; Jenkins demonstrated that the number of serial murders that occurred in the past two decades was quite ordinary, which indicates that serial murder has been a consistent problem for most of the century. But, in the 1980s, serial murder became more notorious because it became more useful than other social problems to political and bureaucratic officials (Jenkins, 1994).

Two famous serial murder cases are presented in this volume. Both are extraordinary in the number of victims killed as well as the span of time from their first murder to capture. First, in chapter 2, Tomas Guillen discusses the murders committed by the Green River Killer—one of the largest, longest, and most notorious serial murder cases in the history of the United States. Starting in 1982, Gary Leon Ridgway began killing young prostitutes in the Pacific Northwest. It is estimated that he murdered at least sixty young women before he was apprehended. Just recently, he agreed to plead guilty to the charges to avoid execution for the crimes. The case of the Green River Killer also highlights an important issue described in several other chapters: The adversarial relationship between the news media and police departments that festers during coverage of a celebrated case. Research suggests that media and police mutually benefit from working together on most crimes. Police organizations are provided an opportunity to highlight issues that are important to them and present cases in a way that minimizes criticism about the police department, and news organizations have access to enough crimes to satisfy the story demands of a reporter's daily routine (Chermak, 1995; Ericson, Baranek, and Chan, 1989). However, this relationship is often put to a test when a famous case occurs. Many more journalists get interested in the case and compete for the presentation of unique angles. As Guillen demonstrates in chapter 2, both the media and law enforcement will make mistakes under the pressure of a high-profile case.

The revelations provided by Ridgway, as stated in chapter 2, give readers insight into the mind of a serial killer. These understandings parallel the discussion of serial murderer Henry Lee Lucas in chapter 3. Some people refer to Lucas as America's worst serial killer—the highest estimate, which was based on confessions by Lucas, was that he murdered over 3,000 victims. The problem, however, is that it is always difficult to find the truth in criminal justice, particularly in high-profile cases. Public perceptions of Lucas have been fueled by news and entertainment media coverage of the case are consistent with the most extreme version of Lucas's crimes. The public wanted to believe the horrors in his confession. Knox describes how these expectations, which had been created by the media about who Lucas was, were far different from reality.

White-collar crimes have generally been devalued in the U.S. criminal justice system. In general, white-collar crimes are not considered to be very serious, and defendants—the individuals or businesses—seem to receive minimal punishment. Thus, it is very rare that such criminal activity evolves into a famous trial. There have been exceptions, however, and of the several famous cases that have occurred in the past twenty-five years, volume 5 presents two of those. Gray Cavendar, Francis Cullen, and William Maakestad discuss the Ford Pinto trial. This case demonstrates the arrogance and the horrors of corporate decision-making. Executives had decided that changing the design of the Ford Pinto would be more expensive than fixing a flaw that led to countless deaths and injuries. It was more cost-effective to pay victims than to fix the problem. The case was ground breaking because rarely do prosecutors attempt to hold corporations accountable for such decisions. Although the defendants in the case were found not guilty, the case sent notice that corporations were not completely above the criminal law.

Another legally complex corporate case is discussed in chapter 6. T. David Evans discusses the wreck of the *Exxon Valdez*, the damage it did to Prince William Sound, and the legal minefield that had to be negotiated. The captain of the *Valdez* was demonized in the media for his drinking, which had contributed directly to the accident. The *Exxon Valdez* case is intriguing also because of the large number of criminal and civil actions against corporations that had been involved. The media's coverage of this case was also quite interesting, as the media presented stunning footage of the damage to the environment and wildlife; however, the legal battles that followed were ignored. Evans, in chapter 6, effectively describes why the media lost interest in the case.

THE POLITICS OF RACE

Racism, and its impact on case processing, is one of the most troublesome issues in criminal justice. The race of the suspect and victim has been consistently shown to impact criminal justice decision-making. In short, minorities are treated differently, and they are more likely to be arrested, convicted, and sentenced to longer periods of incarceration compared with whites. The media also portray white and black defendants differently: Black defendants are depicted as being more dangerous and threatening than whites (Entman, 1994). Public expectations about who is most likely to commit violent crime are shaped in part by the presentation of race in famous cases. Several cases in volume 5 illustrate these expectations. The public accepted Susan Smith's explanation on why her children were missing uncritically: She said that a black man "carjacked" her automobile with her children in it. Smith was the killer, however, and she had murdered her children to spend more time with her lover (see Russell [1998] on racial hoaxes in American culture). Willie Horton became the poster child for the dangerous black man during George Herbert Walker Bush's presidential campaign in 1988. Bush's opponent had supported a program that released Horton back into the community, and then he committed a horrible crime. Horton and black criminality became the central issue that contributed to Bush's landslide victory. Finally, the case of the Central Park Jogger became famous soon after a series of very contentious race-related cases that had occurred in New York: The Tawana Brawley hoax, the trial of Bernard Goetz, and the murder of Yusef Hawkins. The media depicted the juveniles charged in the attack on the jogger as a mob of uncontrollable and indifferent criminals. The criminal justice system was quick to respond to the public pressure generated by media coverage: Arrests were made, charges filed, and verdicts and sentences were delivered. As often in a famous case, however, a rush to justice leads to an injustice. The juveniles were convicted of a crime they did not commit.

Two other cases discussed in this volume directly confront the issue of whether justice can be served when media interest and scrutiny is intense. The case of Rodney King and the trial of O. J. Simpson might lead readers to answer "no." The King case was famous because an amateur photographer captured his beating by Los Angeles police officers on videotape. The videotape provided clear evidence that the police officers had gone too far. It was not surprising when the charges were filed against some of the officers that most of the public had already concluded that they were guilty. The African American community saw the beating of King as only one example of what is a frequent occurrence. The public was shocked when the jury returned a verdict of not guilty. People poured out into the streets to riot in protest of the verdict.

Simpson was a well-known celebrity and a hero to many. He was charged with murdering Nicole Brown Simpson and Ronald Goldman. Greg Barak discusses this case in what is generally considered the most famous and watched trials of all time in chapter 11. The Simpson acquittal was potent because of the diametrically opposed reactions to the verdict. "Race mattered in how respondents judged the guilt or innocent of O.J. Simpson," as 65 percent of whites disagreed with the not guilty verdict and 77 percent of blacks agreed with the verdict (Brownstein, 2000, p. 138).

PRECURSORS TO SEPTEMBER 11

In 2001, the terrorist attacks on the towers at the World Trade Center and the Pentagon occurred just outside the time period covered in volume 5. What had happened on September 11 is briefly mentioned here because there was a series of terrorism-related attacks that had occurred between 1980 and 2000 that had laid a particular foundation for how Americans now think about terrorist attacks.

Damphousse, Lawson, and Smith discuss how most people have forgotten that terrorists first attacked the World Trade Center in New York in 1993. It is an unfortunate oversight because the case is packed with significant legal and media issues, and chapter 13 demonstrates the complexity of terrorism cases. The authors do a masterful job of discussing how each individual involved in the case contributed to its outcome, the successful efforts by law enforcement and prosecutors to bring this group to justice, and the long sentences that had been delivered. How the media depicted the case helped the public come to understand the complexities of the attack on the World Trade Center in 1993. The case changed how the United States responds to terrorism, how law enforcement agencies attempt to prevent similar attacks, and how Americans think about terrorism and the Middle East.

One chapter focuses on the work of individual terrorists. Chapter 14 addresses the bombing of the Alfred F. Murrah Building in Oklahoma City, Oklahoma. Timothy McVeigh was eventually captured, convicted, and eventually confessed to his involvement in the bombing that killed 168 people. His target appeared random and thus feelings of vulnerability increased dramatically. There are two issues of particular interest in the media coverage of this famous case. First, reporters initially guessed that the bombing was the work of terrorists who were of Arab origin. Although there was no supporting evidence, reporters and the American public immediately jumped to this conclusion because it was consistent with the media and public's expectations of the nature of terrorist acts and the type of people most likely to be terrorists. Second, like so many other famous cases, McVeigh's links to right-wing extremists set off a storm of media coverage searching for other individuals and groups that supported his viewpoint.

The public's fear that the number of terrorist acts would increase dramatically grew, law enforcement cracked down on militia and other paramilitary groups, and politicians supported legislation to respond more effectively to terrorism.

NOTE

1. A short list of web resources that include Famous Trials: (http://www.law. umkc.edu/faculty/projects/FTrials/ftrials.htm);

CourtTV's CrimeLibrary (http://www.crimelibrary.com/);

History Matters (http://historymatters.gmu.edu);

Library of Congress American Memory (http://memory.loc.gov/ammem/collections/finder.html);

Man or Monster?: Merchandising Murder in the Nineteenth Century American Popular Press (http://www.oneonta.edu/academics/cgp/murder/welcome.html); and PBS (http://www.pbs.org).

REFERENCES

Brownstein, H. H. (2000). *The social reality of violence and violent crime.* Boston: Allyn and Bacon.

Bureau of Justice Statistics. (2004). Key facts at a glance. Retrieved on February 20, 2004, from http://www.ojp.usdoj/bjs/

Chermak, S. M. (1995). *Victims in the news: Crime and the American new media.* Boulder, CO: Westview Press.

CNN. (1999a). Bullet-scarred Columbine High opens doors to the media. Retrieved on February 15, 2004, from http://www.cnn.com/US/9906/15/columbine.tour/

CNN. (1999b). Crews work to erase signs of massacre at Columbine. Retrieved on February 15, 2004, from http://www.cnn.com/US/9906/16/columbine/

Entman, R. (1994). Representation and reality in the portrayal of blacks on network television news. *Journalism Quarterly, 71* (3), 509–520.

Ericson, R. V., Baranek, P. M., and Chan, J. B. L. (1989). *Negotiating control: A study of news sources.* Toronto: University of Toronto Press.

Harrison, P. M. and Beck, A. J. (2003). *Prisoners in 2002.* Washington, DC: Bureau of Justice Statistics.

Jenkins, P. (1994). *Using murder: The social construction of serial homicide.* New York: Aldine De Gruyter.

Kennedy, H. (1997, November 10). Trial fans keeping Internet buzzing. *New York Daily News,* p. 7.

Lee, E. (1997, November 11). The au pair decision. *Atlanta Journal and Constitution,* p. 11a.

Mauer, M. (2001). The causes and consequences of prison growth in the United States. *Punishment and Society, 3*(1), 9–20.

Russell, K. (1998). *The color of crime: Racial hoaxes, white fear, black protectionism, police harassment, and other macroaggressions.* New York: New York University Press.

1

Jack Henry Abbott:
An Author from behind Bars

Lee Bernstein

Born in Oscoda, Michigan, in 1944, Jack Henry Abbott rose to national prominence in 1981 when Random House published *In the Belly of the Beast*—a collection of autobiographical, political, and philosophical writings. *In the Belly of the Beast* is grounded in Abbott's experiences in and interpretations of his time behind bars. Abbott spent only nine and a half months of the previous twenty-five years outside of prison.

Abbott first entered a youth detention facility—the Utah State Industrial School for Boys—at age twelve, after numerous failed attempts to place him in foster homes. He described himself as a "state-raised convict," which he defined as anyone who is "reared by the state from an early age after he is taken from what the state calls a 'broken home'" (Abbott, 1981a, p. 10). Abbott did not know his father, and his mother was too impoverished and in trouble with the law to care for Abbott and his sister, Frances. Abbott believed that being "state-raised" implicated the state itself in his crimes and provided a context for him to interpret his experience.

After a childhood spent shuttling between foster homes and juvenile detention facilities, Abbott moved on to an adult prison after leaving the juvenile system. In 1963, Abbott was sentenced to a maximum of five years in the Utah State Penitentiary in Draper, Utah, after being convicted of

Convicted author Jack Henry Abbot is on his way for a hearing in federal court in New Orleans, Louisiana, on Thursday, September 24, 1981. (AP/Wide World Photos)

check forgery. He stole some checks from a shoe store and wrote them out to himself. This five-year sentence would extend to over seventeen years, except for a brief period in the spring of 1971 when he escaped from a Utah prison. In 1966, Abbott killed James Christensen in a knife assault; Christensen was a fellow inmate whom Abbott allegedly made sexual advances towards. He received a twenty-year sentence to run concurrent with his forgery sentence. In addition, during his 1971 escape, Abbott robbed a savings and loan association in Denver, Colorado. After capture and conviction, Abbott entered the federal prison system to serve a nineteen-year sentence (Farber, 1981a).

Despite never finishing sixth grade and a refusal to attend prison schools, Abbott was widely read in European philosophy, especially the political and economic theories of Marx, Lenin, and other communists. Like many convicts of the 1970s, Abbott was convinced by Marx's arguments and by the deep commitment of Communists to the plight of incarcerated men and women. Communists, he wrote, "do everything legally possible to help reform these prisons and to rescue prisoners from insanity, injury, death. . . . No one else does a thing" (Abbott, 1981a, p. 96). During the 1970s, education in radical politics and philosophy helped Abbott develop the critique of the prison system that appears in his book *In the Belly of the Beast.* In the book, Abbott critiqued the justice system as irrational: "A system of justice that does not instruct by *reason,* that does not rationally demonstrate to a man the error of his ways, accomplishes the opposite ends of justice: oppression" (Abbott, 1981a, p. 118).

His politics also led him to rarely cooperate with prison administrators or correctional officers, as Abbott received numerous disciplinary charges during his incarceration. "So long as classes are not equal," he wrote, "men are not equal, and there is no way I can reach any agreements with the enemies of my class—particularly since these enemies hold the power of life or death over us" (Abbott, 1981a, p. 98). Because of Abbott's frequent participation in political resistance and his history of violence toward correctional officers and other inmates, he spent fourteen years of his sentence in solitary confinement. He read books received from his sister and from the PEN American Center, a writer's organization based in New York City (Cohen, 1981; Farber, 1981a).

During the 1970s, Abbott began corresponding with many American writers, first with Jerzy Kosinski, who was, at the time, president of PEN. Later, he would correspond with Pulitzer Prize–winning author Norman Mailer. His relationship with Mailer would prove central to later events in Abbott's life. Well known for such works as *The Naked and the Dead* (1948), *Advertisements for Myself* (1959), and *Armies of the Night* (1968), Mailer announced in 1978 that he would write a nonfiction work on the life and execution of Gary Gilmore, a Utah man who was to be the first person executed since the U.S. Supreme Court suspended the practice in 1972 (*Furman v. Georgia*, 1972). Abbott saw an item in the newspaper about the project and wrote a letter to Mailer offering to help. This project would become Mailer's Pulitzer Prize–winning *The Executioner's Song* (1979). Abbott believed that he could offer unique insight into the experiences and mind-set of Gilmore, who, like Abbott, was a state-raised convict (Abbott, 1981a, p. ix).

Mailer encouraged Abbott's correspondence and received, according to his own estimation, 1,000 pages of letters over a two-year period (Abbott, 1980). Mailer found the information helpful for his writing project. He also felt strongly that Abbott was the best convict-writer since Eldridge Cleaver, the writer and activist best known for *Soul on Ice* (1968). In an effort to make Abbott's work more widely available, Mailer showed the letters to Scott Meredith, his literary agent (Farber, 1981a). At Meredith's urging, the *New York Review of Books* published several excerpts from these letters in 1980 (Abbott, 1980). The letters would also serve as the basis for much of Abbott's book *In the Belly of the Beast*.

In addition to Marx and Lenin, *In the Belly of the Beast* contains references to modern philosophers, including Sartre, Camus, Dostoyevsky, Spinoza, Kierkegaard, and Jung. His second book, *My Return* (1987), coauthored with philosophy professor Naomi Zack, showed a continued interest in continental philosophy but a new familiarity with classical drama. *In the Belly of the Beast* was released in early 1981 to great fanfare. Random House heavily promoted its new author, and early reviews of the book ranged from favorable to raves. Abbie Hoffman reviewed the book in the *Soho News*, linking the book to literary giants like Aleksandr Solzhenitsyn and Jacobo Timmerman (Kakutani, 1981). *The Nation* magazine featured Abbott's contention that the American prison system was worse than the Soviet gulags (Kakutani, 1981). Terence Des Pres offered perhaps the most positive and prescient review. "Now that his letters have been published," Des Pres wrote in the *New York Times Book Review*, "we have before us the most intense, I might even say the most fiercely visionary book of its kind in the American repertoire of prison literature. *In the Belly of the Beast* is awesome, brilliant, perversely ingenuous; its impact is indelible, and as an articulation of penal nightmare it is completely compelling" (Des Pres, 1981, p. 3). Although he was deeply moved by Abbott's account, Des Pres made clear that Abbott's previous life experience left him completely unprepared for life outside of prison. Abbott's precision about "evil and human ugliness" did not allow for the kind of romanticized attention to violence that his work was sure to engender. Although Des Pres did not think that Abbott's anger would lead to future violence, he did point out that "in Abbott's view, convicts kill to gain respect, to establish moral superiority," which is a worldview that could led to tragic consequences inside and outside of prison (Des Pres, 1981, p. 14).

As *In the Belly of the Beast* was nearing release, Abbott was nearing the end of his sentence on the federal bank robbing charges. He applied for and received early parole in 1981, expecting to be returned to Utah to finish his sentence on the 1966 murder of Christensen. Mailer, along with Erroll McDonald from Random House, *New York Review of Books* editor Robert Silvers, and literary agent Scott Meredith, wrote letters to the Utah Board of Pardons attesting to Abbott's literary talents and potential for full-time work as a writer. According to Thomas R. Harrison, then serving as chairman of the parole board, these letters testified to Abbott's "sensitivity, talent, goals, and accomplishments" (Farber, 1981b, p. A1). Harrison was convinced that Abbott had "a great deal going for him" and that he no longer posed a violent threat. With the prospect of a lucrative and productive writing career in front of him, on June 5, 1981, Abbott was placed in a halfway house in New York City, pending his full parole date of August 25.

BRIEF FREEDOM

Abbott's parole from the federal prison in Marion, Illinois, would normally have been to Denver, which was the location of the 1971 savings and loan robbery that resulted in Abbott's federal conviction. However, because of the promise of a $150-per-week job as a research assistant for Mailer, a resident of Brooklyn, New York, federal authorities agreed to parole Abbott to a halfway house that was run by the Salvation Army on New York's Lower East Side. In a flurry of activity, Abbott was interviewed on *Good Morning America* and in *People* magazine, and he was feted by well-known writers and the editorial brass of Random House. He also made a point of learning to dance, something he never had the opportunity to do in prison. Early in the morning of July 18, 1981, after a night of dancing, Abbott and two women—Susan Roxas and Veronique de St. Andre—went to the Binibon restaurant on the corner of Second Avenue and Fifth Street, which was several blocks from his halfway house on Third Street. That night, Abbott was involved in an altercation that resulted in the death of Richard Adan, and Terence Des Pres' review of *In the Belly of the Beast* appeared in the newspaper that next day.

The altercation between Adan and Abbott is clouded by inconsistent versions of the story. Abbott, media accounts, and trial testimony are consistent on some details. Abbott entered the Binibon restaurant with Roxas and St. Andre. Adan, a 22-year-old Cuban-born dancer and actor, was working as a waiter and night manager at the restaurant, which was owned by his father-in-law, Henry Howard. After several tense exchanges between Abbott and Adan, Abbott asked to use the bathroom. According to some accounts, Adan explained that because the bathroom was through the kitchen, it would be a violation of health codes to allow access to customers. According to Abbott, Adan merely told him that he could not use the bathroom. Depending on who told the story, either Adan or Abbott asked the other to step outside. The two men then left the restaurant and went around the corner. In the midst of a brief altercation, Abbott stabbed Adan once in the heart with the knife he began carrying after seeing several muggings in the neighborhood. Adan staggered, slumped to the pavement, and died.

Abbott fled the scene, phoned Mailer (who asked that he call back at a later hour), and then returned to the halfway house for the daily 7:30 a.m. "face-to-face" roll call. Later that morning, he ate brunch at the apartment of French writer Jean Malaquais, and Abbott made no mention of the altercation with Adan. He then fled New York, and he traveled to Philadelphia and Chicago before crossing the U.S.-Mexico border at Nuevo Laredo with the goal of going to Cuba. Unable to gain work on a ship destined for Cuba and with funds running low, Abbott hitchhiked to New Orleans, where he worked in a series of odd jobs before gaining employment as a roustabout for offshore oil rigs near Morgan City, Louisiana. After several weeks, an informant contacted New York Police Detective William J. Majeski with information about a man with the letters "J A C K" tattooed across the fingers of his left hand. Federal authorities arrested Abbott on September 24, 1981 (Farber, 1981c, p. A1).

THE TRIAL

Abbott was quickly transferred to New York City where he faced first-degree murder charges. The trial lasted from January 9 to January 21, 1982. Under heavy media scrutiny, the case for the prosecution was argued by James H. Fogel, a New York City assistant district attorney. Ivan S. Fisher defended Abbott and argued that Adan's death was an accident occasioned by Abbott's attempt at self-defense. On the first day of the trial, Fogel asked the judge, Acting Justice Irving Lang, if he could introduce excerpts from *In the Belly of the Beast* as a partial explanation of Abbott's motive (Montgomery, 1982a). Lang ruled against the prosecution, but when Abbott chose to take the stand in his own defense on January 15, the judge allowed the prosecution to use previously agreed-upon excerpts in questioning as long as no passage referred to any of Abbott's previous crimes, including the 1966 stabbing. However, upon taking the stand, Howard, Adan's father-in-law, shouted from the observers' seats, "It's just like in the book, Abbott, just like in the book!" prestaging the prosecution's own strategy (Montgomery, 1982b). The judge barred Adan's family from the remainder of the trial.

Under questioning from his attorney, Abbott described Adan's death as a "tragic misunderstanding" brought about by paranoia. Adan, he admitted, was probably just leading him to a hidden spot around the corner so that Abbott could relieve himself. Abbott testified that he mistakenly interpreted all of Adan's benign gestures as hostile, and when Adan approached him, he pulled out a knife. Instead of pulling away, as Abbott expected, Adan leaned into the knife and unluckily walked into a fatal stabbing (Montgomery, 1982b). During his cross-examination, Fogel read several excerpts from *In the Belly of the Beat*, including Abbott's discussion of the importance of using deadly force when behind bars: "Here in prison the most respected among us are those who have killed other men, particularly other prisoners. Beneath all relationships in prison is the ever-present fact of murder. It ultimately defines our relationship among ourselves" (Abbott and Zack, 1987, pp. 59–60). Abbott insisted that, while based in fact, the book was a fictionalized account of his experiences and views (Montgomery, 1982c).

In one sense, the trial acknowledged the importance of Abbott's writing in Adan's murder. The prosecutor and Adan's family directly implicated Abbott's writing in his murderous acts. They did not argue that his writing made him a violent person; however, they used his published work as proof that, as Fogel remarked after sentencing, Abbott was a "killer by habit, a killer by inclination, a killer by philosophy and a killer by desire" (Montgomery, 1982d). The writing, then, became a key context to understand the interior philosophy of Abbott.

The jury had five options. They could acquit Abbott of all charges. They could convict him, as the prosecution wished, of first-degree murder, which would require evidence of premeditation. In addition, Lang gave the jury other options: second-degree murder (causing a death with intent to kill), first-degree manslaughter (causing a death but where blame is mitigated by "extreme emotional disturbance"), or second-degree manslaughter (causing death because of recklessness). After deliberating for two days, the jury found Abbott guilty of first-degree manslaughter on January 21, 1982, which was also Abbott's thirty-eighth birthday. Lang handed down a sentence of fifteen years to life, but he could have given him a life sentence under New York's Persistent Felony Offender Statute (Montgomery, 1982d).

The manslaughter conviction can be seen at face value: Abbott killed Adan while in a state of paranoia. His history in prison—which included long periods of solitary confinement and time in the early 1970s when he was prescribed heavy doses of Valium, Prolixin, and Mellaril, a tranquilizer—made it impossible for Abbott to see Adan's actions as anything but a threat (*New York v. Abbott*, 1982). However, perhaps they saw Abbott's experience as much as his mental state as a mitigating factor. Abbott's lawyer argued as much in his appeal of his sentence; in the appeal, Abbott's lawyer wrote that prison "is the only 'society' that the defendant has ever known" (*New York v. Abbott*, 1982). As a state-raised convict, Abbott was acting within the rules of his society rather than in the new context of New York's Lower East Side.

RETURN TO "THE BELLY"

Because his altercation with Adan was also a violation of his parole, Abbott returned to Marion, Illinois, to complete his federal sentence for the 1971 bank robbery conviction. After completing this sentence, he was transferred to the New York State Department of Corrections with little public attention. In 1987, he and Zack released *My Return*. The book includes a play, *The Death of Tragedy*, about the altercation with Adan and the trial that followed. The play refutes the idea that either Mailer or Abbott's prison experience played any role in the altercation with Adan. In her introduction, Zack made an assertion that proved particularly offensive to Adan's family. Arguing that it "takes two to tango," Zack contended that "had [Adan] known to be more careful with strangers, he would probably not be dead today. But from his appearance, his words, his behavior, the night manager must not have realized any problem existed and that he could not handle the man in the manner he did" (Abbott and Zack, 1987, p. 10). In addition to holding Adan partially responsible for his own death, *My Return* raised many objections to the prosecution's use of his writings during the cross-examination and summation, reiterating Abbott's comment at the time of the trial that *In the Belly of the Beast* was a fictionalization of his life rather than an autobiography. "The Leader," a character in *The Death of Tragedy*, which is based on a traditional role in Greek drama, says, "Abbott had been tried for writing a book. His book has been used as evidence against him. But Abbott and his book are two different things. Abbott's ability with a pen should not be taken as ability to kill" (Abbott and Zack, 1987, p. 61).

Despite Abbott's continued reluctance to connect his literary creations to the altercation with Adan, the two would remain intertwined inside and outside the courts. In December 1981, Ricci Adan, Adan's widow, filed a $10 million wrongful death suit against Abbott. A jury found Abbott liable for damages in 1983, but a civil court would not decide damages until June 1990. In the interim, Abbott's two books had earned more than $100,000 dollars in royalties and film rights, and he had signed a $150,000 contract to write an autobiographical film script. Although he had hoped that his sister would benefit from these earnings, the money was held by the New York County Sheriff's Office and the New York State Crime Victims Board under the New York's "Son of Sam" law, which prevented convicted felons from profiting from their crimes. In addition, Abbott and Zack had married in 1989 (Sullivan, 1990, p. B2). The jury awarded Ricci Adan $7.5 million, ensuring that she would receive all future royalties from the sale of Abbott's work (Silvestre, 2002, p. 1).

In March 2000, while incarcerated in Attica Prison in Attica, New York, Abbott was severely beaten in an attack by fellow inmates. After recovering from seven hours of surgery, he was transferred to Wende Correctional Facility, which was near Buffalo, New York. Abbott was denied parole at his first parole hearing in August 2001, and he continued to have difficulty behind bars. According to his letters to Michael Kuzma, Abbott's lawyer at the time, he faced continued harassment from correctional officers and fellow inmates through early February 2002. Abbott was found dead of an apparent suicide in his cell at Wende on February 10, 2002. Correctional authorities refused to release his last written work: a suicide note.

RADICAL CHIC

According to the media coverage of Abbott's trial, Abbott was the beneficiary of "radical chic" and Adan was its victim. A phrase coined by novelist and social commentator Tom Wolfe, radical chic refers to the courting of political radicals, convicts, and criminals by cultural and economic elites (Wolfe, 1970, p. 6). In an essay about a 1970 fundraiser for the Black Panther Party at the New York apartment of conductor Leonard Bernstein, Wolfe lampooned the efforts of wealthy and influential people to connect with experiences deemed "authentic" or "hip." According to the application of radical "chic" by the mass media, Mailer's mentorship of Abbott could be compared to Bernstein's sponsorship of the Black Panthers, Bob Dylan's efforts to get a new trial for boxer Ruben "Hurricane" Carter, William F. Buckley Jr.'s help in gaining the release of Edgar Smith, Jean Paul Sartre's mentorship of Jean Genet, or Nelson Algren and William Styron's mentorship of James Blake. One author from the *Washington Post* wrote, "Jack Henry Abbott wasn't so much Mailer's literary protégé as a feather in his cap: A real live crook—one who writes with his fists!—to be put on exhibit in the salons of radical chic" (Yardley, 1982, p. B1). The *Washington Post* urged readers to "keep one's distance" and leave criminals to the penal system. The radical chic argument would long outlive the public visibility of Abbott. The *New York Daily News*, for example, singled out Mailer and literary agent Scott Meredith as "fancies and nellies and swells" fussing over a "noble savage" almost two decades after Abbott's return to prison (Maeder, 1998, p. 33).

The radical chic theory drew on several important factors. First, many media accounts proclaimed that Mailer and the others who wrote letters to the Utah Board of Parole should be held partially responsible for Adan's death. In his efforts to connect with an "outsider," Mailer let his passions get away from him (Farber, 1981a, p. A1). None said that Abbott no longer posed a threat; however, Mailer wrote in his preface to *In the Belly of the Beast*: "It is certainly time for him to get out" (Abbott, 1981a, p. xvi). A dinner held in Greenwich Village honoring Abbott also influenced the belief that Abbott was a beneficiary of radical chic. The dinner celebrating his release—attended by Jason Epstein (a Random House editor), Silvers, Mailer and his wife Norris Church, and Kosinski and his partner Katherina Von Fraunhofer—was used to cast aspersion on the literary crowd who championed Abbott's talents. His promotional appearance on *Good Morning America* attested to the extent of the publicity Abbott received in the short period of his freedom. One newspaper even transformed the early morning meal at Binibon—an inexpensive café on the Lower East Side—into the more glamorous sounding: "he walked into an East Village restaurant, a woman admirer on either arm" (Davis, 2002, n.p.).

The implication of radical chic is that Abbott should never have been released from prison and that he received preferential treatment because of his connections to literary giants. Some reporters went beyond radical chic by noting Mailer's literary fascination with strong men who meet tragic outcomes. From essays like "The White Negro" (1959) to *The Executioner's Song* (1979)—the book that led Abbott to Mailer—Mailer documented his identification with marginalized men and his view of them as appealingly masculine. Mickiko Kakutani, the influential cultural and literary reviewer for the *New York Times*, traced the many ways Mailer's characters assert their "identity in the face of an arbitrary system of officially regulated morality" and "kill without apology." According to Kakutani, Mailer had long "equated violence not only with virility but also with creativity and moral courage" (Kakutani, 1981, p. 36). Kakutani heralded the use of "the man on the fringes" as a literary device that defines "the perimeters of bourgeois society" in writers like Blake, Nietzsche, Baudelaire, Rimbaud, Dostoyevsky, Kafka, Sartre, Cheever, and even ex-convict Genet. However, Kakutani thought that the championing of Abbott replaced literary and philosophical exploration with a dangerous experiment. In interviews with leading cultural critics and novelists like H. Bruce Franklin, Irving Howe, Joyce Carol Oates, and Richard Slotkin, Kakutani builds the argument that it was "wishful impulse to see Mr. Abbott's life as a store not just of crime and punishment, but of crime and punishment and redemption; and it was the fervently held belief that talent somehow redeems, that art confers respectability, that the act of writing can somehow transform a violent man into a philosopher of violence" (Kakutani, 1981, p. 37). Kakutani stopped far short of blaming the literary establishment for the death of Adan, but she used the opportunity of his death to show the consequences of the romanticized view of violent men with radical politics.

Mailer's attention to violent themes both predated his relationship with Abbott and outlived Abbott's connection to the author. Many pointed out that Mailer had stabbed a previous wife in 1960, and as recently as a 2000 interview, Mailer revealed his ongoing belief that "we are as ugly as animals in our fashion, and unless we deal with the ugliness in ourselves, unless we deal with the violence in ourselves, the brutality in ourselves, and find some way to sublimate it, just to use Freud's term, into something slightly higher, we're never going to get anywhere with anything" (Weinraub, 2000, p. E1). Mailer had a literary interest in the themes explored in Abbott's letters, but he and Kosinsky also saw Abbott's talent as indicative of an inner transformation. Kosinsky reflecting on this view, agreed with Kakutani's central point: "Maybe I share with my intellectual friend Norman Mailer the feeling that talent redeems" (Wadler, 1981, p. C1). Both men felt partially to blame for not seeing that Abbott had frequently used both philosophical and physical violence. Many of Abbott's early letters to Kosinsky were "an unremittant litany of spiritual and intellectual abuse." So, Kosinsky did not ignore Abbott's justification of violence in his book *In the Belly of the Beast* but saw it as evidence that the physical propensity to violence had been channeled into a literary form. "We preferred to see him as a man who is going to become an intellectual of violence," Kosinsky said (Wadler, 1981, p. C1).

Other news writers found the sharp critiques of Mailer oversimplified. They recognized that politically engaged writers like Mailer and Kosinsky placed great importance on their relationships with convict writers for a variety of literary, political, and personal reasons rather than simply as an attempt to be "chic."

"It is easy to dismiss [Mailer's] efforts on behalf of Mr. Abbott as radical chic," the *New York Times* editorialized, "or the overly romantic celebration of his literary ability. But perhaps too easy. Mr. Abbott's writing may be unusual, but his state-sponsored rearing in rage and murder are not. For that, we all must bear some responsibility" (1981, p. A22). The attention to the radical chic of left-leaning elites ignored important aspects of the larger context for Abbott, *In the Belly of the Beast*, and the killing of Adan. Much of the mass media focused attention on the predictability of Abbott's violence based on his own words and criminal record. The media ignored or discounted Abbott's implication of the state, and the *Times* opined, the general readership of newspapers—in creating the conditions within which this violence occurred. In one of the more powerful passages in Abbott's *In the Belly of the Beast* (and thus before the altercation with Adan), he argued that "to say you are *not* responsible for the life of someone you killed in self-defense, not responsible for the circumstances that brought you to prison (and kept you there for two decades)—to say all that in the face of your accusers, accusers who also justify their mistreatment of you by those accusations, is to be really responsible for your words and deeds. Because every time you reject the accusations, you are held responsible *further* for things you are not responsible for" (Abbott, 1981a, p. 18). Instead of holding himself at fault—or blaming well-meaning intellectuals—Abbott insisted that the penal system (and the capitalist economy) held responsibility for placing him in a brutalizing context for much of his life. Des Pres, in his *Times* review, found Abbott's view compelling, but thought that Abbott's interpretation of society as a whole was limited by his confinement: "Abbott uses Marxist theory to generalize his own experience, assuming that what happens in American maximum security prisons must be a sort of paradigm for oppression everywhere" (Des Pres, 1981, p. 14).

Media coverage of the crime and trial paid close attention to the role Abbott's talent made in misleading well-meaning, if naïve, writers and editors.

There was a larger subtext to this critique that called into question the scrutiny the prison system had received since the black power movement of the 1960s. The very idea of radical chic connoted a critique of the embrace of the Black Panther Party by white conductor and composer Leonard Bernstein. Wolfe coined the phrase to cast cynical aspersion on the alliance between moneyed New Yorkers and black radical activists. Although Abbott was, in contemporary terms, biracial (Chinese and white), he was frequently compared with African American radical writers and activists. Abbott's politics placed him closer to incarcerated African Americans such as Eldridge Cleaver, George Jackson, and Angela Davis than to incarcerated white writers like Caryl Chessman or Nixon coconspirator Charles Colson. Abbott would have been comfortable with Black Panther Party Chairman Huey P. Newton's claim that "there are no laws that the oppressor makes that the oppressed are bound to respect" (Newton, 1970, pp. 322–323). Abbott was part of a political and cultural renaissance behind bars, one that had deep and lasting connections to political activists without the elite pedigree of Mailer, Bernstein, or Kosinsky.

A PARADOX AT THE CORE OF PENOLOGY

The historical period provides evidence of a more complicated link between Abbott's celebrity and the murder of Adan. Mailer was not alone; there was a profound fascination with prison writers and intellectuals during the 1970s. Many prisoners benefited from the sharp rise in writing and artistic opportunities available in correctional facilities. In addition to Cleaver, Jackson, and Davis, writers like Etheridge Knight, Jimmy Santiago Baca, and Miguel Piñero would achieve widespread acclaim for their creative works. Prisoners who were less inclined to pursue literary efforts exposed a legacy of injustice within penal institutions by rioting. From 1970 to 1986, there were approximately 300 prison riots in the United States, many of which—like the Attica Prison riot in 1971—placed an insistence on access to education and literary programs as a condition of negotiation (Useem and Kimball, 1989).

During the years leading up to *In the Belly of the Beast*, many prisoners sought to participate in social and political debates occurring in the "free" world despite their incarceration and the need to overcome obstacles like illiteracy or poor writing skills. Learning to write, for many prisoners, became a political and cultural act as much as one of individual improvement. Between 1965 and 1973 the number of college-level programs in U.S. prisons increased over fifteenfold to 182. By the time Abbott returned to prison, there were 350 programs in 45 states, with roughly 10 percent of all inmates attending a prison college. In addition, the National Endowment for the Arts funded the publication of prisoner works, and other organizations began major initiatives to create freestanding programs behind prison walls. There were unprecedented joint projects between state departments of corrections and arts commissions throughout the United States. In the private, not-for-profit sector, the PEN American Center—the organization that Kosinsky once headed—founded its famous Prison Writing Program and literary competitions, and the Black Emergency Cultural Coalition started a Prison Arts Program. Many individuals started small-scale courses, workshops, and performances, which were often at their own expense (Bernstein, 2004).

Abbott's politics and literary talents, while not in the mainstream of American political life, were representative of a period of tremendous upheaval in U.S. prisons. Leonard Munker, the attorney who represented Abbott at his 1981 parole hearing, pointed out that "the [1970s] were a turbulent time in prisons and Jack was leader of the pack" (Wadler, 1981, p. C1). Abbott's time in solitary, Munker observes, should be seen in relation to the political nature of his violence. For example, in 1975, to protest the heavy doses of tranquilizers the prison administered, Abbott punched a doctor in the face, which led to a long stint in solitary confinement. Munker asked readers of the interview to consider if Abbott's action was an example of a violent nature or an act of political and personal resistance. For most readers, this would require an interpretive leap they were not yet ready to take. However, Abbott provided an opportunity to ask difficult questions about how Americans understand criminality and incarceration.

The crime, trial, and media coverage of Jack Henry Abbott's release and return to prison provided an opportunity to debate the relationship between art and redemption, prisons and reform, and radical chic among the cultural elite. Many observers remarked that Abbott's parole, continued violence, and return to prison showed the excesses of the prison movement and their well-heeled friends. According to the critics, prison writers and activists were no more than gifted con artists—liberal reviewers, teachers, and readers were easy marks for their wily ways. As Abbott's prosecutor pointed out, cues to their deceptions and the true threat they posed could be deduced in their own writings.

Few media accounts drew attention to Abbott's critique of the prison system. Instead the media chose to find fault with the literary establishment in general and Norman Mailer in particular for mentoring, publishing, and celebrating Abbott. The media used the killing of Adan as an opportunity to call for the further marginalization of incarcerated people. The *Washington Post* urged an imaginary "Author's Guild" to stick to their typewriters: "The rehabilitation of convicted criminals is for the penal system, not for the city desk of the book-review department" (Yardley, 1982, p. B1). Others, like Terence Des Pres, observed that many of the conditions that Abbott wrote of were eliminated only after a series of reforms in the 1960s and 1970s. Abbott had been active in the Marion Prisoners' Rights Project, which was an organization founded during the period of reform (Farber, 1981b, p. A1). These reforms, according to the *Christian Science Monitor*, did not occur because of a self-critique by correctional facilities. Prisoners, activists, and eventually, the courts, demanded that torture, extended solitary confinement, and many of the other practices described by Abbott be stopped. The *Monitor* reported in 1981 that Supreme Court Chief Justice Warren E. Burger urged that these reforms needed to go further. The *Monitor* also argued that Abbott needed to remain part of the debate about prison reform. To at least one observer, Abbott's continued violence did not negate the brutality of his experience nor did his reincarceration prevent others from going down that path (Nordell, 1981, p. B4). Although the film of Abbott's life has yet to be made, few discussions of Norman Mailer fail to mention his connection to Abbott; *In the Belly of the Beast* has remained in print since 1981. In addition to these impacts on popular culture, Abbott had a long-term impact on the prison system in a way rarely mentioned. In 1972, Abbott was the lead plaintiff in a class action lawsuit seeking to reform prison regulations of mail delivery. With support from the National Prison Project of the American Civil Liberties Union (ACLU), the suit prompted prison authorities to give increased access to personal correspondence. Although Abbott never shook his reputation as a misguided prophet who did not deserve the faith of the New York literary crowd, his reputation as a reformer and self-defined troublemaker has also not been forgotten.

In the introduction to *In the Belly of the Beast*, Mailer revealed more than his own glorification of violent men when he wrote that "it is not only the worst of the young are sent to prison, but the best—that is, the proudest, the bravest, the most daring, the most enterprising, and the most undefeated of the poor" (Abbott, 1981a, p. xii). Mailer called this the "paradox at the core of penology." According to his defenders, Abbott, in his crimes as well as his writings, was among the greatest chroniclers of the brutalization of a life behind bars. According to the critics, the story of Jack Henry Abbott is a cautionary tale to leave the penal system as it is.

REFERENCES

Abbott, J. H. (1980, June 26). In prison. *The New York Review of Books, 27* (11). Retrieved November 15, 2003, from http://www.nybooks.com/articles/article-preview?article_id=7349

Abbott, J. H. (1981a). *In the belly of the beast.* New York: Random House.

Abbott, J. H. (1981b, March 5). The condemned. *The New York Review of Books, 28* (3). Retrieved November 15, 2003, from http://www.nybooks.com/articles/article-preview?article_id=7105

Abbott, J. H. (1981c, June 11). Two notes by Jack H. Abbott. *The New York Review of Books, 28* (10). Retrieved November 15, 2003, from http://www.nybooks.com/articles/article-preview?article_id=6973

Abbott, J. H., and Zack, N. (1987). *My return.* Buffalo, NY: Prometheus Books.

Bernstein, L. (2004). Prison writers and the black arts movement. In A. M. Beane (Ed.), *New thoughts on the black arts movement.* New Brunswick, NJ: Rutgers University Press.

Broyard, A. (1981, June 20). A life imprisoned. *New York Times*, p. 15.

Cleaver, E. (1968). *Soul on ice.* New York: McGraw-Hill.

Cohen, R. (1981, July 30). A killer who writes or a writer who kills. *Washington Post*, p. B1.

Davis, C. (2002, March 1). The killer instinct. *The Times* (London). Retrieved November 15, 2003, from Lexis/Nexis database.

Des Pres, T. (1981, July 19). A child of the state. *New York Times Book Review*, pp. 1, 14.

Farber, M. A. (1981a, July 26). Killing clouds ex-convict writer's new life. *New York Times*, p. A1.

Farber, M. A. (1981b, August 17). Freedom for convict-author: Complex and conflicting tale. *New York Times,* p. A1.

Farber, M. A. (1981c, October 11). The detective vs. the fugitive: How Jack Abbott was found. *New York Times*, p. A1.

Furman v. Georgia, 408 U.S. 238 (1972).

Kakutani, M. (1981, September 20). The strange case of the writer and the criminal. *New York Times Book Review*, pp. 1, 36–39.

Maeder, J. (1998, Noveber 12). The worth of culture. *New York Daily News*, p. 33.

Mailer, N. (1959). The white negro: Superficial reflections on the hipster. *Advertisements for myself.* New York: Putnam.

Mailer, N. (1979). *The executioner's song.* Boston: Little, Brown.

Montgomery, P. L. (1982a, January 9). Murder trial of Jack Abbott is begun. *New York Times*, p. B28.

Montgomery, P. L. (1982b, January 16). Abbott, on witness stand, admits fatal stabbing. *New York Times*, p. B27.

Montgomery, P. L. (1982c, January 19). Abbott rejects account of him as violent man. *New York Times*, p. B3.

Montgomery, P. L. (1982d, April 16). Abbott is sentenced to 15 years to life in slaying of waiter. *New York Times*, p. A1.

Newton, H. P. (1970, August 15). Eulogy for Jonathan Jackson and William Christmas. Delivered at St. Augustine's Church, Twenty-Seventh and West Streets, Oakland, California. In G. Louis Heath (Ed.), *Off the pigs! The history and literature of the Black Panther Party.* (1976). Metuchen, NJ: The Scarecrow Press.

New York v. Jack Henry Abbott. 113 Misc. 2d 766; 449 N.Y. 2d 853; LEXIS 3378. (1982, April 15). Supreme Court of New York. New York County. Retrieved November 15, 2003, from Lexis/Nexis database.

Nordell, R. (1981, August 10). Prisons: View from behind the bars. *Christian Science Monitor,* p. B4.

Radical rage and chic [Editorial]. (1981, August 18). *New York Times,* p. A22.

Silvestre, E. M. (2002, February 21). Fil-Am widow fearful no more. *Filipino Reporter,* p. 1.

Sullivan, R. (1990, June 6). Author facing damages for murder. *New York Times,* p. B2.

Useem, B. and Kimball, P. (1989). *States of siege: U.S. prison riots, 1971–1986.* New York: Oxford University Press.

Wadler, J. (11 August 1981). Violence's intellectual. *Washington Post,* p. C1.

Weinraub, B. (2000, October 4). Mailer tells a lot. Not all, but a lot. *New York Times,* p. E1.

Wolfe, T. (1970). *Radical chic & mau-mauing the flak catchers.* New York: Farrar, Straus, and Giroux.

Yardley, J. (1982, January 25). Risking society for literature? *Washington Post,* p. B1.

2

Green River Murders Case:
The Hunt for a Killer

Tomas Guillen

For many decades, the Green River in western Washington State enjoyed a reputation for attracting life and vivacious communities. In the dense forest where it originates in the Cascade Mountains in Washington, the serene Green River beckoned elk that were thirsty for fresh water. As the river meandered to lower lands, it pulled at fishermen in search of trout and farmers seeking water to irrigate crops. Where the Green River reached the edges of small, populated suburbs, its strong currents entertained families in inner tubes looking for a suntan.

All that changed in the summer of 1982. That summer, the Green River's murky waters and high banks, overgrown with blackberry vines, attracted a man in search of a secluded spot to hide dead girls and women. Since then the Green River has been linked with death and the infamous Green River Murders Case, which was one of the largest serial killer cases in U.S. history. Two decades would pass before the mystery would unravel to reveal the man who had killed over sixty women. The killer was a truck painter who had lived and worked south of Seattle, Washington, near the Seattle-Tacoma International Airport (Sea-Tac) prostitution strip—his name was Gary Leon Ridgway, and he was fifty-four years old. He was married, but

Gary L. Ridgway is led out of a King County courtroom in Seattle, Washington, after his arrest in late 2001 in the Green River Murders case. (Photo by Natalie G. Guillen)

he still sought prostitutes, partly, to satisfy a voracious appetite for sex ("Ridgway's Habits," 2001).

The Green River serial murders officially surfaced on July 15, 1982. Two children, who were riding their bicycles, had noticed a nude body in the Green River just south of Kent, which is a community located about thirty miles southeast of Seattle. The girl was sixteen-year-old Wendy Lee Coffield, a chronic runaway. On August 12, 1982, a twenty-three-year-old woman, identified as Debra L. Bonner, a prostitute from Tacoma, Washington, was found floating—nude and dead—in the Green River. Although both women were white and both were found in the Green River within a mile or so of each other, King County Police investigated the slayings as unrelated murders. It was not until August 15, 1982, that investigators and the public began to question if the killings were caused by a serial murderer.

On August 15, a Seattle man, who was traveling on the Green River, had used a hook to reach in the river to pull at what he had thought was a mannequin. He quickly realized it was a real body that was under water. As his small craft shifted on him, he discovered the body of a second woman under water. When King County Police arrived at the scene, Detective Dave Reichert found a third body on the bank of the river. The victims, all black women, were identified as Marcia Faye Chapman, thirty-one years old; Cynthia Jean Hinds, seventeen years old; and Opal C. Mills, sixteen years old. At first, it appeared that the first two victims were simply placed in the river; however, the killer had tried to conceal these victims—the two bodies that were found in the water were weighted down with rocks.

From the autopsies that were performed on the five women, investigators concluded the victims had died from some type of asphyxia. A pair of pants was still wrapped around the neck of Coffield. Nevertheless, the slayings would be termed to be polite deaths, in which the killer abstained from using extreme violence or mutilation. Autopsies also revealed what appeared to be a signature of the killer: rocks had been placed inside two of the victims' vaginas.

Investigators compiled information to help provide a profile of the victims and the killer's modus operandi (MO). All the victims frequented the streets at night, either as runaways or prostitutes. In police jargon, they were "high-risk victims" or "victims of opportunity." The killer appeared to be roaming areas that prostitutes frequented, convincing the women to get in his car, killing them, and then dumping their bodies in the Green River. To better understand the killer's potential propensities, King County Police asked the FBI for a psychological profile. After analyzing the investigative work and the crime scene, John E. Douglas, a profiler with the FBI, offered a lengthy report that contained the following observations (Douglas, 1982):

He does not want his victims to be found, and if they are eventually found, he has the mental faculties to understand that they are items of evidentiary value because of the bodies being found in the river.

His efforts to secure victims to the bottom of the river by placing rocks on top of them demonstrate that he spent a considerable period of time in or at this location.

The offender, in all probability, has a prior criminal history and comes from a family background that includes marital discord between his mother and father.

The suspect is white.

Amid the observations from Douglas's report and the FBI's discussions with King County Police, investigators concluded that these types of killers liked to "inject" themselves in the investigation. In other words, offenders tend to find an excuse to help, either by claiming to have contact with a victim or knowing something about the case. This resonated strongly with a twenty-five-person task force created to investigate the murders. It so happened that a feisty Seattle cab driver named Melvin Foster fit many of the characteristics outlined in the FBI profile. Most importantly, Foster had "injected" himself in the case by revealing that he had given the women rides throughout Seattle and that he was intimately familiar with the street life of the victims. Almost certain that Foster was the killer, Detective Reichert and the Green River Task Force followed Foster's every move and served search warrants on him and his property. Foster was interrogated repeatedly (Nalder, 1882; Norton, 1983). The investigators discovered that Foster was an odd man but not the man they were seeking. The task force's dependence on the profile and Foster, however, cost them valuable time and resources. While investigators wasted their time on Foster, the real killer remained at large. As fall turned to winter, the investigation stalled and investigators were slowly sent back to their units. Two primary reasons caused the demise of that first investigative effort. First, no matter how many search warrants were served on Foster and no matter how many hours police followed him, the investigators had been unable to create a viable case against their number one suspect. Second, when no more bodies were found in the Green River, King County Police assumed the killer had stopped killing or had left the Seattle area, but they were very wrong.

In the coming years, observers of the serial murder case would be surprised that King County Police, specifically Major Richard Kraske, virtually stopped all investigative efforts because, after all, it had been King County Police who spent years trying to solve the Ted Bundy slayings throughout the 1970s. Kraske had played an integral part in the Bundy investigation. Based on other serial killer cases, police should have known better than to assume a serial killer would stop killing (Cahill, 1986; Carpozi, 1977; Egger, 2002; Frank, 1966; Michaud and Aynesworth, 1983). An unsympathetic view of "street walkers"—both by police and the public—also seemed to play an important role in the killer's success. The killer regularly abducted victims from the prostitution strip near Sea-Tac. King County Police undercover vice officers frequented the strip, but they focused on gambling arrests and picking up the potential victims rather than looking for the man responsible for the slayings. An analysis of records related to vice unit activities during the years in which the Green River serial murders occurred demonstrated clearly that vice officers acted as if there was no serial killer at work (Smith and Guillen, 1987). Vice expenditure records were the most revealing. For instance, during one evening, two vice officers doing a "vice investigation/ prostitution" visited one business and each bought a "mixed drink." The two then moved to a second business and each bought a "soft drink." The officers then visited a third establishment and one officer purchased a "mixed drink" and the second one bought a beer.[1] Not only were King County Police vice officers not looking for the killer, they were wasting money drinking and frequenting dance clubs and gambling houses.

During that lull in the investigation, the Green River serial murderer killed repeatedly in 1982 and 1983. From the day the fifth victim was discovered in the Green River to the end of 1982, at least nine young women were abducted and killed, with most of them from the Sea-Tac prostitution strip. Twenty-seven more women disappeared during 1983. The killer seemed to be streetwise and picked up women at will. One woman named Carol Christensen, twenty-one years old, was abducted off the strip in the middle of the afternoon. Five days later Christensen's body was found staged in the woods: there was a paper bag over her head, a clean trout over her throat, another on her shoulder, and a sausage substance was sprinkled about the body. An odd-shaped wine bottle was also found resting on her crotch. Another woman, Mary B. Meehan, twenty years old, disappeared while taking a walk at night on the strip. Meehan, nine-months pregnant, was found two months later in a shallow grave near Sea-Tac. A third victim, Denise D. Bush, twenty-three years old, had vanished in October 1982 while walking to a convenience store on the strip. Most of her skeletal remains were found in June 1985 near Tigard, Oregon, a suburb that is south of Portland, Oregon. Some time later a portion of her skeletal remains was found in a wooded area right off the strip south of Seattle, near where she disappeared. The killer, obviously, intended to toy with police by moving bones (Barber and Hessburg, 1990).

It was not until the fall of 1983 that police and residents of the Pacific Northwest began, once again, to sense something amiss. Hikers and mushroom hunters wandering in wooded areas began coming across skeletal remains of women. When identified, the women fit the profile of women killed in 1982 by the Green River Killer. So many remains were discovered that King County Police quietly laid plans for creating a second Green River Task Force. In early 1984, the King County Police announced that they had formed a task force of forty-five investigators, which included Detective Dave Reichert, who was the first King County Police detective on the Green River case. The Green River Task Force investigators set themselves apart from the rest of the department by wearing green jackets with the letters "GRTF." In their headquarters, which was at a precinct near the strip, the task force designed efficient investigative units to examine tips, suspects, and missing women reports to grasp the enormity of the serial case. A "proactive" unit also was formed to meander through the strip undercover in case the killer was still active. In short, if the proactive unit failed to snag the killer with "john patrols," the task force sought to find the "needle in the hay stack" by recreating the killings that occurred in 1982 and 1983 through interviews of thousands of strip residents, business employees, and criminals. For months and years, the task force toiled at trying to uncover missing women and their acquaintances while reviewing tips of potential suspects. Often, their task was interrupted by the discovery of skeletal remains. Few weeks went by without media reports depicting investigators wearing GRTF jackets at a wooded site. It seemed investigators were spending more time excavating skeletal remains than connecting together the pieces that would lead to the killer's identification. The killer, knowing or unknowing, inundated police with victims. The time-consuming excavations of remains stole valuable time from the investigation, but the experience working on the excavations made King County Police national experts at processing outdoor scenes and the disarticulation of remains by wild animals. Eventually, the task force arbitrarily concluded that the total number of potential victims was forty-nine, and the killer had been active between the summer of 1982 and March 1984. Only two women who disappeared after the task force was formed were believed to be victims. As the investigation continued forward, the task force also found itself drowning in suspects. It seemed that many residents of King County between 1982 and 1984 emphatically thought that their husband, boyfriend, or a date had been the Green River Killer. Tips came in from all over the United States.

After two years in operation, the Green River Task Force relied heavily on the FBI's profiling skills to sift through the suspect files to generate a suspect. The suspect fit the FBI's profile: he was white, he hunted, he frequented the woods near where the bodies had been found, and he lived right off the prostitution strip near the airport. In February 1986, the Green River Task Force converged on the suspect's home in Riverton Heights with search warrants and an interviewing approach they hoped would yield a confession (Guillen, 1986). The arrest was played out over and over again by the news media. Within a matter of hours after arresting the suspect, however, investigators knew they had the wrong man.

In late 1986 and early 1987, task force investigators relied more on investigative information to analyze hundreds of suspects. One individual, Gary Leon Ridgway, a truck painter, caught the eye of one of the investigators, Matt Haney. The suspect's name was on the "inactive" list, but Haney thought the suspect merited another look. Ridgway lived and worked near the prostitution strip, and, in April 1982, he had been arrested for soliciting a police decoy prostitute. In May 1984, after the task force's formation, Ridgway had contacted the task force and said that he might have known one of the victims. He was simply trying to help, Ridgway said. In April 1987, the Green River Task Force gathered all its resources and went after Ridgway with search warrants and evidence technicians. Again, the arrest was broadcast nationwide. But, again, the task force came up empty, as investigators were unable to find the evidence to file charges. Although Ridgway was not charged, his initial arrest earned him the nickname "Green River Gary" among his peers at work.

The apparent false alarms revealed how little evidence the investigators possessed to arrest and convict the perpetrator, and by the late 1980s the Green River Task Force was disbanded. For a short time, two King County Police detectives were assigned to handle tips that trickled in. Then, there was one: Detective Tom Jensen.

Jensen spent his days babysitting the case. Some days he organized disorganized files. Other days he spent hours on the phone explaining to women why their husbands or boyfriends could not be the Green River Killer. While Jensen spent long days "Green Rivering," many of those who had worked on the task force parleyed their efforts into prestigious promotions; Detective Reichert became the commander of the King County Police.

At the end of 1991, the *Seattle Times* published a front page story that carried the headline: "Green River killer back?" (Guillen, 1991). After examining stacks of missing person reports and reviewing several years of murders in the Seattle area, the *Seattle Times* concluded that there was evidence the Green River Killer had not stopped killing in 1983, and the serial murderer was continuing his rein of terror, although at a reduced rate. King County Police remained adamant that the killings had ended in 1984. Bob Keppel, a serial killer expert who for years assisted the Green River Task Force, stated, "Some other person could be doing the same thing. It would be unbelievable to me that the Green River killer would risk detection by starting over again. He has spent his life trying to avoid detection" (Guillen, 1991, p. 2).

For Detective Tom Jensen, days rummaging through the Green River case files turned into weeks, weeks turned into months, and months turned into years. Eventually, Jensen settled on trying to identify the skeletal remains of several suspected Green River victims. Using DNA seemed the most reliable way to give the eight sets of bones names. Suddenly, something serendipitous occurred. Amid all the talk about using DNA, a suggestion was made in 2001 to apply the latest DNA technology to a saliva swab taken in 1987 from suspect Gary Leon Ridgway. His DNA matched DNA taken from several suspected Green River victims, including Carol Christensen and those found in the Green River.

On November 30, 2001, King County Police arrested Ridgway at his job (Ith, Miletich, and Wilson, 2001). Simultaneously, detectives served search warrants at several homes he had lived in since 1982. This time, investigators knew that they had the right man. The King County Prosecutor's Office agreed and charged Ridgway with seven counts of aggravated first-degree murder. Ridgway quickly hired one of the top defense attorneys in Seattle. Everyone began preparing for a lengthy trial in the year 2004. Years of appeals were expected to follow. The King County Police formed the third Green River Task Force—eleven detectives—to exhaust every lead to help link Ridgway to all the suspected Green River victims. Although Detective Haney had left King County Police, he was invited to participate in the new task force.

THE NEWS MEDIA

Short newspaper stories ushered in coverage of the case of the Green River murders in 1982. One of the articles in the *Seattle Times* that summer consisted of a few paragraphs and simply stated that a young woman had been found dead in the Green River just south of Kent and that the police were investigating. By the time the case was solved and adjudicated over two decades later, it had been the focus of stories and broadcasts of every major newspaper, magazine, and television station in the United States. Many major newspapers, magazines, and broadcast networks in Europe, too, reported on the case several times. In the end, the media had helped give the case of the Green River murders status accorded such historic cases as Jack the Ripper and the Zodiac of San Francisco.

What factors contributed to the Green River murders becoming a high-profile case and attracting sustained media attention? The sheer number of victims probably was the most important factor. For over two decades, the case of the Green River murders was known as the biggest unsolved serial case in U.S. history. The police's inability to catch the killer for so long also added an element of intrigue and mystery. Although extensive media coverage elevated the case to international prominence—especially in law enforcement and criminal justice circles—sometimes it translated into a blessing for investigators and other times a curse. Overall, during the duration of the Green River case, the relationship between the news media and investigators could only be described as acrimonious.

The confrontations between the media and investigators started at the beginning of the case. When bodies were first discovered in the Green River in 1982, Major Richard Kraske made a conscious decision not to notify the media. He feared they would get in the way and ruin evidence, as he thought they had done years earlier during the Ted Bundy investigation. The lack of notification infuriated journalists and set the tone for the relationship with investigators (Smith, 1989). After the women were found in the Green River, investigators set up a stakeout at the Green River in case the killer came back. According to police, a television news helicopter flew over the river while doing a live broadcast, exposing the stakeout. Early in the investigation, investigators also complained that news organizations were assigning too many journalists to the case and that they were getting in the way.

With the creation of the second Green River Task Force in 1984, relations seemed to improve between the media and investigators. The task force assigned a detective as a public information officer, and the detective provided the media with regular briefings on the case. Relations improved so dramatically that at one point the task force worked with one of the network's local affiliates to offer a $100,000 reward for information leading to the arrest and conviction of the Green River Killer. Interestingly, the television station offered the money during the rating season—the station could not lose. If the case was solved as a result of the reward, the station would get the credit and more viewers. If the case was not solved, the station did not have to pay out the money. Although the reward offer had little effect on the case, the media's coverage of the arrest of the Riverton Heights suspect in early 1986 had a great impact on the investigation.

The events leading to the "media circus" during the arrest began in the first days of 1986. In January 1986, the task force was excavating more skeletal remains on a steep, wooded bluff when the task force commander told a reporter that by "this time next year" the killer would be caught (Guillen, 1986). The commander's prediction and subsequent story essentially sounded an alarm for the news media to prepare for a conclusion of the long-unsolved serial murder case. When the task force arrived at the home of the Riverton Heights man—Ernest W. "Bill" McLean—two months later in March of 1986, the media surmised it was the beginning of the end. That evening hordes of journalists from scores of news organizations camped out at the suspect's home as investigators gathered evidence. When the Riverton Heights man turned out to be the wrong man, the subsequent criticism of police and the media's accusatory coverage resulted in political decisions to disband the task force (Curry, 1986).

The *Seattle Times* was the only news organization to assign journalists to the Green River Murders Case full time. The two reporters' jobs began early in the case and called for them to follow the investigation to better report on developments and try to ensure that the wrong man was not charged. Each day, the reporters interviewed relatives and friends of the women on the official Green River victim list, compiled their own lists of other potential victims, and evaluated what police did or did not do to solve the case. At times, the two *Seattle Times* reporters discovered information that investigators did not have and passed it on to the Green River Task Force. The reporters were the only members of a news organization who had weekly meetings or debriefings with the task force commander during the mid-1980s. Occasionally, the reporters had assignations with a task force lieutenant in restaurants and golf course cafes. Still, the task force could not dictate what the reporters wrote, be it positive or negative. Hence, the task force decided to circumvent the *Seattle Times* and all other news organization in 1988 in an effort to appeal directly to the public for help in identifying the killer. The task force needed to control the spin on all the information it wanted to provide—including psychological suggestions aimed at the killer—so it decided to create its own "media" following its unsuccessful attempt to build a case against Gary Leon Ridgway. The task force hired a producer from New York to create a Green River murders case "docudrama," a documentary with some reenactments. Shown on national television, the docudrama included a room full of detectives from around the United States taking telephone tips from those watching the docudrama, which was dubbed *Manhunt Live: A Chance to End the Nightmare.* The docudrama did not end the nightmare; it only succeeded in provoking local journalists at being bypassed. The acrimony and distrust that the media and investigators had surfaced at the beginning of the investigation in 1982 never really went away.

THE RESOLUTION

One late summer day in 2003, a journalist in Seattle reported that Gary Leon Ridgway had been secretly moved from the King County Jail, where he had been held since his arrest in November 2001. According to the reporter, Ridgway was transferred to an unknown location as part of negotiations for a plea agreement. Ridgway reportedly was willing to confess and promised to reveal the location of missing skeletal remains in exchange for avoiding the death penalty. The public had trouble believing the news report since King County Prosecutor Norm Maleng announced emphatically shortly after Ridgway's arrest that he would not bargain with the death penalty.

The report sparked spirited public debates in school classrooms and coffeehouses. Some of the victims' relatives even spoke publicly on the issue of a plea bargain. "I don't think they should," Virginia Coffield told a Kent newspaper. Her daughter, Wendy Lee Coffield, was the first victim found in the Green River. "The girls he killed, they didn't get a chance to bargain for their life" (Archbold, 2003, p. A1). Kathy Mills, the mother of victim Opal Mills, stated, "He didn't give the girls a chance" (Archbold, 2003, p. A1). Tim Meehan, whose sister Mary was abducted and killed in 1982, favored a deal and made public a letter he sent to King County Prosecutor Norm Maleng. In his letter, Meehan wrote, "We have a big opportunity to find out from him if he killed our family members and that opportunity shouldn't be passed up for shortening his life by a couple of years or even him passing away naturally before the time of his execution" (Archbold, 2003, p. A1).

After the television broadcast, the rest of news media—including the *New York Times* and the *L.A. Times*—chased the story, but neither the King County Police, the King County Prosecutor's Office, nor Ridgway's attorneys would confirm or negate the report of a negotiated deal. However, unexpectedly, task force investigators began showing up at sites near wooded areas where Green River victims were found in the 1980s. For several months in 2003, investigators spread out across the United States cutting down blackberry bushes and sifting dirt at close to twenty sites. In August and September 2003 alone, task force investigators searched at least seven different locations. At several of those sites, investigators found pieces of human bones. Through DNA comparisons, the DNA laboratories working with the police and the King County Medical Examiner's Office identified some of the bones as belonging to Pammy A. Avent, sixteen years old. Another set of bones found in a bog in a secluded area were those of April D. Buttram, seventeen years old. Both teenagers disappeared in mid-1983 and were on the list of Green River victims (Ith, 2003). Not since 1989 had investigators discovered skeletal remains related to the serial case. Asked about the renewed activities and identities, King County Police spokesperson Kathleen Larson claimed the task force was identifying new potential victim dump sites based on the case evidence. Larson refused to say directly if Ridgway had a hand in the latest discovery of human remains. Neither the public nor the media believed Larson or the sheriff's office explanation.

Gary Leon Ridgway had been pointing out new dumpsites, which came to light November 5, 2003, when prosecutors, defense attorneys, and investigators appeared in court to announce the plea agreement. To avoid being put to death if convicted, Ridgway confessed to being the infamous Green River Killer. Finally, investigators had found a conclusion to a case that had begun two decades earlier. The plea agreement brought closure for many families. However, Ridgway's confession introduced renewed pain to most of the victims' relatives and friends. The thousands of people around the world had logged on to the internet to read the Summary of the Evidence were stunned by Ridgway's view of his victims and the efforts he took to elude capture. At the beginning of the Summary of the Evidence, readers were warned by the following: "These crimes are unspeakably cruel and depraved and cannot be described in an antiseptic manner. Language in this document is graphic and disturbing because the crimes are horrific. The authors of this document are sensitive to the suffering of the victims, their families and survivors. With a full account of these terrible crimes, we hope that our community can find some resolution to the Green River case, and can take steps to prevent unnecessary suffering by its most vulnerable members" (King County

Prosecuting Attorney Norm Maleng, 2003, p. 2). Some of Ridgway's revelations:

Ridgway did not stop killing in 1984. He killed as late as 1998 and claimed he killed over 60 women. He would have killed more but it was time consuming to abduct and hide bodies.

Ridgway used a number of ruses to get women to trust him. He carried beer, offered to become a regular customer, feed them, and give them jobs. He had in his wallet a picture of his son and let his victims see the picture.

Ridgway killed dozens of women at his residence a few blocks from the prostitution strip. He used his son's room to reassure the women that he was not dangerous: "They look around and everything, they're getting more secure as you go. They look in the bedrooms, nobody's in there, nothin's, you know, there's my son's room, hey, this guy has a son, he's not gonna hurt anybody. His name's written on the door and it's empty and it's got his bunk bed there, toys on the floor" (King County Prosecuting Attorney Norm Maleng, 2003, p. 20). On one occasion Ridgway sneaked a victim out of his house in his son's footlocker.

Ridgway usually killed his victims by getting behind them during sexual intercourse and compressing their necks in the crook of his arm. Sometimes he strangled women with towels, a belt, a necktie, socks, jumper cables, and his T-shirt.

Ridgway's victims existed simply to satisfy his needs: "like I said before, they don't mean anything to me . . . once I've killed 'em, I didn't kept it in memory . . . I just knew where they . . . I dumped 'em . . . the women's faces don't . . . don't mean anything to me . . . There were . . . the bodies, if they had a . . . had a pussy, I would screw and that was it . . . I'd much rather have white, but black was fine. It's just . . . just garbage. Just somethin' to screw and kill her and dump her" (King County Prosecuting Attorney Norm Maleng, 2003, pp. 14, 17).

Often, Ridgway had postmortem intercourse with some of his victims and "he admitted that a few of these women had been decomposed enough that maggots had begun to appear on the bodies" (King County Prosecuting Attorney Norm Maleng, 2003, p. 25). On one occasion, Ridgway had intercourse with a dead body about thirty feet from his truck, where his son was sleeping.

Ridgway regularly took his victims' jewelry and placed it in women's bathrooms where he worked. He enjoyed thinking about women wearing the jewelry.

The horrific details of the confession were still fresh in the minds of the victims' relatives and friends and journalists from around the world when they gathered at the King County Courthouse in Seattle on December 18, 2003. On that day the plea agreement—a confession in exchange for no death penalty—was consummated. Before accepting the agreement, however,

Judge Richard A. Jones allowed relatives and friends of the victims to address Ridgway. Although some relatives told Ridgway they would forgive him, most tearfully detailed their pain before shouting hateful words at the accused. Tim Meehan, brother of victim Mary Meehan, who was murdered while nine-months pregnant, stated, "I can only hope that someday, someone gets the opportunity to choke you unconscious [forty-eight] times, so you can live through the horror that you put our daughters, our sisters, our mothers through . . . May God have no mercy on your soul" (King County Superior Court Sentencing, 2003). Gary was allowed to make a short statement. In a halting voice, he read, "I'm sorry for killing all those young ladys [*sic*]. I have tried hard to remember as much as I could to help the detectives find and recover the ladys. . . . I know how horrible my acts were" (King County Superior Court Sentencing, 2003). Gary wiped tears from his eyes during his presentation. No one seemed to believe his words or tears. Judge Jones concluded the historic sentencing with a few words for Ridgway: "The remarkable thing about you, sir, is your Teflon-coated emotions and complete absence of genuine compassion for the young women you murdered. . . . There is nothing in your life of any significance other than your own demented, calculating, lustful passion of being the emissary of death. . . . The women you killed were not throwaways, or pieces of candy in a dish, placed upon this planet for the sole purpose of satisfying your murderous desires" (King County Superior Court Sentencing, 2003). Because Ridgway claimed to have trouble recalling some of his many victims and details of his misdeeds, some of the locations of his victims' bodies remain unresolved.

SOME OF THE ISSUES

A plethora of serious issues surfaced in the case of the Green River murders and it seemed the enormity of the case and the length of the investigation tended to heighten the importance of each issue. One of the most volatile and potentially harmful issues to the investigation was the relationship between investigators and the media. Clearly, each side was to blame for creating an atmosphere so antagonistic that the public was not served. Police must methodically investigate murders to ensure they can discover the evidence for a successful prosecution. However, it is also the police's duty to be honest with the public and to provide enough information to make the public aware of a potentially serious issue of public safety. Police should have contacted the news media when more victims were discovered in the Green River. Police, who had been concerned with reporters walking through crime scenes, could have dealt with those concerns at the crime scenes, as intentionally not notifying the media only angered journalists and caused deep distrust throughout the investigation. The Green River Task Force, too, probably erred in creating its own docudrama. The task force had provided producers, who were not law enforcement officers, with sensitive investigative information that the police had refused to reveal to mainstream journalists for fear of reportedly compromising the investigation. Seattle journalists were justifiably upset at the double standard and of being usurped by a "media" that the police had created. Interestingly, as providers of information to the public, the police had acted irresponsibly, which was the opinion of some news media organizations. Investigators had believed that someone close to the killer knew he was killing, and the investigators used the docudrama to attempt to prompt that individual to contact police. They did this by showing a task force video of the excavation in the woods of Mary Meehan, who was nine-months pregnant when she was murdered. Investigators had hoped the video would lead to the identification of the killer; however, the police did not meet the outcome that they had hoped. Instead, the video left the Meehan family with an excruciating image of their daughter and her unborn baby.

The news media had a duty to inform the public of the dangers of a serial killer, and to some extent, the media ensured that investigators were doing their best to solve the murders and not wasting public expenditures. The investigation into the Green River Murder Case was costing about $2 million per year. However, from the start the news media seemed irresponsible in their coverage of the case. The television helicopter incident and reporters interviewing witnesses before the police did hindered the investigation. Journalists were interfering and apparently lacked concern for what they published. Most of the news organizations had not assigned reporters to the ongoing investigation; instead, news organizations sent out anyone who was available when a victim was found. Frequently, those individuals were unfamiliar with the case and asked ignorant questions. Too many of those journalists detested covering crime and felt uncomfortable interviewing police officers.

Neither the media nor investigators communicated their needs and how those needs could have been met during a time in which there was extreme pressure on both investigators and journalists. Because there was little or no communication between the media and investigators, problems during the Green River murder case went unresolved—they simply festered. Because the acrimony between the two sides was never addressed, similar serious problems between the media and investigators can be expected when another high-profile case arises in Seattle. Despite their problems dealing with investigators, journalists acted from a position of power and had relative success obtaining information from police. However, the victims' families and friends had no power and had regularly found themselves receiving little compassion from law enforcement.

Nearly every mother, father, brother, sister, and friend of a Green River victim became frustrated by and infuriated with investigators when trying to report one of the victims missing. Whether reporting a missing victim to the Seattle Police Department, King County Police, or one of the many small police departments in the suburbs, the victims' families and friends met with the same results; law enforcement cited a multitude of reasons for refusing to take a missing person report: The missing person had not been missing for over forty-eight hours; the missing person was too mobile and could have disappeared from any jurisdiction; and the missing person had a history of running away. When they accepted a missing person report, the police customarily assigned the reports with low priority, and it was not uncommon for police to completely ignore reports. Considering the factors that affected how the police handled missing person reports, the Green River Killer was able to abduct women at will without arousing much suspicion.

Parents would file several missing reports with the same police department or law enforcement agency in the hope of encouraging the police to look for their daughter. One couple found their daughter's photograph in a vice arrest album after being told repeatedly that the vice unit had had no contact with their daughter.[2] In the eyes of many families, police inaction translated to a lack of sympathy for young women who had lived an at-risk lifestyle. Police seemed to show little compassion because many of the Green River missing had been known to frequent the streets, and some did so as prostitutes. Some victims' relatives became so upset at police inaction that they took to the street to demonstrate. During a demonstration, Kathy Mills, mother of victim Opal Mills, carried a sign that read: "My daughter murdered, attitude—to bad [sic]. Policeman's daughter murdered, attitude: Killer found next day" (Smith, 1989).

IMPACT ON LEGAL AND POPULAR CULTURE

It will be imprudent for prosecutors, defense attorneys, and elected officials across the United States to ignore the Green River Murders Case when examining the possible cost of resolving a murder case, especially a complicated one that includes many victims and a multitude of records and evidence. The Green River case seems to have set a precedent in how all sides viewed the fiscal aspect of justice. The most unusual aspect was the appointment of a "special master" to mediate budget disputes. A King County Superior Court judge appointed the special master based on defense arguments for needing extensive funds and resources to guarantee Gary Leon Ridgway's constitutional right to a fair trial. Even after Ridgway hired one of Seattle's top defense attorneys, the judge ruled that King County was obligated to provide funds for several more defense lawyers, investigators, and legal staff. What made the appointment of a special master even more unusual was the judge's insistence that the arbitrator make decisions in secret without having his or her name revealed. The entire arrangement seemed absurd as an anonymous attorney was helping dictate how King County should spend money when there were public elected officials to make those decisions.

King County Councilman Kent Pullen stated during a hearing that "I think this amounts to judicial theft. Those are strong words, but isn't that what it amounts to? . . . King County Councilman Kent Pullen stated during a hearing . . . It sets a terrible precedent. What do we do when someone else says, 'I want a secret special master for my case?' Do we raise taxes or do we take money away from other defendants?" (Merrill, 2002, p. A1).

Eventually, news organizations challenged the judge's order to keep the special master's name secret and won. The special master turned out to be a former U.S. Attorney for western Washington, Kate Pflaumer. The use of a special master in judicial proceedings was not a new practice; however, it was unusual to use one in a criminal case and have the identity of the special master remain secret.

With the help of Pflaumer, the defense received millions of dollars to create a team of twenty-three individuals that included several attorneys, investigators, paralegals, and a transcriptionist. The public complained bitterly to King County officials since the allocations for a hefty defense team came amid budget cuts for services such as keeping swimming pools in public parks open. During 2002, the costs for police investigators, prosecutors, and defense attorneys to prepare for the trial, which never came about after a plea agreement was reached in 2003, reached over $6 million.

Ridgway's success at negotiating an agreement that ruled out the death penalty sent the wrong message to the criminal justice system and society: A serial killer could avoid the death penalty by confessing and assisting in finding his victims—to bring closure for relatives of the missing—while an individual who killed only one person could be put to death. In the end, the case of the Green River murders seemed to have little impact on society's understanding of such human atrocities. Why had Gary Leon Ridgway killed? How could he kill so many women? Why were there so many men like Ridgway crisscrossing the country? The Green River Murders Case and everyone associated with it had failed—similar to many other high-profile serial cases since the 1970s—to help society realize that the real problem seemed to be that there are too many men willing to assault and kill women. Why so much abuse? Why so much hatred? In the Green River murders, society, once again, primarily focused on the blood and guts and the film ready mystery that took over two decades to solve.

NOTES

1. This information was found in the King County Police Expense Reports, 1982, 1983, and 1984.

2. T. Estes and C. Estes (personal communication, 1990).

REFERENCES

Archbold, M. (2003, September 27). Families of victims differ on possibility of plea bargain. *King County Journal*, p. A1.

Barber, M., and Hessburg, J. (1990, February 17). Grisly twist in Green River case, remains found near Tukwila match skull discovered five years ago in Oregon. *Seattle Post-Intelligencer*, p. A1.

Cahill, T., and Ewing, R. (1986). *Buried dreams*. New York: Bantam Books.

Carpozi, G. Jr. (1977). *Son of Sam, the .44 caliber killer*. New York: Manor Books.

Curry, B. (1986, April 17). Green River killer case: TV "near-hysteria" mars "suspect" and news media. *Los Angeles Times*.

Douglas, J. (1982). Green River murders. Federal Bureau of Investigation Profile, Seattle, Washington.

Egger, S. A. (1985). *An analysis of the serial murder phenomenon and the law enforcement response*. Doctoral dissertation, Sam Houston State University. University Microfilms International Dissertation Information Service, 8605112.

Egger, S. A. (2002). *The killers among us*. Upper Saddle River, NJ: Prentice Hall.

Frank, G. (1966). *The Boston strangler*. New York: New American Library.

Guillen, T. (1986, January 4). Hunter of serial killer optimistic. Task-force leader predicts capture of slayer this year. *Seattle Times*. p. A1.

Guillen, T. (1991, November 21). Green River killer back? New murders show some similarities. *Seattle Times*, p. A1.

Hickey, E. (1997). *Serial murderers and their victims*. Belmont, CA: Wadsworth Publishing.

Ith, I. (2003, September 27). Bones linked to Green River case. *Seattle Times*, p. B1.

Ith, I., Miletich, S., and Wilson, D. (2001, December 1). Green River arrest, *The Seattle Times,* p. A1.

King County Prosecuting Attorney Norm Maleng. (2003, November 5). Prosecutor's summary of the evidence, King County Superior Court. Seattle, WA.

King County Superior Court Sentencing. (2003, Dec. 18). *State of Washington v. Gary Leon Ridgway* 01-1-10270-9 SEA. Seattle, WA: King County Superior Court.

Merril, R. (2003, August 4). Ridgway's purse strings. *King County Journal*, p. A1.

Michaud, S., and Aynesworth, H. (1983). *The only living witness*. New York: New American Library.

Nalder, E. (1982, October 5). Man reports he's a suspect in 6 deaths. *Seattle Post-Intelligencer.*

No new clues found in Green River problem. (2003, September 25). *King County Journal*, p. A2.

Norton, D. (1983, January 26). Lacey man now is only suspect in Green River Killings. *Seattle Times.*

Ressler, R. K., Burgess, A. W., and Douglas, J. E. (1988). *Sexual homicide: Patterns and motives.* Lexington, MA: Lexington Books.

Ridgway's habits, life detailed. Affidavit: Penchant for prostitutes. (2001, December 6). *Seattle Times*, p. A1.

Smith, C. (1989, October). Interview with Major Richard Kraske of King County Police.

Smith, C., and Guillen, T. (1987, September 13, 18). Green River: What went wrong? [A Special Report]. *Seattle Times*, p. A1.

Smith, C., and Guillen, T. (1990). *The search for the Green River killer.* New York: New American Library.

3

The Confessions of Henry Lee Lucas: High Numbers and Higher Stakes

Sara L. Knox

In 1984, Henry Lee Lucas was convicted of capital murder in Texas. Lucas's conviction—the third of ten eventual convictions across Texas, Florida, and Virginia—had Lucas set to serve whatever nature would allow of a 216-year term, even after the 1998 commutation of the death sentence by Texas Governor George W. Bush.[1] But in 1987, Lucas—the man the media had tagged "the one-eyed drifter" and "America's worst serial killer," and the man who had once claimed to have killed more than 600 people—died of a heart attack at sixty-four years old.

Lucas's quiet death in the Ellis Unit outside Huntsville, Texas, contrasted the noisy beginning of his long, last stretch of confinement. Arraigned in 1983 in Montague County, Texas, for the murder of an elderly neighbor, Kate Rich, Lucas was asked by the district judge if he understood the seriousness of the charge against him. According to Mike Cox,[2] Lucas stunned the court by indicating he did and that such things were nothing new to him—he had "about a hundred of them" (Cox, 1991, p. 167). But after the arraignment—according to the evidence of a taped session with his attorney of record—Lucas admitted he had made up the claim about murdering hundreds. The pattern of on-the-record sensation and off-the-record recantation was typical in the case of Henry Lee Lucas. Lucas's admission in open

A January 1984 photo of Henry Lee Lucas being escorted into the Williams County Courthouse in Georgetown, Texas. (AP/Wide World Photos)

court in Montague County, in which he attested to a decade-spanning career in serial killing, is to true crime what Joseph McCarthy's Wheeling, West Virginia, speech was to cold war anticommunism.[3]

Lucas's admission to Judge Thomas Douhitt was the first in a series of confessions. After a little while of Henry's laconically bloody tale-telling confessions to Texas Rangers and out-of-state law enforcement, 100 seemed a modest figure. In 1983, the year of Lucas's confessing, the number of killings he claimed to have committed quickly escalated. The most conservative of the credulous put the figure at 360; less cagey analysts stopped counting at 600. The most critical assessor, Brad Shellady,[4] revealed the ceiling of Lucas's confessed murders as 3,000—a figure so large that the conclusions to be drawn were that Lucas's confessions were coaxed or that Lucas was a fantasist (Shellady, 2002, p. 67).

Whatever statistic people believed, the number of *claimed* kills was simply astonishing. Lucas's confessions put into motion successive administrative and legal mechanisms: The year-long work (1984) of the Texas Ranger–led and Georgetown-based Lucas Task Force, which was the gateway for investigators from other jurisdictions seeking Lucas's cooperation in closing cases; the three-month long convening in 1985 of a grand jury in Waco, Texas, to investigate the investigators and—by implication—the basis for Lucas's confessions; and the "Lucas Report" issued by the Office of the Texas Attorney General, Jim Mattox, making public the findings of the grand jury doubtful about the reliability of Lucas's confessions and critical of the procedural ethics of the task force.

These were only the most obvious and immediate responses to the phenomenal claims of Henry Lee Lucas. Stakes—both personal and political—were high for all involved. Lucas's life depended on how his admissions were weighed. The Texas Rangers in charge of his custody had reputations to protect and—as the "gateway" to Lucas in the clearinghouse of out-of-state investigations—had a process to defend. In 1984, a great deal was at stake for state and federal law enforcement, as investigators converged on Henry Lee Lucas's "office" in the Williamson County Jail in Georgetown, Texas.[5] The cases subsequently cleared on the basis of those visits[6] represented a wide cross section of a growing minority of homicides—those flagged on supplementary homicide report forms by a tick in the box for "Assailant: Unknown" or still more ominously, "Stranger." District and state attorneys were nervous about criticisms being leveled at them for poor judicial oversight of investigative procedures—and what if tainted confessions threw doubt on the confession, per se, as an evidentiary tool? Criminologists and forensic psychologists took great interest in Lucas on the pathological end of one continuum or another: serial confessor or serial killer. However he was regarded, Lucas was the man to interview, the perfect subject for profilers, or for psychological and biometric testing. And, of course, there was the media, which was cued to the growing appetite of readers and viewers for the baroque violence of serial killing.

With interests such as these at stake, the Lucas case was destined for controversy, and—despite the eventual death of the principal actor—Lucas's case remains controversial today. So great were the stakes in play that even a matter indirectly involving the Lucas confessions has made U.S. legal history. The largest amount of damages ever awarded in a libel suit went to Vic Feazell, a former McLennan County district attorney. In 1991, Feazell was awarded $58 million in punitive damages in his suit against Belo Broadcasting, the parent company of WFAA, a television station in Dallas, Texas, for the "malicious distortions" of Feazell's character as a public official. The jury believed Feazell's claim that a series of reports WFAA aired were a smear campaign—punishment for Feazell initiating the grand jury sessions that had cast such doubt on the Lucas Task Force and raised questions about the validity of Lucas's confessions. After the trial, jury members indicated that the amount of punitive damages awarded related directly to the degree by which truth diverged from "reality," that is, public knowledge of the case. Just as WFAA's representation of Feazall's character as a public servant was far from the truth, so too was the popular conception of the Lucas case. Ironically, it was in the libel suit alone that the "myth" of Henry Lee Lucas, serial killer, was formally adjudicated.

SOMETHING ABOUT HENRY

In terms of the popular rather than public record, which is an important distinction,[7] it is almost impossible to separate the real crimes of Henry Lee Lucas from the apocryphal. Lucas had promise as a villain but was none too prepossessing—that skinny, rank, ill-shaven, chain-smoking suspect who was jailed in Montague County on a felony firearm charge in 1983 because Montague County Sheriff, Bob "Hound Dog" Conway could not help but to see Lucas as the key to something bigger. Conway had Lucas in mind for the suspicious disappearances of two people—Kate Rich, an elderly woman with whom Lucas had shared a house and for whom he had worked as general handyman, and Frieda "Becky" Powell, Lucas's traveling companion (frequently remembered in literature on Lucas as his "common-law wife"), who Lucas claimed he had last seen hitchhiking south from a truck stop in Bowie, Texas. According to the numerous sources retelling versions of the story of Lucas's 1983 arrest, Conway thought there was more wrong with Lucas. After all, Lucas had a previous murder conviction to his name: the 1960 murder in Michigan of his mother, Viola. There is another way of looking at Conway's suspicion of Lucas: Stoneburg was a small community and that "something" that had alerted Conway may well have been that Lucas was the *only* stranger in this tiny, settled community.[8] More significant still was that Lucas was a stranger with a prior record. There was just something about Henry.

The time Henry Lee Lucas spent in the Montague County Jail marks the beginning of the myth. It was at the jail that the scant and sorry but relatively easy to verify facts of his life started to be slowly eclipsed by something else. Some might call that something the truth revealed: the strange life of a serial killer laid bare (Call, 1985; Cox, 1991; Norris, 1991).[9] For the majority of the public and for a surprising number of experts, the image of a serial killer is the regnant image of Henry Lee Lucas. A minority of others, however, see the "disappearance" of the drifter/casual laborer under the persona of the serial killer as the result not of a truth revealed but of a story let loose—a hardy, adaptable story with multiple grounds for its institutional and popular appeal; a story with its roots in the wrong-headed or manipulative attempts of a man to say what he thought his jailers wanted to hear; or a story that—if told right—would secure him a more comfortable confinement (Shellady, 2002). According to critics of the Lucas myth, the tales he told found a receptive audience because they tallied with already potent cultural narratives about who serial killers were, what childhoods they had, and how they acted both in and out of custody (Knox, 2001). Philip Jenkins has suggested that Lucas, in 1984, personified the much-publicized "dark figure" findings of Arlen Specter's Senate Juvenile Justice Subcommittee. The drifter/killer figure that Lucas embodied gave a frightening and vivid face to what that subcommittee had warned were unknown (but large) numbers of predatory killers roaming the United States and taking the lives of an equally unknown (but large) number of innocent people (Jenkins, 1994).

TELLING THE STORY

The tale of serial killing told—fantastically—by Henry Lee Lucas with such brutal eloquence in 1984 has two principal areas of impact: two related and powerful audiences. The significance of the confessions to law enforcement and to groups with broader and often politicized concerns with "law and order" was one facet of the Lucas phenomenon. The other facet was Lucas's place as a figure of infamy in true crime and popular culture. To discuss either facet of Lucas, it is necessary to précis the Lucas myth itself.

Generally, the tale of Henry Lee Lucas is told in conventional narrative terms: Beginning with an awful childhood and ending with his confinement, after the controversial recantations, in Huntsville, Texas. Between those two imbalanced poles (there being much more interest in his childhood than his life after recantation) is a world of woe and a life packed with bloody encounters, Satanic rituals, and predatory drifting of a less dangerous kind.[10] One of Lucas's biographers, Joel Norris, stated:

Did [Lucas] become a hopeless drifter who worked at odd jobs here and there, mooched off relatives, and generally did very little while accomplishing even less? Or, as law enforcement agencies believe, did he set out on one of the longest serial killing sprees in the annals of American crime? (1991, p. 61)

Despite setting the question (and devoting half a chapter to a view of the life of mooching without murder), Norris, like so many others, goes on to explore at length the life of Lucas as one of an itinerant killer.

The remainder of this chapter is, then, by its very nature apocryphal and controversial. There is no single authoritative account of the life and crimes of Henry Lee Lucas. However, the basic elements of Lucas's story and its infinite small variations have been so influential, popularly persuasive, and memorable that it is necessary to précis them in order and then proceed with a discussion of why the mythic tale of Lucas's serial killing has had such longevity.

THE STORY

Henry Lee Lucas was born August 23, 1936, in Montgomery County, Virginia. Lucas was the youngest child of nine and was raised in a dirt-floored cabin in a wooded holler between Brushy and Get Mountains on Craig Creek. Lucas later expressed doubts about his true paternity, but as far as he knew, his father was Anderson Lucas, who was an alcoholic double-amputee and violently dominated (like the rest of the family) by Lucas's mother, Viola. Viola Lucas had earned income as a prostitute, drank incessantly, and beat her husband, her children and—as legend has it—customers unwise enough to attempt to shortchange or otherwise disrespect her. Like his brothers and sisters, Lucas was neglected: ill-clothed, ill-shod, and undernourished. The attention the children did receive was unwelcome and often abusive. It is said that when Lucas began his schooling he appeared at the schoolhouse dressed in a girl's clothes and his hair so long it had formed natural curls.[11] His early years were punctuated by physical and emotional misery, some purposeful and some accidental (all versions of his life agree that the two injuries to Lucas's left eye resulted in him being fitted with a glass replacement that was too small).

At sixteen years old, Lucas was arrested for burglary and served the first of successive indentures in state institutions: first at a vocational school for juveniles and then—a year after his release—in the Virginia State Penitentiary. One prison break later and after time was added to his sentence, Lucas was released for a brief stint of liberty, during which he stayed with his older sister, Opal, in Michigan. It was in Michigan, during Viola's Christmas vacation visit with her children, that Lucas stabbed his mother during an argument. Lucas inflicted just one wound, not particularly deep, with the small bladed knife that he habitually carried. Viola Lucas may have survived had she been tended to; however, Lucas left the elderly woman bleeding, fled the house, stole a vehicle, and left Michigan.

Detained in Ohio, Lucas—like so many other indigent defendants—did not resist the extradition order and was returned to Michigan to stand trial in March 1960. Both sides agreed that Lucas had killed his mother but wrangled over the intent behind the blow, and it was probably that doubt that had softened the jury's finding: guilty of second-degree murder. After hearing evidence to mitigate punishment, the presiding judge sentenced Lucas to a minimum of twenty years of a forty-year life term.

Early in his confinement, Lucas was transferred out of general population to the Ionia State Mental Hospital. Lucas spent four years heavily drugged and subject to a therapeutic regime that included days of being made to walk on tiled corridors with rags strapped to his feet: a perambulating human floor polisher (Norris, 1991). In 1966, he was transferred back to the state prison in southern Michigan to serve the rest of his term. During the 1960s and early 1970s, prisons in the United States were becoming overcrowded and new correctional facilities were being built and early release programs were being institutionalized to ease the overcrowding. After serving just ten years of his sentence, Lucas was released under parole supervision. Not long after his release, Lucas was arrested again on a charge of attempted kidnapping, and he spent another four years incarcerated.

Lucas's confessions deal most thoroughly with a relatively short period of his life; from winter 1975 to fall 1983 when he was taken into custody in Montague County. These are the years filled, in his cumulative account in the confessions, with a busy schedule of murder: people stabbed, shot, strangled, eviscerated, drowned, beaten to death, or—in a rarer and less "hands-on" method—run over with one of the long succession of used cars that the mechanically gifted Lucas maintained and drove.[12]

In the first year of his freedom, Lucas stayed with relatives, got married (although it did not last and he is said to have abused the children from his wife's first marriage), and worked odd jobs throughout Maryland, Pennsylvania, and Texas. By 1979 he was single again, and Lucas found himself in Florida. There, in the line at a Jacksonville soup kitchen, Lucas met Ottis Toole. Toole, who was ever generous, suggested Lucas come stay with him and his family, and the two quickly struck up a close relationship that offered companionship on the road and true domesticity. Lucas soon became close not only with Toole but to Toole's mother and his sister's children, Frank and Frieda.

Two versions of the story of the meeting of Lucas and Toole in the Jacksonville soup kitchen are told by Norris (1991). Lucas and Toole met in 1978 while both were picking cups at a mushroom farm in Pennsylvania, which was a job both soon ditched in favor of a run across six states robbing "small stores and gas stations along the townships roads," and—when it suited them—killing those who worked there (Norris, 1991, p. 73). On that early trip Toole told Lucas that he was working for an outfit willing to pay for the kind of killing that they were doing for free, an outfit dedicated to chaos and to Satan himself.

For writers like Max Call (author of the earliest and most outrageous account of Lucas's crimes), this last version of the meeting of Toole and Lucas is the telling one. The idea had been planted that would soon grow into Lucas's commitment to a Satanic cult—the Hand of Death—that inducted Lucas in an Everglades boot camp for Satanists that was complete with blood rituals, human sacrifice and orgiastic sex. The Hand of Death then supposedly sent Lucas—with Toole or alone—across the Texas border into Mexico with carloads of drugged children for illegal adoption, contracted the two to kill apostate cult members or snooping law enforcement, and tracked their mayhem by a "code" that was contained in the patterned arrangement of bodies at the crime scenes or by strange postmortem markings on the corpse (Call, 1985).[13] For Call and others who followed the account of the Hand of Death's impact on Lucas's life, the following years of violence were at least partly in service to this "higher" calling.

In early 1979, Toole and Lucas separated only to reunite in Jacksonville, where they would enjoy a quiet period of domesticity until they again took to the road, this time with Toole's niece and nephew.[14] The string of killings in that 1980 sojourn through Alabama and Georgia was long: uncooperative storekeepers, single women stranded by the roadside or making calls at an isolated phone booth, and an old woman in her trailer. That year of wandering was punctuated by another stay in Jacksonville, where Lucas got even closer to Toole's niece, Frieda, or "Becky," as he liked to call her. Then he was off to Maryland by himself, returning to find that Becky had been placed in a juvenile home. Determined not to be without her, he and Toole broke Becky out of the juvenile home and left Florida again, this time headed for Texas. Not much later, it was just Lucas and Becky Powell, as Toole left them to return to Florida.[15] The couple traveled through Texas, and Becky calmly watched as Henry gave in to his less than occasional fancy for killing. Becky was the Carol Ann Fugate to Lucas's older, grizzled Charlie Starkweather.

In early 1982—after a long period of drifting and hand-to-mouth existence that (as myth has it) had random killing and robbery as the only relief to that monotony (Norris, 1991)—Lucas and Becky ended up in Hemet, California, where a good Samaritan by the ironic name of Smart found the couple on a roadside—footsore and ragged. He offered them a place to stay and offered Lucas some temporary work in a furniture shop. When the temporary work ended, Smart asked that the couple take on a job as casual companions or caregivers to his wife's aging mother in Ringgold, Texas. Lucas and Becky found a home and a vocation living with Kate Rich.

Lucas fixed things around Rich's home, and the couple would drive into town to collect groceries and do the everyday business that Rich was getting too frail to do. The items charged to Rich's account soon changed from her usual staples to items that included crates of beer and cartons of cigarettes. Suspicious, the storekeeper phoned nearby relatives of the elderly Rich and suggested they check in on her and her new houseguests. When the relatives arrived they found the house in an appalling state, and they promptly (if politely) asked the couple to move on.[16]

Lucas and Powell did move on, though not very far. The last "home" for Lucas and Powell was the House of Prayer in Stoneburg, Texas, a small Christian community presided over by the Reverend Reuben Moore. As this part of Lucas's story is generally told, the couple's stay at the House of Prayer was a watershed in their relationship; it was the scene of Becky Powell's religious conversion and the source of a more thoroughgoing change of heart about her wayward life. In this telling, Lucas's other commitments stayed firm. He was happy to work on the roof and other casual labor for Reverend Moore, and the accommodation and food offered as payment were also welcome. However, Lucas did not want to commit to staying at the Stoneburg community, and the idea of taking Powell back to Florida so she could pay her dues (in evading juvenile justice) seemed both foolish and dangerous to him. The arguments had over this commitment to the community wore down Lucas's resolve, and late in the summer of 1982, he decided to take Powell back to Florida. Reuben Moore sent them with his blessings and some traveling cash, which the couple dealt sparingly with, as they decided to hitchhike rather than take the bus. They did not get far, and Lucas returned alone to the House of Prayer just a few days later. Distraught, he told Moore that Powell had left him.[17]

Later, during the early stages of his confessing, Lucas—no less distraught—told another story of his parting with Powell, which is the story that would stick so well in the public's imagination and would give director John McNaughton the shocking end to his infamous and acclaimed serial killer biopic, *Henry: Portrait of a Serial Killer* (1989). Not able to find a ride or find a hotel room for the night, Lucas and Powell slept in a field. They started drinking; then he and Becky argued, and an infuriated Lucas stabbed Becky Powell repeatedly in the chest. After he took a few hours to recover from the shock of what he had done, he hacked her body to pieces, sorted these pieces by size into pillowcases, and scattered them around the field. Lucas then walked back to the House of Prayer.

In the period after his return to the House of Prayer, a quiet Lucas worked off his debt to Moore. According to his confessions (the story of sudden violence and casual cruelty so persuasively paired with the account of his killing of Becky Powell), Lucas went to visit Kate Rich to drive her to church one Sunday evening, but when Rich assailed him with one too many concerned questions about the whereabouts of Becky Powell, Lucas stabbed her to death. After having sex with her dead body, he stuffed Rich into a culvert where time and the still warm late summer air did its work. Weeks later, after Lucas had returned to the House of Prayer after yet another stint of worried wandering and bothered by the sense of a job still undone, Lucas moved Rich's remains and burned them in a wood stove at the House of Prayer.[18]

It is Lucas's departure from his chosen style of murder (of strangers and strangers at some safe distance form his home or work) that his criminal biographers have tended to suggest was the proximate cause of his capture. He had become sloppy in his grief at having killed Becky Powell—now there were two disappearances in Montague County of women Lucas had known. Certainly, it was the association of the Rich disappearance with Lucas's murder of his mother (another elderly woman on whom he had been dependant) that had stirred the suspicions of Montague County Sheriff Conway and Texas Ranger Phil Ryan.

Conway and Ryan had connected the disappearance of Kate Rich and concerns of her relatives to the couple sent to care for them. Ryan then went to talk to those at Lucas's last known address, the House of Prayer, where he had learned from Reuben Moore that Lucas and Powell's contentment had turned into regular arguments; these arguments culminated in the couple leaving and Lucas returning, alone. Ryan and Conway then attempted to locate Becky Powell, discovering that they could not and that she had—in any case—been a young person at risk, and one whose disappearance was, therefore, even more worrisome. Law enforcement had traced the car Lucas had been driving at the time he was staying at the House of Prayer to its new owner in Needles, California, and they had found bloodstains on the front seat, which gave them grounds to detain Lucas as a material witness in what they were treating as a murder back in Montague County. Lucas was in Beaumont, California, once again staying with the Smarts. Not taken aback by the blood on the front seat of what once had been his car, Lucas claimed it as his own; subsequent tests were ambivalent.[19]

It was not until the firearms charge that Lucas was brought into custody for what would be the last time. In the mythic account, Lucas was slippery and evasive until a change of heart in his jail cell late one night; he had found himself visited by a blue light from out of which a voice spoke to him that had asked him to cleanse himself by providing a true and full account of his wicked life. Not able to get all of the details into one account, Lucas simply wrote a note saying he had killed Powell and Rich. This tale of the conversion came from Lucas himself, but after the fact, the conversion is not supported by the account of the deputy responsible for the jail that night. (Lucas may well have stated his admissions to please one of his only non-law enforcement visitors, "Sister Clemmie" Schroeder.) Nevertheless, it was this apocryphal story of dramatic religious conversion that provided the ongoing motive for the confessions: Lucas's desire to set both the record and his soul straight.

WEIGHING THE CONFESSIONS

For much of 1984 and 1985 (when the process of recantation started), Lucas was "booked solid" with law enforcement (Call, 1985, p. 158). His confessions provided the district attorneys of several jurisdictions with enough evidence to prosecute him for multiple counts of homicide, one of them capital, and to secure those convictions. Those convictions emboldened others to seek the Lucas cure for stubbornly unsolved cases. Steve Simmons, the district attorney for El Paso, Texas, was one of those emboldened. Facing reelection, Simmons was tempted by the headline-catching Lucas and the prospect of solving cold cases for which the killer's identity remained unknown. Even one such case settled would be a victory, but Lucas's history of clearing cases offered bigger, better, and more promising numbers. Simmons thought he should review some of the cleared cases first to check the process before he committed his own jurisdiction and his own cold cases to the pile. He requested 100 cases of the total cleared to that point. What Simmons discovered was unsettling at best: many of those cases that had been cleared and accounted to Lucas had since been reopened. Still, other cases were questionable on other grounds. In one case, the victim had since turned up alive. Simmons not only abandoned hope of the "Lucas cure" for the cold cases in his jurisdiction, but he brought the irregularities he had discovered to the attention of Jim Mattox, the attorney general for Texas.

From early on in the Lucas case, there had been various moves afoot to weigh the basis in fact of his confessions, but the Lucas story itself had snowballed to such an extent that—for over ten years—the power of the confessions grew apace with the amassing of the documentary material available to debunk them. As Lucas's defenders have observed, Lucas was his own worst enemy: He was no help to his defense and—even after his recantation began—he was still willing to help out visiting law enforcement by "taking cases."[20] However, even without the morass of documents, the Lucas defense eventually assembled to debunk the confessions and convictions—Lucas's own inimitable storytelling provided proof enough not just that he was a fantasist but that he narrated his confessions in tune with the world as he saw it. Lucas was a man with a poor education but a powerful audience. In 1984, Lucas told the Texas Rangers that he had delivered the poison that killed hundreds of the faithful in Jim Jones's compound in Guyana. When asked how he had got the poison to Guyana, Lucas told his interrogators that he had driven his deadly cargo straight through.[21] For Lucas, the answer was logical: his was a world navigable by road—never mind the Panama Canal.

Lucas's willingness to tell a story and his facility for the recall of detail (both of things experienced and things he had read) generally worked against him. However, those uncannily precise powers of recall were also what eventually saved him from lethal injection. In June 1998, Lucas was scheduled to be executed for the rape and homicide of an unidentified woman whose body had been found dumped near Interstate 35. The unidentified woman, who still remains unidentified today, was dubbed "Orange Socks" for the fluorescent socks she was wearing.

In June 1983, Lucas confessed in what Shellady and Hansen noted as his stylistically signature "conditional third person" narrative point of view: "She would have been sexually assaulted. She would have several stab wounds, probably some through the breasts, probably, and some through her chest cavity. . . . And she would have been in a sort of a field, grassy area" (Shellady and Hansen, 1994, p. 169). The detail chosen and the style of narrative revealed a great deal about the background of this particular interview and the procedure of many of the Lucas interviews. When Sheriff Boutwell came to see Lucas about the Orange Socks case, he arrived with the medical examiner's report in hand. Was this why Lucas—a man confused enough about geography to think he could drive to Guyana—described the wounds in anatomical jargon: "Several stab wounds . . . through her chest cavity"? Even the description of the victim was telling: "Five foot seven to five nine, 140 pounds, with long brown hair, eighteen to twenty years old"— information on the first page of the report Sheriff Boutwell brought with him to his interview with Lucas (Shellady and Hansen, 1994, p. 170). The narrative point of view, with its "she would haves," presented an odd combination of eagerness to please and reticence in the person confessing, and strong, too, was the sense that what was happening was a story reinterpreted, rather than one that was retold. Whatever the statements reveal, they pleased Sheriff Boutwell at the time. According to Shellady and Hansen (1994), Boutwell secured a signed confession before Lucas's lawyer joined his client for the interview.

It was not until early 1998 that Lucas's penchant for yarning and his impressive powers of recall actually did him any good. Lucas's defense team had had years worth of their own solid research to help in the battle for commutation of his death sentence, which included a meticulously documented time line of Lucas's activities and whereabouts that proved he could not have done most—if not all—of the killings he had confessed to; however,

Lucas's alibi for the Orange Socks murder had been seriously undermined during the trial.[22] Then, during one consultation in Huntsville, Texas, Lucas breezily told someone on his defense team that, one late October evening in 1979, Toole, Powell, and Lucas had seen a fiercely burning Cadillac doused by the Jacksonville fire department on a street near his home. Without realizing it, Lucas had finally provided himself an alibi for October 30, 1979. Subsequent research by Lucas's defense produced police and fire department records that detailed the response on October 30 to the rekindle of a 1974 Cadillac Eldorado. The fire was 1,100 miles from where the Orange Socks killing had occurred just two hours later (Shellady and Hansen, 1994).

There is one final element of the confessions that requires detailing, because it provides a clue to the cultural power of the Lucas confessions to capture the popular imagination and shape Lucas as the prototypical, emblematic, and predatory killer. Many of Lucas's confessions detailed terrible violence, but they also stressed a perverse, insatiable sexual appetite both in the violence of the killings and in his "ordinary" life. In many of his confessions, as in his most incriminating statements (to the killings of Kate Rich, Frieda "Becky" Powell, and the unidentified woman known as Orange Socks), Lucas said he had penetrative sex with his victims postmortem, often after having had consensual or nonconsensual sex with them previously. In his statement on the murder of Orange Socks, Lucas said he had "come inside" her (Shellady and Hansen, 1994, p. 188). Of Powell, Lucas said he had "taken advantage of her" after the murder, and just to make sure his meaning was clear he added, "taking advantage of her means I had sexual intercourse" (Shellady and Hansen, 1994, p. 342). The confessions portray Lucas as a man who had a lot of sex, much of it violent and some of it not. But, while in prison in 1956, Lucas was stabbed in the groin area. He sustained such serious nerve damage that he was rendered functionally impotent. When tested in the mid-1990s, Lucas showed no penile response to stimulus whatsoever.[23] Such evidence suggested that Lucas used the *confessions* to act out a fantasy of sexual dominance and, more banally, to prove his virility.[24] This is a radically different interpretation from that of the more culturally persuasive myth of Henry Lee Lucas, as an exemplar of the class of serial killing sexual sadists more generally and that he used the killings to act out a fantasy of sexual dominance.

THE CULTURAL MOMENT

In 1986, Elliot Leyton published his study of what he termed "mass" killing, *Compulsive Killers*. It became an immediate bestseller in the United

States, Canada, and United Kingdom, where *Compulsive Killers* was published under the much more evocative title—*Hunting Humans*. In the following decade from 1985 to 1995, the serial killer became one of the preeminent figures of popular culture: the subject of documentary and sensational true-crime studies, the stalker villain in "slasher" movies, and foe to detective protagonists in thrillers on film and in popular literature—most famously so in Thomas Harris's *Silence of the Lambs* and Jonathan Demme's direction of the film version of the novel. Philip Jenkins (1992) noted that such was the serial killer craze that true-crime titles that were once destined for remainder shelves reappeared in print and sold quickly. Old crimes were rehashed in print and in film, and talk show and magazine format shows turned, with gusto, to stories not just of serial killers but of the women who love them.

Lucas was arrested in 1983, and his confessions have remained a hot topic for more than two decades since his arrest. Lucas burst onto the cultural scene at the height of what Jenkins identifies as the bureaucratic and jurisdictional construction of the "serial killer problem" (Jenkins, 1992, pp. 55–80). Lucas's appearance on the cultural stage coincided with the start of a period of unprecedented popular cultural ascendancy of the serial killer and thoroughgoing rise in a fear of, and fascination with, crime and the looming threat of random violence (Best, 1999, pp. 4–5). In such an historical context, Lucas's infamy cannot be regarded as coincidental. His place in the limelight was secured by the very same fantastical quality to the confessions that created doubt about their truth. Only a minority of people found Lucas's tales of infinite variations in killing techniques incredible because his audience of law enforcement, jurists, psychiatrists, criminologists, journalists, and the worldwide public were already primed to read about the serial killer as the most exotic and dramatic of killers. Were not the favorite subjects of true-crime compendiums and thrillers in fiction and film notorious for just such baroque feats of violence—garroting their victims, for eviscerating and hacking, for staging the display of bodies reversed over by cars, or burned or beaten into unrecognizable shapes? Throughout the later 1980s and into the 1990s Henry Lee Lucas personified the popular cultural figure of the serial killer, and—for criminologists like Joel Norris—provided the perfect example of the type. Lucas, therefore, summed up in one the worst the world had to offer: a monstrous drifter-drinker-killer with a Taylorist efficiency for violence.

A CULT CLASSIC FILM FOR A CULT KILLER

Just as it is impossible to separate Lucas the man from Lucas the myth, it is difficult to separate the myth of Lucas from the lead character in the cult classic biopic of his crimes. John McNaughton's *Henry: Portrait of a Serial Killer* was a controversial film, just like the film's subject. The film's release to cinema was banned in certain countries, and the version in greatest circulation has been purged of the worst of its violence. McNaughton's film captures the myth of Lucas evocatively, for—as most critics have observed—its shock value lies in the banality of the violence it portrays. McNaughton's Henry was Henry Lee Lucas in McNaughton's words: a killer who once called the act of killing "as easy as walking outdoors,"—if he ever "wanted a victim," he would "just go get one" (Fox and Levin, 1994, p. 49). In *Killers among Us*, Steven Egger wrote of Lucas once protesting that "except for killing" he had been as "nice as he could be." On film, as in the confessions, this portrait of lackadaisical violence compelled audiences because it packaged their worst fears about the sociopathic fabric of the world into the fame of one man. And, just as the still unclosed cases in life put to account a bewildering array of losses to just one cause, the body count on film has a single, busy source: Henry Lee Lucas, serial killer extraordinaire.

NOTES

1. Consecutively: six life sentences, two seventy-five-year sentences and one sixty-year sentence. The convictions were for the deaths of: Frieda Powell, Kate Rich, Police Officer Clemmie Curtis, Lillie Pearl Darty, Linda Phillips, Diana Bryant, Glenna Biggers, "Orange Socks" (the sole capital conviction), and Laura Jean Domez.

2. The reliability and impartiality of Mike Cox's account is questionable. Cox, prior to and during the writing of his study of Lucas, was the public relations officer for the Texas Rangers.

3. On February 9, 1950, at the Ohio Countrywomen's Republican Club, Senator Joseph McCarthy's claimed to have a list of "205" Communists in the State Department. The figure fluctuated in his later speeches, but the idea contained by it (a dark figure of 'Red' infiltrators undermining American society) made his name and, briefly, his career.

4. Shellady is by far the most well-informed commentator on the Lucas case. He worked as an investigator for a various number of Lucas's successive court-appointed attorneys between 1988 and 1998, and Shellady compiled in that time a vast archive of official documents pertaining to the investigation of the cases credited to Lucas, transcripts, interrogation and interview tapes from police files.

5. The flood of offices giving their unsolved cases to Lucas in the hope that he'd claim one or other as one of "his" slowed, but did not stop, until his death in 2001.

6. The figure given for the cases cleared varies—like most numbers at play in the published accounts of the case. One hundred and ninety-eight and 213 are the

numbers most commonly cited. One figure may attempt to include the convictions (but even so the sum is not accurate).

7. The public record comprises an enormous amount of official documentation containing information that the popular, or commonsensical, account of the crime cannot take into account. Facts are often the least visible elements of the fabric of narrative of a given crime (Knox, 1998).

8. Brad Shellady (personal communication September 23, 2003).

9. Joel Norris (1991), to his credit, does construct parallel narratives for Henry Lee Lucas: One of a life of itinerant drifting and odd jobs, and one of that same itinerant life punctuated regularly by murders.

10. The story of Lucas's life as a serial killer survives only in secondary forms, all of which reorder his life into a conventional biographic structure. Although some people have accessed the documentary sources, there are no published records that tell Lucas's "life" this way. There would, nevertheless, be great value in a reconstructed narrative centered on the order in which Lucas narrated the events of his early life and killing career, a reconstruction that could include the missing side of conversations with jailers, and visitors, could include the strategic context of the confessions.

11. Another contentious element of the Lucas story, the tale of his being "dressed in girl's clothes" also varies in terms of how long Lucas was dressed this way, and where (home or school) and for what reason he was dressed like that. Although some authors suggest that it was Henry Lee Lucas's teacher who tells the story of his being dressed that way, the story comes primarily, it seems, from Lucas's mouth.

12. It is Lucas's record of vehicle ownership that provides the best basis in evidence to debunk the confessions. Brad Shellady and the Lucas defense team spent days and weeks searching licensing, purchase, and insurance records to compose an alternative timeline for Lucas's activities in the supposed "killing" years (Brad Shellady, personal communication, September 23, 2003).

13. Call wrote his book with the full cooperation of Lucas, basing it largely on a full forty hours of taped interviews. The primary work was done before his subject's recantations and entirely on Lucas's account. Call clearly believed in the moral lesson of Lucas's confessions as a brave and Christian act. By inference, Call takes their content to be true: "Under Divine inspiration, Henry's talking" (Call, 1985, p. 162) and "setting the record straight" (p. 17). For a compressed account of the role played by the Hand of Death in the confessed murders, also see Norris (1991, pp. 86–109) and Cox (1991).

14. Frank Powell, a key witness to the alleged "crimes" of Lucas in this period, was for years keenly sought for interview by the Lucas defense team. According to Brad Shellady, Frank Powell was hard to find. He was cosseted by the Texas Rangers, and it would seem (from the brief statements Powell eventually made) that he was heavily influenced by them. Powell would later describe those years as empty; he could remember nothing of them or only vaguely recalled murders he was "told" about rather than witnessed (the implication being not that Henry or Ottis described them but that the Texas Rangers had) (Brad Shellady, personal communication, September 23, 2003).

15. Cox tells this story differently in his study of Lucas. Toole was not in on the "break-out" and was left in Jacksonville, "bewildered that Lucas had left him behind" (1991, p. 99).

16. There is a telling alternative account of these keys events. There is evidence to suggest that Kate Rich offered to buy the beer and cigarettes for Lucas and Powell because she liked them and they were her houseguests. She knew what the deliveries comprised. In this account, Powell and Lucas were asked to leave by Rich's relatives because their stay was compromising Rich's welfare payments. The house was a "mess" but not unusually so, as Rich had never been too scrupulous a housekeeper (Brad Shellady, personal communication, September 23, 2003).

17. There is evidence to suggest Becky Powell did leave Lucas this way. Witnesses testified by affidavit to having seen Lucas at the Country Square truck stop in Alvord, "hanging around" and waiting for something. One of the waitresses at the attached diner testified that she had seen a girl answering Frieda (Becky) Powell's description get into a Red Arrow semi-trailer (Brad Shellady, personal communication, September 23, 2003).

18. Another unlikely detail. The temperatures required for the burning of human remains simply could not have been reached, let alone maintained, in this type of oven (Brad Shellady, personal communication, September 23, 2003). Even assuming they could have been, the published accounts differ on where the oven was at the time Lucas used it. Norris wrote that Lucas burned the remains down to a few tiny fragments of bone and ash in "the wood stove in the communal kitchen" (1993, p. 173) of the House of Prayer—one would think a rather public place to choose for such a time-consuming endeavor. Cox's account, however, is of Ranger Phil Ryan and a deputy finding (at Lucas's prompting) "a wood-burning stove like the one described by Lucas . . . [b]ehind Lucas's trashed out apartment behind the converted chicken barn," where he and Powell had stayed (1991, p. 161). From the communal kitchen to the trashed back lot was quite a distance.

19. The high temperatures and the passing of time had degraded the blood evidence to such an extent that any attempt at correlation would have been next to useless.

20. Brad Shellady, personal communication, September 23, 2003.

21. Brad Shellady, personal communication, September 23, 2003.

22. The prosecution had brought witnesses to testify to the common practice of forging work records, thus undermining the Lucas defense's evidence that Lucas had been signed in and out of a roofing job in Florida on the day Orange Socks had been killed near san Antonio.

23. The Lucas defense team conducted the tests and had independent corroborative evidence in prison record detailing the original attack and in the medical report of the physician who treated Lucas (Brad Shellady, personal communication, September 23, 2003).

24. It would be naïve to suggest that rape necessarily involved penile penetration and ejaculation but, significantly, these were elements of the sexual violence that Lucas constantly stressed. Despite the baroque and endless variations of violence Lucas

confessed that there's a distinct lack of that kind of violence sadly routine to rape: the use of objects as a proxies for the penis.

REFERENCES

Best, J. (1999). *Random violence: How we talk about new crimes and new victims.* Berkeley, CA: University of California Press.

Call, M. (1985). *Hand of death: The Henry Lee Lucas story.* Lafayette, Louisiana: Prescott Press.

Cox, M. (1991). *The confessions of Henry Lee Lucas.* New York: Pocket Books.

Fox, J. A., and Levin, J. (1994). *Overkill: Mass murder and serial killing exposed.* New York: Bantam Doubleday Dell.

Jenkins, P. (1994). *Using murder: The social construction of serial homicide.* New York: Aldine de Gruyter.

Knox, S. (1998). *Murder: A tale of modern American life.* Durham, NC: Duke University Press.

Knox, S. (2001, May). The productive power of confessions of cruelty. *Postmodern Culture, 11*(3). Retrieved October 1, 2003, from http://www.iath.virginia. edu/pmc/text-only/issue.501/11.3knox.txt

McNaughton, J. (Writer/Director). (1989). *Henry: Portrait of a serial killer* [Motion Picture]. United States: Maljack Productions.

Norris, J. (1991). *Henry Lee Lucas: The shocking true story of America's most notorious serial killer.* London: Constable and Company.

Shellady, B. (2002). Henry: Fabrication of a serial killer. In R. Kick (Ed.), *Everything you know is wrong; the disinformation guide to secrets and lies* (pp. 64–71). New York: The Disinformation Company.

Shellady, B., and Hansen, G. (1994). *Things only the killer knew: The framing of Henry Lee Lucas.* Unpublished manuscript.

4

The *State of Texas* v. *Karla Faye Tucker:* Death Row Inmate #777

Heidi Ahl-Quanbeck

The execution of Karla Faye Tucker drew media attention, as the execution epitomized violent youth, excessive drug use, profuse hatred, incriminating confessions, and alleged sexual overtones. When she had participated in one of the most brutal and violent murders in Houston, Texas, Tucker was twenty-three years old and had a severe drug addiction. On the morning of June 13, 1983, Tucker, along with her accomplice, Daniel Garrett, murdered Jerry Lynn Dean and Deborah Thornton with a pickax. The victims were struck more than forty times, and the pickax was left embedded in Thornton's chest. The defendants went to the Dean residence with the intent to commit robbery; when they left, however, two people had been murdered. The victims were two very different people. Tucker knew Jerry Dean, and it was apparent that Tucker and Dean disliked each other. The other victim, Deborah Thornton, a complete stranger, was a mother with a young family who was simply in the wrong place at the wrong time. These innocent victims were brutally murdered, suffering horrendous deaths at the hands of Tucker and Garrett.

The murder investigation took approximately five weeks, and the case was solved when Doug Garrett, Daniel Garrett's brother, stepped forward and provided the evidence necessary to make an arrest (BBC News, 1998a).

In the end, both Tucker and Garrett would be convicted of capital murder and sentenced to death for these gruesome crimes. Garrett would later die in 1993 from liver disease while awaiting a new trial (BBC News, 1998a), but Tucker was executed on February 3, 1998, which was fourteen years after sentencing (Geringer, 2003). Even though the murders were extremely shocking and disturbing, the case, from its initial discovery through the trial, received only moderate regional attention. The case did not capture the full glare of the media until Tucker's execution was imminent. Tucker's execution grabbed the media's attention and led to numerous debates regarding the constitutionality of the death penalty and, ultimately, its essential purpose.

Tucker was a self-proclaimed, born-again Christian who pleaded for mercy, requesting commutation of her sentence and to have her now repentant life spared. Support to spare Tucker from the death penalty was voluminous and included requests for judicial intervention, pleas to the governor's office, and Tucker's own use of the media, granting interviews to several news organizations and networks, in an attempt to gain support and leniency. She was deemed, by some, a "media darling" who presented a sweet and wholesome facade proclaiming religion and repentance for her sins, and by all accounts she was a changed person. She requested leniency on the premise that the person who had committed the horrendous acts of violence several years earlier was not the person who would ultimately be executed. The case fueled debate over the death penalty, with those in support and those in opposition coming out in strength. Aspects surrounding the debate, excluding challenges encompassing constitutionality, centered on Tucker's gender, repentance, religious conversion, and retribution for the crime of murder and the lives that were taken. Tucker's gender was particularly important to the debates that ensued. Religious conversion, while not an atypical issue in a death penalty case, also became a focal point in Tucker's case with the premise being that the execution of a changed person gained no essential purpose. In the end, public opinion and extralegal factors would be considered extraneous to the rulings and proceedings of the judiciary as well as its statutory requirements.

KARLA FAYE TUCKER: A TROUBLED LIFE

On November 18, 1959, Karla Faye Tucker was the third child born to Larry and Carolyn Tucker (Memorial, 2001). In the early years, by all accounts, Tucker's childhood appeared happy and relatively normal. By the time Tucker was ten years old, her parents would divorce for the last and final time (Geringer, 2003). Larry and Carolyn had married and divorced several times, which created an environment of instability and confusion for their children. Pursuant to their divorce, Larry Tucker was awarded custody of the three children, and the children primarily resided with him throughout their adolescent years. Although he attempted to provide stability for his children, given limited supervision, Tucker would engage in a disruptive and addictive lifestyle.

There were several critical points in Tucker's life that ended tragically. At the age of eight, Tucker started smoking marijuana, and by ten, she was injecting heroin intravenously and experimenting with other hard drugs (*Tucker v. Texas*, 1988). By age twelve, she was sexually active and was engaging in orgies and a risky sexual lifestyle. Tucker dropped out of school in the seventh grade, which left her with limited legitimate career options (Geringer, 2003). At thirteen, Tucker traveled with the Allman Brother's Band and engaged in a lifestyle that was well beyond her years (Geringer, 2003). While most young girls at her age still play with dolls, Tucker's life consisted of sex, drugs, alcohol, and other self-deprecating behavior.

Tucker's behavior simply became problematic, troublesome, and uncontrollable. When she was fourteen years old, Tucker went to live with her mother. Tucker's mother was a prostitute herself and attempted to teach her the tricks of the trade ("Justice Delayed," n.d.). Tucker reluctantly engaged in the lifestyle, reportedly wanting to please her mother. It was during this time that Tucker would also come to learn that the father who had raised her was not her biological father (Geringer, 2003). Instead, she was the product of an affair by her mother. The physical differences between Tucker and her sisters were obvious. Tucker had a dark complexion and dark curly hair, and her sisters had light hair and fair complexions.

Just before she turned sixteen, Tucker met and married Stephen Griffith, a mechanic (Geringer, 2003). Their relationship was tumultuous at best, and the couple engaged in frequent and mutual physical and verbal confrontations. The couple would remain married only for a short period of time. By twenty-one years old, Tucker had left Griffith and was again working as a prostitute (Obbie, 1984h). Tucker embraced the rambunctious party lifestyle that she had become accustomed, and she became further immersed in the drug subculture.

Another event that deeply affected Tucker was the death of her mother. Carolyn Tucker died on December 24, 1979, from problems associated with her drug abuse ("Justice Delayed," n.d.). Tucker was twenty years old at the time. Tucker would go on to meet Danny Garrett and her life, along with the lives of numerous others, would be changed forever. Tucker and Garrett became intimately involved and reveled in a world of drug addiction and destructive behavior. Tucker's addiction to prescription and illegal drugs was exacerbated by her acquaintance with Garrett. Garrett, who was more than ten years older than Tucker, was a Vietnam veteran who had boasted about training Tucker to be "the first hit women in the mafia" (BBC News, 1998b). Tucker and Garrett's relationship would prove to be a catalyst for disaster.

THE PICKAX MURDERS

Before committing the murders, Tucker and Garrett partied excessively with drugs. Tucker had used Valium, Placidyl, Percodan, Soma, Wygesic, Dilaudid, and methamphetamines at various times before the murders, and she had not slept for days (*Tucker v. Texas*, 1988). On the evening before the murders, Tucker came into contact with Shawn Dean, the estranged wife of Jerry Dean and one of Tucker's good friends ("Justice Delayed," n.d.). Shawn and Jerry's marriage had ended recently because of numerous on-going domestic assaults and other problems. Shawn was sporting a broken nose and busted lip that had been inflicted by Jerry Dean (Geringer, 2003). Tucker, who was hyped up on drugs, commiserated with Shawn Dean, Daniel Garrett, and James Leibrant regarding potential retaliatory acts against Jerry (*Tucker v. Texas*, 1988). Tucker wanted revenge: Tucker and Jerry's past relationship had been tumultuous, and the two strongly disliked one another. There had been several past episodes between the two; one encompassed a situation where Jerry destroyed one of the few photographs that Tucker had of her mother (*Tucker v. Texas*, 1988).

Later that evening, Garrett left to go to his job as a bartender. At approximately 2 a.m. the following morning, June 13, 1983, Tucker, accompanied by James Leibrant, picked Garrett up from his place of employment (Geringer, 2003), and they devised a plan to get even with Jerry—they would steal his beloved motorcycle that he was restoring.

Sometime between 2:30 a.m. and 4:30 a.m., Tucker, Garrett, and Leibrant went to the residence of Jerry Dean (*Tucker v. Texas*, 1988). For protection, or in case Dean resisted, Garrett brought along a .38-caliber gun and placed it in one of his boots (Geringer, 2003). Allegedly, Garrett also brought along rubber gloves, but it is unclear if they were actually used during the crime (*Tucker v. Texas*, 1988). On arrival at Dean's residence, Leibrant stayed in the vehicle to keep watch while Tucker and Garrett entered the residence using a key Tucker had stolen from Shawn Dean (*Tucker v. Texas*, 1988). Leibrant would later testify that he went to Dean's residence with the intent to commit theft but not for the purpose of committing murder (Obbie, 1984b).

Once inside the residence, Tucker and Garrett listened for Dean but there were no sounds. Garrett took out his flashlight and the two maneuvered in the darkness until they located the motorcycle (Geringer, 2003). They examined the bike only to discover that Dean was still restoring his motorcycle, as parts and tools were strewn throughout the apartment. A shovel and a pickax were lying against the wall (Geringer, 2003). Kari Ann Tucker, Karla Faye Tucker's older sister, would later testify that the two proceeded to Dean's bedroom where Tucker "put a pickax up to Jerry Dean's head and told him not to move" or he would die (*Tucker v. Texas*, 1988). Garrett then began to repeatedly strike Dean with a hammer, rendering him backwards. Blood started to flow from Dean's nostrils and mouth. During this time, Deborah Thornton, who had been lying next to Dean, was attempting to hide herself on the side of the bed (Geringer, 2003). Tucker, seeing the woman, took the three-foot-long pickax and plunged the ax into both Thornton and Dean's bodies (*Tucker v. Johnson*, 1992). At some point during the murders, Leibrant entered the residence to witness Tucker as she lifted the ax over her head, she turned to smile at him, and then plunged the ax into one of the victims who was covered by a sheet (Obbie, 1984b). Seeing this, Leibrant left the Dean residence and fled the scene of the crime. In the end, Dean suffered more than twenty strikes to his body, and the pickax was found embedded in the body of Thornton (*Tucker v. Johnson*, 1992).

After the bloody and murderous act, Tucker and Garrett fled the scene with stolen merchandise from the Dean residence. Tucker drove Dean's vehicle, an El Camino, with his motorcycle in the back, to Doug Garrett's residence. Tucker and Garrett bragged to Doug about what they had done (*Tucker v. Texas*, 1988). Tucker and Garrett went to the residence that they shared with Kari Ann, and again they relayed their story about the murders. Eventually they disposed of some of the incriminating evidence in an attempt to hide their crime. The El Camino was abandoned in a parking lot near the Houston Astrodome, and the motorcycle was eventually thrown into the Brazos River (*Tucker v. Texas*, 1988). Doug Garrett would admit to helping dispose of some of Dean's property, although he was never charged with any criminal violations (Obbie, 1984b). Tucker gave Thornton's wallet to Kari Ann as a birthday gift; Kari Ann "threw it away in disgust" (*Tucker v. Texas*, 1988). Kari Ann eventually moved out of the residence and moved in with Doug, as she became frightened of the couple (*Tucker v. Texas*, 1988).

The couple bragged about the murders to both friends and family members and reveled in the media coverage of the case—this would be to their detriment. Tucker would make incriminating statements that she received sexual gratification with every swipe of the pickax to Dean's body (Court TV, 1998). She later recanted the statements, claiming that she only made such comments in an attempt to appear tough in front of her friends

(Memorial, 2001). Tucker, by her own account, claimed that she had not felt any guilt during the days following the assault on Dean and Thornton.

The bodies of Jerry Lynn Dean and Deborah Thornton were discovered the following morning by Gregory Traver, a friend of Dean's. Traver went to Dean's apartment after Dean had failed to pick him up for work (*Tucker v. Texas*, 1988). Traver found the bodies in one of Dean's bedrooms. Traver immediately contacted police, and the investigation commenced.

THE INVESTIGATION OF THE PICKAX MURDERS

The investigation into the murders of Jerry Lynn Dean and Deborah Thornton began immediately. Upon identification of the bodies, homicide detectives with the Houston Police Department spoke with friends and family members associated with the victims, and they found no viable leads. A thorough examination of the Dean residence revealed no evidence of forced entry (Amended Writ of Habeas Corpus, 1992). Several items were identified as stolen from the scene of the crime, including Dean's motorcycle, his El Camino, and wallets that belonged to both Dean and Thornton (*Tucker v. Johnson*, 1997). Investigators searched the residence for evidence that would lead them to the killers. The investigation took approximately five weeks, and investigators did not have any suspects until they received vital information that would lead them to the individuals responsible for the horrendous crimes.

The break in the case came when Doug Garrett, Danny Garrett's brother, contacted the Houston Police and spoke with his long-time friend, J.C. Mosier, a homicide detective. Doug Garrett, along with Kari Ann Tucker, met with Mosier the following day (*Tucker v. Texas*, 1988). The two relayed their knowledge of the crime as provided to them by their siblings. They disclosed that Tucker and Garrett had committed the pickax murders and that another friend, James Leibrant, had also been involved (*Tucker v. Texas*, 1988). Doug agreed to assist detectives with the investigation in an attempt to solicit a confession from the couple and to obtain critical details of the murderous night. Doug was subsequently wired with a tape recording device, and he went to the residence that Tucker and Garrett shared together on McKean Street (*Tucker v. Texas*, 1988). Doug spoke with the couple about the murders and obtained the detailed information and probable cause necessary for the police to execute an arrest. The conversations, which lasted approximately one to one and one-half hours, were recorded and would become crucial evidence for the prosecution during the trial (*Tucker v. Texas*, 1988). Later that same day, after Doug had exited Tucker and Garrett's residence, police rushed in and arrested them for the murders of Dean and Thornton

(Geringer, 2003). James Leibrant and Ronnie Burrell, Kari Ann's ex-husband, were also arrested but on different charges.

On September 13, 1983, Karla Faye Tucker was indicted for capital murder and entered a plea of not guilty to the charges (Amended Writ of Habeas Corpus, 1992). Both Tucker and Garrett's crimes were eligible for the death penalty. They had committed murder during the commission of a felony—robbery. Tucker was twenty-three years old at the time of her arrest, and surprisingly, she had no documented criminal history (*Tucker v. Texas*, 1988).

THE TRIAL OF KARLA FAYE TUCKER

A bifurcated process is used in cases that are determined to be "death eligible." Given this process, cases are broken down into two stages. The first stage is the trial stage where there is a determination of the defendant's guilt. The second stage, if the defendant is found guilty, is the sentencing and punishment phase in which aggravating and mitigating circumstances are considered and a sentence is imposed (Death Penalty Information Center, 2003a). The prosecution of Tucker proceeded in such a manner.

The Guilt/Innocence Phase

On March 2, 1984, the guilt/innocence phase of the trial in the case of the *State of Texas v. Karla Faye Tucker* began in the 180th Judicial District Court of Harris County Texas with Judge Patricia Lykos presiding. Prosecutors Joe Magliolo, Keno Henderson, and Jim Peacock represented the State of Texas (Obbie, 1984a), and Mack Arnold and Henry Oncken were appointed to represent Tucker (Amended Writ of Habeas Corpus, 1992). Voir dire, jury selection, commenced on March 2 and concluded on April 9. Once the jury was established, the trial began on April 11 and ended on April 19. The trial had lasted nine days, and a verdict of guilty was rendered the same day that the jury had begun deliberations (Geringer, 2003). Although Tucker was indicted on two counts of capital murder, the state proceeded against Tucker only with respect to the murder of Jerry Lynn Dean (Obbie, 1984a). Given Tucker's subsequent conviction and sentence, a trial for the murder of Thornton was deferred. The defense conceded to Tucker's participation in the murders, yet argued that the defendant was "temporarily insane due to drug and alcohol use the night of the killings" (Obbie, 1984e). This tactic was used by the defense in an attempt to gain credibility and presumably mercy for Tucker although such a concession was seen as a somewhat controversial strategy. Critics of the insanity plea argued that it was the defense's legal responsibility to advocate and protect the rights of Tucker, who was their client, while supporters thought that the strategy was brilliant given the culmination of evidence against them (Obbie and Wittenberg, 1984).

The trial was filled with numerous witnesses and exhibits, including the tape-recorded confession obtained by Doug Garrett. This piece of evidence was overwhelmingly damaging to the defense, as it contained Tucker's confession. Doug Garrett and Kari Ann Tucker testified for the prosecution regarding their involvement as well as to statements made to them by Tucker. During the trial, Doug Garrett had referred to the murders of Dean and Thornton as the work of the devil, which led defense attorneys to challenge his mental competency (Obbie, 1984c). Doug was determined competent and his testimony was admitted.

One of the more controversial prosecution witnesses was James Leibrant, who had accompanied Tucker and Garrett to the Dean residence on the morning of June 13, 1983. The prosecution and defense would argue the motivation of Leibrant's testimony in subsequent appeals, with the defense contending that the testimony was provided in exchange for leniency pertaining to his criminal charge of burglary of the Dean residence (*Tucker v. Texas*, 1988). By challenging the motivation of Leibrant's testimony, the defense created a motive for Leibrant to lie. Leibrant's account of the tragic night would be particularly damaging to the defense, as he relayed his account of Tucker's struggle to remove the ax from one of the victim's bodies only to subsequently strike another blow (Obbie, 1984b). Leibrant testified about Tucker's satisfaction with such brutality, as he relayed that she had looked up to smile at him as she committed murder (*Tucker v. Texas*, 1988). Leibrant further testified to comments made by Tucker, in the weeks before the murder that she had wanted to kill Dean and steal his motorcycle (Obbie, 1984b). Leibrant's testimony helped establish premeditation to murder. He went on to state that he only went to the Dean residence to intimidate Dean and collect on a debt (*Tucker v. Texas*, 1988). Leibrant testified about Tucker's excitement of the media coverage of the murders, as she appeared to be thrilled about her criminal acts. Tucker cried throughout most of Leibrant's testimony (Obbie, 1984b).

A pathologist testified for the state that both Dean and Thornton suffered more than twenty wounds each (Obbie, 1984b). These wounds included injuries inflicted by both Tucker and Garrett. Sergeant J.C. Mosier testified how Doug Garrett provided him information that had led to the subsequent arrest of the defendants and how Doug admitted to assisting his brother in destroying evidence from the crime (Obbie, 1984b). He commended Doug for coming forward to assist detectives with the investigation and leading detectives to his brother and Tucker.

The state had presented a case proving that, by all accounts, Tucker had killed Dean as a result of hatred and vengeance; however, the murder of Thornton was a different matter. Thornton was simply at the wrong place at the wrong time and was a stranger to both Tucker and Garrett. She was presumably killed to eliminate a potential witness. The prosecution easily covered all of the essential elements necessary to obtain a conviction. They provided motive, a tape-recorded confession, an eyewitness, and established premeditation. Furthermore, they had proven that Tucker's actions had resulted in deadly culpability in the crime, meaning that the murder "was committed deliberately and with reasonable expectation that death would result" (*Tucker v. Texas*, 1988. p. 524). Challenging the evidence that the state presented would prove difficult for the defense.

Once the state rested, the defense presented its case. The defense attempted to call two witnesses: one who would testify to a "deal" between the prosecutor and Leibrant in an attempt to establish prejudice and prosecutorial misconduct for impeachment purposes; and the other would testify to "an alleged murder contract placed on the defendant's life by one of the victims" (Obbie, 1984d). The testimony of these witnesses was heard outside the presence of the jury to determine admissibility. Donna Wages, a jail confidant of Tucker's, testified that she overhead an unknown man and District Attorney Charlie Davidson discussing a "deal" offered to Leibrant of less than ten years imprisonment in exchange for his testimony during the Tucker trial (Obbie, 1984d). As a witness for the state, Leibrant had testified that the prosecution told him they would tell the judge of his cooperation in the murder trial during the sentencing phase of his trial for burglary in relation to the Dean and Thornton murders, but there was never an offer referencing a specified period of incarceration. At the time, in addition to his current charge, Leibrant also had pending drug charges out of Harris and Austin Counties (Obbie, 1984b). District Attorney Davidson testified denying such misconduct or any offer of a deal (*Tucker v. Texas*, 1988). Judge Lykos ruled the testimony of Donna Wages inadmissible as hearsay evidence. The second witness was Sergeant James Ladd from the Houston Police Department. Ladd testified about conversations he had with Shawn Dean who alleged that Jerry Dean might have put out a "contract" on Tucker's life (Obbie, 1984d). Given that the testimony encompassed information relayed by a second party and not by Shawn Dean herself, again Judge Lykos ruled the testimony as hearsay and inadmissible (Obbie, 1984d). Tucker did not testify in her own defense—the defense rested.

Tucker was convicted of capital murder on April 19, 1984 (Memorial, 2001). A jury of eight women and four men deliberated for seventy minutes before handing down a verdict of guilty ("Justice Delayed," n.d.). The defense conceded Tucker's participation in the murders yet contended that the defendant was temporarily insane as a result of voluntary intoxication (*Tucker v. Texas*, 1988), and, as such, the necessary statutory requirements were not met to elevate the criminal offense to the level of death applicable or qualified—Judge Lykos disagreed.

The Penalty Phase

On April 23, 1984, the penalty phase of Tucker's case began (Amended Writ of Habeas Corpus, 1992). Tucker was found guilty of capital murder, and her defense attorneys now worked to spare her life. During the sentencing phase, the defense concentrated on Tucker's drug use in an attempt to show Tucker as so consumed by drugs that her judgment and behavior were substantially impaired and altered. The defense offered mitigating circumstances for the jury to consider in the contemplation of a sentence of life in prison as opposed to the death penalty. The defense submitted a jury instruction encompassing voluntary intoxication in such that intoxication rose to the level of temporary insanity on the night of the criminal acts (*Tucker v. Texas*, 1988). Jury instruction would later become a critical and contentious issue on appeal alleging the inclusion of the instruction established "egregious harm" (*Tucker v. Texas*, 1988). Under Texas criminal code, voluntary intoxication cannot be used as a defense for a specific crime, although it can be used as a mitigating factor during the sentencing phase but only if it rises to the level of temporary insanity.

Tucker's defense attorney argued that

temporary insanity caused by intoxication means that the defendant's mental capacity was so disturbed from the introduction of a substance into her body that the defendant did not know that her conduct was wrong or was incapable of conforming her conduct to the requirements of the law she allegedly violated. Therefore, if you find, or have a reasonable doubt thereof, that the defendant at the time of the commission of the offense for which she is on trial, was laboring under temporary insanity caused by intoxication, then you may take such condition into consideration in mitigation of the penalty attached to the offense for which the defendant is being tried. (*Tucker v. Texas*, 1988)

In an attempt to spare Tucker's life, eight witnesses were called to the stand in Tucker's defense. These witnesses included Michael Rogers, Zelda Donaldson (Tucker's grandmother), Larry Tucker (Tucker's father), Linda Willett (a deputy sheriff), Rebecca Lewis, Ooudia Dorr, and two expert witnesses: Dr. Barbara Felkins, a psychiatrist specializing in the treatment of drug addictions; and Dr. James W. Hayden, an expert in the field of pharmacology (Amended Writ of Habeas Corpus, 1992). Rogers testified to Tucker's reputation for nonviolence, and Donaldson, Larry Tucker, Lewis, and Dorr testified about positive changes that have occurred in Tucker since her incarceration (Amended Writ of Habeas Corpus, 1992). Willett testified that Tucker had not engaged in disruptive behavior and that she was not seen as a threat to the guards (Amended Writ of Habeas Corpus, 1992). The testimony from these witnesses was presented in an attempt to prove to the jury that Tucker was not a threat to society and that she had become a different person as a result of her abstinence from drugs.

Defense experts were presented to establish Tucker's state of mind at the time of the crime—proving the crippling effect of her drug use and addiction and establishing the necessary elements of temporary insanity based on a drug-induced psychosis (Amended Writ of Habeas Corpus, 1992). Dr. Felkins testified to Tucker's long-term drug use that had started at a very early age and continued, almost without pause, until the time of her incarceration (Amended Writ of Habeas Corpus, 1992). Felkins further testified that, given the nature of the drugs that Tucker had used, "it was probably only two weeks [throughout Tucker's entire adolescence] that she was not on some sort of drugs from the time she was about [ten] until the time the offense occurred" (Amended Writ of Habeas Corpus, 1992). Dr. Felkins testified that Tucker had been using drugs continuously on the days leading up to the crime and on the day of the crime (Amended Writ of Habeas Corpus, 1992). Some of the drugs she used were considered depressants and others were considered stimulants, which created a circular need for more drugs. Dr. Felkins testified, in her professional opinion, that Tucker was in a "drug induced psychosis on the date of the offense" (Amended Writ of Habeas Corpus, 1992), and that as a result of the drug-induced psychosis, Tucker was unable to distinguish right from wrong, nor was she able to discern what was real from what was made up. Dr. Hayden's testimony addressed the pharmacological effects of multiple drug use and elements of a drug-induced psychosis (Amended Writ of Habeas Corpus, 1992).

Tucker did not testify during the guilt/innocence phase of her trial; however, she did testify on her own behalf during the sentencing phase in an attempt to spare her life. Tucker testified to her early drug use and medical history. She relayed that "she did not feel the killings were real to her," in an attempt to describe her state of mind at the time of the murders ("Justice Delayed," n.d.). She testified that she continued to strike Dean with a pickax because she wanted the "gurgling noises" that emitted from his body to stop (Obbie, 1984g). She also testified that Thornton, at one point, actually begged for death to stop the pain (Obbie, 1984g). Tucker's testimony was chilling.

In rebuttal, the state called Dr. James Nottingham to testify about information related to drug-induced psychosis. It was Nottingham's professional opinion that Tucker was not suffering from a drug-induced psychosis during the time of the crimes and that she was, in fact, able to differentiate right from wrong and understand the consequences of her actions (Amended Writ of Habeas Corpus, 1992). The state also called Dr. Jerome Brown, a psychologist, to testify that he determined Tucker to be able to distinguish right from wrong at the time of the offense, despite her drug use (Amended Writ of Habeas Corpus, 1992). The prosecution provided evidence that Tucker not only knew what she was doing when she committed murder but also consciously attempted to cover-up the crime. The state established such motivation by presenting evidence that Tucker obtained a key to Dean's residence with the express purpose of revenge, and then after the murders, she talked about plotting to kill two men "who would testify against her": one of those men was James Leibrant (Obbie, 1984f). Doug and Kari Ann alleged that they took turns sleeping at night for fear of retaliation, even though they knew of no threats made against them (Obbie, 1984f).

1. On April 25, 1984, the prosecution and the defense rested (Amended Writ of Habeas Corpus, 1992). In Texas, the statutory requirements for the determination of death qualified are as follows: whether the conduct of the defendant that caused the death of the deceased was committed deliberately and with the reasonable expectation that the death of the deceased or another would result; and/or whether there is a probability that the defendant would commit criminal acts of violence that would constitute a continuing threat to society. (Amended Writ of Habeas Corpus, 1992)

After nearly three hours of deliberations, the jury answered in the affirmative to requirements and handed down a sentence of death the same day ("Justice Delayed," n.d.). The experts' testimony of both the defense and the prosecution seemed somewhat confusing and conflicting; however, the prosecution's case was overwhelmingly strong. Upon the imposition of sentence, Tucker was transferred to the Mountain View Unit of the Gatesville Penitentiary, where she was placed on death row to await her execution ("Justice Delayed," n.d.).

TUCKER'S LEGAL BATTLE AND FIGHT FOR CLEMENCY

Although Tucker's trial received moderate regional attention, her sentence received international focus and notoriety. As her execution date drew near, media and societal focus exploded. Celebrities, church officials, and death penalty opponents and proponents alike were all captivated by the elements of the penalty and by the offender herself. George McCall Secrest Jr. was appointed as Tucker's attorney to represent her on appeal (*Tucker v. Texas*, 1988).

Fourteen years would pass from the imposition of the death sentence to the time of Tucker's execution. During these fourteen years, Tucker found religion and became a model inmate with an exemplar record. In 1995, Tucker married Dana Brown (by proxy) while on death row; Brown had been involved in a "prison ministry group" (Geringer, 2003). Tucker also worked to assist other inmates, she finished her education, and she concentrated heavily on religious teachings and endeavors, which would, in the end, make her more appealing to the media (Geringer, 2003). The "media darling," as she was deemed, would make several television appearances and grant numerous interviews. These interviews and appearances were highly influential with society at large in bringing attention to her case and gaining support from various organizations and groups.

Throughout those fourteen years, appeals and requests for Tucker's sentence to be commuted to life were abundant. Tucker's attorneys attempted various legal tactics to spare her life. The fight to save Tucker's life encompassed challenges of ineffective assistance of counsel and the absence of premeditation to murder, which is "a requisite for capital punishment in Texas" (Geringer, 2003). After Tucker's initial sentencing, lawyers requested another trial, but Judge Lykos denied those requests (Geringer, 2003). In 1987 and 1988, similar filings were made to the "Court of Criminal Appeals to overrule the client's conviction" (Amended Writ of Habeas Corpus, 1992). However, both of the filings were denied. Attorneys filed a Motion for Rehearing on January 4, 1989, "but the Court of Criminal Appeals stayed issuance of the mandate until April 11, 1989, pending the filing of a Petition for Writ of Certiorari in the Supreme Court of the United States" (Amended Writ of Habeas Corpus, 1992).

In the *Tucker v. Texas* appeal, the request for stay filed by Tucker's attorneys and the petition for Writ of Certiorari was denied. U.S. Supreme Court Justices Brennan and Marshall dissented, stating that "adhering to our views that the death penalty is in all circumstances cruel and unusual punishment prohibited by the Eighth and Fourteenth Amendments, *Gregg v. Georgia* (1976), we would grant certiorari and vacate the death sentence in this case" (Memorandum Decision, 1989). Justice Brennan and Justice Marshall were in the minority.

On appeal, the defense argued the second component of the penalty determination and attempted to prove that Tucker did not, in fact, pose a continuing threat to society (*Tucker v. Texas*, 1988). On review of the evidence, the Court disagreed. The court determined the evidence had demonstrated that Tucker did have a violent past and had the potential for future violence. This evidence was obtained during the sentencing phase; Tucker testified about fights that she had previously engaged in during her life (*Tucker v. Texas*, 1988). She explained how a couple months before the murders, she had engaged in a fight with Dean; Dean's glasses were broken, and he had required medical attention to remove glass fragments from his eye (*Tucker v. Texas*, 1988). Tucker also testified about possibly killing Leibrant and Burnell and going on future raids of drug labs and killing the people and stealing their merchandise (*Tucker v. Texas*, 1988).

Tucker had repeatedly made requests for an "evidentiary hearing in the trial court" to address issues regarding ineffective assistance of counsel (Geringer, 2003, p. 3). "In February 1992, Judge Lykos rejected the request for a new hearing. Rather, she set a tentative date (June 30) for execution" (Geringer, 2003). The execution was stayed by the Texas Court of Appeals, and instead the court ordered an evidentiary hearing to examine the claim that James Leibrant perjured himself during the trial. Judge Lykos filed her "supplemental Findings of Fact and Conclusions of Law and Order" to the court of appeals (Geringer, 2003). While awaiting a final verdict, Lykos scheduled another execution date. The Texas Court of Appeals rejected the legal reasoning of the defendant and lifted the stay. However, Tucker's attorneys continued to fight, subsequently filing an appeal challenging "the constitutionality of the state's clemency procedure" (Geringer, 2003). The final plea was denied on January 28, 1998. Tucker also appealed to George W. Bush, who was the governor of Texas at the time; she wrote him a letter in which she asked for mercy. Tucker and her attorneys had exhausted every legal and personal maneuver available to them. On February 2, 1998, the Board of Pardons and Paroles rejected Tucker's request for clemency (Court TV Online, 1998). The U.S. Supreme Court would deny her request for a stay as well.

In Texas, "the Governor can commute a death sentence only with the recommendation of a majority of the Board of Pardons and Paroles" (Memorial, 2001). The Board of Pardons and Paroles is obligated to review requests for clemency and then make a recommendation to the governor. The board's purpose is to "review the facts of the criminal case to ensure the prisoner received a fair trial" (Memorial, 2001, p.7). Victor Rodriguez, the chairman of the board at the time of the Tucker execution, stated that "commutation of a death sentence should be granted for only two reasons: actual innocence or a lack of due process"; neither reason was determined to be present or factual in the Tucker case (Memorial, 2001, p. 7). By all accounts, Tucker had received a fair and just trial, and all judicial maneuvering and consideration had been exhausted. The execution would be carried out as scheduled.

THE DEATH SENTENCE IMPOSED

In preparation for her execution, Tucker was transferred to the "Walls Unit" in Huntsville, Texas, where the execution would occur (Stem Owens, 1998). A Huntsville resident relayed the following observation regarding the execution: "A week before her sentence was carried out, camera crews, international news teams, Amnesty International representatives, and victims' rights advocates crowded our town to chronicle the event" (Stem Owens, 1998, p. 26). Tucker's execution had society's attention. The race for clemency continued up to and throughout the day of February 3, 1998, when the final request for a thirty-day stay was rejected by Governor Bush (Geringer, 2003). Prison officials received news of the rejection at approximately 5:25 p.m. and proceeded with preparations for the execution (Geringer, 2003).

On the day of her execution, February 3, 1998, Tucker reportedly rejected breakfast, wrote a letter, and spoke with two visitors—her husband Dana Brown, and a spiritual advisor ("Justice Delayed," n.d.). Media crews, families, and demonstrators, both for and against the execution, gathered outside the prison facility. At 6:35 p.m., Tucker was strapped to a gurney and wheeled into the execution chamber (Geringer, 2003). Present as witnesses to the execution were members of Tucker's family, media representatives, and some of the victims' families, including "Richard Thornton, the victim's husband and her son, Bucky David [twenty-four], and stepdaughter, Kathryn Thornton [twenty-six]" ("Justice Delayed," n.d., p. 3). Tucker was asked if she had any final statements to which she replied the following:

Yes sir, I would like to say to all of you—the Thornton family and Jerry Dean's family that I am so sorry. I hope God will give you peace with this.

Baby, I love you. Ron, give Peggy a hug for me. Everybody has been so good to me.

I love all of you very much. I am going to be face to face with Jesus now. Warden Baggett, thank all of you so much. You have been so good to me. I love all of you very much. I will see you all when you get there. I will wait for you. (Texas Department of Criminal Justice—Death Row, 2001)

At approximately 6:37 p.m., the lethal mixture of pancuronium bromide, potassium chloride, and sodium thiopental was injected into Tucker's veins through two IVs, which had been inserted into each of her arms (Memorial, 2001). Reportedly, Tucker took "two deep sighs and then a groan" and then was pronounced dead at 6:45 p.m., February 3, 1998 ("Justice Delayed," n.d., p. 3).

Tucker was the first woman executed in Texas since Chipita Rodriguez was hanged in 1863 (Leung, 2000). Rodriguez was "hanged from a mesquite tree for killing a horse trader during the Civil War" (Obbie, 1984i, p. A3). Furthermore, Tucker was the second woman executed in the United States since the reinstatement of the death penalty by the U.S. Supreme Court in 1976; the first woman executed was Velma Barfield in 1984 in North Carolina ("Man, Woman, Death and God," 1998). For comparison, death row statistics in 1998 for Texas indicate that a total of twenty individuals were executed, nineteen men and one woman—Tucker (Texas Department of Criminal Justice, Death Row, 2003). Of all of these individuals, Tucker's case received the greatest attention and focus, with the majority of the other death row inmates' cases receiving little to no attention at all; their executions were carried out relatively quietly.

THE INFLUENCE OF THE TUCKER CASE

The attention focused on the Tucker case was intense. Media and onlookers alike reveled in the facts of the crime as well as the numerous extralegal factors pertaining to Tucker and her case. The debate was fueled by the person Tucker seemingly was at the time of the offense combined with the gruesome and violent facts of the case. Who Tucker was at the time of the murders and the born-again, repentant Christian that Tucker personified at the end of her life were in stark contrast. The fact that Tucker was a woman only seemed to exacerbate and complicate the issue, as gender was of particular significance.

In general, women account for approximately 13 percent of murderers, 1.9 percent of death sentences imposed at trial, 1.4 percent of the inmates currently on death row, and 1.1 percent of the inmates actually executed since the death penalty was reinstated (Death Penalty Information Center, 2003b). This disproportion appears, at first glance, to be alarming and suggestive of leniency towards women. Some researchers assert that the U.S. criminal justice system itself is inherently chivalrous and biased, and they claim that the system allows women to get away with certain types of crime without being provided similar consequences as received by men. Others suggest that women are being made an example of in an attempt to assert equality. According to Schulberg (2002, p. 278), "The equality theory proposes that females are sentenced to death only when their offenses are particularly egregious and uses their scarcity on death row to suggest that few women commit the type of offense that warrants capital punishment for either gender." All of these assertions apply directly to the Tucker case. Although some individuals and organizations believed that Tucker was being made an example of specifically because she was a woman in an attempt to demonstrate equality, the sheer brutality of her crime was of enormous consequence and could not be overcome. Her behavior had demonstrated "contradicting expectations about gender" (Heberle, 1999, p. 1103). At the time of the murders, Tucker appeared to be out of control, vengeful, and a threat to society—her gender was of little consequence. It was not until her execution was imminent that the issue of gender, in conjunction with religious conversion, became significant. Heberle (p. 1103) would even suggest that "her effort to win forgiveness included refeminizing herself" to be more appealing to the masses.

In the end, Tucker's pleas for mercy were heard worldwide, and the impact of her case was enormous. Governor Bush reportedly received over 700 letters regarding Tucker, with the vast majority opposing her execution (Zewe, 1998). Individuals who, in the past, had supported the death penalty now spoke out in support of Tucker. Supporters of Tucker included Amnesty International, Pope John Paul II, and even Pat Robertson (Leung, 2000). Court-focused television shows such as Court TV documented Tucker's story attempting not only to provide the facts of the murders but also Tucker's transformation as well. Several books were written about Tucker, documenting her life both before and after the murders. Numerous websites were dedicated to Tucker's case, supporting Tucker and condemning her execution as well as denouncing her for her crimes. Members of the victims' families also posted their information on the internet and provided their thoughts on the murders and the execution. Many websites still remain today.

All of this attention provided society with an insight into Tucker's case. Tucker gained notoriety and exposure that she otherwise would not have received. Her case appeared to momentarily have widespread influence on society's perception of the death penalty. While the debate over the death penalty historically focuses on two sides, those for and against, the death penalty as a constitutional sentence, for capital murder has always been an intensely debated topic. Tucker's case was complicated and conflicting, as it encompassed a seemly reformed individual who brutally and tragically took the lives of two innocent individuals. Without the media, Tucker's case would have been relatively unknown. The attention, while justifiable, appeared to have a tremendous impact on the lives of the victims' families. The families were made to endure frequent discussions regarding the facts of the case, which can only exacerbate their pain and suffering. Although the media's attention after Tucker's execution has seemingly halted, it was the media that first expanded society's knowledge about the death penalty and gave Tucker an outlet for discussion. Without the media, society's knowledge of the Tucker case would have been substantially limited.

REFERENCES

Amended Writ of Habeas Corpus. No. 388428-A in the 180th District Court of Harris County, Texas. Ex parte motion. (1992). Retrieved September 11, 22003, from http://www.straightway.org/karla/writofhc.htm

Attorney for woman on death row challenges Texas procedure. (1998, January 20). [Electronic Version]. Retrieved August 31, 2003, from http://www.cnn.com/US/9801/20/tucker.appeal/index.html

BBC News. (1998a, January 30). A crime that shocked America [Electronic Version]. Retrieved September 10, 2003, from http://news.bbc.co.uk/1/hi/special_report/1998/ karla_faye_tucker/48796

BBC News. (1998b, January 30). Portrait of a repentant killer [Electronic Version]. Retrieved September 10, 2003, from http://news.bbc.co.uk/1/hi/special_report/1998/ karla_faye_tucker/48816

Buckley, W. F. Jr. (March 9, 1998). Miss Tucker's plea. *National Review, 50,* 71–72.

Court TV Online. (1998). *Texas v. Karla Faye Tucker,* a question of mercy. Retrieved August 31, 2003, from http://www.courttv.com/archive/casefiles/tucker/background.html

Cruikshank, B. (1999). Feminism and punishment. *Signs, 24* (24), 1113–1118.

Death Penalty Information Center. (2003a). History of the death penalty (Two Parts). Retrieved September 1, 2003, from http://www.deathpenaltyinfo.org/article.php?scid=15&did=410#TheDeathPenaltyinAmerica

Death Penalty Information Center. (2003b). Women and the death penalty. Retrieved September 1, 2003, from http://www.deathpenaltyinfo.org/womenstats.html

Evidentiary Hearing 180th District Court of Patricia Lykos. (1992). Retrieved August 31, 2003, from http://www.straightway.org/karla/1992.htm

Geringer, J. (2003). Karla Faye Tucker: Texas's controversial murderess. Retrieved August 31, 2003, from http://www.crimelibrary.com/notorious_murders/women/tucker.html

Heberle, R. (1999). Disciplining gender; or, are women getting away with murder? *Signs, 24* (4), 1103–1111.

Johnson, H. A. (1988). *History of criminal justice.* Cincinnati, Ohio: Anderson Publishing.

"Justice Delayed," Karla Faye Tucker. (n.d.). Retrieved August 31, 2003 from http://www.geocities.com/trctl11/karla.html

Kaufman-Osborn, T. (1999). Symposium gender and the death penalty. *Signs, 24* (4), 1119–1130.

Leung, R. (1998, February 3). Texas executes Tucker, case raised question about women and the death penalty. ABC News [Electronic version]. Retrieved

August 31, 2003, from http://abcnew.go.com/sections/us/DailyNews/ tucker0202.html

Man, woman, death and God: The death sentence. (1998, February 7). *The Economist, 348*, 28.

McMurry, K. (1998). Illinois law extends death penalty to domestic batterers. *Trial, 34*, 100–111.

Memorandum Decision, 109 S. Ct. (1989). *Supreme Court Reporter, 109*, 3230.

"Memorial" to Karla Faye Tucker Brown. (2001, October 5). Retrieved August 31, 2003, from http://www.geocities.com/RainForest/Canopy/2525/karlamain. html

Obbie, M. (1984a, April 12). Testimony begins in ax-murder trial. *Houston Post*, p. B11.

Obbie, M. (1984b, April 13). Witness in Tucker trial describes pickax slaying. *Houston Post*, p. B6.

Obbie, M. (1984c, April 19). Testimony of defense witnesses thrown out in pickax slaying trial. *Houston Post*, p. B6.

Obbie, M. (1984d, April 20). Tucker convicted in slaying. *Houston Post*, pp. A1, A3.

Obbie, M. (1984e, April 24). Psychiatrist says Tucker psychotic when she killed. *Houston Post*, p. A12.

Obbie, M. (1984f, April 25). No justifying what I've done: Tucker. *Houston Post*, p. A13.

Obbie, M. (1984g, April 26). Tucker to die, jury decides. *Houston Post*, pp. A1, A3.

Obbie, M. (1984h, April 27). Tucker's death sentence won't guarantee execution. *Houston Post*, pp. A1, A3.

Obbie, M. (1984i, April 18). Murder called sexually gratifying. *Houston Post*, p. A6.

Obbie, M., and Wittenberg, P. (1984, April 20). Lawyer explains trial tactic. *Houston Post*, pp. A1, A3.

Schulberg, D. E. (2002). Dying to get out: The execution of females in the post-Furman era of the death penalty in the United States. In R. Muraskin (Ed.), *It's a crime, women and justice* (3rd ed.). Upper Saddle River, NJ: Prentice Hall.

Stem Owens, V. (1998). Karla Faye's final stop: How a city in Texas (Huntsville) deals with being the execution capital of the United States. *Presbyterian Record, 122*, 26–30.

Texas Department of Criminal Justice, Death Row. (2001). Last statements. Retrieved September 8, 2003, from http://www.tdcj.state.tx.us/stat/ tuckerkarlalast.htm

Texas Department of Criminal Justice, Death Row. (2003). Executed offenders. Retrieved September 8, 2003, from http://www.tdcj.state.tx.us/stat/ executedoffenders.htm

Transcript of Larry King Live Interview with Karla Fay Tucker. (January 14, 1998). Retrieved August 31, 2003, from http://www.geocities.com/RainForest. Canopy/2525/ larrykinglive.html

Tucker v. Johnson. (1997, July 2). United States Court of Appeals for the Fifth Circuit. No. 97-20101. Retrieved November 1, 2003, from http://www.ca5.uscourts.gov/opinions/pub/97/97-20101-cv0

Tucker v. Texas, 771 S.W. 2d 523 (Tex. Ct. App. 1988).

Zewe, C. (1998, January 15). Texas prepares to execute woman, governor asked to show mercy. *U.S. News.* Retrieved August 31, 2003, from http://www.cnn.com/US/9801/15/texas.execution/index.html

5

The Ford Pinto Trial: The Criminal Prosecution of a Corporation

Gray Cavender, Francis T. Cullen, and William J. Maakestad

Attorney James Neal called the Ford Pinto case one of the most important trials of the twentieth century.[1] Although Neal and his law firm represented the Ford Motor Company in the trial, his assessment reflected more than self-interest. The Ford Pinto trial was a landmark case, because it addressed the legal issue of whether a corporation could be prosecuted for a violent crime like any other citizen. The trial made legal history and captured the American public's attention.

On August 10, 1978, three Indiana teenagers who were riding in a Ford Pinto were burned to death when their car exploded into flames after being rear-ended by a Chevrolet van. The State of Indiana claimed that there was a design defect in the Pinto and that the Ford Motor Company knew about the defect but still marketed the car without making repairs in a timely manner. In 1980, Indiana prosecuted the Ford Motor Company on three counts of reckless homicide—one count for each of the teenage victims.

This chapter discusses why the Ford Pinto trial is a landmark trial. The chapter begins with a brief look into U.S. legal history and a presentation of the context of the automobile industry in the 1970s. This chapter also addresses the media's role in the case, then describes the Pinto trial, which contained all of the dramatic elements of a first-rate movie. Finally, the chapter concludes with a commentary on why the Pinto case is still important even though the trial occurred almost twenty-five years ago.

LEGAL DEVELOPMENT AND CORPORATE CRIMINAL RESPONSIBILITY

A major reason why the Pinto trial is so significant is that, historically, it was unheard of for a corporation to be prosecuted for a crime like reckless homicide. Criminal law was applied to people, not corporations. Corporations were subject to civil liability; that is, a plaintiff could sue a corporation seeking monetary damages in a tort case if a corporation's negligence had caused a wrongful injury or death.

History contributed to this current state of legal affairs. Centuries ago, when England was developing a process for criminal law (before the United States existed as a nation), the law had been created to apply to individuals. Few organizations were in existence, let alone subject to criminal law. Of course, over the years, organizations emerged: partnerships, joint-stock companies, and, eventually, corporations. These organizations offered a means of amassing large amounts of capital for conducting business, at first on a one-shot deal (e.g., outfitting a ship), and later, on continuing projects (e.g., creating a company that would be involved in colonizing a new territory). As these organizations emerged, they became major players in the political economy. Government was "friendly" to these organizations, as the government was more interested in their growth than in regulation (Commons, 1924/1959).

Because some of the English common laws were retained in the United States after its independence, the same situation of interest in economic growth rather than regulation existed in the United States. As they competed for corporations, states did not want to regulate corporations too severely. As corporations became a dominant economic force in the United States, they also had a tremendous ability to influence legislation. Corporations lobbied lawmakers to assure that the law was in their interest—that the criminal law did not apply to them (Hurst, 1970; Perrow, 2002).

For legal purposes, corporations eventually came to be viewed as a type of person, a juristic person that could transact business (e.g., execute contracts, buy and sell, etc.). However, this type of "person" was not subject to criminal law or to its punishments. The general thinking was that corporations as juristic persons had no mind to form the criminal intent that was a standard element in crimes and that corporations did not exist as a physical body to punish (Edgerton, 1926–1927). Only natural persons were subject to the criminal law and its punishments. Even when corporations were sued in tort cases, they enjoyed legal advantages in the form of tort defenses that precluded or limited liability (Friedman, 1973).

Over the years, reforms did occur, usually prompted by scandal or some gross corporate wrongdoing. For example, David von Drehle (2003) describes the investigatory commissions, the criminal trials, and the reform legislation that followed the Triangle Shirtwaist fire of 1911. Almost 150 young women in New York's garment industry burned to death because they were locked inside a building that had caught fire. Corporations gradually lost some of the immunity from criminal responsibility. With few exceptions, however, the traditional view that corporations were not subject to criminal law persisted, especially with respect to crimes like homicide.

The Context of the Automobile Industry

Just as the legal landscape in 2004 differs from what was described in the preceding paragraphs, today's automobile industry differs from what it was in the 1970s. Today, large and small cars are on the roads—big sport utility vehicles (SUVs), like the Ford Expedition, and tiny imports, like the MiniCooper. It is common to read that the best selling car in the United States in any given year is a Honda or a Toyota (Jensen, 2003).

In contrast, thirty years ago American-made cars ruled the streets in the United States. To paraphrase the lyrics of a Bob Seger song, Americans were making and driving Thunderbirds (Seger, 1982). Although the original Thunderbird was small and sporty, most U.S. cars were big, heavy automobiles, and most got poor gas mileage. But, no one cared: gas was plentiful and cheap.

U.S. automakers correctly saw change looming. The oil embargo of the mid-1970s signaled the end to plentiful, inexpensive gas; and a surge of imports began to appear in automobile showrooms across the United States in the 1970s. U.S. automakers knew that these changes were permanent. Beginning in the late 1960s, U.S. automakers began a race to design small cars for the U.S. market. The term "race" is used because each automaker wanted to have its small car model on the streets first to get a leg up on the competition.

The race to production would become an issue in the Ford Pinto case. Critics argued that Ford pushed too fast to be the first U.S. automaker to market a small car. Critics contended that Ford executives pressed forward with production rather than change or slow production to fix the problem that had been discovered with the Pinto prototype. The problem discovered with the prototype was the Pinto's rear-mounted gas tank. The bumper was directly behind the gas tank on the rear of the vehicle. The problem with this configuration, critics charged, was that if the Pinto was hit hard enough in a rear-end collision, the bumper could penetrate the gas tank causing fuel to leak; or the impact could drive the gas tank forward into the differential housing, which would again cause rupture and gas spillage. An explosion could follow (Stuart, 1978). Ford defended the Pinto, claiming that the car met the federal safety standards applicable at the time (Iacocca, 1984).

Critics claimed that the Pinto was not safe and pressured Ford to recall the Pinto and add a layer of protection, a buffer between the bumper and the gas tank. Critics lobbied the National Highway Traffic Safety Administration (NHTSA) to take some action, for example, to order Ford to recall and repair the Pintos. Ford lobbied against any recall.

Ford began selling Pintos in 1970. The Ford Pinto, which only cost about $1,900 and got better gas mileage than heavier U.S. cars, quickly became a market success. But, the gas tank issue persisted. While critics continued to complain about Pinto-related injuries and deaths, Ford continued to defend the Pinto. Perhaps the situation might have continued in this fashion had the media not been involved.

THE PINTO, THE MEDIA, AND THE LAW

For the most part, the public was unaware of the issue with the Pinto's gas tank. The public would not have known about an internal memo at Ford that had summarized the debate about repairing versus not repairing the fuel system integrity problem. Contained in this memo were the results of a cost-benefit analysis wherein Ford analysts concluded that it would be cheaper and more profitable to settle tort claims involving Pinto-related accidents than to fix the Pinto's design.

However, that internal memo was leaked to the media. On December 30, 1976, *Washington Post* journalists Jack Anderson and Les Whitten reported that the Pinto's gas tank problem had caused thousands of horrible injuries and deaths. They argued that Ford easily could have prevented these tragedies but chose profits over lives (Anderson and Whiten, 1976).

Media exposure did not end with that *Washington Post* article. In the September-October 1977 issue of *Mother Jones* magazine, Mark Dowie wrote an article titled "Pinto Madness" (Dowie, 1977). In the article and in a related press conference that was held on August 10, 1977, Dowie reiterated *Washington Post* journalists Anderson and Whitten's claim that the Pinto's gas tank placement was problematic; Ford knew and could have fixed it but chose not to do so, and the result was needless injury and death (Dowie, 1977). Consumer advocate Ralph Nader attended the press conference; Nader was well-known for his denunciation of another car, the

Chevrolet Corvair (Nader, 1965). Nader's presence guaranteed media coverage of the press conference and of the "Pinto Madness" article.

Dowie's article reported the gas tank issue in detail and described how Ford could have resolved it and at what cost. Moreover, Dowie included the cost/benefit analysis that had been contained in that infamous internal memo from Ford. In stark black and white, there were the calculations and the implication that it was more profitable for Ford to deal with lawsuits generated by serious accidents than to fix the Pinto. Equally stark was the language of the memo in which the predicted tort liability for injured or dead victims was labeled "unit cost," that is, the memo referred to potential victims as "units."

Dowie's allegations, bolstered by Ralph Nader's reputation for consumer advocacy, renewed the pressure on the NHTSA. The day after the Dowie/Nader news conference, the NHTSA opened a preliminary evaluation into the Pinto's safety. Within a month, in November of 1977, the NHTSA began a formal investigation as to whether the Pinto posed a safety defect of the sort that was within the agency's regulatory power.

Once the media got hold of the Pinto story, they did not let go; it became a news theme. Other Pinto-related stories would reference the Dowie article and would be seen as newsworthy. This is common with the news media: once coverage establishes a "hook," future stories on the topic enjoy a ready-made newsworthiness (Chermak, 2002; Tuchman, 1978).

For example, in February 1978, a California jury awarded judgment to a plaintiff who was injured in an accident involving a Ford Pinto. The civil trial was newsworthy because of the amount of damages awarded and because the California story fit the news theme that had started with Dowie's article in *Mother Jones*. In the California case, thirteen-year-old Richard Grimshaw was a passenger in a Pinto that was involved in a fiery rear-end collision. Grimshaw survived but suffered serious burns; the Pinto's owner and driver, Lily Gray, died in the accident. Grimshaw's lawyer introduced into evidence the allegations that Dowie had made in his article, including Ford's internal cost/benefit analysis. Grimshaw's lawyer asked the jury for compensatory damages (e.g., medical expenses and pain and suffering) and for $100 million in punitive damages, which are intended to punish wrongful conduct. The jury awarded Grimshaw almost $3 million in compensatory damages. Moreover, the jury was so angry with Ford that they awarded Grimshaw more punitive damages than his lawyer had requested ($125 million, not $100 million) (Cullen, Maakestad, and Cavender, 1987). In 1978, the combined compensatory and punitive damages awarded to Grimshaw were the largest ever in a personal injury case (Harris, 1978). As is fairly typical in such cases, following an appeal, Ford settled with Grimshaw for $7.5 million (Harris, 1978; "Ford's $128 million headache," 1978).

It was as if legal action generated more legal action. Soon, plaintiffs were seeking large punitive damage awards from Ford for Pinto-related accidents. Pinto owners filed class-action lawsuits against Ford. In May 1978, the NHTSA notified Ford that a safety defect existed. The NHTSA had commissioned crash tests that revealed a number of Pintos had leaked gas or exploded into flames after rear-end collisions were simulated. In June 1978, the NHTSA scheduled a public hearing in which Ford could respond. On June 9, although denying any wrongdoing, Ford announced a recall of the Pinto (models created during 1971–1976) and of the Mercury Bobcat (models created during 1975–1976), which had a similar gas tank configuration (Strobel, 1980).

Perhaps the zenith of the Pinto as a media news theme occurred on June 11, 1978, when *60 Minutes*, the CBS news magazine, aired Mike Wallace's interview of Richard Grimshaw just two days after Ford announced the recall (Hewitt, 1978). Millions of viewers saw host Mike Wallace interview Richard Grimshaw and heard a former Ford executive say that, at Ford, style was more important than safety and that Ford penalized (in terms of career advancement) employees who were too safety-oriented. A Ford representative who appeared on the program to counter these allegations did not fare well against Wallace's questions about profits and safety.

Media coverage may not have caused the verdict in the Grimshaw case and prompted the State of Indiana to prosecute Ford in a criminal trial. This coverage, however, did publicize the gas tank issue, and, equally important, the media publicized the cost/benefit analysis that had angered the jury in the Grimshaw trial. And, each new event—another lawsuit, the NHTSA report, and Ford's recall decision—generated more coverage. With the Pinto as the news theme, each new story was newsworthy.

Other commentators credited the media as a mobilizing force in what would become a crusade against Ford. Criminologists John Braithwaite and Brent Fisse interviewed Ford executives who had said that Dowie's article was the opening salvo against the company (1983). Sociologists Victoria Swigert and Ronald Farrell reached a similar conclusion after an analysis of newspaper coverage of the Pinto (1980–1981). Swigert and Farrell noted that after Dowie's article and the Grimshaw verdict the nature of the news coverage changed as stories focused more on crash victims, which then personalized the harm. It has been suggested that a focus on victims in news stories serves as a representation of victimization and prompts readers to identify with the victims (Chermak, 1995). Swigert and Farrell concluded that over time the news coverage vilified Ford by focusing on "willful harm" and the notion that Ford remained "unrepentant" in the face of Pinto-related accidents. By characterizing Ford in "the language of moral deviance,"

Swigert and Farrell concluded that the newspaper coverage increasingly portrayed the Pinto not as a business or a consumer issue but as a crime problem (1980–1981, p. 172).

The final link in this chain of events was Indiana's criminal prosecution of Ford Motor Company. Here, too, the media coverage of the Pinto mattered.

THE FATAL ACCIDENT IN INDIANA

Ford recalled the Pinto to make the sort of repairs that would satisfy the NHTSA. To accomplish this, Ford had to notify Pinto owners of the recall. Ford began the process; however, unfortunately, one recall notice arrived too late. Three Indiana teenagers had died before the notice of the recall had reached them. The Pinto involved in the fatal accident was a used car, and it had taken Ford longer to trace owners when a car had changed hands.

Sisters Judy and Lyn Ulrich and their cousin Donna were riding in Judy's used 1973 Pinto. They had stopped for gas, but they had apparently forgotten to replace the gas cap and left the cap on the roof of the car. A mile or so later, after the gas cap blew off, Judy Ulrich made a U-turn and drove slowly, looking for the gas cap. Robert Duggar, who was driving about fifty miles per hour, had been feeling around on the floorboard of his Chevrolet van for a pack of cigarettes. A distracted Duggar looked up too late. He rear-ended the Pinto, and it exploded into flames. Lyn and Donna died at the scene of the car crash; Judy died in a hospital a few hours later.

When Indiana State Trooper Neil Graves arrived at the accident scene, he saw the burned-out Pinto. This surprised him because witnesses reported that both vehicles had been moving and that the speed differential between the van and the Pinto was about thirty miles per hour. The speed differential would become an important issue in the trial. State Trooper Graves also smelled gas.

The media again played an important role. The next day, State Trooper Graves received a series of telephone calls from various news services, including CBS News. When they mentioned defects in the Pinto, Graves remembered reading Dowie's "Pinto Madness" article months before. Graves called Dowie, who reminded him about the details of the article.

Later, Graves met with Elkhart County Prosecutor Michael Cosentino and Assistant Prosecutor Terry Shewmaker. What emerged from Graves's meeting with Cosentino and Shewmaker was the sense that this was not a normal traffic accident. Photos of the Pinto and of the victims were shocking, especially because there was so little damage to Duggar's van. Soon, Cosentino began to receive phone calls from lawyers who were suing Ford for Pinto-related accidents—they offered to share information.

In part, Cosentino's decision to pursue a criminal prosecution was motivated by Indiana civil law. In Indiana, when children were accident victims, compensatory damages in wrongful death lawsuits were limited to the amount that the children could have contributed to their parents until they became adults. Because the Ulrich girls were in their late teens, this "contribution" would have been negligible, so the damages that could be awarded to their parents would be minimal. Moreover, Indiana was one of several states that limited or prohibited punitive damage awards in such cases. In other words, unlike the Grimshaw case in California, there would have been almost no damages awarded had the Ulrichs' parents sued Ford, even if they had won.

However, when Cosentino researched the relevant criminal law, he discovered that Indiana had recently amended its reckless homicide statute so that, arguably, criminal responsibility could be imposed on a corporation. Also, reckless homicide did not require proof of intent to kill. The prosecution simply must prove that a death, even if unintended, resulted from reckless behavior of the sort that a reasonable person would regard as life threatening.

Cosentino presented the case to a grand jury in Elkhart County on September 13, 1978, and the grand jury handed down three felony indictments against Ford Motor Company for reckless homicide (Cullen et al., 1987). The indictments named Ford, not individual executives, because Cosentino knew that it would be difficult to prove individual responsibility in the case. The indictments charged that Ford had designed, manufactured, and failed to repair the Pinto, and that Ford's reckless disregard for safety had caused the deaths of the Ulrichs.

PRETRIAL MATTERS

Had Ford been convicted, it would have had to pay a thirty thousand-dollar fine, ten thousand per count of the indictment (Cullen et al., 1987; Strobel, 1980). And, yet, Ford spared no expense in organizing a defense. Obviously, it was not the fine that troubled Ford: The automaker was concerned about its reputation and about sales—of the Pinto and of other Ford models. Moreover, a criminal trial in Indiana might encourage other legal actions against Ford.

Following the indictments, Ford went outside of its own legal departments and engaged the assistance of two prestigious law firms: Mayer, Brown, and Platt; and Hughes, Hubbard, and Reed. The lawyers worked on a series of pretrial motions that were designed to effect a dismissal of the Indiana indictments.

For his part, in addition to Shewmaker, Cosentino added another trial attorney, John Ulmer; two university law school professors, Bruce Berner and

Terry Kiely; a number of law students and other researchers; and State Trooper Neil Graves was assigned to the case as well. Elkhart County gave Cosentino $20,000 to help with the case. A team of volunteers on a small budget would prosecute one of the largest corporations in the United States.

Criminal trials are dramatic and exciting, but, before they begin, important legal groundwork occurs that may affect a trial's outcome. The pretrial phase proved to be important in the Pinto case. Soon, there was a good deal of back and forth of Ford motions and prosecution responses. Although Ford's lawyers had offered several rationales for dismissing the indictments, two key arguments were considered. Ford claimed that the indictments should be dismissed because corporations cannot be prosecuted for crimes such as reckless homicide. The notion that only individuals, not corporations, were subject to criminal law had been discussed earlier in this chapter. However, Indiana's statute had been amended and now read that "a person who recklessly kills another human being commits reckless homicide" (Indiana Code, IC 35-42-1-5).[2] The statute specified that the victim must be a human being, and the killer was designated as a person. As a juristic person, a corporation, arguably, would be considered a "person" within the meaning of the Indiana statute.

Second, Ford claimed an ex post facto prosecution, which violates the U.S. Constitution, because Ulrich's Pinto (a 1973 model) was manufactured before Indiana's amended reckless homicide statute took effect. The prosecution responded that Ford's reckless behavior entailed a continuation of acts that began with the manufacture of the 1973 Pinto but did not culminate until the Ulrichs died—the amended statute was in effect when they died.

On February 2, 1979, after hearing oral arguments, Judge Donald Jones rendered his decision on Ford's motions for a dismissal. Judge Jones referenced the trend toward reducing corporate immunity to criminal prosecution and the specific language in Indiana's reckless homicide statute. Other Indiana statutory language suggested that the Indiana State Legislature no longer granted corporations a carte blanche of immunity. Judge Jones rejected Ford's claim that a corporation could not be prosecuted for reckless homicide in Indiana. Judge Jones rejected Ford's ex post facto claim, although his rationale was a bit complicated. He accepted the prosecution's view that Ford's behavior constituted a continuation of actions; but, Judge Jones emphasized those actions on Ford's part that occurred after the amended reckless homicide statute took effect, that is, the forty-one-day period between when the new statute took effect and the accident. His ruling meant the prosecution had to prove not merely that Ford was reckless in manufacturing and marketing the car, but that Ford was also reckless in its failure to recall and repair the Pinto.

Judge Jones's decision on these motions was significant. He ruled against Ford and for the prosecution, which indicated that there would be a criminal trial, but the rationale for at least a part of the ruling made the prosecution's task more difficult. Even so, Judge Jones's ruling meant that the state had the right to use the criminal law to prosecute a corporation for a violent act. Not only was an important legal precedent set in Indiana, but Judge Jones's decision had implications across the United States.

Ford quickly engaged the law firm of James Neal and Aubrey Harwell. Neal had the reputation as one of the best trial lawyers in the United States. He had a career's worth of stellar legal experience: along with U.S. Attorney General Robert Kennedy, he prosecuted Teamsters boss Jimmy Hoffa, and as a Watergate prosecutor, he helped to convict John Ehrlichman, H. R. Haldeman, and John Mitchell. His Nashville, Tennessee, law firm represented clients ranging from country music stars to major U.S. corporations.

One of Neal's first moves was to request a change of venue. In support of this motion, he presented the results of a telephone survey. Almost 70 percent of Elkhart County residents admitted to some level of prejudice against Ford. The trial was relocated to Pulaski County in Winamac, Indiana, which is over fifty miles from Elkhart.

Neal and his firm drafted a mountain of other pretrial motions. These motions contained relevant legal arguments, but they taxed the resources of the small prosecution team that had to respond as they tried to prepare for trial. The lack of financial resources for the prosecution was another issue that made the Pinto trial unusual. Notwithstanding a defendant's presumption of innocence or the prosecution's burden of proof beyond a reasonable doubt, the state usually enjoys an advantage over most criminal defendants in terms of financial resources. But, in this case, the defendant was the Ford Motor Company, which had financial resources far greater than those available to the prosecution. For example, the telephone survey that Neal used to justify a change of venue cost about as much as Cosentino's $20,000 budget. The resource differential between Ford and the prosecution was a constant issue during the trial.

While preparing for trial, the prosecution was concerned on how to prove Ford's guilt beyond a reasonable doubt. It would not be enough to simply show the Ulrichs' burned-out Pinto. Given the charge of reckless homicide, the prosecution would have to present the jury with the corporate decision-making process at Ford that resulted in the decision to go forward with the Pinto, and until the recall, Ford's decision not to repair the Pinto. Cosentino and his team had some help in this task: numerous lawyers shared internal documents (e.g., crash tests that had emerged during their civil lawsuits against Ford). The prosecution had documents that demonstrated Ford's mind-set in terms of the decision not to repair the Pinto. Cosentino also had commitments from expert witnesses and a former Ford executive who would testify against Ford.

Of the many pretrial motions that Neal introduced, three were especially significant. First, Neal noted that the NHTSA requirement, as of 1977, that cars had to meet a thirty-mile-per-hour rear-end crash test should govern the jury's decision about whether Ford had been reckless. The defense's motion addressed the issue of the speed differential between the Chevrolet van and the Pinto. If the appropriate standard was thirty miles per hour, and if Neal could demonstrate a greater speed differential, it was not reasonable to expect that the Pinto could have withstood the impact. The prosecution responded that the federal standard was a minimum standard, but that an Indiana jury should determine the applicable standard in Indiana. Second, Neal argued that because the accident involved a 1973 Pinto, the prosecution should be limited to using evidence related to the 1973 Pinto. The prosecution responded that the 1973 model was representative of Pintos in general and that the entire Pinto line, regardless of model year, was problematic. Third, Neal stipulated that the victims died from burns and not because of trauma caused by the accident. Accordingly, Neal argued that it would be sensational and distracting for the jury to see photos of the dead Ulrich girls. The prosecution wanted the jury to see the photos, and the prosecution argued that Indiana court precedent upheld the state's right to show such photos even when defendants stipulated the victims' injuries.

These motions may seem fairly straightforward, but because this was a landmark case, many of the issues were being considered for the first time. In other words, there was not much legal precedent for Judge Harold Staffeldt to rely on for his decisions. Judge Staffeldt agreed with the prosecution about allowing the jury to determine the appropriate mile-per-hour standard. However, the judge sided with Neal and Ford about limiting evidence to the 1973 model; however, he left open the possibility that later in the trial he might allow information from other model years to be submitted as evidence. Staffeldt's ruling hurt the prosecution, because they were on a limited budget and much of their information pertained to other than the 1973 model (e.g., the crash test information that other lawyers had shared with Cosentino was not for the 1973 model). Characterizing the photos as "melodramatic," Judge Staffeldt granted Neal's third motion and excluded the photos (and much other information about the Ulrich girls) from evidence. Because some of the prosecution's important evidence was not excluded, Neal's motions weakened the prosecution's case. The legal fireworks had begun even before the trial started.

THE TRIAL

Jury selection began on January 7, 1980, and the trial began on January 16, 1980 (Cullen et al., 1987; Strobel, 1980). In his hour-long opening statement to the jury, Cosentino charged that Ford had known about the Pinto's gas tank problem but had marketed the car and resisted warning Pinto owners about the dangerous situation. He said that the Ulrich girls died because Ford had callously chosen profits over safety.

Neal's opening statement to the jury lasted for about seventy-five minutes. He told the jury that the Pinto met applicable safety standards for rear-end collisions. Moreover, he argued that the speed differential between the Ulrich's Pinto and the Chevrolet van was fifty miles per hour and not the lower speed differential asserted by the prosecution. Neal stated that most U.S. cars could not withstand that level of impact. Focusing on that forty-one-day period that had been created by Judge Donald Jones's ruling on pretrial motions, Neal asserted that Ford had done everything possible during that time period to notify Pinto owners of the recall. Neal concluded his opening statement with the words, "We are not reckless killers" (Strobel, 1980, p. 119).

In a trial, each side has a "theory of the case"; that is, a framework through which the jury is supposed to understand facts and evidence. Each side uses witnesses to establish its points in that theory. The prosecution presents its case first. Cosentino's strategy was to convince the jury that although Ford had known about problems with the Pinto's gas tank and could have repaired it for a fairly modest amount of money per car, Ford had not repaired the problem in time to prevent the Ulrichs' death, and this was reckless behavior.

Cosentino's first witness was Indiana State Trooper Neil Graves. Graves testified that the Pinto's gas tank was almost empty even though Judy Ulrich had just filled it. He also testified that he had smelled gas. During Graves's testimony, Cosentino showed the jury the gas tank from the Ulrich Pinto and the gaping hole in it. The hole in the gas tank demonstrated the rupture caused by the wreck, why the tank was empty, and why there was a prominent gas smell.

Next, Cosentino called Mattie Ulrich, the mother of Judy and Lyn, to the stand. Mattie Ulrich testified that the family had not received a recall notice before the accident. Her presence added a human face to the tragedy, which was important because the prosecution could not show the jury the photos of the victims.

Cosentino called a series of witnesses who had seen the accident. They testified that both the Pinto and the van were moving and that the speed differential between the vehicles was around thirty miles per hour. According to one witness, what appeared to be a "fender bender" instead was more like a "napalm bomb" (Strobel, 1980, p. 127).

Cosentino brought forth and questioned Harley Copp, the retired Ford executive testing engineer who had appeared on *60 Minutes*. Copp testified that Ford could have repaired the Pinto for seven dollars per car, which would have increased the car's ability to withstand a rear-end collision. Ford decided not to effect the repairs, Copp testified, because of its cost/benefit analysis and because of the rush to market the Pinto. He explained the notion of a production cycle in the automobile industry; that is, how the basic design of a model remains essentially the same during the life of that model.

The latter part of Copp's testimony was important to Cosentino, who again argued to Judge Staffeldt that since the basic design essentially was the same from year to year, the Ulrichs' 1973 Pinto was the same as Pinto models. Accordingly, Cosentino reasoned, crash-test information and other evidence should be admissible even though it was not specific to the 1973 model. Judge Staffeldt persisted in his decision about evidence pertaining to the 1973 model. He reiterated that evidentiary matters were more strictly construed in criminal cases.

Through Copp's testimony, Cosentino was able to present to the jury some of Copp's theory of the case about Ford's mind-set with respect to the Pinto. But, much of the prosecution's strongest evidence (e.g., internal documents and crash-test information), was still inadmissible: The evidence pertained to models from other years and not the 1973 Pinto that Judy Ulrich was driving.

There were other witnesses called by the prosecution, but this chapter has presented discussions that demonstrate the main points in Cosentino's theory of the case. After the prosecution rested, Neal introduced a motion for directed verdict, which is a standard practice, for Ford. Neal argued that the prosecution had failed to make a compelling case and that, even before the defense presented its case, the judge should end the trial. Judge Staffeldt ruled against Neal's motion for directed verdict.

Neal opened the defense case with a surprise witness. Levi Woodard was discovered by Neal's partner, Aubrey Harwell, who directed the behind-the-scenes investigation. Woodard had been an orderly at the hospital where Judy Ulrich was taken after the accident. He had long since left his job at the hospital, which is why the prosecution did not know about him. Indeed, Harwell's investigators tracked Woodard across several states. Woodard opened Neal's defense with a bombshell: he testified that he talked with Judy Ulrich before she died, and she told him she had found the gas cap and had stopped to pick it up when the van hit the Pinto. Woodard testified to a key element in Neal's theory of the case. If Ulrich's car was stopped, the speed differential between the Pinto and the Chevrolet van was close to fifty miles per hour and not the smaller speed differential claimed by the prosecution.

Other defense witnesses were automotive experts. Some testified that the Pinto's gas tank configuration was comparable—in terms of placement and safety—to that of other small cars. Other witnesses were Ford employees who testified that the Pinto was a safe car and that their family members drove Pintos. Another Ford employee addressed the all-important forty-one-day period. He described the steps that he and his colleagues had taken to speed up recall notices being sent to owners.

Neal then showed to the jury a crash-test video involving a 1973 Pinto. The Pinto in the crash test was hit in a rear-end collision at about fifty miles per hour. Although the gas tank in the test vehicle ruptured, the rupture was smaller than in Ulrich's Pinto. An expert witness interpreted the difference in rupture size to indicate that the speed differential between the Ulrich Pinto and the Chevrolet van was even greater than the fifty miles per hour differential in the crash test. The expert witness estimated a speed differential of fifty-five miles per hour.

There was symmetry between Neal's closing and opening witnesses. Again, through thorough investigation procedures, Harwell located another witness who talked with Judy Ulrich in the hospital. Nancy Fogo, a nursing supervisor, confirmed Woodard's testimony: Judy Ulrich told her that the Pinto was parked. Neal rested the case for the defense.

After Neal rested his case, Cosentino attempted to present additional information as a rebuttal to the witnesses for the defense. He wanted to call two new witnesses: an accident reconstruction specialist who would testify to the distribution of debris at the accident scene and how it suggested a differential speed impact of considerably less than fifty miles per hour; and a retired Ford employee who would testify that Ford employees sometimes misreported crash-test information.

Neal responded that the prosecution should have examined these witnesses during its original presentation. The prosecution responded that Indiana Supreme Court decisions had permitted new information that specifically rebutted defense evidence. Judge Staffeldt ruled in favor of Ford; Cosentino's rebuttal witnesses were not permitted.

Cosentino offered his closing argument to the jury on Monday, March 10, 1980. He argued that Ford knew about the Pinto's gas tank and could have repaired it for a small amount of money per car, but that Ford chose not to do so. He reminded the jury of the prosecution's view of the speed differential between the Pinto and the Chevrolet van and of the eyewitnesses who said that the Pinto was moving when the collision occurred. Cosentino described Judy Ulrich's physical condition and her heavy sedation in an attempt at discrediting the defense witnesses who testified that she told them that the Pinto was not moving. Cosentino told the jury that although they could not bring the girls back, they could give meaning to their deaths and by so doing, send a message about corporate moral responsibility.

In his closing argument, Neal reiterated the points that he had tried to make through his witnesses during the trial: the Pinto met applicable safety standards, two witnesses testified that Judy Ulrich told them that her car was stopped, the speed differential between the Pinto and the van was so great that few cars—even larger cars—could have withstood the impact, and Ford employees were honest people and not reckless killers. He criticized Cosentino for vilifying Ford, and, by extension, U.S. corporations. Neal also referenced morality, arguing that the jurors had a moral duty to end the practice of blaming business for everything; a practice that Neal said was undermining the U.S. economy.

THE VERDICT

The case went to the jury that Monday afternoon (Cullen et al., 1987; Strobel, 1980). Thursday morning, twenty-five ballots later, the jury returned with a verdict: Ford was not guilty. The trial had lasted twenty-nine days; there were twenty-two prosecution witnesses and nineteen defense witnesses and almost 6,000 pages of transcripts.

Any explanation of the verdict is speculative. However, some jurors who were interviewed offered a sense of the jury deliberations. For the most part, their comments can be characterized by Neal creating a reasonable doubt in their minds as to the recklessness of Ford's behavior. Neal had "put a human face" on Ford employees, and his witnesses convinced jurors that those employees had done everything possible to notify Pinto owners during the forty-one-day period.

The outcome of the case also demonstrates the importance of pretrial activity. Motions from Neal and his predecessors undermined the prosecution's case, specifically those motions that pertained to the forty-one-day period and those that caused the exclusion of non-1973 evidence.

Ford's resources were no doubt a significant factor in the outcome. Throughout the case, Ford engaged excellent legal representation and gave their legal teams the resources to do their work. Nowhere was this more telling than in the prosecution's inability to conduct its own crash test with a 1973 model. Prosecution witness Harley Copp could explain in words Ford's mindset, but Neal's compelling visual crash test was unanswered by a visual presentation from the prosecution. Similarly, Neal's "surprise" witnesses—Woodard and Fogo—resulted from thorough investigation procedures that were made possible by Ford's extensive financial resources. Cosentino presented eyewitnesses, but Neal's witnesses were able to plant the seed of reasonable doubt in the jurors' minds.

Not intended to fault the prosecution: Cosentino and his team did a very good job. Simply getting the case to trial was a major legal outcome. And, given the vast economic differential between the prosecution and the defense, as well as novel nature of the case, the prosecution team demonstrated their own legal acumen and their tenacity.

IMPLICATIONS

Before implications of the trial are addressed, it should be mentioned that this famous trial has been analyzed and reanalyzed many times. Some analyses are critical that the trial even occurred. These commentators argue that the characterization of Ford executives as wanton, reckless people demonstrated a misunderstanding of corporate decision-making. They argue that Ford's internal cost/benefit analysis was not the smoking gun that revealed Ford's recklessness, but rather, the cost/benefit analysis was an appropriate aspect of job performance. They suggested that corporations must be loyal to their stockholders and that they make business decisions through cost/benefit analyses (Schwartz, 1991). Others claim that a review of internal documents suggests that Ford did no wrong in the production of the Pinto; the Pinto's gas tank placement, they argue, was defensible and no worse than other configurations. They conclude that Ford did not put profit over consumer safety (Lee and Ermann, 1999).

Even so, some commentators acknowledge that the Pinto trial has become a part of the public and the legal consciousness, and the trial has come to symbolize dangerous products that are manufactured by corporations (Schwartz, 1991). When new revelations emerge about a defective product, especially if it is linked to the automobile industry, media frequently invoke the Pinto trial as a point of reference. This practice is reinforced by popular movies like *Class Action*, a film that is reminiscent of the events in the Ford Pinto case, and films like *A Civil Action* or *Erin Brockovich* that address other forms of corporate wrongdoing. Moreover, commentators argue that corporations are so embedded in the lives of the American public that they owe a high standard of care (legally and ethically) that ensures that the public is not harmed by their practices or products (Coleman, 2002).

As for the Pinto trial, two observations are offered in the aftermath of this landmark case. First, Indiana's criminal prosecution of the Ford Motor Company for three counts of reckless homicide broke the "legal ice." The trial demonstrated that it is possible for a corporation to be prosecuted for crimes that, until then, ordinarily were thought to be beyond the reach of the criminal law. Second, the Pinto case demonstrated the obstacles to getting a conviction in such a trial; these obstacles relate to such matters as problems of proof, the complicated nature of such trials, the economic power of some corporations, and what those financial resources actually mean in a trial. In other words, a prosecutor who is considering filing criminal charges against a corporation might either be encouraged or discouraged by the Pinto case.

In the years after the Indiana trial, there were a number of criminal prosecutions. In some cases, prosecutions were successful. For example, in 1991, employees of the Imperial Chicken Processing Plant burned to death because they could not escape a fire in the plant; the manager had locked the plant door from the outside to prevent theft (Wright, Cullen, and Blankenship, 1995). The manager of the plant was convicted of manslaughter. Many of these corporate defendants were not the size of the Ford Motor Company. Even so, there were trials and the notion of criminal responsibility for corporations and their managers became more normal.

By the late 1980s and early 1990s, these criminal prosecutions seem to have waned in favor of civil trials, including class-action lawsuits against large corporations. Perhaps this shift is due, in part, to the political context under Presidents Reagan and Bush who were considered to be "corporation friendly" presidents. Perhaps, in part, the focus on tort lawsuits occurred because the burden of proof is less in civil suits than in criminal trials (Coleman, 2002; Simpson, 2002). Perhaps the shift occurred because juries were willing to grant large damage awards against corporate defendants, and it was in the interest of victims and plaintiff lawyers to pursue civil cases. Whatever the reason, successful civil lawsuits have been an important mechanism for redressing corporate wrongdoing.

Recently, new revelations have come to light about corporate wrongdoing. Enron and other related accounting scandals returned the issue of corporate criminal responsibility to center stage. The American public will have to wait and see how the issue of corporate accountability plays out. In any case, two things are certain: first, the public today is more aware of and less tolerant of corporate crime; and second, the Ford Pinto trial in 1980 is a landmark case and its notoriety contributed to the public's awareness of corporate crime.

NOTES

1. Neal made this statement before the Elkhart (Indiana) Bar Association at Elkhart County Prosecutor Cosentino's invitation in 1982.

2. As added by Acts 1976, P.L.148, Section 2. Amended by Acts 1977, P.L.340, Section 29; and Acts 1980, P.L.83, Section 6. Information retrieved from http://www.ai.org/legislative/ic/code/title35/ar42/ch1.html#IC35-42-1-5

REFERENCES

Anderson, J., and Whiten, L. (1976, December 30). Automaker shuns safer gas tank. *Washington Post*, p. B7.

Braithwaite, J., and Fisse, B. (1983). *The impact of publicity on corporate offenders.* Albany, NY: State University of New York Press.

Chermak, S. (1995). *Victims in the news: Crime and the American news media.* Boulder, CO: Westview Press.

Chermak, S. (2002). *Searching for a demon: The media construction of the militia movement.* Boston: Northeastern University Press.

Coleman, J. W. (2002). *The criminal elite: Understanding white-collar crime* (5th ed.). New York: W H Freeman and Company.

Commons, J. (1959). *Legal foundations of capitalism.* Madison, WI: University of Wisconsin Press. (Original work published 1924)

Cullen, F., Maakestad, W., and Cavender, G. (1987). *Corporate crime under attack: The Ford Pinto case and beyond.* Cincinnati, OH: Anderson.

Dowie, M. (1977). Pinto madness. *Mother Jones.* Retrieved from http://www.motherjones.com/news/feature/1977/09/dowie.html

Edgerton, H. (1926–1927). Corporate criminal responsibility. *Yale Law Journal, 36.*

Field, T., Kroopf, S., and Cort, R. W. (1991). *Class action* [Motion picture]. United States: 20th Century Fox/Interscope.

Ford's $128 million headache. (1978, February 20). *Time, 111*(8), 65.

Friedman, L. (1973). *A history of American law.* New York: Simon and Schuster.

Hall, C. H., and Zaillian, S. (1999). *A civil action* [Motion picture]. Burbank, CA: Touchstone Pictures.

Harris, R., Jr. (1978, February 15). Jury in Pinto crash case: "We wanted Ford to take notice." *Washington Post*, p. A2.

Hewitt, D. (Executive Producer). (1978, June 11). Is your car safe? *60 Minutes* [Television Broadcast]. New York: CBS Television Network.

Hurst, J. W. (1970). *The legitimacy of the business corporation in the law of the United States, 1780–1970.* Charlottesville, VA: University of Virginia Press.

Iacocca, L., with William Novak. (1984). *Iacocca: An autobiography.* New York: Bantam Books.

Jensen, C. (2003, January 16). 5 of last year's best selling vehicles were built in Ohio. *Cleveland Plain Dealer*, p. C3.

Lee, M., and Ermann, D. (1999). Pinto "madness" as a flawed landmark narrative: An organizational and network analysis. *Social Problems, 46*, 30–47.

Nader, R. (1965). *Unsafe at any speed: The designed-in dangers of the American automobile.* New York: Grossman Publishers.

Perrow, C. (2002). *Organizing America: Wealth, power, and the origins of corporate capitalism*. Princeton, NJ: Princeton University Press.

Schwartz, G. (1991). The myth of the Ford Pinto case. *Rutgers Law Review, 43,* 1013–1068.

Seger, B. (1982). Makin' Thunderbirds. On *The distance* [CD]. Hollywood, CA: Capitol.

Simpson, S. (2002). *Corporate crime, law, and social control*. Cambridge, UK: Cambridge University Press.

Soderbergh, S. (Director). (2000). *Erin Brockovich* [Motion picture]. Hollywood: Universal Pictures and Columbia Pictures.

Strobel, L. P. (1980). *Reckless homicide? Ford's Pinto trial*. South Bend, IN: And Books.

Stuart, R. (1978, May 9). U.S. agency suggests Ford Pintos have a fuel system defect. *New York Times,* p. 22.

Swigert, V. L., and Farrell, R. (1980–1981). Corporate homicide: Definitional processes in the creation of deviance. *Law and Society Review, 15,* 172.

Tuchman, G. (1978). *Making news: A study in the construction of reality*. New York: The Free Press.

von Drehle, D. (2003). *Triangle: The fire that changed America*. New York: Atlantic Monthly Press.

Wright, J., Cullen, F., and Blankenship, M. (1995). The social construction of corporate violence: Media coverage of the Imperial Food Products fire. *Crime and Delinquency, 41,* 20–36.

6

The Wreck of the *Exxon Valdez*: Oil and Water Don't Mix

T. David Evans

At 12:26 a.m. on March 24, 1989, the captain of the *Exxon Valdez*, Joseph Hazelwood, radioed the U.S. Coast Guard to announce, "We've fetched up hard aground. . . . We're leaking some oil, and we're going to be here awhile" (Little, 2002, p. 1). About twenty minutes earlier, the oil supertanker had run aground in Prince William Sound, about twenty-five miles from the Port of Valdez, Alaska. At 987 feet long and 166 feet wide, the *Valdez* was the newest supertanker and one of the two largest ships in Exxon Shipping's fleet of twenty oil supertankers (Malcom, 1989). The ship had just been loaded with close to 53 million gallons of Alaskan crude oil.

It would be hard to imagine a worse time and place for such an accident. Birds were migrating, the herring run was about to begin, and salmon were spawning in Prince William Sound, a huge and productive pristine bay surrounded by islands (McAllister, 1989). To add further risk of major contamination, the bay was dotted with islands that would keep the oil from going further out to sea and being diluted. The spill threatened the livelihood of commercial fishermen, who depended on the sound's resources for a living, and residents of Alaska, who used the resources for subsistence (Wells and Chase, 1989). The long-term environmental damage from the spill and the ultimate recovery of fish, plants, and other wildlife are still uncertain;

Former *Exxon Valdez* captain, Joseph Hazelwood, arrives
for a relicensing hearing in a California court in this July
1990 photo. (AP/Wide World Photos)

more than twenty-four years after the "accident," civil litigation by private
plaintiffs is still not resolved. Compensation for damages and punitive damages were assessed against Exxon, but the case is currently on appeal for the
third time. As with many white-collar crimes, remedies for damages and
punishment for environmental law violations ran the gamut from civil to
regulatory and criminal approaches to "justice." In the *Exxon Valdez* case,
there was also a wide range of governmental and private parties involved;
all sought relief and retribution in a variety of legal ways.

As Lebedoff (1997) noted, the crash of the *Valdez* was simply a case of
"drunk driving." In fact, Captain Hazelwood had apparently consumed
alcohol within four hours of the ship's sailing—a violation of both U.S.
Coast Guard and Exxon rules. A test of Hazelwood's blood alcohol level
was administered ten hours after the grounding of the *Valdez*; the test results

indicated a level of .061 percent, which was about half of the drunk-driving limit in Alaska, but 50 percent above the 0.04 percent allowed by the Coast Guard (Keeble, 1999). When and how much alcohol was actually consumed or if the captain was drunk, and if so, the extent to which the alcohol impaired his judgment and actions, remain in dispute.

However, more than a year after the incident, the National Transportation Safety Board (NTSB)—a U.S. federal agency charged with investigations of such accidents—ruled that the captain's drinking prior to sailing, the fatigued and overworked crew members, and the inadequacy of Coast Guard tracking of the *Valdez* all contributed to the grounding of the *Valdez*. In addition, the NTSB concluded that the third mate, as the only crew member on the bridge at the time of the collision, was overworked and lost track of the ship's location (Cushman, 1989a, 1989b).

THE EVENT: "FETCHED UP HARD AGROUND"

As it set sail on a routine journey from Valdez, Alaska, to Long Beach, California, the *Exxon Valdez* was captained by a veteran and, by most accounts, capable pilot Joseph Hazelwood, forty-two years old. As required, a port pilot, familiar with the obstacles to navigation and the contours and depth of the channel, steered the ship through the Valdez narrows. The pilot left the bridge at about 11 p.m., and Hazelwood took charge. To avoid ice floes from the Columbia Glacier in the outbound channel, Hazelwood requested and was granted permission by the Coast Guard's Valdez Traffic Control Center to move into the inbound lane (National Transportation Safety Board [NTSB], 1990). Moving into the inbound lane was a common practice at that time of the year when no traffic was incoming and the outbound lane was clogged with chunks of ice.

As the *Valdez* headed out of the outbound and toward the inbound lane of the channel, a course was plotted, and the *Valdez* was set on autopilot. Shortly after midnight, the captain turned command over to Third Mate Gregory T. Cousins, and Hazelwood left the bridge for his cabin below. Cousins took the *Valdez* off autopilot, following Hazelwood's instructions, and piloted it on a course that would avoid the ice but take the *Valdez* completely out of the channel toward Busby Island—about three miles north of treacherous shallower waters at Bligh Reef. Before Hazelwood went below deck, Cousins confirmed that he was told to turn the ship back into the inbound lane at Busby Island (Cushman, 1989a). There is some dispute on the subsequent events before the grounding: apparently after a course correction was made incorrectly by Third Mate William Kagen, the *Valdez* was going past Busby Island and was headed toward Bligh Reef when

Cousins ordered a hard turn to avoid the reef. Unfortunately, under nearly full sail and seriously off course, the attempted last minute corrections by Cousins were unsuccessful in avoiding the grounding at 12:04 a.m. on March 24. After its first collision with the reef, the *Valdez* apparently plowed on for another two miles; a second collision with the reef ruptured more of the ship's hull, and the oil began to leak (Keeble, 1999; NTSB, 1990). At 12:26 a.m., Hazelwood called the Coast Guard to announce the crash and that the ship was leaking oil (Little, 2002).

In less than five hours of the grounding, nearly 11 million gallons of crude oil "flooded one of the nation's most sensitive ecosystems" (U.S. Environmental Protection Agency [EPA], 1989). Barely a day later, a plume of oil 1,000 yards wide extended five miles into Prince William Sound toward the ocean and began polluting the bay, killing fish and threatening marine mammals and plants (McAllister, 1989). Within five days of the grounding and spill, "the currents and wind . . . spread the oil more than [fifty] miles from the stricken tanker, blackening pristine island beaches, coating plant and marine life, and endangering one of the world's largest salmon runs" (Egan, 1989b, p. A1).

Many of the events immediately prior to the grounding were clear violations of Exxon and/or Coast Guard regulations: alcohol consumption by several officers within four hours of boarding the ship and leaving port; the failure to notify the Coast Guard that the ship would be leaving the channel entirely, not just changing to the inbound lane to avoid ice; leaving the ship in command of a third mate who was not licensed to pilot the ship in the sound; and the captain being absent from the bridge before the *Valdez* was sailing in open seas (EPA, 1989; NTSB, 1990). Some of the violations constituted potentially criminal acts; others would be used to support claims for damages in civil suits.

RESPONSE AND CLEANUP: TOO LITTLE, TOO LATE

Alyeska Pipeline Service Company is a consortium of oil companies, including Exxon, that built and continues to operate the Valdez port and the Alaskan pipeline, which brings Alaska crude oil down 800 miles from the North Slope at Prudhoe Bay, Alaska. To end a four-year moratorium on construction of the Alaskan pipeline, win the permits to build and operate the pipeline, and to be relieved of lawsuits in opposition to the pipeline and the Valdez terminal, Alyeska had given strong assurances that an oil spill was remote (Hunter, 1989). The companies "further represented that they would utilize the best available oil spill containment and cleanup technology and that, if an oil spill did occur, they would be able to contain and clean up the oil spill" (Mauer, 1989a, p. A1). The inability of Alyeska and Exxon to respond quickly and effectively to the oil spill was a major issue in litigation.

Alyeska, as the designated first responder to any oil spills in the area, was not prepared for the event. Alyeska's emergency cleanup plans required a response within five hours to any spill; however, it took the consortium twice as long just to get equipment and crews to the scene that was twenty-three miles away. The first response and rescue vessel (a barge) was in dry dock for repairs, and emergency cleanup equipment had been removed at the time of the spill or was buried under snow (Jones and Parrish, 1989). The first "full emergency crew did not arrive at the spill site until more than [ten] hours after the shipwreck (Jones and Parrish, 1989). Also, the *Valdez* was not surrounded by floating oil containment booms for another twenty-one hours. By then, the oil had leaked out and, combined with additional delays over the next two days in trying to burn or disperse the oil, "the deadening fluid was out of any effective control" (Malcom, 1989, p.1).

In the emergency response plans, chemical dispersants were to be used immediately to break up the oil, but these dispersants were neither available nor used when they would have been most effective. Exxon later claimed that the State of Alaska was responsible for the delay in the use of dispersants; the state had claimed that Exxon and Alyeska had neither the chemicals nor the equipment to deliver them when the seas were calm in the first few days. At any rate, use of dispersants is controversial: they are toxic to wildlife, and they may not have worked at all with the thick crude oil in the cold waters or the relatively calm seas right after the spill (Schmitt and Miller, 1989). As with ordinary cleaning detergents, the chemical dispersants require some agitation to be activated, and they work better at higher temperatures. Ultimately, the response was too little and too late to deal effectively with the spreading oil spill (Toomey, 1989b).

Within a few days of the spill, Exxon completely took over the cleanup effort from Alyeska and began pumping the remaining oil out of the *Valdez* and attempting to clean up the oil on the water and the shore. However, Exxon, too, was later accused of being slow and ineffective, thereby allowing the oil to spread beyond the original site and cause more damage than necessary. It is clear that opportunities were missed during the first few critical days when the weather was good and the seas were relatively calm to contain and clean up the spill. The cause and responsibility for the delay would later be disputed by Exxon. At any rate, the botched response became a key issue in the litigation against Alyeska, Exxon, and Exxon Shipping.

By March 29, Exxon officials admitted that the spill could not be contained and that, in fact, containment booms were not put in place until ten hours after the spill and five hours after cleanup plans required (Egan, 1989b). Lawrence G. Rawl, chairman of Exxon, claimed that the delay was due to late authorization by the State of Alaska, but, as noted, the state contended that Exxon was not prepared for the cleanup effort until the winds had picked up and seas became too rough for effective cleanup. The fumbled cleanup effort was summarized in the *Wall Street Journal*:

Nothing much has gone right for Exxon from the very moment the *Exxon Valdez* went aground early in the morning of March 24th, causing the largest oil spill ever in North America and an environmental disaster covering 1,300 square miles. Nor for the Alyeska Pipeline Service Company . . . that operates the Valdez terminal and was supposed to mount the initial defenses against the spill. (Wells and McCoy, 1989, p. 1)

What happened and why in both the cause of the spill and the prolonged cleanup would be subjects of extensive investigation and litigation in the following months and years. Early reports attributed the crash to "human error," at least as the proximate cause of the spill. Exxon Shipping's President, Frank Iarossi, especially promoted the theory that the spill was strictly the result of Hazelwood's errors and possible impaired state of mind due to alcohol consumption prior to sailing (Egan, 1989a). But, the record of litigation and later accounts would show a much more complicated chain of events that preceded the crash.

LITIGATION

State Charges against the Captain

Captain Hazelwood was initially charged with negligently discharging oil, criminal mischief, reckless endangerment, and operating a vessel while intoxicated. Ultimately, the only charge to result in a conviction was negligently discharging oil. His sentence was 1,000 of community service (Wells, 1990). Hazelwood's prosecution was relatively straightforward; however, this was not the case for Alyeska and Exxon.

State and Federal Criminal and Civil Prosecutions

Not unlike many other white-collar crimes, the quest for justice in the *Exxon Valdez* case took many forms. Public and private parties were harmed and victimized; civil and criminal processes were used for remedy and retribution. Captain Hazelwood, Exxon, Exxon Shipping, and Alyeska were the primary offenders and defendants. The State of Alaska, the federal government,

Alaskan populations and corporations, municipalities, fishermen, canneries, related businesses, and businesses that depended peripherally from tourism and other commercial activities interrupted by the oil spill were the main victims and plaintiffs.

Hazelwood and Exxon (including Exxon Shipping) were initially charged with criminal acts by the federal government. Following initial outrage after the spill, Alaska Governor Steve Cowper also considered criminal charges against Exxon. However, Cowper, a lawyer familiar with maritime law, apparently believed that the cost in litigation expenses and delayed justice did not warrant criminal charges (Piper, 1999). Thus, on August 14, 1989, the State of Alaska sued Exxon and Alyeska based on Exxon's negligence before and after the spill and the botched cleanup. The state sought damages for economic and environmental harm and punitive damage for the defendants' deliberate, negligent, and reckless actions before and after the spill. Among other things, the state claimed that the response plan was faulty, the defendants were not prepared for an effective response, and decisions made before, during, and after the spill (for example, man-power reductions and inadequate and poorly maintained equipment) practically guaranteed that, in the event of an oil spill, the response would not be efficient or effective, especially in the critical first two days (Mauer, 1989a).

Exxon countersued Alaska on October 24, 1989, claiming that "the state knew or should have known that its vigorous and active opposition to the use of dispersants would cause the Coast Guard to delay granting permission for the use of dispersants" (Toomey, 1989b, p. C1). Evidence would later indicate, however, that Exxon and Alyeska did not have enough chemical dispersant available on March 24 to use in a big spill and did not have any planes accessible to drop the dispersants on the oil. In addition, it was unlikely that the dispersants would have worked in the relatively calm waters of the first two days (NTSB, 1990).

While the state was pursuing legal action against Exxon, the federal government was also considering charges. On February 27, 1990, a federal grand jury indicted Exxon and Exxon Shipping on five counts, two felonies, and three misdemeanors. The felonies were alleged violations of the Dangerous Cargo Act—specifically the employing of crew members incapable of performing their duties and failure to ensure that the wheelhouse of the *Valdez* was manned at all times by competent crew members (Epler, 1990). The misdemeanors included two counts of discharging pollutants (oil) without a permit under the Clean Water Act and killing migratory birds without a permit, which violated the Migratory Bird Treaty Act. Exxon pled not guilty to all charges (Mauer, 1990).

Unknown to the State of Alaska, the federal government and Exxon began working toward a negotiated settlement—or "global" plea bargain—to resolve all federal civil and criminal claims and charges. When it was discovered that these two parties were nearing a settlement, Alaska contended that the proposed settlement would make the state's litigation much more difficult. Under the terms of the agreement, civil claims would not be pursued for four years, and even more threatening for Alaska, the federal government would not share information with the state or assist the state or private civil claimants (Piper, 1999).

Because the state had already relinquished criminal charges and negotiations between Exxon and the federal government broke down in the fall of 1990, Alaska joined the federal government in pursuit of a "global" settlement of federal criminal charges and state and federal civil claims (Piper, 1999). On March 13, 1991, a deal was struck between the U.S. Attorney General and Exxon for settlement of civil and criminal issues. For its part of the deal, Exxon pled guilty to criminal charges of violating the Clean Water Act, Migratory Bird Treaty Act, and the Rivers and Harbors Act. To settle charges, Exxon agreed to pay a $100 million criminal fine to the federal government, with 50 million passed on to Alaska, and payment of $900 million for damages to be paid in installments over ten years to a restoration fund. The restoration fund would be administered by six trustees—three from Alaska and three from federal agencies. The government retained the right to withdraw if public hearings indicated that the deal was not in the public interest. Exxon could withdraw if the court modified or rejected the agreement (Postman, 1991a). The Alaska State Legislature voiced many objections. A primary contention was that the terms of the settlement were private with no public access to damage studies (Enge and Postman, 1991; Piper, 1999). With the terms of the settlement kept private and no public access to damage studies, there was no accurate way for the public to assess the fairness of the deal.

All objections were moot, however, when federal district court Judge Russell Holland rejected the criminal fine as too low; Exxon exercised its right to withdraw from the agreement (Enge and Postman, 1991; Postman, 1991). However, the settlement was resurrected in a slightly modified form, and on October 8, 1991, a new agreement was reached. It differed only in minor details from the previously rejected offer. Exxon pled guilty to violating the Federal Migratory Bird Treaty, and Exxon Shipping pled guilty to the same charge plus violations of the Clean Water Act for spilling the oil, which had been deemed a pollutant. The criminal fine was increased from $100 million to $150 million, and all but $25 million was remitted back to Exxon for cooperating in reporting the incident, payment of many civil claims, cleanup efforts, and post-spill precautions instituted to prevent such future oil spills (Frost, 1991a, 1991b). Because Exxon was responsible for the cleanup, it was also able to deduct its expenses related to cleanup activities from its payments owed as restitution for the damages.

One advantage of the new agreement for existing civil claimants was that Alaskan groups and other private plaintiffs agreed to drop all lawsuits against the state and federal governments in exchange for government data that would be assembled for use against Exxon in their respective investigations and trial preparations (Frost, 1991b). Judge Holland approved the deal that resolved all federal and state criminal and civil charges on October 10, 1991 (Frost, 1991a). This deal only settled issues regarding damages to the general environment. Economic losses of fishing and other marine wildlife were pursued by private claimants as civil lawsuits.

PRIVATE CIVIL CLAIMS

Although all government cases against Exxon have been resolved, most private claimants have yet to receive any compensation. Although a jury awarded the private parties $287 million in compensatory damages and $5 billion in punitive damages, the matter has been successfully appealed twice by Exxon and—as of this writing—a third reduction in the punitive damages just ordered by Judge Holland is likely to be appealed. Not surprisingly, the issue in contention is the amount of punitive damages in proportion to actual damages, especially in light of recent U.S. Supreme Court rulings that suggest limits on such awards.

In the civil lawsuits, it was alleged that losses in fishing stock and other marine mammals and wildlife were due to the negligence of Exxon for leaving Hazelwood in command of the tanker and the negligence of Alyeska for being ill-prepared for the disaster and failing to respond as quickly and effectively as promised (Toomey, 1989a). Hazelwood was said to be negligent for his failure to "operate the *Exxon Valdez* in a safe and prudent manner in accordance with accepted navigational practices" (Toomey, 1989a).

The civil claimants include commercial fishermen, Alaska Natives, Alaska corporations, private land owners, municipalities, tenders, cannery workers, processors, recreational users, and others ("Exxon trial," 1994). According to one of the attorneys representing some of the plaintiffs, "From the beginning, Exxon pursued a complicated and sophisticated legal strategy. In the early stages, Exxon and Alyeska fought off efforts for class-action suits and sought to dismiss claims of large numbers of injured parties on technical grounds" (Hirsch, 1999, p. 272). Exxon and Alyeska also sought to have cases transferred from Judge Brian Shortel in Alaska Superior Court in Anchorage,

Alaska, to a federal district court where many charges were dismissed by Judge Holland. The state suits were based on common law negligence, nuisance, and misrepresentation; claims in federal court were based on strict liability under the Trans-Alaska Pipeline Environmental Conservation Act (Hirsch, 1999).

Normally, common law tort (damage) claims are made under state laws, but federal court jurisdiction extends to all cases of admiralty and maritime law. Judge Holland's "Order no. 38" was crucial for the defendants because Holland found that the spill was a "maritime tort" (legal harm) and that maritime jurisdiction applies to injuries at sea and on land, if the proximate cause of the land damage is caused by a vessel at sea (Hirsch, 1999). Next, Judge Holland applied the Robbins Dry Dock Rule, which he interpreted absent physical injuries to persons or property to mean that a party may not seek a pecuniary remedy or recover damages. Holland's interpretation meant that liability was limited only to those who were in fact directly touched by the oil. The final ruling was the death knell for many of the cases: Maritime law preempts state common law, which meant that claims of most plaintiffs had to be pursued under federal maritime law (Hirsch, 1999). Claims for negligence under federal law permit recovery for all damages that are proximately or indirectly caused by the wrongful act.

By Order no. 38, claims of processors, cannery workers, fishery tender operators, area businesses, and municipalities were all dismissed. Judge Holland also dismissed claims of "unoiled" property owners for devaluation of their property and claims of Alaska Natives for injury to subsistence culture. Even though Alaska State Judge Shortell ruled that state law was not preempted by maritime law under Supreme Court rulings in other cases, most of the state filed suits were transferred to the more hospitable—for Exxon—federal court. Many of these cases were the ones dismissed due to Holland's ruling on Order no. 38 (Hirsch, 1999).

When a settlement could not ultimately be reached, the case went to trial—over five years after the spill in May 1994. Over 10,000 claimants sought compensation for damages in the amount of $1.5 billion and as much as $15 billion in punitive damages (Schneider, 1994a). There were four phases in the trial. In the first phase, the jury had to decide if Exxon was liable for punitive damages. This determination hinged on whether the jury believed that Exxon was negligent *and* reckless to continue employing a captain who was known by Exxon to have had alcohol problems that led to convictions for drunk driving on land, treatment, and drinking aboard ship, which was a violation of Exxon policy. For punitive damages, it was essential that the prosecution prove that Exxon acted not only with negligence but that their conduct constituted a reckless course of action. Negligence supports a lesser form of culpability than recklessness. Recklessness implies total disregard for safety issues and it approaches intention, or at least that the company "knew or should have known" that its decisions and actions were very likely to lead to a catastrophe. On June 14, 1994, the jury determined that the spill was due to the negligence and recklessness of Hazelwood and Exxon (Schneider, 1994a).

In the second phase of the trial, the jurors reviewed evidence concerning the actual fishing and other seafood and wildlife losses to fishermen and residents of Alaska. To determine fair compensation for the losses, the jurors heard testimony from biologists and economists concerning the value of the losses attributed to the oil spill. On August 11, 1994, the jury awarded the plaintiffs $286.8 million for the harm they suffered (Schneider, 1994b).

In the third phase of the trial, the jury determined punitive damages. This was only possible because they had found that Exxon and Exxon Shipping had been negligent and reckless in phase one. On September 16, 1994, the jury awarded the assorted plaintiffs $5 billion in punitive damages, which was the largest such award at that time (Schneider, 1994c). Phase four of the trial was used to "mop up" any leftover claims.

Not surprisingly, Exxon appealed the punitive award, vowing to "use every legal means available to overturn this unjust verdict, which is not a final judgment. It will be reviewed and we trust it will be modified by the trial court or appellate courts" (Phillips, 1994, p. A1). In siding with Exxon and rejecting the punitive damages award, the U.S. Court of Appeals for the Ninth Circuit decided that punitive awards should be relative to other similar cases, proportional with actual damages, and scaled to reprehensibility of the behavior ("Judge reconsiders," 2002). When issued, the punitive damage award—seventeen times the actual damages of $287 million—was the largest ever to be awarded in a U.S. court. A recent Supreme Court ruling in *State Farm v. Campbell* suggested that punitive damages should not be grossly disproportionate to actual damages; in fact, they suggested a ratio that should not exceed single digits—a maximum of 9:1 and as low as compensatory damages ("Exxon's payout cut," 2003). In addition, the ruling of the U.S. Court of Appeals for the Ninth Circuit suggested that the wealth or size of a business should not be a determining factor.

In the original appeal, the case was sent back to Judge Holland in the federal district court for reconsideration of the $5 billion punitive award, in part, because the court could find no "aggravating factors" identified in previous cases by the U.S. Supreme Court such as violence, intentional spilling of oil, or trickery to hide spill ("Exxon's payout cut," 2002). Judge Holland then reduced the award by 1 billon dollars. Exxon appealed again and in August 2003, the U.S. Court of Appeals for the Ninth Circuit again rejected the punitive damages award and sent the case back to Judge Holland for reconsideration (Gold, 2003).

MEDIA PRESENTATION OF THE EVENT

The *Exxon Valdez* oil spill was very big news: "In 1989, no topic other than the politics of Eastern Europe and the Soviet Union commanded as much sustained U.S. press attention as did the oil spill of the *Exxon Valdez* in the Alaskan waters of Prince William Sound" (Dailey and O'Neill, 1999, p. 239). The tragic images of oil-covered and dead birds, fish, and other wildlife were quickly and widely broadcast. The vivid and visceral pictures of the tragedy evoked an immediate impact on the public. Unlike many more complex white-collar crime cases, which lack sympathetic and clearly identifiable victims, the aftermath of the *Valdez* oil spill provided clear and incontrovertible proof of serious and extensive harm.

The "reality" of the spill—its causes, consequences, and attributions of responsibility—was largely created by the news accounts or narratives. In the telling of the oil spill story, certain viewpoints and cultural biases were projected. Some corporate and political sources were quoted, while other sources with vested interests were not. Some victimization was reported on; others were ignored. Also, in telling the *Valdez* story—in "making sense" of the events leading up to and following the spill—the issues were framed in certain ways. In short, "journalistic accounts allow some competing narratives to become news and preclude others; these narratives give us vantage points from which to understand the world" (Daily and O'Neill, 1999, p. 239).

White-collar crime especially lends itself to conflicting interpretations. Is white-collar crime considered to be "real" crime? How can reputable business people and legitimate corporations be "criminals"? Certainly the managers and executives of Exxon did not intend to do so much harm. Surely the oil spill was a tragedy. But, are such events accidents, disasters, or crimes (Reiman, 2004)? If an accident, was it a "normal" accident to be expected sooner or later with such complex technological systems as on the *Valdez* (Perrow, 1984)? How do some harmful acts come to be labeled crime, while others are accidents beyond human control? How do some individuals come to be labeled as criminal, while others escape or avoid such a label (Reiman, 2004)?

Critical criminologists seek to understand why the law criminalizes some acts and not others, even when the harm is equivalent. Much of what is now white-collar "crime" was once normal and acceptable business practice.

Just as critical criminologists attempt to understand the origins of criminal law and criminal justice policy, critical news analysts (e.g., Luke, 1987; Tuchman, 1978) seek to understand how news is shaped by ideologies and how it includes some viewpoints while excluding others. News is not "neutral" in the sense of reporting only on "the facts." The facts must be put in a context, to be given meaning in the narrative. Narratives may change as stories unfold. According to Farrell and Goodnight (1981), the disaster narrative was the first and most sustainable story type used by news sources that covered the *Valdez* story. In this news narrative, the clean up was slow and ineffective, and opportunities were missed for halting the spread of the oil and subsequent damage. The disaster narrative presents an event as an "accident" or an event outside human control in which no one or no organization is responsible or ultimately blameworthy (Tuchman, 1978).

Early accounts stressed the roles of victims, especially fishermen in Cordova and Valdez. Residents of Alaska, who depended on the sound for subsistence and whose culture was intricately and intimately intertwined with the natural world of Prince William Sound, were not given much voice by the mainstream media (Dailey and O'Neill, 1999). Similarly, attributions of blame focused on "human error" and individualistic causes rather than the more complex chain of events that led to the spill. In this narrative, Captain Hazelwood became the scapegoat. Hazelwood as the scapegoat served Exxon well early on since it was in their interests to have attention diverted from corporate decisions to reduce the crews on supertankers and to overlook violations of Coast Guard and company work rules, which led to fatigue and "human error." Exxon's own "organizational error" allowed for Hazelwood's "human error" by allowing him to remain in charge of the supertanker, despite his record of alcohol-related problems and treatment.

As events unfolded and when news of the extensive damage came out and after it was reported that Hazelwood may have been impaired at the time of the accident due to earlier alcohol consumption, environmental and crime narratives began to compete with the disaster story. A crime narrative is a narrative "in which legal officials tended to individualize blame and an environmental narrative [is one] in which environmental groups contested the statements and practices of industrial spokespersons and the Bush administration" (Dailey and O'Neill, 1999, p. 243). Furthermore, crime narratives serve to "assess blame and ritually purify the disorder crime has created" (Dailey and O'Neill, 1999, p. 243). Such stories serve to point a finger and individualize the incident. The shift to the crime narrative focused on Hazelwood, and not—at least initially—on Exxon, Alyeska, or Exxon Shipping as "criminals." This is a much simpler story and an uncomplicated way to understand what happened and why. In effect, Hazelwood was demonized and became the central focus of news attention for a time. And, accordingly, the responsibilities of Exxon to oversee the ship's captain and operation and the Coast Guard for failing to adequately track the *Valdez* were minimized. Some of these factors generic to the marine transport industry include the social organization of the personnel, economic structure and pressures within the industry, and compliance with (or defiance of) national and international regulation (Perrow, 1984). Risk is exchanged for profit and "normal accidents" occur.

Early reports ignored underlying events that led up to the "accident." Another big part of the "story" not told by the mainstream press was the suffering and victimization of the residents of Alaska and especially the damage to their way of life and culture (Gill and Picou, 1999; Rodin, Downs, Petterson, and Russell, 1999). The "native narrative" in which both subsistence and culture were damaged could not compete effectively to become a dominant frame of reference. Residents of Alaska were integrated with the natural world, and they depended on the resources of Prince William Sound for more than mere subsistence. Their way of life and existence were intimately bound to the natural world around them. But, they could not "define the situation" in a way that would give them a public voice. It was easier to understand and report on the plight of commercial fishermen in Cordova and Valdez as victims.

Over time, media coverage diminished. The prolonged legal contests were not as dramatic or exciting as early events following the spill, and the early powerful images of the environmental damages were no longer newsworthy. The complex legal issues were also not so easily captured compared with the initial images of extensive environmental damage. The simple narrative centering on Captain Hazelwood—who acted as an isolated and impaired individual who made some bad decisions—was a more succinct and palatable explanation then the more remote connections between the "accident" and decisions to reduce crew members, reductions in Coast Guard monitoring, incompetent planning for and response to a major spill, and failure to monitor Hazelwood's rehabilitation.

THE LEGACY

The *Exxon Valdez* civil case continues; the *Valdez* supertanker has been renamed *SeaRiver Mediterranean* after Exxon spun off its shipping subsidiary. After it was repaired and banned from Prince William Sound, the *Valdez* hauled oil among Europe, Asia, and the Far East for twelve years. "The changing economy and a lifetime ban from the Alaskan oil trade . . . finally overwhelmed the notorious vessel, and it is a multibillion-dollar headache that its owners are no longer willing to bear" (Little, 2003, p. 1). The *Valdez*, which had been built specifically for transport of North Slope oil from the Valdez oil terminal, is apparently inefficient for use in other areas of the world and has been mothballed. The man who captained the ship during its Alaskan service, Joseph Hazelwood, was fired by Exxon, lost his pilot's license, and never returned to the merchant marine service. He has earned a living primarily as a maritime consultant and claims adjuster for the same law firm that represented him throughout his civil and criminal litigation. The judge who sentenced Hazelwood on charges of discharging oil without a permit noted that "he'll never pursue his career anymore . . . he has been vilified more than most who commit a misdemeanor" ("Where are they now?" 1999b).

The person who had been actually steering the *Valdez*, helmsman Robert Kagen, who had failed to make the correction order by Third Mate Gregory Cousins to avoid the Bligh Reef, retired in 1995 with twenty years service in the Exxon fleet. Another key player in the spill and its aftermath, Exxon Shipping President, Frank Iarossi, resigned a year after the oil spill, and he was still working for American Bureau of Shipping, a nonprofit organization that classifies ships for insurers and certifies that ships are seaworthy ("Where are they now?" 1999a).

Controversy still abounds on the extent and permanence of damages to Prince William Sound. For example, studies show that "only bald eagles and river otters are recovered among the [twenty-eight] damaged species and resources. Among the [thirteen] still recovering are animals with signs of ongoing exposure to hydrocarbons" ("Where are they now?" 1999c). A spokesperson for Exxon said, "We see the sound as essentially recovered" ("Where are they now?" 1999c). The director of an aquaculture research institute, Ernest Brannon, believes that there is a "fixation on a very minute amount of very degraded oil that's left at very few places in the [s]ound that doing very little damage [*sic*]" ("Where are they now?" 1999c).

Beyond actual immediate and lingering damages to Prince William Sound and its plant and animal life, the spill clearly disrupted the lives and livelihoods of fishermen, residents of Alaska, and others dependent on the fish and marine and other wildlife—fishery workers and tourist-related businesses. The *Valdez* oil spill made hardly a dent in Exxon profits; although changes have been made by Exxon and other supertanker operators that ostensibly should make future spills less likely, or at least less damaging, to the environment. One of these changes include the requirement of double hulls to minimize future spills—once promised for supertankers in operating in Prince William Sound but not required by the Coast Guard.

The *Valdez* oil spill illustrates a number of points regarding how corporate crime's causes and consequences are interpreted, reported, and prosecuted. The oil spill also illustrates the complexity of such cases and why it is inappropriate to focus on individual factors and ignore or downplay decisions and actions of corporations and industries that are likely to lead to harmful consequences. The complicity of regulatory bodies in these events cannot be overlooked. The Coast Guard was deficient in its monitoring of such ships as the *Valdez* as they navigated in such sensitive waters as Prince William Sound. And state and federal agencies were responsible for failure to properly oversee preparedness and cleanup capabilities and responsibilities.

The case of the *Exxon Valdez* is not simply a case of "drunk driving." It was a case of corporate negligence and even recklessness in failing to minimize the risk of a spill of this magnitude in such an environmentally rich and sensitive area. The case was also a case of government neglect and acquiescence to corporate interests. The Coast Guard failed to adequately monitor the progression of the *Valdez* toward the treacherous Bligh Reef. The State of Alaska bears some responsibility when it had failed to use considerable powers to take control of the cleanup when the state became aware that Exxon and Alyeska were failing in their responsibilities.

The *Valdez* oil spill is also an exemplar of the violation of trust, the hallmark of white-collar crime, according to Friedrichs (2004). Exxon and Alyeska had assured opponents of the Alaskan pipeline and Valdez terminal that a spill of this magnitude was highly unlikely and that, in any event, would be able to control and contain any spill. When Hazelwood failed as a scapegoat in framing the event as simply a result of human error and when Exxon tried to shift part of the blame to the State of Alaska for its hesitation in allowing the use of chemical dispersants in the first few days of the spill, the corporation used every avenue available to receive the most favorable hearing (in federal court) and to seek a new trial when evidence surfaced, later largely discredited, of jury tampering and other roadblocks to a fair trial.

Was justice done in this case? Hazelwood lost his license, was vilified and demonized, and he eventually served a reasonably light sentence of community service. Alyeska escaped with the payment of civil damages; Exxon pled guilty to relatively minor criminal charges, was ordered to pay for studies and restoration of Prince William Sound, and was found liable for damages and ordered to pay a huge punitive damages award. Although the results are debatable, Exxon spent billions on cleanup efforts and agreed to pay for ongoing research and restoration. However, the punitive damages award continues to be appealed and is likely to be significantly reduced, especially in light of recent Supreme Court rulings noted earlier in the chapter. Exxon, which has since merged with Mobil Oil, appeared to suffer no long-term economic consequences.

Clearly, fishermen and fishery workers lost at least part of their earnings and livelihood for a period of time. How much of the fish stock and value was damaged by the oil and how much by other factors such as lower market prices is not really clear. Native Alaskans, whose subsistence and culture depended on the wildlife of the sound, may never recover fully and their "narrative" has been relatively neglected. Oil continues to flow from the North Slope, and efforts continue to open more wilderness area in Alaska for oil exploration and drilling.

Justice, of course, is relative—an approximation. In civil cases, the remedy is generally to require the damaging activity to stop or compensate those who were harmed. This is to make the victims "whole" again—to restore them to a previous state. In reality, this is never entirely possible. Commonly, most "justice" in white-collar crime cases is received in civil settlements. Of course, Prince William Sound will never be the same again—not only due to the oil spill but also due to other ongoing changes typical for such a natural ecosystem. The human victims cannot be made entirely whole again even if the civil case is finally resolved.

Despite the status of the *Exxon Valdez* oil spill as the worst in U.S. history and possibly the worst environmental disaster ever, there is no clear evidence that the spill and its aftermath induced any long-term interest in or attention to environmental issues. For a time, the *Valdez* oil spill was the major news story, and it may have raised consciousness about the potential for great harm to the environment. However, deeper connections were not made— in the media or politically—relative to our dependence on oil and the trade-offs we make between risk and safety in acquiring and transporting it. Exxon, as noted, escaped relatively unscathed, and no one in the corporation was formally punished or fired, except Captain Hazelwood.

REFERENCES

Cushman, J. H., Jr. (1989a, May 7). With disaster as grist, safety board seeks "sense out of chaos." *New York Times*, p. B7.

Cushman, J. H., Jr. (1989b, May 17). Board is told tanker failed to report change in route. *New York Times*, p. A14.

Dailey, P., and O'Neill, D. (1999). Sad is too mild a word: Press coverage of the Exxon Valdez oil spill. In J. S. Picou, D. A. Gill, and M. J. Cohen (Eds.), *The* Exxon Valdez *disaster: Readings on a modern social problem* (pp. 239–254). Dubuqe, Iowa: Kendall/Hunt Publishing Company.

Egan, T. (1989a, March 17). High winds hamper oil spill cleanup off Alaska. *New York Times*, p. 17.

Egan, T. (1989b, March 29). Exxon concedes it can't contain most of oil spill. *New York Times*, p. A1.

Enge, M., and Postman, D. (1991, April 25). Judge rejects Exxon deal. *Anchorage Daily News*, p. A1.

Epler, P. (1990, February 28). Federal grand jury indicts Exxon. *Anchorage Daily News*, p. 1.

Exxon trial on oil spill starts Monday. (1994, April 30). *New York Times*, p. 1.

Exxon's payout cut by a billion. (2002, December 8). *Juneau Empire*, p. 1.

Farrell, T. B., and Goodnight, G. T. (1981). Accidental rhetoric: The root metaphors of three mile island. *Communication Monographs, 48.*

Friedrichs, D. O. (2004). *Trusted criminals: White-collar crime in contemporary society.* Belmont, CA: Wadsworth/Thompson Learning.

Frost, G. (1991a, October 1). 2nd spill settlement looks like the 1st. *Anchorage Daily News*, p. A1.

Frost, G. (1991b, October 9). Judge ok's oil spill settlement. *Anchorage Daily News*, p. A1.

Gill, D. A., and Picou, J. S. (1999). The day the water died: Cultural impacts of the *Exxon Valdez* oil spill. In J. S. Picou, D. A. Gill, and M. J. Cohen (Eds.), *The* Exxon Valdez *disaster: Readings on a modern social problem* (pp. 167–192). Dubuqe, Iowa: Kendall/Hunt Publishing Company.

Gold, R. (2003, August 25). U. S. court rejects punitive award for Exxon spill. *Wall Street Journal*, p. B2.

Hirsch, W. B. (1999). Justice delayed: Seven years later and no end in sight. In J. S. Picou, D. A. Gill, and M. J. Cohen (Eds.), *The* Exxon Valdez *disaster: Readings on a modern social problem* (pp. 271–308). Dubuqe, Iowa: Kendall/Hunt Publishing Company.

Hunter, H. (1989, March 29). Seeds of Alaskan catastrophe promises broken, warnings ignored, spill was preordained. *Los Angeles Times*, p. 7.

Jones, T., and Parrish, M. (1989, March 26). Oil spill cleanup effort in Alaska drawing fire; industry response called slow and inadequate. *Los Angeles Times*, p. 1.

Judge reconsiders *Exxon Valdez* award. (2002, October 13), *The Olympian*, p. A1.

Keeble, J. (1999). The imaginary journey of Captain Joseph Hazelwood. In J. S. Picou, D. A. Gill, and M. J. Cohen (Eds.), *The* Exxon Valdez *disaster: Readings on a modern social problem* (pp. 23–38). Dubuqe, Iowa: Kendall/Hunt Publishing Company.

Lebedoff, D. (1997). *Cleaning up: The story behind the biggest legal bonanza of our time.* New York: Free Press.

Little, R. (2002, October 15). Even renamed, *Exxon Valdez* can't outlive stain on its past. *Maryland SunSpot*, p. 1.

Luke, T. W. (1987) Chernobyl: The packaging of transnational ecological disaster. *Critical Studies in Mass Communication*, 4(4), 351–375.

Malcom, A. H. (1989, April 16). How the oil spilled and spread: Delay and confusion off Alaska. *New York Times*, p. 1.

Mauer, R. (1989a, March 16). State sues Exxon. *Alaska Daily News*, p. A1.

Mauer, R. (1989b, March 16). Exxon responds to 140 lawsuits. *Alaska Daily News*, p. A1.

Mauer, R. (1990, April 10). Exxon arraigned, pleads not guilty. *Anchorage Daily News*, p. B1.

McAllister, B. (1989, March 25). Millions of gallons of oil spill into Alaskan sound; waves hampering containment efforts. *Washington Post*, p. A1.

National Response Team. (1989). *The* Exxon Valdez *Oil Spill: A Report to the President.* Washington, DC: Environmental Protection Agency.

National Transportation Safety Board. (1990). NTSB Report Number: MAR-90-04. (Grounding of the U.S. Tankship *Exxon Valdez* on Bligh Reef, Prince William Sound near Valdez, AK, March 24, 1989).

Perrow, C. (1984). *Normal accidents: Living with high risk technologies.* New York: Basic Books.

Phillips, N. (1994, September 17). 5,000,000,000 jury sets oil spill damages. *Anchorage Daily News*, p. A1.

Piper, E. (1999). The *Exxon Valdez* oil spill: Government settlement and restoration activities. In J. S. Picou, D. A. Gill, and M. J. Cohen (Eds.), *The* Exxon Valdez *disaster: Readings on a modern social problem* (pp. 255–270). Dubuqe, IA: Kendall/Hunt Publishing Company.

Postman, D. (1991a, May 4). Spill deal dies as Exxon, Hickel pull out. *Anchorage Daily News*, p. A1.

Reiman, J. (2004). *The rich get richer and the poor get prison.* Boston: Pearson.

Rodin, M., Downs, M., Petterson, J., and Russell, J. (1999). Community impacts of the *Exxon Valdez* oil spill. In J. S. Picou, D. A. Gill, and M. J. Cohen (Eds.), *The* Exxon Valdez *disaster: Readings on a modern social problem* (pp. 193–210). Dubuqe, Iowa: Kendall/Hunt Publishing Company.

Schmitt, R. B., and Miller, J. P. (1989, March 28). Exxon liability for oil spill may grow due to crew behavior, cleanup delays. *Wall Street Journal*, p. 1.

Schneider, K. (1994a, June 13). First decision of *Exxon Valdez* trial is expected in days. *New York Times*, p. B8.

Schneider, K. (1994b, August 12). An Exxon verdict of 286.8 million. *New York Times*, p. A1.

Schneider, K. (1994c, September 17). Exxon is ordered to pay $5 billion for Alaska Spill. *New York Times*, p. A1.

Toomey, S. (1989a, March 30). 2 fishermen file first lawsuit over spill; more suits likely. *Anchorage Daily News*, p. C1.

Toomey, S. (1989b, October 24). Exxon lawsuit blames state for delay in oil spill response. *Anchorage Daily News*, p. A1.

Tuchman, G. (1978). *Making news: A study in the construction of reality.* New York: Free Press.

Wells, K., and Chase, M. (1989, March 31). Paradise lost: Heartbreaking scenes of beauty disfigured follow Alaska oil spill. *Wall Street Journal*, p. 1.

Wells, K., and McCoy, C. (1989, April 3). Out of control: How unpreparedness turned the Alaska spill into ecological debacle. *Wall Street Journal*, p. 1.

Where are they now? The boss: Frank Iarossi. (1999a, May 13). *Anchorage Daily News*, p. A1.

Where are they now? The captain: Joseph Hazelwood. (1999b, May 13). *Anchorage Daily* News, p. A1.

Where are they now? The helmsman: Robert Kagen. (1999c, May 13). *Anchorage Daily News*, p. A1.

7

William "Willie" Horton:
Presidential Campaign
Controversy

Benjamin Fleury-Steiner

Willie Horton is perhaps most remembered for his appearance in a series of controversial political advertisements in the last two months of the U.S. presidential campaign of 1988. The first ad titled "Weekend Passes" presented a picture of George H. W. Bush, and a voice-over announced, "Bush supports the death penalty for first-degree murderers." A photo of former Massachusetts governor and Democratic presidential candidate Michael Dukakis appeared, and the voice-over continued, "Dukakis not only opposes the death penalty, he allows first-degree murderers to have weekend passes from prison." The ad then showed Willie Horton's mug shot, and the voice continued, "One was Willie Horton, who murdered a boy in a robbery, stabbing him [nineteen] times." With Horton's face still on the screen, the voice continued, "Despite a life sentence Horton received [ten] weekend passes from prison. Horton fled, kidnapping a young couple, stabbing the man and repeatedly raping his girlfriend." Then the words "KIDNAPPING," "STABBING," and "RAPING" slowly appeared on the screen.

Two other ads, which were perhaps less memorable but no less effective, furthered the attack on Dukakis's furloughing of Horton and Dukakis's so-called "liberal" punishment policy. One ad—"George Bush and Michael Dukakis on Crime"—showed a revolving-door turnstile with running text displaying that 268 convicts escaped while on furlough, while a voice-over stated that many leave prison early to commit crime again. The other ad— "Governor Dukakis's Liberal Furlough Program Failed"—followed the same themes as the other two advertisements; however, this ad provided emotionally charged testimony by the sister of Michael Fournier, a teenager who was killed in a robbery that reportedly involved Horton and two accomplices.

At the time, no one in the Bush campaign knew just how effective publicizing the Horton incident would be for rejuvenating George H. W. Bush's stagnating presidential campaign. Bush's campaign manager, Lee Atwater, was unknowingly foretelling when, weeks before, he predicted that Willie Horton would be Dukakis's "single biggest negative."

THE MURDER OF MICHAEL FOURNIER

Despite the image of Willie Horton's escape from a Massachusetts furlough program that was captured in the Bush campaign's infamous thirty-second advertisements, less is known about Horton's involvement in the murder of Michael Fournier and his subsequent trial and first-degree murder conviction. Fortunately, Steve Takesian (2002), a police lieutenant from Horton's hometown, has written a very detailed insider account of these events. In this section, the chapter draws extensively from Takesian's account.

Shortly after 9:40 p.m. on Saturday, October 26, 1974, three men in a blue 1963 Chevrolet arrived at the Marston Street Mobil Station in Lawrence, Massachusetts. The three had intended to rob the station; one of the men remained in the vehicle as the lookout and getaway driver. The other two men, one armed with a knife, walked toward the station. After entering the station, the two men confronted attendant Michael Fournier, a seventeen-year-old high school student. Confronting Fournier in the corner of the room, the two men, one with the knife drawn, demanded that Fournier empty the cash registers. Complying with their demands, Fournier, as official records have it, begged the men to take the money and not hurt him; however, such pleas were ignored. The unprovoked accomplice with the knife stabbed Fournier repeatedly. The two men then left the building and joined their third accomplice in the vehicle.

On November 7, 1974, after a housemate had notified police that he confessed to killing Michael Fournier, Alvin Wideman was brought in for questioning by the Lawrence Police Department. Although it is clear from Takesian's analysis of police reports that Wideman eventually confessed to police on that evening, it is not completely clear if Wideman or his housemates identified the two other accomplices (Takesian, 2002, pp.16–17). However, the next day at 3:30 a.m., Roosevelt Pickett, the driver of the blue 1963

Chevrolet was taken into custody. Less than two hours later, Lawrence police officers arrested the last accomplice—twenty-three-year-old Willie Horton of 18 Acton Street.

For the next three hours, each suspect was questioned separately by police. During the interrogations, Willie Horton stated that he remained in the getaway car while his accomplices Wideman and Pickett entered the gas station. According to Takesian (2002), Horton stated, "Pickett returned to the vehicle and said, 'I had to get rid of the evidence, just another dead honky'" (p. 18). Horton then told police that the money was divided evenly between the three of them and that he then went home for the night. Having all the evidence they now needed, the police booked all three men for the murder of Michael Fournier, which had occurred twelve days earlier.

THE TRIAL

The trial of Horton, Pickett, and Wideman began on May 2, 1975. The trial was marked by several controversial events. First, each of the defendants' defense attorneys claimed that his client had been coerced by the Lawrence police into confessing to crimes they did not commit. The crime details provided appeared to indicate guilt; however, at the trial, each of the defendants' testimony, including Willie Horton's, complicated matters:

Horton . . . said that he was threatened [by police]. He testified that he had been in a cell prior to the group interrogation. According to Horton, two officers approached him and asked if he knew that Mr. Wideman said he did it. Horton told the officers that if Wideman did say that, he was lying. One of them then said, according to Horton, "If you stand up and say that again I'm going to blow your head off." (Takesian, 2002, p. 36)

Horton's testimony, however, was given only to the trial judge outside the presence of the jury. Thinking that Horton's testimony was "possibly irrelevant," the judge chose to evaluate it during a recess in the trial (Takesian, 2002, p. 35). After his review of the testimony, the judge did not find Horton and his accomplice's testimony believable and blocked the defense from presenting it to the jury. In a little over three hours later, the jury returned with three guilty verdicts of first-degree murder and robbery. Horton, Pickett, and Wideman were each sentenced to life without the possibility of parole.

WILLIE HORTON BECOMES A HOUSEHOLD NAME

Whether Willie Horton was coerced by Lawrence police officers into confessing to a crime he did not commit, his conviction for the murder of

Michael Fournier was not the crime that would later make Willie Horton a household name. It was not until slightly more than a decade later that a second unexpected set of horrifying events would lead to the infamous Horton spectacle of the presidential election campaign of 1988.

It was the events that took place in early April 1987 that the Bush campaign would capitalize on in tarring Michael Dukakis as "soft on crime." Horton's decision to run from a Massachusetts furlough program ten months earlier culminated in his desperate invasion of a Maryland couple's home. The terrifying invasion ended with Willie Horton robbing Clifford and Angela Barnes, stabbing Clifford Barnes multiple times, and brutally raping Angela Barnes.

In addition to the devastating effectiveness of the national and local media's widespread publicizing of these events for the Bush campaign, the publicizing of the Barnes' victimization by a black murderer "let out of prison on vacation" by a "weak" governor of largely Democratic state made Willie Horton a powerful new symbol for racial fears of crime and punishment in the United States. The publicity also emphasized the need for the federal government to play a larger role in "fighting" crime. Horton (as a black murderer) was a racially constructed symbol of the crime problem in the United States, which has had widespread effects on public perceptions of crime and punishment since 1988.

Willie Horton and the Public's Perception of Crime and Punishment

In the more than fifteen years since the Horton spectacle and the so-called "war on crime" that was fought in its wake, an imposing collection of social science studies have documented significant links between racial stereotypes (Barkan and Cohn, 1994; Sweeny and Haney, 1992) and racial fears (Hurwitz and Peffley, 1997, 1998) with the public's increased support for punitive criminal justice policies. The most sophisticated of these studies demonstrated that respondents presented with media-adapted vignettes of violent crimes committed by black offenders yield stronger correlations between the factors of race and punitiveness than the diffuse indicators of crime and punitiveness.

A collection of such studies is presented in the award-winning book *Perception and Prejudice: Race and Politics in the United States* by political scientists Jon Hurwitz and Mark A. Peffley. Based on data from the Race and Politics Study (RPS) conducted by the Survey Research Center, which is acclaimed to be one of the most extensive scientific surveys of race ever conducted, Hurwitz and Peffley demonstrated the strong influence of media images of crimes committed by blacks on public fears of criminal victimization. Specifically, Hurwitz and Peffley observe that public fears are conflated by the media, by individuals like Charles Stewart and Susan Smith (both of whom blamed black men for crimes that they had committed), and by cynical political messengers who "Willie Hortonize" campaigns (Hurwitz and Peffley, 1997, pp. 395–396; Hurwitz and Peffley, 1998).

Studies done with focus groups have also documented the link between racial images of criminals in the media and public fears of crime. In an analysis of attitude change in focus groups conducted by Kathleen Hall Jamieson, a nine-member focus group from Dallas that had favored Dukakis 5 to 4 in early September 1988 shifted in favor of Bush 7 to 2 shortly after the airing of the Horton ads. Specifically, Jamieson found a hardening of attitudes among respondents in favor of a "get tough" on crime policy and the death penalty. The Horton ads directly influenced the focus group respondents' fear of victimization, beliefs that such criminals must be kept in prison or be executed, and feelings of blameworthiness toward Dukakis. After asking respondents' to indicate the source of their information regarding the Horton incidents, Jamieson instructed respondents to write a "PN" for print news, "BN" for televised broadcast news, "RN" for radio news, "A" for advertising, "H" if they had heard it in conversation, and "NS" to indicate that they were unsure where they had heard, read, or saw it. Consider the response of one focus group member:

Willie Horton was a killer and wasn't electrocuted (H/PN) . . . He kept raping the wife (BN). He [Horton] was black and the wife [*sic*] was white . . . Her husband went crazy . . . He [husband] still can't forgive himself. That's why he is against Dukakis (BN). Her husband says that she is afraid that he will come back (BN/NS). He [Horton] killed a boy in a supermarket in Maryland (H) . . . I believe in the death penalty for people like that . . . George Bush opposes gun control and favors executing Hortons (Radio—I think it was an ad). I would guess Willie Horton doesn't. (Jamieson, 1992, p. 34)

It is clear from this respondent how influential the media was for antagonizing public fears of both so-called "black crime" and a faulty criminal justice system. The durability of the underlying story of a faulty criminal justice system presented in the Horton ads was also evident in another aspect of Jamieson's study. In particular, over time, respondents refused to question their beliefs, even in the face of evidence that undermined the claims against Dukakis. Specifically, statistics documenting the overall success of the Massachusetts furlough program, as well as statistics from the federal government showing higher rates of early release and recidivism in California under Governor Ronald Reagan, provoked one group member to respond: "You can't change my mind with all of that. . . . When you support the death penalty, the really bad ones get killed. That's . . . the problem with . . . liberals" (Jamieson, 1992, pp. 31–32). Another focus group member dismissed statistical evidence, "We should ship all our criminals to the college liberals in College Station . . . or Austin. Crime's not statistics, honey" (Jamieson, pp. 31–32).

In her analysis of the responses from focus group members, Jamieson blamed the media as complicit in the deception. The media, Jamieson suggested, did little to "disabuse the public of the misimpression that Dukakis promoted an irresponsible and failed policy of early release or to get the details or context of the Horton story across" (Steiner, Bowers, and Sarat, 1999, p. 470). Whatever the reason for its profound impact, the Horton incident was one of a criminal justice system out of control; a system that is freeing dangerous black criminals to prey on innocent white victims (Hurwitz and Peffley, 1997, 1998).

"HORTONIZED" FEDERAL CRIMINAL JUSTICE

The Horton spectacle had very direct effects on both policymakers and principal actors in the U.S. criminal justice system. As legal scholar Joseph E. Kennedy observed, "That [Horton] crime story may have influenced the outcome of the 1988 presidential election and established the power of a simple theme in criminal justice policy: Any politician, judge, or prosecutor who authorizes the release of a potentially violent offender will be held politically accountable for any future crimes committed by him" (Kennedy, 2000, p. 847).

Indeed, a consensus that transcends political ideology on "tough-on-crime" policies was formally ushered in during the U.S. presidential election campaign of 1992. The Democrats acceptance of "Hortonized" criminal justice policies was given national attention when then Arkansas governor and Democratic presidential candidate Bill Clinton decided to leave the campaign trail to preside over the execution of a mentally retarded prisoner, Ricky Lee Rector.

Likewise, the next eight years of the Clinton presidency (1992–2000) proved that the legacy of Willie Horton had a major influence on the increased role of the federal government for enforcing "tough" criminal justice policies. Perhaps, the most sweeping new policy was the passage of the federal "crime bill" known as The Violent Crime Control and Law Enforcement Act of 1994. Despite significant declines in the rate of violent crime in the United States (Mauer, 2001), the Clinton-led passage of this legislation significantly expanded the use of the death penalty, weakened Fourth Amendment protections against search and seizure, increased spending for the largest prison expansion in U.S. history, and instituted punitive determinant sentencing frameworks and policies such as "Three Strikes and You're Out."

Similar to the Bush campaign's media coopted marketing of the crime problem in the form of the Horton ads, "Three Strike sand You're Out"— perhaps more than other federal crime policies—demonstrated the effectiveness of a catchy and memorable phrase or name (i.e., Willie Horton) for playing on public fears of crime through the practice of putting repeat offenders in prison for life. However, in the case of Three Strikes and You're Out laws, both the "Hortonization" of criminal justice attitudes by the public and policymakers have collided in ways, perhaps, once thought unimaginable. Writing about the passage of Three Strikes and You're Out in California and in the rest of the United States, criminologist Franklin E. Zimring and his colleagues cogently observed:

Three Strikes was an extreme, but by no means isolated, example of the kind of law produced when very little mediates antioffender sentiments. The 1994 federal anticrime legislation is another example of the direct reflection of public sentiments. At the federal level, the kind of expertise that used to write crime commission reports in the 1960s was considered a drawback to federal criminal justice administration in the 1990s. (Zimring, Hawkins, and Kamin, 2001, p. 15)

Another "Hortonized" criminal justice practice that has recently received a tremendous amount of public exposure has been the disproportionate targeting of nonwhite populations for illicit drug crimes by the police, that is, racial profiling. Like the other expanded law enforcement roles the federal government has fashioned for itself post-Horton, the widespread use of racial profiling as a law enforcement tool at the local and state levels was influenced by the federal government's expanded role in the so-called "war on drugs" (Harris, 2002). Created by the Drug Enforcement Agency (DEA) in the early 1990s, the drug courier profile was used as a training tool in police departments across the United States. Federal agents trained local law enforcement to focus explicitly on, among other factors, the offender's racial characteristics (Buckman and Lamberth, 2001; Harris, 2002). In addition to detailing the use of openly racial discriminatory DEA training tools by state police departments, William H. Buckman and John Lamberth (2001) detail in their powerful sociolegal critique how the federal government's zeal to "win" the drug war has spilled over into more blatantly discriminatory tools used by state police departments, including the New Jersey State Police:

A training video entitled "The Jamaican Posse" was produced by the New Jersey State Police (NJSP) and shown, at least, to all 2700 members of that force. To show the supposition that all "Jamaican Posse" members are "violent" the video employed, without permission, portions of the movie *The Harder They Fall* starring Jimmy Cliff. One inflammatory scene depicted Cliff slashing another man's face with a straight razor. On cross examination the NJSP author of *Jamaican Posses* admitted that the sections from *The Harder They Fall* were entirely fictional and that he knew of no case or investigation that remotely resembled those scenes. Nevertheless, he had used those scenes to instruct troopers on how violent the "Jamaican Posse" members are and how they should be on their guard when encountering suspected posse members. The "training" video further instructed that "Jamaican Posse" members are astute enough to shed their dreadlocks and appear like any African American, thus converting all blacks to potentially violent suspects. (Buckman and Lamberth, 2001, p. 89 fn34)

"HORTONIZED AMERICA"

The case of Willie Horton was most certainly not your typical crime. The Bush campaign's effective use of the case fostered the perception that being black was synonymous with rising criminality in America, and "tough on crime" policies that target offenders like Horton (i.e., disproportionately of color) must be mandated by the federal government.

The chapter details how the federal mandate to "fight crime" spawned into what has been called the "Willie Hortonization" of U.S. criminal justice (Anderson 1995; Robinson 1993). But, the "Hortonization" of U.S. criminal justice also has broad consequences for American society, especially if a more open acceptance of a multiracial American public is a goal worth pursuing.

An ominous indicator of how the "Hortonization" of criminal justice in the United States profoundly undermines the goal of multiracial acceptance is the marked increase in "racial hoaxes." Coined by criminologist Kathryn Russell (1999), a racial hoax occurs when a person fabricates a crime then blames it on a black or other nonwhite person or when an actual crime occurs but someone falsely blames a black or other nonwhite person. Although recent racial hoaxes such as the Susan Smith case have received wide publicity, Russell documents dozens of racial hoaxes that have received far less media attention. Racial hoaxes and other disturbing trends such as federal law enforcement's recently heightened focus on Arab Americans since September 11, 2001, may only deepen the pernicious effects of the Horton legacy on the future of democracy in the United States.

REFERENCES

Anderson, D. C. (1995). *Crime and the politics of hysteria.* New York: Times Book.
Barkan, S. E., and Cohn, S. F. (1994). Prejudice and support for the death penalty by whites. *Journal of Research in Crime and Delinquency, 31*, 202–209.

Buckman, W. H., and Lamberth, J. (2001) Challenging racial profiles: Attacking Jim Crow on the interstate. *Temple Political and Civil Rights Law Review, 10,* 387–409.

Harris, D. (2002). *Profiles in injustice: Why police profiling cannot work.* New York: New Press.

Hurwitz, J., and Peffley, M. (1997). Public perceptions of race and crime: The role of racial stereotypes. *American Journal of Political Science, 41,* 375–401.

Hurwitz, J., and Peffley, M. (1998). *Perception and prejudice: Race and politics in the United States.* New Haven, CT: Yale University Press.

Jamieson, K. H. (1992). *Dirty politics.* New York: Oxford University Press.

Kennedy, J. E. (2001). Monstrous offenders and the search for solidarity through modern punishment. *Hastings Law Journal, 51,* 829–888.

Mauer, M. (2001). *Race to incarcerate.* New York: New Press.

Robinson, L. (1993). Prison policy. *Federal Sentencing Reporter, 5,* 207–213.

Russell, K. (1999). *The color of crime: Racial hoaxes, white fear, black protectionism, police harassment, and other macroaggressions.* New York: New York University Press.

Steiner, B. D., Bowers, W. J., and Sarat, A. (1999). Folk knowledge as legal action: Death penalty judgments and the tenet of early release in a culture of mistrust and punitiveness. *Law & Society Review, 33*(2), 461–505.

Sweeny, L. T., and Haney, C. (1992) The influence of race on sentencing: A meta-analytic review of experimental studies. *Behavioral Sciences and the Law, 10,* 179–195.

Takesian, S. (2002). *Willie Horton: True crime and its influence on a presidential election.* Lawrence, MA: Steve Takesian.

Zimring, F. E., Hawkins, G., and Kamin, S. (2001). *Punishment and democracy: 3 strikes and you're out in California.* New York: Oxford University Press.

8

The Central Park Jogger: The Impact of Race on Rape Coverage

Laura L. Finley

Shortly after 9 p.m. on April 19, 1989, a young woman on her nightly run through New York's Central Park was bludgeoned, raped, sodomized, and left for dead. She was twenty-eight-year-old investment banker Trisha Meili, but she came to be known as the Central Park Jogger. At the time, several teenage boys were arrested for various crimes related to the attack on Meili and other incidents on the same night. Approximately thirty boys were involved in some way in these incidents, but the seven main suspects and the focus in this chapter were as follows: Antron McCray, Raymond Santana, Kevin Richardson, Kharey Wise, Steve Lopez, Yusef Salaam, and Clarence Thomas. All were black or Hispanic, ranging in age from fourteen to sixteen; five were convicted in two separate trials (Sullivan, 1992). More recently, however, their convictions were vacated because another man, Matias Reyes, confessed to the assault and rape of Trisha Meili.

The case of the Central Park Jogger received amazing amounts of press coverage in 1989. According to Hap Hairston, then city editor of *New York Newsday* and later city editor of the *Daily News*, "The story was New York. It was upwardly mobile New York attacked by the not so upwardly mobile; the working class attacks the upper class. It was every wealthy Manhattanite's nightmare to be attacked by a group of black kids" (Benedict, 1992, p. 189).

Interest in the case was recently reignited due to Reyes's confession and the publication of Meili's autobiography, *I Am the Central Park Jogger* in 2003.

THE INCIDENT

Friends had been warning Meili not to run alone at night in Central Park for some time, but that only seemed to have made her more determined to do it. On the night of the incident, a friend from work, Pat Garrett, was supposed to have come over to look at Meili's new stereo system at 10 p.m. after her run. When Garrett arrived, Meili was nowhere to be found. Although he thought it curious that she had stood him up, he was generally unconcerned. The next morning, however, when Meili failed to appear for work at Salomon Brothers, Garrett as well as many others became concerned. Garrett eventually called the police, and the police decided that the "Jane Doe" in the hospital was likely to be Meili. Garrett identified her from a distinctive bow-shaped ring she frequently wore (Meili, 2003a).

Meili was discovered at 1 a.m. on Thursday, April 20, in a muddy ravine. Linda Fairstein, chief of the sex crimes division of the prosecutor's office, assigned Elizabeth Lederer as prosecuting attorney to the case. Homicide detectives investigated the case, as it was not clear Meili would survive the attack. The initial picture of the crime provided to Lederer by the investigators was that fifteen boys met in front of Schomburg Plaza, a housing complex near the northeast corner of Central Park. They were joined between 8:30 p.m. and 9 p.m. by another group of approximately fifteen boys from the Taft House complex. The group went to the park to steal, beat people up, and create havoc. During the night of April 19, they allegedly committed several misdemeanors and felonies that involved at least twelve people (Couric, 2003). For example, they surrounded a Latino man in the park, but they decided to let him go because someone in the group knew him. They beat and left unconscious a drunken Latino man, Antonio Diaz, whom they referred to as "the bum." The group tried to dismount several cyclists, including one couple on a tandem bicycle. The group of thirty split up after the police arrived to investigate these incidents.

Although this string of incidents was significant, what made these boys notorious was the accusation that they raped and sodomized Meili. The attack on Meili occurred in the midst of several inflammatory racial incidents in New York. In 1986 and 1987, the focus was on Howard Beach in Queens, where a gang of whites beat three black men, then chased a black man, Michael Griffith, into the street where he was struck by a car and died. Tawana Brawley, a black teen from upstate New York, falsely accused six white police officers of raping her, writing racist insults on her body, smearing her with dog excrement, and leaving her in a plastic trash bag in 1987. Trials were ongoing for the murder of a black teenager Yusef Hawkins, fourteen years old, by whites in Bensonhurst, Queens. Blacks were organizing a boycott of two Korean grocery stores. Spike Lee's racially inflammatory *Do the Right Thing* was released, and the city replaced their white mayor, Ed Koch, with a black mayor, David Dinkins (Benedict, 1992).

The Central Park Jogger case became an instant national news story. New York City Mayor Ed Koch and New York State Governor Mario Cuomo both spoke frequently about the case. Donald Trump purchased $8,000 worth of news advertisements that called for New York to reinstate the death penalty (Sullivan, 1992). All three of the major women's magazines, *Ladies' Home Journal, Good Housekeeping,* and *McCall's* featured articles about the assault. In December, 1989, the Central Park Jogger was chosen as one of *Glamour* magazine's Women of the Year, and *People* magazine selected her as one of the year's most interesting people. It also made international news, appearing in papers in London and Lebanon (Meili, 2003b).

RAPE AND THE MEDIA

Rape is a hard crime to understand, to prosecute, and to discuss. Despite numerous theories, there is still no clear understanding of why someone commits rape. Prosecuting rape offenders is difficult because, in many cases, the only witnesses are the victim and the alleged offender. Exacerbating the difficulties is the way that society has been socialized to discuss, and, consequently, think about rape. The Central Park Jogger case was particularly difficult because of the racial environment surrounding the incident. Race intersected all aspects of the case, including the media coverage, the police tactics used, and ultimately the verdicts.

According to Benedict (1992), there are ten myths about rape that are presented in the media and used in the courtroom that shape public understanding of a crime. The result of these myths is that portrayals of rape victims often become dichotomized—victims are either "virgins or vamps." The description of the Central Park Jogger, as described by most people and in the mainstream press, was consistent with the virgin paradigm. Most of the early stories focused on the seriousness of the attack and the symbolic value of Central Park for New Yorkers. Some coverage brought up the social class and physical appearance of Meili in a flattering rather than stigmatizing way. For instance, the tabloids began early on to use a "beauty and the beast" theme. As Miller, Like, and Levin assert, "the image of the young, attractive, middle-class, white (often blonde) female rape victim is the epitome of our society's construction of the innocent victim of street crime" (2001, p. 101). The Central Park Jogger exemplified this "ideal" victim.

Of Benedict's ten rape myths, several were employed in some way during the Central Park Jogger case. Some black newspapers, as well as a few people who zealously defended the innocence of the accused, described Meili in terms more consistent with the vamp ideology. Many blacks were disturbed by the largely positive coverage of Meili, as they asserted that black victims do not receive such flattering coverage. Many blacks thought the myth that assailants are usually black and/or lower class and their victims are generally middle or upper class and white was clearly emphasized in the Central Park Jogger case. In reality, most rapes occur within the same race or same class. The rapes that vary from the majority such as black/poor on white/wealthy description are given much more press coverage. The coverage of the Central Park Jogger case is especially problematic when compared with coverage of cases involving white offenders. For instance, there were twenty-eight other first-degree rapes or attempted rapes in the same week as the assault and rape of Meili, yet these received little, if any, coverage. The gang rape of a twenty-six-year-old prostitute who was also stabbed 138 by eight youths received scant attention, arguably because both the victim and offenders were black (Benedict, 1992).

Another myth of Benedict's used in the Central Park Jogger case was that the victim provoked the rape through her sexuality or that she deserved to be raped based on her careless behavior. These are part of a larger myth, referred to as the "Just World" ideology, which instructs people that bad things do not happen to good people. By default, if a bad thing, like rape, happens to a woman, she must have done something to warrant it. In this case, Meili's decision to run alone in the park provided some reporters with an opportunity to apply those myths related to the victim's behavior. Many of the articles had a punitive tone, and several seemed to imply that Meili's privileged background should have ensured that she knew better (Benedict, 1992). It was as if the press struggled with how much to use the traditional blame-the-victim tactics versus how much sympathy to show for such a heinous assault. Of all the newspapers, the *New York Times* ran the least amount of victim-blaming coverage; they even included a piece with advice from runners about safety in the park (Benedict, 1992).

Coverage of the case intensified with the defendants' first trial. Most of the later coverage continued using the virgin ideology, describing Meili as a heroine and emphasizing her amazing recovery. New York tabloids focused on Meili's recovery. By the end of the first trial, there were clearly two camps. The black press stressed that no one involved in the case could be trusted, alleged that the police had coerced the boys' confessions and lied on the witness stand, claimed that Meili lied about her boyfriend, and contended that the white press covered up facts and slandered the suspects. In sum, the black press portrayed the accused as innocent martyrs. The white press, however, presented the accused as guilty thugs, depicted the demonstrators at the trial as crazed by racial resentment, and stressed that Meili was a noble victim (Benedict, 1992).

RACE AND THE MEDIA

There were three main race-related concerns with media coverage of the Central Park Jogger case: negative depictions of the black defendants, overemphasis on the white victim, and differential coverage by white versus black presses. Most of the quotes from authorities, as well as editorials, claimed the case was *not* about race. Such coverage, by the sheer amount and lack of perspective offered by the largely white authors, merely served to inflame race-related issues (Benedict, 1992).

Early media coverage coined the term "wilding" to describe the incident. Some claim "wilding" was a "ghetto term," although many blacks say there is no such term used in the ghetto and that authorities made it up, mishearing the boys singing "Wild Thing." Welch, Price, and Yankey (2002) maintained that use of the term "wilding" was about news sensationalism and helped to create a moral panic about youth violence, particularly violence committed by young men of color. Virtually all the coverage emphasized the boys' lack of remorse. The press continually used animalistic descriptions of the accused, something not done when defendants are white. A study of the first two weeks of newspaper coverage, for instance, found that there were 390 instances of "emotional negative language," with 185 references to animals (Benedict, 1992). A *San Jose Mercury News* columnist captured the theme of animalistic savage versus innocent victim when he wrote, "They were predators. She was Bambi" (Miller et al., 2001, p. 101). Blacks were especially upset by some of the news coverage, which they thought presented the behavior of the accused as generalized to all of Harlem. It was racist to ignore the sympathy for Meili expressed by many Harlem residents. Some even held a vigil at the hospital for her (Sullivan, 1992). Several editors said they received more angry phone calls about the coverage of this case than for any other (Benedict, 1992). Further, the press was racist, because they treated the suspects as guilty from the start and profiled the accused by providing their names, schools, and addresses. This type of coverage did not occur in the Howard Beach or Bensonhurst cases where the accused were white (Benedict, 1992). According to Welch, Price, and Yankey (2002), the media hostility and reliance on racial criminal stereotypes adversely affected the way the suspects were initially processed by police.

Use of the black rapist myth has occurred throughout history. The fear originates in stereotypes of black criminality, as well as in concerns about race mixing or miscegenation. Ironically, miscegenation was common but had largely been between white masters and black slaves. Of the 455 men who were executed for rape (before the use of the death penalty for the rape of an adult woman was declared unconstitutional), 405 of them were black (Mann and Zatz, 2002). The myth appears in contemporary media coverage as well. The Central Park Jogger case provides an example, especially when juxtaposed with coverage of sexual assaults committed by whites. On the same day that Meili's assault and rape made the front page of most daily newspapers, at least ten other rapes occurred in New York City, with two ending in fatalities. The difference was less about the brutality of the attacks—one of the women was pushed from a ten-story building—than it was about race. In these cases, both the victims and offenders were black or Hispanic (Mann and Zatz, 2002). One example is the difference between coverage of the Central Park Jogger case, and the rape and sodomy committed by a group of suburban white teens of a mildly retarded girl in Glen Ridge, New Jersey, just six weeks later. Both cases were brutal; in Glen Ridge, eight teens watched as the young woman was forced to perform sex acts and was raped with several objects, including a broomstick and a miniature baseball bat. The first difference is that the Glen Ridge case received much less coverage. Second, the Central Park Jogger defendants were described as "vicious, sadistic terrorists," and the boys involved in the Glen Ridge assault were referred to as "collegiate," "former captain of the football team," and "honor student" (Mann and Zatz, 2002, p. 75). The boys from New York were described as a gang; the descriptions of the boys from New Jersey emphasized their grade point averages, sports achievements, and post–high school plans, sometimes not even mentioning the assault. The tone of the coverage implied that such vicious behavior was normal for the black and Hispanic suspects, but the behavior of the white assailants was surprising and unusual. A reader who encountered these images repeatedly can easily internalize the notion that these images are true and representative of minorities (Mann and Zatz, 2002).

The media proposed a variety of reasons why the New York boys might have committed such brutal offenses: race, drugs, class, the "culture of violence," music, lack of father figures, a soft-on-crime justice system, poor schools, popular culture, and boredom. No one in the media, however, emphasized that the attack on Meili was a sex crime and could and should be explained by societal sexist attitudes toward women. None of the journalists wrote about this as a gang rape, nor did they seem at all familiar with research literature on this topic. Yet, the callous views toward women that were elicited through interrogations and testimony are common in cases of gang rape (Benedict, 1992).

The two main black newspapers to cover the case, the *City Sun* and the *Amsterdam News*, were both weeklies. Both papers compared the coverage of this case with the coverage of the Tawana Brawley case, claiming that Brawley, as do other minority victims, received much less favorable coverage. Although this is generally true, as Benedict (1992) asserted, these two cases are not really analogous. There was generally no doubt that Meili was raped; however, there was doubt that Brawley had been, and in fact, a grand jury had dismissed her case. The mainstream media was criticized for identifying Brawley as the victim and for generally not identifying Meili, but Brawley's name was given with the permission of her family. Furthermore, the *Amsterdam News* did publish Meili's name; the editor claimed he was redressing the racism of naming the black accused but not the white victim (Benedict, 1992).

PREPARING FOR TRIAL

Most of the boys gave written and videotaped statements, some doing so several times. The conflicting statements made during the interrogations of the boys, both between and within statements, made preparing the case somewhat difficult for the prosecution. Most of the defendants claimed during the trial that the videotaped and written statements they made had been coerced, adding another element for the prosecution to address in their case. Anticipating the issue, the tapes had been used both to gather information and to preclude certain defenses. Further, because it had already been determined that the prosecution would seek convictions based on the acting-in-concert rule, the videotapes were used to get information about other defendants (Sullivan, 1992).

The attitude of the boys during their interrogations, as well as the degree of involvement each admitted, varied tremendously. Each was relatively quick to implicate others, however. Various individuals questioned if the police had coerced the boys into saying things they did not want to, both about themselves as well as others. The concern that the police coerced the boys seems to have even more merit in light of the recent developments with the case.

Antron McCray acted meek and embarrassed throughout his videotaped session, while Raymond Santana maintained a defiant attitude. Kevin Richardson was devoid of emotion. Steve Lopez, who was identified as the leader in the attacks by many of the boys, appeared smarter and more mature than the others, according to Lederer. Kharey Wise was the least coherent, providing conflicting statements that made little sense. No tape was made of the interviews with Jermain Robinson, who was fifteen, because his father refused permission (Sullivan, 1992).

McCray was the only one to confess to actual penetration. He had done so in a written statement before his videotaped session. In the videotaped session, however, he denied that his penis was ever in Meili, claiming that he was acting like he penetrated her to impress the others. He implicated Lopez, Santana, and Richardson in the assault and Richardson and Salaam in the rape. Although there was no videotape of Robinson, he told one of the detectives who drove him to the booking that his intent that night was to "get some whites." He was the only defendant identified by a witness or victim (Sullivan, 1992).

Santana confessed to sexual abuse by admitting that he "grabbed her tits" while Robinson and Richardson allegedly penetrated Meili. Santana also implicated McCray in the rape. Santana described Lopez as the primary assailant, claiming in his video that Lopez was kneeling on her arms, covering her mouth, smacking her, and hit her twice with a brick.

After initially denying ever seeing the Jogger, Lopez eventually admitted being present, but he never admitted any involvement in the attacks. Richardson also claimed to be merely a tagalong. Richardson primarily implicated McCray and Santana. Wise admitted assaulting "the bum" and kicking another jogger, as well as playing with Meili's legs while Lopez, Santana, and Richardson "started a little rape."

After all of the interrogations, Lederer, who was assisted by Arthur "Tim" Clements, decided on the formal charges. Wise, Richardson, Lopez, Salaam, McCray, Santana, and Thomas were all charged with several counts of assault, riot, rape, sodomy, sexual abuse, robbery, attempted murder, and assault with intent to do serious damage. As juveniles, all but Wise faced a maximum sentence of three and one-third to ten years unless they were convicted of murder, arson, or kidnapping. The prosecutors were disappointed with this, but they knew that they could at least up the minimum years with multiple convictions, so they decided to indict the boys on as many felonies as possible. While in the holding cells jail staff were appalled to find the boys joking, comparing stories, singing "Wild Thing," and making cat calls at a female detective. The grand jury heard evidence about attempted murder, assault with intent to cause serious injury, rape, sodomy, riot, and two counts of robbery (related to John Loughlin's headset). Despite having a hard time finding victims or witnesses who could identify the boys, the prosecutors got thirteen grand jury indictments on Lopez, Wise, Richardson, McCray, Salaam, and Santana. Robinson was indicted for the assaults, robbery, and riot. The grand jury did not return any indictments for Clarence Thomas (Sullivan, 1992).

The case was assigned to Judge Thomas Galligan, rather than a judge being selected at random, as was normal practice. Both the defense attorneys and the prosecution objected, but Galligan remained on the case. Galligan had a reputation as being fair, although he was referred to as "Father Time" due to his heavy sentencing (Sullivan, 1992).

The prosecution was able to reach a plea bargain with Robinson. He first had to provide them with a blood sample to ensure that he was not involved in the rape, the deal was off if his DNA showed up on the victim. He was then interviewed a total of five times, where he primarily implicated Lopez (Sullivan, 1992).

Other Pretrial Issues

The primary pretrial issue revolved around the admissibility of the videotape statements for each defendant. Galligan also considered motions for separate trials. These pretrial issues were much less significant for the prosecution, however, than the scientific evidence.

Santana was represented by Peter Rivera, McCray by Mickey Joseph, and Richardson by Howard Diller. Lopez's attorney was Jesse Berman, Bobby Burns represented Yusef Salaam, and Colin Moore represented Wise. The defense attorneys were all very concerned about the tapes, especially after *Newsday* received a copy and printed much of the information, although Richardson's had actually been released by Diller to allegedly debunk the myth that all the defendants had confessed on tape. In the days following, virtually every station aired pieces of the tapes.

The motions for separate trials were based on the Sixth Amendment right to cross-examine witnesses; such a right is impossible if the witness is a codefendant because of self-incrimination issues. Also at issue was whether the videotapes would self-incriminate or would unfairly prejudice the case against codefendants. Galligan allowed the prosecution three weeks to edit the tapes in such a way so as not to prejudice the jury, as well as to propose which defendants would be tried together (Sullivan, 1992).

DNA results indicated that the semen on the Jogger's tights matched her boyfriend, but the two other samples were not matched. This was a significant blow to the prosecution's case, as they had no conclusive physical evidence linking the boys to the victim. The lack of DNA prompted some to suggest that the Jogger never was raped and had engaged in rough sex with her own boyfriend, a position largely held by a group known as the "supporters." This group included such well-known figures as Alton Maddox, Vernon Mason, and Al Sharpton (Sullivan, 1992).

Galligan finally made his ruling on the admissibility of the tapes, much to the chagrin of the defense attorneys. He determined that all written and videotaped statements were admissible. Galligan also denied the motions for separate trials. The prosecution came up with the trial combinations of Santana, Salaam, and McCray for the first trial and Lopez, Wise, and Richardson for the second. Galligan determined that the editing they did of the videotaped statements would not be prejudicial to the codefendants in these combinations. Some people, especially members of the black community, thought that the pretrial issues would have been handled differently if the defendants had been white and that the case was pushed forward absent physical evidence because of the boys' race (Sullivan, 1992).

TRIAL ONE: McCRAY, SANTANA, AND SALAAM

Judge Galligan granted a seven-week delay before the trial began, so the prosecution could get the DNA results on semen found on the Jogger's sock. This time the sample was clearly strong enough to obtain a result, but it still did not match any of the defendants. Not only did this further weaken the prosecution's case, but it likely meant that at least one guilty party was going free. Lederer maintained that it was possible one of the defendants masturbated on the sock, but many did not believe that explanation. To some, the lack of a DNA match reinforced the defense and "supporters" contentions that the boys were innocent scapegoats. The city of Harlem was split by the case; much of Schomburg Plaza was appalled by the violence and had even held a vigil for the Jogger, but others resented the media's trashing of the neighborhood and their tendency to blame blacks (Sullivan, 1992).

Three hundred potential jurors had to be called, due to the publicity about the case, to select a jury. Jury selection proceeded smoothly at first, until a supporter, Paul Antonio Williams, was caught passing out fliers to potential jurors claiming Judge Galligan was biased. He later pled guilty to disorderly conduct. After eight days of voir dire a jury was seated; the jury included ten men, two women, four whites, four blacks, three Latinos, and one Asian.

Lederer's opening statement emphasized that the defendants were guilty, and the jury would be able to hear their confessions to the crime. She also stressed that their individual actions were less important than their collective actions. This was critical in presenting the notion of acting-in-concert, which requires that defendants share in the intent to commit the act and aid in some way, even if they do not commit the crime, per se. Rather than the victim identifying the accused, in this case, the accused would be identifying their victims. Lederer also provided a chronology of the case where the rape occurred before some of the attacks (Sullivan, 1992).

Joseph and Burns requested permission to call experts to testify that their clients were susceptible to psychological coercion. McCray allegedly had an IQ of 87. Although Salaam's IQ was above average, he supposedly suffered from low self-esteem. Galligan denied both requests. Joseph was the better attorney of the three and ended up leading the other two attorneys. Burns's opening statement was disjointed and largely ineffective. Rivera stressed that overzealous police violated his client's Miranda rights. He also suggested that his client was only arrested because he was Latino and brought up whether his client's father and grandmother understood English well enough to consent to the interrogation (Sullivan, 1992).

The prosecution began their case by calling seven joggers and cyclists who were in Central Park that night. Each personified the significance of the case—all were middle class New Yorkers who had survived the nightmarish urban onslaught. Probably the most important testimony came from John Loughlin, a physical education teacher. The boys had thought Loughlin was a cop at first because of the fatigue jacket and camouflage pants he wore. He initially stopped when he saw the group beating Robert Garner. Loughlin recalled someone calling him a vigilante and then being facedown on the pavement and hit twice in the head. He was unconscious for a while. He suffered damage to his head, shins, right arm, ankle, right knee, back, and rib cage. His eyes were so injured they looked like they had been "outlined in charcoal" (Sullivan, 1992, p. 122). He testified that he had lasting pain in his right knee and the left side of the back of his head. Loughlin identified Robinson as one of his assailants during the lineup.

Witnesses who found Meili were next to testify. The first was Patrolman Joseph Walsh. He was with his partner when two men approached them and said they had found a man beaten and tied up in the woods. When they arrived at the scene, Walsh and his partner discovered a woman, otherwise naked, with a dirty bra pushed up around her breasts. Walsh testified that her head was beaten, her eyes were swollen shut, and there was a significant amount of blood. A cloth was tied around her wrists and neck and stuffed in her mouth. The two men who found her, Charles Colon and Benicio Moore, also testified (Sullivan, 1992).

Several of the doctors who treated Meili testified. Robert Kurtz was the surgeon who supervised Meili for the seven weeks she was at Metropolitan Hospital. He stated that she was barely alive when she was brought in; they could not get a blood pressure reading, she had lost almost 80 percent of her blood, and her body temperature was eight-five degrees. Meili could not breathe on her own, so a technician had to pump oxygen into her body through a throat tube. Brain damage made her thrash around in her bed. She was bleeding from five major head cuts and had several skull fractures. The jury was also shown pictures of Meili's injuries (Sullivan, 1992).

The jury next heard from the officers who collected evidence or found the suspects. A major issue was whether McCray's statements to police could be used or whether a Miranda violation had occurred. Joseph managed to cast some doubt on the credibility of Officer Rosario. Lederer also called a DNA expert with the intent to make the DNA results look inconclusive; however, Joseph got the expert to admit on cross-examination that the results were conclusive and definitely did not match McCray. Throughout most of the witnesses' testimony, the defendants appeared bored (Sullivan, 1992).

Meili herself testified to refute the claim that the semen was from a voluntary partner. Lederer also wanted to put a face on the crime for the jury. She testified that she did not remember the incident. She last had sex with her boyfriend three days before the incident. Press coverage praised her for her courage; the *New York Times* placed the story on the front page (Sullivan, 1992).

Detective Hildebrandt was called to describe the interrogation of McCray. He described McCray's family as cooperative. He said that McCray acted nervous, so he eventually asked his mother to leave the room. Then, McCray told of the attack on Antonio Diaz and how he kicked Meili and jumped on her. The jury saw McCray's videotape, where he said he rubbed his penis on the Jogger. On cross-examination, Joseph tried to persuade the jury that McCray's statements were not made voluntarily but were induced by promises and threats made by cops. Several of the jurors said they had doubts about Hildebrandt's testimony (Sullivan, 1992).

Detective McKenna was the primary witness against Salaam, and he mainly focused on the interrogation. McKenna was allowed to testify even though his testimony was hearsay because of Salaam's admission of guilt. McKenna described how he tried to trick Salaam into confessing by telling him they had his fingerprints. He said Salaam admitted to being there but said he did not rape her. Salaam also said that Richardson hit the Jogger with a pipe and raped her, as did Wise and two others. According to McKenna, Salaam said, "it was something to do. It was fun." Burns, who was already in trouble for making disparaging comments when McKenna was testifying, tried to depict Salaam as an innocent kid who had been coerced, but he also tried to argue that his client made no incriminating statements. The jury had to believe that McKenna and the others tried to trap him and failed, so they fabricated his statement, a fairly unlikely combination (Sullivan, 1992).

Detective Hartigan testified about his interrogation of Santana. He said that Santana admitted to participating in the rape and also implicated

McCray. McCray signed a statement, but his grandmother refused to sign it. Santana drove with officers to where the pipe was supposed to be and said he had "touched her tits." He came across on the videotape as a smart aleck, trying to portray himself as a leader (Sullivan, 1992).

The Defense Strategy

Joseph tried to explain why McCray would confess to crimes he did not commit, even when his parents were present. His argument was that the McCrays were made promises by the police. McCray's dad testified that he told his son to lie or else he would go to jail.

Burns began his case amidst a spectacle. Reverend Sharpton and Vernon Mason brought Tawana Brawley to court with them. Sharpton, Mason, and Alton Maddox had represented Brawley until a grand jury dismissed her case. Burns presented the same case he had at the preliminary hearing. Several witnesses testified that Salaam was only fifteen and was thus questioned in violation of the requirement to have a guardian present. Salaam testified that what he told McKenna was secondhand. Lederer tried to expose him as malicious and belligerent. The jury later said he seemed too cool and detached, so they did not find him very believable. Burns was lambasted in the press for allowing Salaam to testify. Rivera also put forward virtually the same case as in the preliminary hearing (Sullivan, 1992).

In his closing statement, Joseph focused on the fact that no one identified McCray and that there was no physical evidence tying him to the crime. He reiterated that McCray's statements were not voluntary but were coerced by the police based on their pressure to solve the case. Burns suggested that Meili might not have been raped and that there was no physical evidence against Salaam. Rivera argued that Santana was framed by the police, pointing out the errors in his client's description of the crime. The prosecution reiterated the evidence of acting in concert and reviewed the sequence of events. Lederer managed to maintain her composure despite that a group of supporters silently marched out of the courtroom during her closing (Sullivan, 1992).

The Jury

After hearing the law on all thirteen counts, the jury began deliberations. The deliberation process was made more difficult because most of the jurors had fallen asleep during the trial (Sullivan, 1992). The jurors considered the lower charges first and had little trouble deciding on most of them. During their deliberations about the more serious charges, they asked for a review of the acting-in-concert principle, and they also reviewed the tapes many times. As the defense attorneys had worried, the editing failed to protect their clients. The jury was easily able to guess whose name had been bleeped out (Sullivan, 1992). Salaam suffered the most from guilt by association. Another problem was that some of the jurors had seen press coverage of the case.

The jury convicted all three defendants of rape, assaults, robbery, and riot, although some jurors had doubts about McCray and rape. Each defendant was sentenced to three and one-third to ten years for the rape and robbery (Sullivan, 1992).

The Deal with Lopez

The prosecution wanted to try Lopez separately because of the editing of the tapes that would be required if they did not would hurt the case against Richardson and Wise and because they needed time to build a stronger case. Jesse Berman represented Lopez. Lopez denied everything but witnessing the crimes, and because the tapes could not be used Berman felt fairly confident that Lopez would not be convicted. However, he was concerned with how much the other defendants might reveal. Before the trial, the prosecution lost a mystery witness who would have placed Lopez at the rape, so they were left with no conclusive evidence against him. The prosecution could not make any kind of offer to those who were already convicted, so they were unwilling to testify. In the end, Lopez took a plea just as jury selection was beginning. He pled guilty to one count of robbery against Loughlin and was sentenced to one and one-half to four and one-half years (Sullivan, 1992).

TRIAL TWO: RICHARDSON AND WISE

The two remaining defendants, Richardson and Wise, were tried together next. It took seven days to seat a jury of five whites, four blacks, two Latinos and one Asian (Sullivan, 1992). Lederer's case was essentially the same as in the first trial, but she did not focus on the chronology. Colin Moore represented Wise, and Howard Diller represented Richardson. Moore was known to have an ambitious political agenda and had been referred to as an anti-white activist. Diller offered little in the way of a coercion defense, focusing more on that acting in concert requires intent and Richardson had none. Moore stressed the chronology problem, and he embraced the boyfriend theory. He also argued that psychological and physical stress was what made Wise's four statements differ from one another. Throughout the trial Kharey

Wise was agitated, fidgeting in his chair and mumbling. At several times during the trial, he even yelled out in court (Sullivan, 1992).

Diller and Moore had dramatically different styles. Diller approached the state's witnesses respectfully, while Moore was much more aggressive. Moore assumed the trial was all a part of a racist plot. Although animated, sometimes he failed so badly during cross-examination that the jurors actually laughed. He was also very aggressive in his cross-examination of Meili, stressing the boyfriend theory and accusing her of not doing enough to regain her memory. The press praised Meili and criticized Moore. Midway through the trial Richardson's family, the Cuffees, wanted to switch to Moore because they thought Diller was dull and ineffective. Diller was eager to leave, as he had been receiving death threats, but Justice Thomas Galligan would not allow it (Sullivan, 1992).

To no avail, Moore had tried to get the detectives to admit that Wise had a hard time understanding what was happening. Both of the defendants' mothers testified, and both were very hostile toward Lederer. Two teenagers, Al Morris and Raheim Fladger, were called to testify, but both pled the Fifth Amendment. The supporters bashed both Morris and Fladger for failing to help the defendants. Moore also argued that Wise had an alibi; he was at a neighbor's house with his girlfriend. He could have been present for the rape, however, but not for the assaults at the reservoir. Wise claimed he was told what to say by the detectives. He, too, was hostile on cross-examination and kept having outbursts. In closing, Moore emphasized that this was a case of the powerful versus the powerless. He compared the New York Police Department to storm troopers and pointed out the leading nature of Lederer's interrogations (Sullivan, 1992).

The Decision

The jury found Richardson guilty of all charges. They did not buy the coercion arguments, as his sister and father were present during the interrogations. The jury found Wise guilty of sex abuse, the assault of Meili, and riot. As the only adult tried, Wise received a lengthier sentence of five to fifteen years (Sullivan, 1992).

AFTER THE TRIALS

Immediately after the crime, Manhattan borough president and then-mayoral candidate David Dinkins responded to the attack by calling for an "anti-wilding law," which was to increase the penalties for anyone who committed a crime as part of a group. Dinkins also advocated hiring more police. Incumbent Mayor Ed Koch called for the death penalty for those involved in "wilding" incidents (Welch et al., 2002).

In June 2002, thirty-one-year-old Matias Reyes, a convicted murderer and serial rapist serving thirty-three years to life, said that he alone raped Meili and left her for dead. His DNA matched the semen on the Jogger's sock, yet he could not be charged because the statute of limitations had expired ("It's Time," 2002). Reyes was already in custody at the time of the trials. He had been arrested on August 5, 1989, and he confessed to raping four women and murdering one of them, a pregnant woman, while her three children called to her from another room. Reyes stabbed some of the victims in the eye, hoping they would not be able to identify him ("It's Time," 2002).

The prosecutor's office has been criticized for not following up on leads relating to Reyes at the time of the attack, as it was clear that the assault on Meili fit his modus operandi. At least one police officer and one assistant district attorney worked on both cases, and Judge Galligan presided over both (Allah and Little, 2002). On December 19, 2002, Judge Charles Tejada vacated the convictions of McCray, Santana, Salaam, Richardson, and Wise for the attack on Meili (Meili, 2003a). Salaam, Richardson, Santana, and McCray had served seven years, and Wise had served twelve years (McQuillan, 2003). The Manhattan district attorney said he would not seek a retrial on any of the other charges (Meili, 2003a). The new developments brought the case renewed media attention, as did the publication of Meili's book in 2003. Meili spoke about the case with Katie Couric, and A&E aired a special about the Central Park Jogger case.

Reyes's confession has also brought scrutiny to the issue of false and coerced confessions. The Supreme Court has ruled that coerced confessions are inadmissible, but what constitutes coercion is not always clear. Torture and beatings were outlawed in 1936 in *Brown v. Mississippi,* but psychological coercion remains on shakier ground. According to *Haynes v. Washington,* allegations of psychological coercion must be evaluated on the totality of circumstances. The result is that police are often trained in the use of psychological tactics designed to get a suspect to confess. For instance, training manuals instruct officers to use the physical environment to their advantage, interrogating suspects in small, sterile, and brightly lit rooms. Officers learn how to extend interrogations over lengthy periods of time and to ignore the suspects' food, bathroom, and sleep needs. Officers also learn that they can use deceptive tactics to obtain confessions. They are allowed and encouraged to suggest to suspects that they will get a better deal if they talk, they can tell them a passing polygraph test will provide for their release, and they can lie to suspects about the evidence they have or what others allegedly told them (Cassel, 2002). All but the polygraph lie test were used with the suspects in the Central Park Jogger case. For instance, the interrogations lasted for more than thirty hours (Allah and Little, 2002). Of course, these tactics are sometimes successful in breaking down guilty parties, but they may be even more successful with vulnerable and innocent populations.

Playing suspects off one another is also a tactic police use to gain confessions and evidence. In this case, each boy tended to minimize his own involvement while implicating others. Individually there was little evidence against any of the boys, but their statements seem to have been taken as some sort of collective confession (Cassel, 2002).

The case has become emblematic of problems in the New York Police Department, the prosecutors office, and the U.S. criminal justice system in general. The case has called attention to the race-based approach to investigations that are often employed by the police (Hayes, 2002). In recent years, the New York Police Department has faced several major setbacks regarding their treatment of racial minorities. Abner Louima was tortured and sexually assaulted by police officers. While some of the officers were initially convicted, their convictions have since been vacated. Amidou Diallo, a Haitian immigrant, was shot forty-one times by officers. Unfortunately, neither these cases nor the Central Park Jogger case brought about necessary reforms. Disregarding the decision by the Manhattan district attorney and a state supreme court judge to vacate the charges against the five teens, the New York Police Department began its own reinvestigation of the case to determine whether policy or procedures needed changing. The resulting report focused on the incident and virtually ignores the interrogations and other potential police misconduct (Allah and Little, 2002). These cases have brought some public attention to the issue of racial profiling and police abuse of authority, albeit still quite limited.

With the resurgence of interest since Reyes's confession, it is surprising little attention has been paid to the many race-related issues involved in the Central Park Jogger case, especially those involving the media. Little has changed in the ways that the media covers crime and has covered this important case. Nonwhite offenders are still often demonized by the press in ways that white offenders are not, and white victims fare better in the media than nonwhite victims do. For instance, the press gave an excessive amount of attention to Robert "Yummy" Sandifer Jr., a black boy from Chicago who was eleven years old when his stray bullet hit a fourteen year old instead of the gang member it was intended for. A rival gang killed Sandifer shortly thereafter. Yet, little attention was paid to other crimes committed by white youths around the same time, such as the Washington twelve-year-olds who shot a migrant worker who had yelled at them (Rome, 2002). In 1991, Alfred Jermaine Ewell, a black seventeen year old, was attacked and seriously wounded. *New York Newsday* described the assailants as a "gang of white toughs." Black community members questioned why the attack was not labeled a wilding. They insisted that term is only used for black suspects (Welch et al., 2002). Although the term wilding is not used as frequently now, other terms with negative connotations are used to describe groups of blacks. For instance, a group of black males is often described as a gang, which connotes violence and mayhem (Welch et al., 2002).

Perhaps, most importantly, media coverage influences how people think about crime and, consequently, the adjudication of criminal cases. Surveys have shown that more than one-half of all Americans think blacks are prone to violence (Robinson, 2002). Many people are quick to believe that blacks commit an inordinate amount of crime due to stereotypes of the black male criminal, like those employed in the Central Park Jogger case. Such media coverage creates a hierarchy of victims. Researchers have found that the harshest sentences for rape are assigned to black men who rape white women, while white men who rape black women receive the most lenient sentences (Miller et al., 2002). The disparity is especially true when a black stranger or strangers, as in the Central Park Jogger case, assault a white woman (Miller et al., 2002).

REFERENCES

Allah, D., and Little, R. (2003, February 18). New York dodgers. *Village Voice*, p. 29.

Benedict, H. (1992). *Virgin or vamp? How the press covers sex crimes.* New York: Oxford University Press.

Cassel, E. (2002). How to stop false confessions such as in the Central Park jogger case. [Electronic version] CNN. Retrieved August 10, 2003, from http://cnn/law.printthis.clickability.com

Couric, K. (2003, April 6). The Central Park jogger. *NBC Katie Couric Exclusive.*

Hays, T. (2002, December 6). Central Park jogger case upsets families. Retrieved August 12, 2003, from http://www.kansas.com/mld/kansas/news/nation/4675364.html

It's Time. (2002, September 26). [Electronic Version]. ABC News. Retrieved August 20, 2003, from http://abcnews.go.com/sections/primetime/DailyNews/centalpark—rape—020926.html

Mann, C., and Zatz, M. (2002). *Images of color, images of crime* (2nd ed.). Los Angeles: Roxbury.

McQuillan, A. (2003, March 28). Park jogger tells of road back from hell. *Daily News*, p. 22.

Meili, T. (2003a). *I am the Central Park jogger.* New York: Scribner.

Meili, T. (2003b, April 20). Central Park jogger: Symbol of hope [Electronic edition]. CBS News. Retrieved on August 10, 2003, from http://www.cbsnews.com/stories/2003/04/29/earlyshow/books/leisure/main/551524.htm

Miller, J., Like, T., and Levin, P. (2002). The Caucasian evasion: Victims, exceptions, and defenders of the status quo. In C. Mann and M. Zatz (Eds.), *Images of color, images of crime* (2nd ed.) (pp. 100–114). Los Angeles: Roxbury.

Robinson, M. (2002). *Justice blind?* Upper Saddle River, NJ: Prentice Hall.

Rome, D. (2002). Murderers, rapists, and drug addicts. In C. Mann and M. Zatz (Eds.), *Images of color, images of crime* (2nd ed.) (pp. 71–81). Los Angeles: Roxbury.

Sullivan, T. (1992). *Unequal verdicts.* New York: Simon and Schuster.

Welch, M., Price, E., and Yankey, N. (2002, September). Moral panic over youth violence: Wilding and the manufacture of menace in the media. *Youth and Society, 34*(1), 3–30.

9

Rodney King Beating Trial: A Landmark for Reform

Shelley L. Schlief

A fire needs oxygen ... From the very beginning, the oxygen that has given life to the Rodney King story is television.

(Alter, 1992, p. 43)

On March 4, 1991, at 10:15 p.m., a local Los Angeles television station, KTLA, aired a sixty-eight second video clip known commonly as the "Holliday videotape," named after the maker of the video, George Holliday. The videotape showed a black man, Rodney Glen King, being beaten by four white Los Angeles police officers. Because KTLA had an affiliation agreement with CNN, the video was shown simultaneously at 1:15 a.m. at CNN's Atlanta headquarters. Shortly after viewing the video, CNN producers obtained a microwave feed of the KTLA tape and began airing it in the early morning hours of March 5, 1991. By Wednesday, March 6, the video became the focus of Los Angeles media and received more attention than the just-ended Persian Gulf War (Cannon, 1997, pp. 22–23). Additionally, CNN gave the video national and international exposure; CNN aired the story everywhere it was syndicated. The Holliday videotape, in a very short period of time, had made Rodney King a household name around the world.

The media exposure that the Holliday videotape received was the sole driving force behind the investigation and trials that would follow. Had there been no video, this probably would have been just another quiet, unreported incident of police misconduct. Instead the beating of King would prove to be the most shocking footage of police brutality ever seen on television. In addition, the video would provide the evidence needed to incite investigations of police brutality across the United States, as police chiefs in at least ten other police departments recognized that excessive force was pervasive across the country (Independent Commission on the Los Angeles Police Department, 1991). Hence, the videotaped beating of King was a landmark in the history of law enforcement, and the basis for police reform across the nation.

THE INCIDENT

On the evening of March 2, 1991, King and two of his friends, Bryant "Pooh" Allen and Freddie Helms, sat in King's wife's car in Altadena County, California, and drank forty-ounce bottles of Olde English 800 (Skolnick and Fyfe, 1994). After a few hours, with King driving, they left Altadena County on Interstate 210, also known as the Foothill Freeway. King was intoxicated and also on parole from a two-year prison term for robbery.

At 12:30 a.m., a husband-and-wife team of the California Highway Patrol (CHP), Troopers Timothy and Melanie Singer, observed King's 1988 white, two-door Hyundai driving behind them at a high speed. The Singers exited Interstate 210 at the Sunland Boulevard off-ramp, and they returned to the freeway behind King's Hyundai. Melanie Singer, who was driving, observed King's car speed to be between 110 and 115 miles per hour. The troopers initiated a traffic stop on the freeway with red lights, sirens, and they ordered King to pull over through a loudspeaker. King ignored the warnings and continued off an exit ramp. Timothy Singer radioed for help. A car from the Los Angeles Unified School District was the first to aid the troopers by joining the pursuit. Units from the Los Angeles Police Department (LAPD) also joined the chase (one operated by Laurence Powell and Timothy Wind), as well as an LAPD helicopter. King continued to drive recklessly for about eight miles, reaching up to eighty-five miles per hour on residential streets and running a red light, in which he nearly caused an accident. Shortly after, King came to a stop in front of the Hansen Dam Park, at the intersection of Osborne Street and Foothill Boulevard.

Timothy Singer ordered the occupants out of the vehicle and to lie facedown on the ground, with their legs spread and arms behind their backs. Allen and Helms complied, but King remained in the car. Timothy Singer quickly handcuffed Allen and Helms; both offered no resistance. He then continued to order King out of the car until King finally exited. Two more LAPD cars arrived; one with Officers Theodore Briseno and Roland Solano, the other with Sergeant Stacey Koon. After King exited, Melanie Singer described him as smiling and watched him wave to the helicopter overhead. Timothy Singer ordered King to show his hands and back away from the car. King moved away from the car and put his hands on his buttocks, causing Melanie Singer and the other officers to suspect he was going for a gun. Instead, Melanie Singer testified that "he grabbed his right buttock with his right hand and he shook it at me" (Alter and Palumbo, 1992). Singer drew her weapon and directed King to move his hands away from his buttocks and lie down. King complied and she moved toward him with her gun drawn in an attempt to handcuff him. When she was within five or six feet of King, Koon ordered her to stop and that he would handle the situation. Koon feared that, by moving toward him, she increased the likelihood that shots would be fired: "She was going to shoot Rodney King or he was going to take her gun away and shoot her" (Koon and Deitz, 1992, p. 34).

Sergeant Koon and the other LAPD officers involved took notice of King's erratic behavior, which included dancing around, talking gibberish, and swaying back and forth. Additionally, King was glistening with sweat and it was a cool night, leading the officers to believe that King was drunk and "dusted" or under the influence of PCP (Koon and Deitz, 1992). Any individual suspected of using PCP is feared by the police because of its effects of making a person impervious to pain and giving them superhuman strength. Koon also observed that King was "buffed out," with a large muscular upper body. He concluded that King was probably an ex-convict who had developed his muscles working out with prison weights.

Koon ordered King to lie flat on the ground with his hands behind his back. King got on his hands and knees, but he did not lie down. Koon ordered the officers watching King—Powell, Wind, Briseno, and Solano— to holster their weapons, and surround King in order to "swarm" him. Swarming the suspect is a level 3 on the LAPD use of force chart, and this is the first level in which there is contact with the suspect. Swarming is taking the suspect to the ground (Koon and Deitz, 1992). Powell and Briseno grabbed King's arms, while Wind and Solano took his legs. Powell placed his knee into King's back as he attempted to handcuff his left wrist. Then, in a swift motion, King threw his arms out, and Powell and Briseno flew off King. Because of the strength King exhibited, which provided further evidence of the possibility of King on PCP, Koon ordered Wind and Solano to step back. Koon continued to shout at King to lie down, but when he failed to listen, Koon fired his 50,000-volt TASER (Tom A Swift Electric

Rifle), which was the next level of force, level 4. The taser darts hit King in the back. Normally, a taser would drop a person and subdue them so that they could be handcuffed, but King fell to his knees and rose again. He turned toward Koon, who reactivated the taser and fired again. The darts hit King in the chest. King groaned and collapsed, but once again came to his feet.

It was at this time that George Holliday began filming his infamous tape from his bedroom terrace. The incident was occurring about ninety feet away. By this time, the officers had been ordered by Koon to have their PR 24 metal batons in hand, level 5. The first scene on the tape would display one of the most disputed actions; after King rose, it appears as though he charges toward Powell. Powell (which he would later claim he had no room or time to swing) swung to protect himself and hit King on the right side of his head or collarbone. Melanie Singer, Briseno, and Wind would state it was a head blow, and Koon and Powell believed contact was made at the collarbone. The tape was blurred. Powell's blow knocked King to the ground, and he would not reach his feet again for the duration of the tape. During the blurry beginning seconds of the tape, which was cut from the segment KTLA aired, an undetermined number of blows are delivered to King. Once the tape comes into focus, no blows are being delivered to King. For the duration of the tape, the officers would alternate between beating and pausing. Officer Briseno is seen restraining Powell, by pushing his baton arm away from King. About fifteen seconds later, King appeared to rise again, and Powell delivered more blows. King continued to roll around on the ground and never got facedown with his arms extended and legs spread. Powell and Wind continued to deliver baton blows and kicks. Blows were delivered first to the chest region and later to the lower extremities. Pauses by the officers are seen throughout the tape, as they assess the force they have used. It is clear that Wind took the time to evaluate King's condition, but the pauses that Powell took lasted only a second or two. For twenty seconds, Powell can be seen hitting King repeatedly in the lower extremities—one blow causing a fracture to King's leg. King then rolls over onto his back and Powell strikes him in the chest. Eight seconds later, Powell reaches for his handcuffs. Two seconds later, Briseno comes in and appears to stomp King with his foot, in the upper shoulder area. King moves in response to the blow, which causes Powell to deliver five to seven baton blows and Wind to deliver four baton blows and six kicks. Koon hears King plead "Please stop" and orders his officers to jump him. Shortly after, King was handcuffed and hog-tied (cuffed at the ankles with both sets of handcuffs cuffed together). During the course of the videotape, an average viewer would see King receive fifty-six blows of the metal baton and six kicks to his entire body (Alpert,

Smith, and Watters, 1992). Later analysis during King's suit against the City of Los Angeles would demonstrate that King only received thirty-three blows and that twenty-three did not make contact.

Before 1 a.m., Sergeant Koon typed a message into his car's on-board computer: "U (meaning 'You,' the lieutenant) just had a big-time use of force. TASED and beat suspect of CHP pursuit. 'Big Time'" (Koon and Deitz, 1992). He waited for Lieutenant Patrick Conway to arrive and assess the situation, but he did not. Koon returned to the station to get a new taser and inform Conway about the incident. Koon would then leave for the hospital to check on King's condition.

Shortly before Koon left, Allen and Helms were released at the scene, and Officer Powell radioed the fire department for a rescue ambulance at Foothill and Osborne:

Powell: (laugh) They should know better than to run. They're going to pay a price when they do that.
FD: What type of incident would you say this is?
Powell: It's a . . . it's a . . . battery, he got beat up.
FD: Okay, by assailants unknown?
Powell: Ah, well . . . sort of.
FD: Okay, any other information as to his injuries, anything at all?
Powell: Nope. (Owens and Browning, 1994, pp. xvii–xviii)

Powell also talked about the incident on his car's on-board computer to Officer Corina Smith, who was patrolling in another area of the city.

Powell: Oops.
Smith: Oops what?
Powell: I haven't beaten anyone this bad in a long time.
Smith: Oh, not again. Why for you do that? I thought you agreed to chill out for awhile. What did he do?
Powell: I think he was dusted . . . many broken bones later. (Cannon, 1997, p. 38)

Officer Smith was making a reference to an incident that she and Powell were involved in on October 1, 1990. They had been accused of using excessive force on a handcuffed suspect. Sergeant Koon investigated the incident, but the suspect later dropped the accusations. These brief statements would only represent a few of the comments that would haunt Powell during the trials of the officers.

Of the twenty-five (some report twenty-three) officers that were present at the scene over the course of the incident, Officer Briseno was the only known officer to criticize the incident.[1] He stated to Solano shortly afterwards, "Sarge really fucked up out there tonight" (Cannon, 1997, p. 37).

King was taken to Pacifica Hospital, where Dr. Antonio Mancia, who told Sergeant Koon that King had ingested PCP and had superficial lacerations, was the first to take a cursory look at King. After Koon had left, Powell and Wind took over and Dr. David Giannettoa thoroughly examined King around 6:30 a.m. He found a right leg fracture, multiple facial fractures, numerous bruises, and contusions. A urinary analysis showed that there was no PCP in King's system, but the results were inconclusive due to the high alkaline content of King's urine, which masks the presence of PCP. Three other doctors would also examine King. After King was treated, he was taken to the police station by Officers Powell and Wind for booking.

THE INITIAL REACTION

On the Monday after the incident, both King's brother Paul and Holliday attempted to file complaints with the LAPD but did not succeed. Paul King went to the Foothill station to file a complaint about his brother being beaten. He was forced to wait for a couple of hours, and once it seemed as though he was finally going to be able to file a written complaint, the sergeant that was "helping" him became more interested in Paul King's arrest record. King's brother even informed the sergeant of the possibility of a videotape, but the sergeant did not seem to care. He was essentially forced to leave the station, and he was never given the opportunity to fill out a complaint form.

Holliday telephoned the Foothill station in an attempt to give his videotape to the police. He told the desk officer he had witnessed the incident and then asked about the motorist's condition. The desk officer informed Holliday that the information cannot be released and did not ask any questions about what Holliday had seen. Once off the phone, a discouraged Holliday tried a different tactic, one that would prove to be infallible: television.

The first LAPD personnel to view the tape were senior officers located in downtown Los Angeles at LAPD headquarters; KTLA had dropped off a copy of the video shortly after receiving it. Immediately, an investigation began. Police Chief Daryl Gates was out of town, and Assistant Chief Robert Vernon was in charge. Investigators were still trying to identify the officers on the videotape when it first aired on KTLA at 10:15 p.m. on March 4. Chief Gates arrived in Los Angeles around midnight, but he did not view the tape until the next morning. Once he viewed the tape, he stated that it made him physically ill but refrained from making snap judgments. Los Angeles Mayor Tom Bradley, a former police officer, said the beating was "shocking and outrageous" and promised "swift prosecution" (Coffey, 1992,

p. 35). Additionally, President George Bush was also appalled by what he saw, and the FBI launched an investigation on March 5.

Reaction to the tape was swift and sharp. Those who saw the tape had a hard time forgetting the brutality that King endured, especially the public. The tape had provided tangible evidence of brutality and racism. Most of the residents of South Central Los Angeles were not surprised by what they saw. Such incidences were considered to be commonplace. A March 10 poll, taken by the *Los Angeles Times*, found that 92 percent surveyed believed the officers used excessive force against Rodney King (Skolnick and Fyfe, 1993, pp. 15–16). Additionally, two-thirds of those polled thought that police brutality was common. Although initial reactions of anger and repulsion were present, some members of the African American community thought that some good may come of the incident—now the public might believe that police often beat or harassed African Americans and the incident brought a sense of unity; "the savage beating of King has inspired Los Angeles' Black community to speak with one voice" (*Los Angeles Sentinel*, 1991, as cited in Jacobs, 1996, p. 1251).

Issues surrounding the incident of police brutality, indictment, and rioting are not a first in Los Angeles history. Other incidents include the "Sleepy Lagoon" incident in the 1940s that demonstrated concerns about discrimination towards Latinos; the Furman Tapes of the 1970s, which led the LAPD to develop a policy against spying on citizens; Eulia Love's death in 1979 from an officer's gun, and the Watts riots of 1965, which led to the creation of the McCone Commission.

The widespread coverage of the Holliday videotape brought about swift action against Officers Koon, Powell, Wind, and Briseno. On March 6, Rodney King was released from jail due to insufficient evidence. On March 7, Chief Gates announced that the officers involved in the King beating would be prosecuted. The next day, District Attorney Ira Reiner announced that he would seek indictment against the four officers. Additionally, Chief Gates suspended fifteen officers that were present at the scene. On March 11, a grand jury watched the videotape and listened to testimony from King (who later would not testify at the state trial) and others, as District Attorney Terry White sought indictments against Officers Koon, Powell, Wind, and Briseno. White succeeded on March 14.[2]

THE SIMI VALLEY STATE TRIAL

Attorneys for the four officers immediately filed a motion for a change in venue from Los Angeles County. They feared that the publicity of the tape would infect the jury pool and would lead to a biased trial. On

March 16, trial Judge Bernard Kamins denied the defense motion, but his decision was appealed. On July 23, 1991, the California Court of Appeals unanimously granted the change of venue motion. Additionally, Judge Kamins was removed from the case because of bias. The case was reassigned to Judge Stanley Weisburg. On November 22, Weisburg met with all the attorneys to determine an appropriate venue. There were three choices: Ventura County, Orange County, and Alameda County. Alameda would have been ideal for the prosecution, because the majority of population of its largest city, Oakland, is black. On the other hand, Ventura was ideal for the defense due to the predominately white conservative population. However, both Michael Stone (Powell's lawyer) and John Barnett (Briseno's lawyer) voted for Orange County, which seemed to be a fair compromise. Orange County was the preferred site for the trial. Unfortunately, there were no courtrooms available, so Judge Weisburg chose Ventura, because Alameda was "inconvenient and costly" (Cannon, 1997, p. 180).

Even better news came to the defense attorneys with the selection of Simi Valley—the community in which the trial would take place—and with the selection of the jury. The announcement of the transfer to Simi Valley brought about immediate objections from prosecutors as well as the NAACP. Their fear was that an all-white panel, which would favor police officers, would hear the case ("Town, Too, Feels Eyes of Nation," 1992). The town was the epitome of white conservatism, with only 1.5 percent of the city's black population residing there. Additionally, there is a large contingent of law enforcement officers that live in the community as well as in the neighboring community of Thousand Oaks.

Jury selection began on February 5, 1992, and it was understood by both sides that the jury's composition would be critical to the outcome of the trial. The jury pool consisted of 260 people (almost all of which had seen the Holliday video), including only six blacks, five of whom were uninterested in serving in a community they felt hostility from on a daily basis. Stone, Powell's defense attorney, used a peremptory challenge to strike the only black who was willing to serve as a juror. District Attorney White stated that he "remember[ed] thinking as we were rating these jurors that we were going to lose this case" (Cannon, 1997, p. 187). On March 2, 1992, the jury was selected and consisted of six males and six females, ten whites, one Hispanic, and one Filipino-American.

Unfortunately, the media failed to report the significance of the jury's composition. The media stated that there were no blacks on the jury but that was all that was mentioned about the jury. There was never any analysis of the pro-law enforcement jury, and the significance that it could play in the outcome. Black community leaders, who closely watched the case, knew that the jury was going to affect the outcome in a way in which the public was unprepared for. It was predicted that riots, like the Watts riots of 1965, would most surely happen again.

The trial began on March 5, 1992, with Chief District Attorney White's opening statement. He showed the Holliday video in its entirety—close to three minutes—not just the small segments that had been aired on various news networks (Owens and Browning, 1994). Over the course of the trial, the jurors would see the video numerous times, and the video was broken down frame by frame.

Opening statements by the four defense attorneys revealed different defense strategies. Darryl Mounger, Koon's attorney, was the first to open. Sergeant Koon was faced with the most numerous charges, including assault with a deadly weapon, assault under color of authority, filing a false police report, and accessory after the fact to a felony (Koon and Deitz, 1992). The main aspect of Mounger's opening statement was that King was actually in control of the beating—not Koon. He argued that King, at any time, could have chosen to follow orders, but he had failed to do so. Stone, Powell's attorney, also took the same direction. Officer Powell was charged with assault with a deadly weapon with great bodily enhancement, assault under color of authority with great bodily enhancement, and filing a false report (Koon and Deitz, 1992). Stone had the most difficult case because Powell was the one in the video shown applying the most beatings to King. Paul DePasquale, Wind's attorney, used inexperience as a defense: Wind had only been with the LAPD for four months, and he had no experience dealing with suspects who are under the influence of PCP. Wind was a police officer in Kansas for seven years before transferring to Los Angeles. The attorney for Officer Briseno, John Barnett, focused on Officer Powell's excessive behavior and how Briseno was the only officer shown to intercede in the beating. Both officers Wind and Briseno were charged with assault with a deadly weapon and assault under color of authority (Koon and Deitz, 1992, pp. 120–121).

The first two witnesses called for the prosecution were George Holliday and Bryant Allen. Holliday was the first witness, and he basically testified that he had shot the video. Additionally, it was a chance for the prosecution to show the videotape once again. Allen was called next, but he had helped the defense more than the prosecution. He had trouble understanding the questions and had not witnessed the beating because he was handcuffed at the time. When the defense cross-examined him about the chase, Allen said that King was acting "strange" and not listening to Allen's pleas to stop.

The next day, Melanie Singer was called to the stand. She was the prosecutor's star witness because King was not going to testify due to his mental state at the time of the incident (drunk and badly beaten). Additionally, King's attorneys had thought that he had suffered enough and should not have to be retraumatized by testifying. Singer claimed the blow to King's head caused a laceration the length of his ear to his chin but that laceration did not appear in any of the photos taken of King after the incident. Her testimony was also diminished when she claimed that Powell struck King four or five more times in the head after the first blow, which did not appear on the videotape.

The media had been present for the first two days of trial. Daily news conferences were being conducted during the lunch hour, and after the day ended, the prosecution and defense summed up their sides for the media. Judge Weisburg did not like the idea of trying the case in the media, so he banned the news conferences. Unfortunately, this led inevitably to misleading coverage of the case on the media's behalf.

Timothy Singer was also called to the stand, but his testimony focused around the blow to King's head and how it is against CHP policy to strike the head. Subsequent testimony consisted of the doctors who treated King to explain the extent of his injuries, but testimony from the doctors revealed that it was inconclusive on telling how the injuries were sustained.

Prosecutors next focused on Powell's callousness with the King incident and with prior incidents. They were essentially attacking his character. Chief White called two emergency room nurses that had treated King, Carol Edwards and Lawrence Davis, who testified about a conversation that took place between King and Powell. Edwards claimed that Powell said, "we played a little hard ball tonight . . . we won and you lost" (Alter and Palumbo, 1992). Davis also said he heard a similar conversation about "playing a game" and also added that Powell said, "we hit quite a few home runs" (Alter and Palumbo, 1992). On cross-examination, Stone suggested that perhaps they had heard another officer having the conversation with King. The prosecution rested their case on March 17.

The first witness for the defense was Catherine Bosak, a paramedic with the Los Angeles Fire Department. She was the first to attend to King's injuries, and she testified that they were minor, including the broken cheekbone. The next witness was LAPD Officer Susan Clemmer, who was at the scene shortly after the incident ended. She also accompanied Officer Wind and King in the ambulance. She said that King repeatedly laughed, spit blood, and said "fuck you" as he lay handcuffed on the ground. He continued spitting blood on her in the ambulance. She said King appeared to be alert but was acting in a bizarre manner. The last witness to be called before the defendants was LAPD Officer David Love, the only black officer present for the incident. Love testified that he arrived to see taser wires in King, and he believed that the force may have been excessive. There were some discrepancies, however, between his grand jury testimony and his state trial testimony. Love concluded that the video had influenced his memory of the event and created details that he had not originally seen during the event.

Koon was the first of the defendants to take the stand. Wind and DePasquale, his attorney, had decided two days before he was scheduled to take the stand that he would not because much of the trial had not focused on Wind's behavior. Sergeant Koon provided strong testimony. In addition to explaining step by step the incident, which he took full responsibility for, he explained the LAPD's policy on escalating use of force. The one contrary piece of testimony was Koon's belief that Powell had not hit King in the face but that as King went to the ground he fell on his face. Koon repeated that the use of force applied the early morning of March 3, 1991, on Rodney King was appropriate and controlled. His concern for escalation came through in his objection to Melanie Singer bringing a gun into the situation, as well as his adamant testimony that he would not have drawn a weapon but would have instead applied a choke hold himself if taking the last step of the use of force chart (level 6, use of deadly force) had been necessary. As of 1982, choke holds were not approved of by the LAPD.

Veteran LAPD officer Sergeant Charles Duke provided the next testimony. Duke demonstrated in a frame-by-frame analysis how Koon properly escalated the use of force. He said that all of the fifty-six swings were justified and were appropriate within policies and procedures. Additionally, former LAPD Captain Robert Michael took the stand after Duke, and he testified about the proper uses of escalation and de-escalation techniques that were employed at the scene. He stated that the "officers were following the rules" based on the suspect's behavior. District Attorney White was unable to shake either witness.

Next to testify were Officers Powell and Briseno, both of whom gave some leverage to the prosecution, but not enough to win the case. Powell's testimony was plagued with a number of contradictions. At first, Powell stated that he had no time to react when King was charging at him and was not able to swing. However, after more questioning from his lawyer, Powell stated that, "I didn't have time to react I was starting to swing" (Alter and Palumbo, 1992). It was unclear if Powell was in the process of swinging or if King just "fell" into the baton. Especially troubling was Powell's testimony during cross-examination by White. Earlier in the evening, Powell had gone out on a call to a disturbance at a black household, and afterwards, he had typed into his on-board computer in his patrol car that "it was right out of *Gorillas in the Mist*" (Alter and Palumbo, 1992).

White: Okay, now this call that involved these [blacks] was in a jungle?
Powell: In what?
White: A jungle.
Powell: No.
White: Was it at the zoo?
Powell: No.
White: Were there any gorillas around?
Powell: I didn't see any . . .
White: But you referred to that call as right out of Gorillas in the Mist?
Powell: Yes . . .
White: Okay . . . did you see anything regarding Gorillas in the Mist while you were at that location?
Powell: Did I see anything?
White: Yes.
Powell: No.

Additionally during cross-examination, Powell first said that he was doing what Koon had told him to do, but he later said, "everybody out there was responsible for their own actions" (Alter and Palumbo, 1992).

Officer Briseno also helped the prosecution more than the defense. From his lawyer's opening statement, it was clear that Briseno was not in the same mind-set as his fellow officers, or so he would convey it that way. He testified that he thought Powell "was out of control" and pointed out that in one part of the tape he tried to stop Powell from swinging his baton (although at that time Koon had just fired a taser and was thought to be warning Powell to not touch King). He stated, "Every time he moved, they hit him. . . . I didn't understand" (Alter and Palumbo, 1992). The only use of force shown on the video by Briseno is a single stomp to the shoulder area of King. Briseno testified that he was not trying to hurt or punish King, but he was trying to help King by pushing him down so he would stop moving. It was also interesting that Briseno had delivered the stomp when no batons are being swung, and while Powell had been getting ready to handcuff King under the assumption that it was safe to do so. Unfortunately, Briseno's plan backfired because the force of the kick caused King to move and gave Officers Powell and Wind a signal that he needed more baton blows and that King was still dangerous.

District Attorney White called LAPD Commander Michael Bostic, who was also head of the use of force review board, as part of his rebuttal. Bostic testified about the use of escalation and de-escalation just as Captain Robert Michael, and he dissected the videotape for the jurors. Instead of justifying all use of force, Bostic testified that the force applied after Briseno stomped King was excessive and should have never been applied. After cross-examination, it was revealed that Bostic had no field experience with the use of force, and he had never had to apply the techniques while out in the field.

Closing arguments were similar to the opening arguments, with the exception of White's. District Attorney White delivered a much more passionate closing, where at one point he walked over to Powell and stuck his finger in his face exclaiming, "This is the man . . . and look at him. This man laughed" (Alter and Palumbo, 1992). After an objection from Stone, Judge Weisburg ordered White back to his podium.

After thirty-five days of testimony from fifty-four witnesses, the jury began deliberations. They deliberated for seven days, with the main focus being on Powell. To the public, who had only gotten tiny glimpses of what was going on inside the courtroom but they knew what they had seen on the video, it was an open and shut case. The officers were guilty. At 3:15 p.m. on April 29, 1992, the clerk announced the jury's verdicts. The defendants were found not guilty on all charges except for one: the jury was hung on Officer Powell's charge of assault with a deadly weapon. The jury did not think that the prosecution proved beyond a reasonable doubt that the officers were criminal. The anger generated by the verdict was intense.

THE RIOTS

About a year after the media "wallpapered"[3] the Holliday videotape into various media for the world to see, a television news helicopter would film another brutal incident that would symbolize the riots of South Central Los Angeles in 1992. At 6:46 p.m., at the intersection of Normandie and Florence, a trucker driver by the name of Reginald Denny was pulled from his eighteen-wheeler onto the street by a group of black men. Henry Watson held Denny's head down with his foot as another man kicked him in his stomach. Another man hurled a piece of medical equipment that had been taken from a looted vehicle just minutes before at Denny's head and then hit him three times with a claw hammer. The most vicious attack came from Damian Williams. Williams had smashed a block of concrete on Denny's head and then proceeded to do a victory dance around a now unconscious Denny. Anthony Brown spit on Denny as he walked away with Williams. As Denny lay helpless in the street, various other men hurled liquor bottles at him, and a local drug user rummaged through his pockets. Eventually, two local residents who were watching what was happening came to Denny's rescue. Denny made it to the hospital just in time to save his life (Coffey, 1992).

The brutal beating of Denny was publicized like the King video, and it was usually shown in conjunction with the Holliday video. Many commentators and activists drew parallels between the incidents, but the assailants should not be equated. King had refused to listen to police commands after a high-speed chase, and many attempts were made to take King into custody before force was applied. Denny was a victim and did nothing to deserve the injuries (which were more severe than King's) that were inflicted by some local gang members.

Before the beating of Reginald Denny, there was an incident that occurred sixty-two minutes after the verdicts were announced and can be considered the official beginning of the riots. Five black male youths entered a Korean-owned liquor and deli store at Florence and Dalton Avenues; each took bottles of malt liquor. The son of the store owner had tried to prevent them from taking the booze, and one of the men smashed a bottle on his head, while two others shattered the store's front windows with their bottles. One of the youths shouted, "This is for Rodney King!" (Cannon, 1997, p. 281).

Two hours after watching the verdicts from his office, Mayor Bradley appeared on television and described the verdicts as "senseless." He stated, "I was speechless when I heard the verdict. Today the jury told the world that what we saw with our own eyes is not a crime" (Coffey, 1992, p. 45). He continued by saying, "today the system failed us" (Mydans, 1992, p. 7). The mayor's words gave a city that was succumbing to violence justification. Bradley was speaking on behalf of those frustrated with months of tension since the Holliday videotape aired, and he had contributed to the mayhem that would persist over the course of the next five days.

Police Chief Gates, who was a field commander during the Watts riots, stated that the LAPD would be ready if it happened again and "would stop it the first night" (Cannon, 1997, p. 263). But, Gates was not prepared. The LAPD was preoccupied with Gates's pending retirement in June, and by the time the riots had begun, it was apparent to news crews flying over head and to patrol officers within the area that there was not enough manpower to control what was happening. Street violence, looting, and fires broke out all over South Central Los Angeles. No one was safe from rioters. The first shooting occurred at 8:15 p.m., at a Korean-owned swap meet at the corner of Vernon and Vermont. Louis Watson Fleming was helping two elderly women when he was hit in the head by a bullet.

By 9 p.m., every police officer in the city had been ordered to report for duty, and Mayor Bradley had declared a local state of emergency and ordered a city-wide curfew. Within minutes, Governor Pete Wilson called on the National Guard to activate 2,000 reservists. Although extra manpower was called in, immobilization took longer than expected. By midnight, 1,790 officers had reached their command posts and were still awaiting orders on what to do (Cannon, 1997). Additionally, the first contingent of the National Guard was not deployed on the streets until mid-afternoon the next day

(Reinhold, 1992). Due to the lack of a police force, many fires were left un-attended because there were not enough fire engines, and members of the fire department were being attacked by rioters. There were barely enough officers able to control an attempted overturn of the Parker Center—police headquarters in downtown Los Angeles.

By late afternoon on May 1, forty-eight hours after the verdict was an-nounced, thirty-eight people were dead. Of these, fifteen were black. The media reported that 1,419 people were injured, 4,000 had been arrested, and the fire department had responded to 3,767 calls associated with riot-related fires (Koon and Deitz, 1992). Also on this day, Rodney King addressed the city, surrounded by 100 reporters, begging for peace saying his infamous words, "Why can't we all just get along?"

Monday, May 4, at 5:15 p.m. signaled the end of the riots when Mayor Bradley lifted the city-wide curfew. Once the riots had ended, fifty-four people had been killed, including twenty-six blacks. This was the biggest death toll in an American civil disturbance since 1863. Over 2,000 people, including sixty firemen, had been injured. Over $900 million in property damage was done from looting and fires, including 862 incinerated buildings and homes. In all, over 7,000 people were arrested. The Los Angeles riots of 1992 had earned the title of the "worst riots of the century" (Coffey, 1992, p. 49).

During the rioting, and not long after the verdicts were announced, President Bush and Attorney General William Barr began the process of bringing federal charges against the four LAPD police officers. In a televised address to the nation on May 1, President Bush announced that he had begun the process of filing charges against the officers for violating Rodney King's civil rights to bring some calm to a disturbed public. On August 4, the grand jury returned indictments against the four officers. Officers Powell, Wind, and Briseno were charged with violating King's Fourth Amendment protection against unreasonable arrest, and Sergeant Koon was charged with violating King's Fourteenth Amendment rights for failing to restrain his officers.

THE FEDERAL CIVIL RIGHTS TRIAL

The decision to try the four officers in federal court after their acquittal in state court brought large debate among the public, media, and courts on the issue of double jeopardy. The Fifth Amendment of the U.S. Constitution protects citizens from double jeopardy, which is protection from being tried for the same offense twice (Woods, 1994). Many people and the media thought that the federal trial was in violation of the officers' Fifth Amendment rights. Additionally, a Gallup poll found that 30 percent of state judges and

10 percent of federal judges thought the second trial constituted double jeopardy (Hengstler, 1993). However, the majority of the judges polled clearly thought that the federal trial was not a violation of the double jeopardy because of the dual sovereignty expectation based on an earlier court decision, *United States v. Koon, Powell, Wind, and Briseno*. The Court decided that the state and federal government are separate bodies, and a single offense can violate the sovereignties of both bodies. Therefore, the four officers could be tried for their offense where the act occurred (state) and in federal court because the act is considered a violation against the United States (King's civil rights).

The U.S. Department of Justice assembled a "dream team" of four prosecutors to try the case. Steven Clymer would serve as lead prosecutor. At the time, he was considered to be the best trial lawyer in the U.S. Attorney's Office in Los Angeles. Jury selection began on February 3, 1993, in District Judge John Davies's courtroom. Judge Davies sent out "invitations" to 6,000 residents of seven different counties in Southern California. He was vague in his description of the case, and only about 380 responded. Of those, only 333 actually showed up on the first day of jury selection. Each juror was given an extensive questionnaire asking about their attitudes on a variety of topics, including police misconduct and interracial marriages (Cannon, 1997). Unlike the Simi Valley jury, the federal jury was racially mixed, including two blacks. The defense had attempted to remove one black juror, because she was overheard criticizing the treatment of the defense during their questioning of other potential black jurors. Judge Davies denied the motion to remove her from the jury. Although it was a media frenzy outside the court house, no media were allowed in the courtroom, which is typical of federal trials.

The prosecution team was prepared to win this trial. Clymer made sure to exclude witnesses he thought were weak during the state trial, and he brought in a number of witnesses that proved to be more capable. The first witnesses to be called were two civilian witnesses, Dorothy Gibson and Robert Hill, who lived in the same apartment complex as George Holliday. Upon cross-examination of Gibson, defense attorneys found that there were discrepancies between what she told investigators and her testimony, which led the attorneys to conclude that the videotape had influenced what she remembered. Other civilian witnesses were brought in to make the case more human to the jury.

Additionally, the prosecution brought in a number of new experts on the use of force and medical examiners. Most important of the experts was LAPD Sergeant Mark Conta. Conta had been brought in to testify about the proper use of force and to evaluate the videotape. Conta excelled where

Commander Bostic failed—he had seventeen years of experience as a patrol officer. As Conta walked the jury though the videotape, he stated that the defendants had acted in a lawful manner until King was lying on the ground. According to LAPD policy, it was unlawful to strike a man who was on the ground. He also stated that Sergeant Koon was violating policy because he had failed to intervene. Upon cross-examination, the defense was able to refute some of Conta's testimony because all but Wind had not received the same academy training that was currently in place.

The next two witnesses would testify about King's injuries. Dr. Charles Aronburg, an ophthalmologist who treated King, took the stand first. He described King as suffering from a broken right cheekbone, damage to the eye socket, and extensive sinus damage. Aronburg also concluded, through bad cross-examination, that King's injuries were caused by blows to the head from batons. The second witness, Dr. Stanley Cohn, a neurologist who also examined King after the beating, testified that he found evidence of memory loss, which was key to the prosecution's case. Any contradictory testimony provided by King would be supported by medical evidence.

The most important testimony came from King himself. More media showed up on March 9, 1993, than any other day of the trial. When King took the stand, he was able to erase the images of a dangerous and erratic criminal that the defense had painted in the minds of the Simi Valley jurors. On the stand, King was seen not as a liar, but as a man who was either too drunk or confused to remember the events of the night of March 3, 1991. In the Simi Valley trial, the defendants had claimed they were in fear; however, now King had the opportunity to show the jurors that he feared for his life. King also introduced the issue of race, where it had not been addressed at Simi Valley. He testified that the officers were chanting at him as they were beating him, calling him either "killer" or "nigger" (Cannon, 1997, p. 426). When questioned which name he thought he was being called, he simply stated he was unsure. When defense attorney Stone was asked about King's testimony, he stated, "He looked good. He was very mild-mannered and polite and thoughtful. All of these things spell credibility to me" (Mydans, 1993, p. A1).

The defense strategy was not nearly as effective during this trial. Two different attorneys, Ira Salzman and Harland Braun, represented Koon and Briseno, respectively. Once again the defense relied on Koon as their key witness, but, unlike the first trial, Koon displayed emotion. Some of the jurors thought that Koon came off as "cocky" but also respectable for consistently standing by what he did. Powell, still represented by Stone, chose not to testify; he had just finished his retrial for the state charge of assault with a deadly weapon and was exhausted. To compensate for Powell not testifying, Stone focused on King's facial injuries and called Carley Ward, a biomedical engineer, to testify on the King's injuries. She concluded that the injuries were caused by a fall. The defense also made the mistake of recalling Melanie Singer to the stand. Singer had already been humiliated in the first trial and made even more noticeable contradictions than before. Braun did not fair so well either. After examining the evidence, he pushed for a unified defense among the officers. He thought it best to minimize the differences between the officers' testimonies. Briseno decided not to testify, so Clymer asked the court if they could show Briseno's testimony at Simi Valley. Judge Davies granted their request. Of course this did not favor well, as Briseno's testimony before was clearly not unified with the other officers. By this point, there was little hope for the defense.

On April 10, 1993, the jury began deliberations. Deliberations were later reported to have been highly stressful, with three of the jurors heavily leaning toward convictions. Arguing ensued and some name-calling took place. After six days of deliberation, the jury came back with its verdicts. Judge Davies decided to postpone the announcement of the verdicts until the morning, in the event they would produce a similar reaction to the verdicts of Simi Valley. At 7 a.m., the next day, the clerk read the verdicts. The jury acquitted Wind and Briseno but found Koon and Powell guilty. Although it was not a sweeping victory for the public, it was enough to keep the streets of Los Angeles quiet.

JUDGMENT

On August 4, 1993, Judge Davies sentenced Powell and Koon to thirty months in a federal correctional camp. Shortly after, the U.S. Department of Justice announced that the sentence was too light and that it would appeal the sentence. The case was sent to the Ninth Circuit Court of Appeals, and the court ruled that the sentences by Judge Davies were too lenient and sent the case back for resentencing. On September 28, 1995, the U.S. Supreme Court decided to hear Koon and Powell's appeal of the Ninth Circuit Court of Appeal's decision of sending the case back to Judge Davies. On June 13, 1996, the U.S. Supreme Court reversed the Ninth Circuit Court's decision and upheld the sentences of Judge Davies on most points, with the exception of two errors. Finally, on September 26, 1996, Judge Davies refused to extend the thirty-month sentence, which effectively ended the case (Cannon, 1997).

In October 1993, Koon and Powell began serving their sentences in separate federal work camps. On October 16, 1995, Koon was moved to the Rubidoux halfway house, where he served the rest of his time. During the Thanksgiving holiday, an armed black man broke into the halfway house and demanded to see Koon. He blatantly stated that he was going to kill Koon, but fortunately Koon was home for the holiday. The armed man was later gunned down in a police shoot-out (Deitz, 1996). By the time their federal case was settled, Koon and Powell had already been released from serving their sentences in December 1995.

CONCLUSION

The trials discussed were not the only two Rodney King was involved in. King also filed two civil suits—one against the City of Los Angeles and another against Officers Koon, Powell, Briseno, and Wind. He won a settlement from his first suit against the City of Los Angeles on April 19, 1994. The jury awarded King $3.8.million in damages. Shortly after, on April 22, 1994, a civil suit before Judge Davies against the officers began. King asked for $15 million in damages, but the jury awarded King no monetary compensation in damages on June 1, 1994.

Rodney King has not been able to escape the press and will continue to make headlines as long as he maintains interactions with the police force. After the incident of March 3, 1991, King has interacted with the police on at least nine different occasions. He has had three violations for driving under the influence (DUI) of alcohol and three incidents involving domestic assault. For most of the incidents, charges were reduced or he was acquitted. One of his latest involvements with law enforcement involved his arrest for indecent exposure and the use of PCP (Cannon, 1997).

As mentioned previously, the King incident changed the way police departments across the United States regarded their police forces, particular in terms of police reform. Prevalence in use of force had not been measured until after the King incident, and now many police departments collect information on incidents involving use of force. Additionally, in 1996 both the Bureau of Justice Statistics and International Association of Chiefs of Police started an ongoing nationwide collection of data on use of force (Adams et al., 1999).

Specifically for Los Angeles, criticisms of the LAPD were substantial. In response to the publicity and scandal surrounding the beating of King, Mayor Bradley developed the Christopher Commission (Independent Commission on the Los Angeles Police Department, 1991). Warren Christopher, senior staff member of the McCone Commission, was to lead the investigation into the causes and contributions of the use of excessive force The Christopher Commission found that there were a number of officers who continuously misused force and ignored the LAPD's written policies and guidelines regarding use of force. In addition, these "problem" officers were well known throughout the department (Independent Commission on the Los Angeles Police Department, 1991). Some of the suggested reforms by the Christopher Commission and the Kolts Commission (which reviewed Los Angeles Sheriff's Department) have become law (Bandes, 1999). A connection between the findings of misconduct within the LAPD to other police departments was highlighted in the media, which prompted various types of reform and prevention strategies across the United States. Changes to federal law include the 1994 Violent Crime Control and Law Enforcement Act, which gave the Justice Department's Civil Rights Division authority to investigate local law enforcement agencies and bring forth civil action if a pattern of police misconduct was established. At least eleven cities have had action brought against them (Anderson, 2003).

One popular prevention measure was the development of what is now known as the "early warning system."[4] Police departments are able to monitor—through civilian and internal complaints—use of force reports and other disciplinary measures such as officer conduct. Officers, who exhibit warning signs by exceeding limits set by the disciplinary measures, can be targeted for various interventions before their behavior becomes out of control. These systems have been implemented in many police departments nationwide.

The Holliday videotape, the Denny news coverage, Rodney King, and the officers involved will be forever embedded within the media. The media fueled the events surrounding this case and have impacted society in ways that people never imagined. The impact the case had on the future of policing, race relations, the American public, and the courts was immense, and it will forever remain a prime example of police brutality tried through the media and society at large.

NOTES

1. The chronology of events was abstracted from media and trial reports.

2. Sequence of events taken from various sources but also found in Cannon (1997).

3. CNN executive vice president Ed Turner stated, "Television used the [Holliday] videotape like wallpaper" (Cannon, 1997, p. 21).

4. For further information see Walker, Alpert, and Kenney (2000).

REFERENCES

Adams, K., Alpert, G. P., Dunham, R. G., Garner, J. H., Greenfeld, L. A., Henriquez, M. A., et al. (1999, October). *Use of force by police: Overview of national and local data* (NCJ 176330). Washington, DC: National Institute of Justice and Bureau of Justice Statistics.

Alpert, G. P., Smith, W. C., and Watters, D. (1992). Law enforcement: Implications of the Rodney King beating. *Criminal Law Bulletin, 28,* 469–478.

Alter, J. (1992, May 11). TV and the "firebell." *Newsweek, 119,* 43.

Alter, J. (Senior Producer), and Palumbo, D. (Director). (1992). *The "Rodney King" Case: What the jury saw in California v. Powell* [Television Broadcast]. Los Angeles: Courtroom Television Network.

Anderson, D. C. (2003). *Managed force: Civilian police experts pursue the nitty-gritty of reform, in the patrol car and on the street* (Ford Foundation Report). Retrieved October 30, 2003, from http://www.fordfound.org/publications/ff_report/view_ff_report_detail.cfm?report_index=452

Bandes, S. (1999). Patterns of injustice: Police brutality in the courts. *Buffalo Law Review, 47,* 1275–1341.

Cannon, L. (1997). *Official negligence: How Rodney King and the riots changed Los Angeles and the LAPD.* New York: Times Books.

Coffey, S., III. (1992). *Understanding the riots: Los Angeles before and after the Rodney King case.* Los Angeles: Los Angeles Times.

Deitz, R. (1996). *Willful injustice: A post-O.J. look at Rodney King, American justice, and trial by race.* Washington, DC: Regnery Gateway.

Hengstler, G. A. (1993, August). How judges view retrial of L.A. cops. *ABA Journal, 79,* 70–72.

Independent Commission on the Los Angeles Police Department. (1991, July). *Report of the Independent Commission on the Los Angeles Police Department.* Los Angeles: Author.

Jacobs, R. (1996). Civil society and crisis: Culture, discourse, and the Rodney King beating. *The American Journal of Sociology, 101,* 1238–1272.

Koon, S., and Deitz, R. (1992). *Presumed guilty: The tragedy of the Rodney King affair.* Washington, DC: Regnery Gateway.

Mydans, S. (1992, April 30). The police verdict; Los Angeles policemen acquitted in taped beating [Electronic version]. *New York Times,* A1.

Mydans, S. (1993, March 10). Rodney King testifies on beating: 'I was just trying to stay alive' [Electronic version]. *New York Times,* A1.

Owens, T., and Browning, R. (1994). *Lying eyes: The truth behind the corruption and brutality of the LAPD and the beating of Rodney King.* New York: Thunder's Mouth Press.

Reinhold, R. (1992, May 1). Riots in Los Angeles: The blue line; Surprised, police react slowly as violence spreads [Electronic version]. *New York Times,* A1.

Simi Valley Journal. (1992, February 22). Town, too, feels eyes of nation for a trial [Electronic version]. *New York Times.*

Skolnick, J. H., and Fyfe, J. J. (1994). *Above the Law: Police and the excessive use of force.* New York: The Free Press.

United States v. Koon, Powell, Wind, and Briseno, 833 F.Supp. 769 (C.D. Cal. 1993).

Walker, S., Alpert, G. P., and Kenney, D. J. (2000). *Responding to the problem police officer: A national study of early warning systems, final report* (NCJ 184510). Washington, DC: U.S. Department of Justice.

Woods, C. G. (1994, Fall). The dual sovereignty exception to double jeopardy: An unnecessary loophole. *University of Baltimore Law Review, 24,* 177–210.

10

The Kidnapping and Murder of Polly Klaas: An Atypical Crime Yielding Controversial Reforms

Amy Kearns

On October 1, 1993, Polly Klaas, a twelve-year-old seventh grader at Petaluma Junior High School in Petaluma, California, decided on the spur of the moment to have a Friday night slumber party. She invited three friends to join her. One of the girls was sick and could not make the sleepover, but Gillian Pelham and Kate McLean, also seventh graders at Petaluma Junior High, joined Klaas for the familiar slumber party ritual of games, giggling, and staying up late. However, on this night in Petaluma there would be no traditional slumber party. Klaas's mother, Eve Nichol, checked on the three friends around 10 p.m., as she readied for bed. Klaas shared a bedroom with her younger half-sister, six-year-old Annie Nichol, so their mother took Annie to bed with her to give the older girls some privacy. Eve Nichol later recounted that she left the girls playing a game, and she fell asleep just a room away to the sound of giggling. It would be the last time Nichol would ever see her daughter. Less than an hour after she drifted to sleep, Pelham and McLean awakened her, and Nichol's whole world changed. Klaas was gone, and what was left was the chilling story told by her two friends.

The kidnapping and murder of Polly Klaas was the embodiment of a "celebrated" case, an atypical crime that deeply impacts the public (Chermak, 2002). Stranger abduction and murder is the most frightening type of crime and also the least likely to occur. The Office of Juvenile Justice and Delinquency Prevention performs national studies to determine the number of and circumstances surrounding children who are reported missing in the United States. Because the Klaas abduction and murder occurred in 1993—after the first and before the second such study—the chapter provides estimates from both studies in an attempt to place stranger perpetrated abduction and murder in perspective.

In 1988, the First National Incidence Studies of Missing, Abducted, Runaway, and Thrownaway Children (NISMART) estimated that 200 to 300 missing children each year were victims of stereotypical stranger kidnappings (Finkelhor, Hotaling, and Sedlak, 1990). A stereotypical kidnapping is defined as an incident in which a child is abducted by a stranger and taken overnight, transported more than fifty miles, held for ransom, or killed. The second NISMART, which was performed in 1999, found that although 12,100 children were victims of nonfamily abductions in which the incident was reported to the police or a missing children's agency, there were only 115 cases of stereotypical stranger kidnappings such as what happened to Polly Klaas. Of those stereotypical stranger abductions, children were murdered 40 percent of the time, and an additional 4 percent were never found. Sexual assault is a factor in about half of stereotypical stranger abductions, as well as in nonfamily abductions (Finkelhor, Hammer, and Sedlak, 2002).

Forty-eight percent of missing children reported to authorities in 1999 were runaways or thrownaways, and 43 percent of children reported missing to authorities were classified as "benign missing" or missing as a result of such things as miscommunication with their parents (Sedlak, Finkelhor, Hammer, and Schulz, 2002).[1] Because the 12,100 nonfamily abductions accounted for only 2 percent of missing children known to authorities and only 115 of those abductions fit the stereotypical kidnapping profile, stereotypical kidnappings capture the public's attention because they are out of the ordinary. Stereotypes are, by nature, oversimplified images, and the stereotypical image of child abduction, which is held by many, is not a realistic representation of the dangers that children face.

Klaas's kidnapping was stereotypical: an innocent victim, a child playing in her bedroom with two friends, snatched away by a stranger in the night—a repeat criminal, who was out on parole at the time—with her mother sleeping just one room away. Her kidnapping contained every necessary ingredient for a notorious crime. For the public, Klaas was the embodiment of the chaste victim, and her killer was the epitome of the wicked—the most striking of crime genre. The abduction, and subsequent revelation of the murder of Klaas, struck deep into the hearts of a nation, tapping into the most latent fears about crime and the most salient streams of anger toward criminals. The aftermath of Klaas's murder changed the way law enforcement responded to missing children, heightened the role of the media in such cases, catalyzed California's "Three Strikes and You're Out" initiative, and turned Klaas into a national symbol for politicized crime and justice debates.

THE "BOGEYMAN"

On the night of October 1, 1993, a man—later identified to be 39-year-old Richard Allen Davis—entered Klaas's home shortly after Eve and Annie Nichol went to bed, either through the back door or an open window.[2] He carried a satchel that contained a hood and strips of cloth. As the three friends played inside Klaas's bedroom, Davis stood outside her bedroom door. When Klaas opened the door of her bedroom, according to one report, "to move the slumber party to the living room so the girls could spread out their sleeping bags . . . the bogeyman was waiting" (Bortnick, 1995, p. 24). Davis threatened the three girls with a knife, ordered them to lie down, placed hoods over their heads, and tied their hands behind their backs. Davis had cut the straps off Klaas's purse and the cords off a Nintendo game system to help secure the girls. The scene was so surreal that it took the girls several moments to comprehend the gravity of the situation; the girls were so shocked that they were not immediately frightened. When Davis threatened to slit their throats if they made noise, the girls began to realize that what was happening to them was no joke.

Davis asked why so many people were there, and he stated that there were not supposed to be that many people in the house. Davis was also said to not believe the girls when they told him that an adult was sleeping nearby (Bortnick, 1995). He asked which girl lived in the house, and when Klaas identified herself, Davis asked her about what money and jewelry were in the house. Klaas pointed him towards both the jewelry and cash. However, in the end, the only thing Davis took was Klaas, carrying her out of the house as her friends were ordered to count to a thousand. After freeing themselves from the bindings, the girls made their way to Nichol's bedroom. Nichol reported that at first she thought the claim that a big man with a knife had come and taken Klaas away was a joke, but after fully awakening, she saw the face of one of the girls and heard the other whimpering Klaas's name. Nichol called 911.

Nichol's call for help was heard across the country. The search for Klaas and then the discovery of her murder when Davis led authorities to her body sixty-five days after her abduction gripped the town of Petaluma and the nation. The abduction and murder of Klaas set in motion reverberations that are still felt today.

PETALUMA RESPONDS

Petaluma is thirty-two miles north of San Francisco in Sonoma County. In 1993, 45,000 residents called Petaluma—deemed by some the "quintessential American hometown—home. Petaluma's quaintness made it the perfect setting for the 1973 film *American Graffiti*, and its weathering of the 1906 earthquake has made Petaluma's Victorian architecture a prized asset to numerous other films over the years. By all accounts, Petaluma was a quiet, tranquil town until October 1993. Former President Ronald Reagan even used Petaluma to illustrate the essence of "All-American," as the town was the backdrop for his 1984 "Morning in America" presidential campaign commercials. Klaas lived in Petaluma with her mother and little sister on 4th Street. Her mother and father, Marc Klaas, divorced when she was two. Marc Klaas lived in nearby San Francisco, owned a rental car business and maintained a close relationship with his only daughter. Nichol remarried after her divorce from Klaas, but she was separated from her husband and Annie's father, Allen Nichol, at the time of the abduction.

Joining her immediate family and local and federal authorities, over 4,000 volunteers pored themselves into the search for Klaas, bringing not only the community of Petaluma together, but also the nation. The Polly Klaas Center was quickly established by a local print shop owner, Bill Rhodes, who became the zeal behind the efforts to find Klaas by organizing and inspiring the army of volunteers energized by "Polly power" (Bortnick, 1995). Even as the days passed and stress mounted, the volunteers did not give up on finding Klaas. In the sixty-four days between her disappearance and the discovery of her body, 9 million posters and fliers with a picture of Klaas and an FBI sketch by the famed facial identification artist Jeanne Boylan of her kidnapper had been disseminated across the United States. According to one report, local companies donated eight computers that were used to fax 1,000 posters per minute across the country, and the emerging power of the internet was also harnessed to disseminate information about Polly's abduction to the nation (Smolowe and Lafferty, 1993).

Many volunteers spent their days, hours, or even minutes between breaks at their regular jobs printing and disseminating fliers; others manned a bank of telephones taking tips, formed search teams, and raised money for the efforts through bake sales and donations. Actress Winona Ryder, a Petaluma native, offered $200,000 for information leading to Klaas's return, and Ryder drove from Seattle to join in the search for the missing twelve year old. Ryder indicated that she felt a special connection to Klaas—not only because Klaas, like Ryder, attended Petaluma Junior High School—but because Klaas had aspirations of becoming an actress. Ryder dedicated her role in the 1994 film adaptation of *Little Women* to Klaas. The volunteers were consumed by their search for the missing girl, never giving up, and even after her body was found, they kept their purpose through the Polly Klaas Foundation in the hopes of helping other missing children.

On November 19, 1993, Rhodes, who had fueled the energy behind the search for Klaas for weeks, stepped down as head of the volunteer search when a woman named him in a civil suit charging that he molested her in 1971 when she was a child. Reports then surfaced indicating that Rhodes was convicted of indecent exposure in 1968 and acquitted in a separate case of molestation that same year. The circumstances around the molestation charges—four girls, held at knifepoint, eyes covered, molested, and told to count to 200—were similar enough to the Klaas incident to increase friction in Petaluma, even though Rhodes was not a suspect in Klaas's disappearance. Residents of Petaluma were outraged that they had learned about Rhodes's background and the pending civil suit against him through the media rather than the authorities. The residents were less than satisfied with the reason they were given as to why they were not made aware of Rhodes's background and current civil suit given the nature of Klaas's abduction (Spolar, 1993b, p. A3).

With pressure increasing on law enforcement to find Klaas, the revelation that the authorities knew and kept Rhodes's background secret did nothing to ease an already frustrated public. Today, those convicted of crimes can expect their convictions to follow them for the rest of their lives; however, in 1993, the FBI and local authorities were prevented from disclosing Rhodes's past based on California laws that ensured the privacy of criminal backgrounds. Klaas's family and the residents of Petaluma did not, however, forget the energy Rhodes put into the search, and he remained a well-regarded community figure even after his past and the current lawsuit became public knowledge. However, as Bortnick (1995, p. 93) wrote, "Rhodes dramatics only added more spice to the abduction saga. Stress was mounting, fingers were being pointed, and authorities were being blamed for failing to locate the child."

RICHARD ALLEN DAVIS

It is unclear exactly when Davis came to Petaluma. What is known is that his presence on October 1, 1993, when he kidnapped and murdered Klaas, forever changed this sleepy town situated in the heart of the Sonoma Wine Country.[3] Davis was paroled to San Mateo County from the California Men's Colony in San Luis Obispo on July 27, 1993, after serving time on a sixteen-year prison term resulting from a 1985 conviction for kidnapping and robbery. Davis maintained that he had arrived in Petaluma on October 1 in search of his estranged mother. During his time in prison, Davis had learned the sheet metal trade and wanted to locate his mother in hopes that she might assist him with getting the resources he needed to find work in the sheet metal business. According to Davis, he was unable to find his mother in the phone book when he arrived in Petaluma. He then drank two quarts of beer in Wickersham Park, which was located near Klaas's home. While drinking beer in the park, Davis said that he was approached by a man who offered to sell him some marijuana. After declining at first, Davis said that he did buy a joint from the man and smoked it in the park. Davis later claimed that, unbeknownst to him, the joint was laced with PCP, which left him in a drugged state and vulnerable to perpetrating the crime against Klaas while he was not in full control of his facilities.

Witnesses, however, indicated that Davis had been seen in the area throughout the day and placed Davis standing in front of Klaas's home, staring. Furthermore, interviews by the *San Francisco Chronicle* with Petaluma transients and other marginal individuals, shortly after Davis was taken into custody and charged with the murder of Klaas, indicate that Davis did not simply arrive in Petaluma on October 1. Rather, Davis had been a regular in Petaluma since his parole in late July. Those who said they came into contact with Davis in areas that were frequented by the homeless, drunks, transients, and occupants of a local drug house remembered quite clearly their encounters with Davis, and that even among these "fringe" groups, Davis was considered trouble. According to individuals that frequented an area under one of Petaluma's bridges where Davis was said to have come to "party" in September 1993, Davis would get drunk and rowdy, often singing Creedence Clearwater Revival's "Bad Moon Risin'." One man who recalled Davis's visits under the bridge said, "We knew he was an ex-con, but a lot of us down here are ex-cons so nobody cared. We just didn't like him. He was an ass" (Fagan, 1998, p. 5). Another respondent said that Davis was eventually chased off from the area by his fellow transients (Fagan, 1998, p. 5).

Davis had spent most of his life on the margins, showing early signs of trouble. He had a history of setting cats on fire, and dogs were his target to practice knife-throwing (Enders, 1993). His official criminal record indicated that his crimes had become increasingly serious. Although Davis had many prior run-ins with the criminal justice system for drunkenness, trespassing, and burglary, his first prison sentence was in 1974 for burglary. In 1977 he was given a sentence of one to twenty-five years for kidnapping; in 1978 he was sentenced six months to life for an assault with a deadly weapon; and in 1985 he was sentenced to sixteen years for robbery, kidnapping, and assault.

At the time of Klaas's murder, Davis was on parole for the 1985 conviction of robbery, kidnapping, and assault.

After Davis was charged with the murder of Klaas, authorities began taking a closer look at a 1973 suicide of a friend of Davis's. Marlene Voris was eighteen years old when she died of a gunshot wound to the head. According to the investigation that ruled Voris's death a suicide, Voris killed herself at the end of a party celebrating her acceptance into the U.S. Navy. Those attending the party, including Davis, all left at the same time, but Davis broke away from the group and returned to Voris's house. Moments later, a gunshot was heard, and Voris was dead. Suicide notes found by investigators seem to have sealed the determination that the gunshot wound was self-inflicted, but friends had long had their suspicions that Davis killed Voris. Although authorities agreed even after reviewing the case that Voris did commit suicide, her death, which Davis said was nearly in his presence, had a profound impact on him. The week after her death Davis embarked on a crime spree, subsequent to which he served his first time in incarceration as an adult. In the years following Voris's death, Davis told psychiatrists at times that he heard her voice comforting him (Martin and Hoover, 1993).

LAW ENFORCEMENT IN BOLD RELIEF

There is nothing like a sensational, emotion-filled case such as the kidnapping and murder of Klaas to bring every movement of law enforcement into bold relief.[4] One of the most haunting incidents of the case—the one that law enforcement will be most remembered for in regard to the kidnapping and murder of Klaas—occurred just an hour after Klaas's abduction when Sonoma County Sheriff's Department Deputy Thomas Howard and his partner, Michael David Rankin, were called to rural Pythian Road the night of October 1, 1993, in response to a trespasser by property owner Dana Jaffe. Jaffe had arrived home shortly after 11 p.m. that night, and she talked briefly with her babysitter, Shannon Lynch, who had left Jaffe's shortly before midnight. Sometime between Jaffe's arrival home and Lynch's exit, Davis rolled through Jaffe's gate and onto his property, getting his 1979 white Ford Pinto stuck in a ditch just off Jaffe's driveway. As Lynch drove down the driveway, she noticed the strange car. With her doors locked and window cracked, she questioned Davis, who told her that his car was stuck. Lynch was suspicious of Davis, and she drove to a nearby payphone where she called Jaffe to warn her of a stranger on her property.

Jaffe—who was readying her daughter and herself for bed—grabbed a bat and drove down the driveway with her daughter. As she passed the Pinto, Davis was nowhere in sight. Jaffe continued on down the road until she also found a payphone. There she called the Sonoma County Sheriff's Department to report the trespasser. Jaffe waited on Pythian Road until Howard and Rankin arrived, and she then led the deputies through the gate and to the Pinto. There, they found Davis with the Pinto. He said that he had accidentally driven onto Jaffe's property and gotten stuck. Rather than asking that Davis be arrested for trespassing (there were "no trespassing" signs posted at the gate through which Davis entered), Jaffe told Howard and Rankin that she simply wanted Davis off her property. She then continued up the driveway to her home, leaving Howard and Rankin to deal with Davis. Although Klaas had been reported missing by this time, Howard and Rankin were unaware of it because an alert had not been broadcast on their radio channel. After questioning Davis, Howard and Rankin helped Davis free the Pinto from the ditch, even though he opened a beer in their presence. They followed him for a little while down Pythian Road until they were satisfied that Davis was moving along, and then Howard and Rankin veered off in another direction.

Although the search for Klaas would saturate the entire region for the days and weeks to come, neither Lynch or Jaffe nor the sheriff's deputies would connect the events that occurred that night on Pythian Road to Klaas's abduction until late November. On November 27, 1993, Jaffe was walking on her property when she saw something bright near the base of a tree. What Jaffe found was a pair of red tights, a man's black sweatshirt, strips of binding tape, and a piece of cloth shaped like a hood. Jaffe's memory shot back to Davis and the night of October 1, nearly two months before. The next day, Jaffe described what she had found to Deputy Michael McManus at the Sonoma County Sheriff's Department. McManus decided to follow up with Jaffe, and she led him to the area where she found the items. There, McManus also found an unrolled condom, which further increased his suspicion. McManus reviewed the trespassing report filed by Howard and Rankin and searched Davis's criminal history. It was then, after nearly two months and millions of posters and thousands of tips, that the pieces of the puzzle began to fall into place. McManus contacted authorities in Petaluma. When the lead investigator in the Klaas case, Mike Meese, saw the evidence collected by McManus, he was certain that the cloth found on Jaffe's property would match the cloth that was used to tie up Pelham and McLean the night of Klaas's abduction. An analysis of the evidence performed by an FBI laboratory confirmed that the cloths found on Jaffe's property were an exact match to those found in Klaas's home. Now that investigators had their suspect, they were able to match a palm print found on the rail of Klaas's bunk bed to Davis. The palm print placed Davis in Klaas's bedroom.

On November 30, 1993, law enforcement descended on the home of Darlene and Dick Schwarm—Davis's younger sister and brother-in-law—who lived on a reservation just north of Ukiah, where Davis sometimes stayed. Although no one was in the home at the time authorities arrived, Davis soon returned along with the Schwarm family and was apprehended without incident (Bortnick, 1995). Davis was technically arrested for violating his parole as a result of a drunken driving charge he received on October 19, 1993, just over two weeks after Klaas was abducted. Davis was held in the Mendocino County jail, and he pled guilty to the drunk driving charge on December 2, 1993. Word was already out—even though no official charges had been filed—that Davis was the suspect in Klaas's kidnapping, and the press was there as Davis was whisked off to serve a thirty-day sentence as a result of the drunk-driving conviction.

On December 3, 1993, the palm print placing Davis in Klaas' bedroom became public. Shortly after, Davis, who had invoked his Miranda rights heretofore, contacted Mike Meese. In a videotaped interview that lasted nearly ten hours, Davis confessed to the kidnapping and murder of Polly Klaas to Meese, telling at least a version of how events had unfolded on the night of October 1, 1993. Davis told Meese that he abducted Klaas in an alcohol- and drug-induced state, and when he finally realized what he had done, he killed Klaas because, "if I let her go, I'd be goin' back to the joint" (Hoover, 1996a, p. A1). Davis said that he strangled Klaas after stopping near Cloverdale, California, off Highway 101. He let Klaas out of the car to go the bathroom, and when she came back to the car he strangled her from behind, stating that Klaas "didn't know what hit her" (Hoover, 1996a, p. A1). While Davis overtly denied sexual assault, some comments made by him regarding how he did not "remember" or "think" he sexually violated Klaas were interpreted by some as raising questions about the validity of that claim. After his confession, Davis led Meese and a small group of authorities to nearby Cloverdale and to Klaas's body, which was covered by a piece of plywood under a spot of berry bushes (Bortnick, 1995). Davis was officially charged with the murder of Klaas on December 7, 1993.

THE TRIAL OF RICHARD ALLEN DAVIS

The preliminary hearing to determine whether there was enough evidence for Davis to stand trial began on May 10, 1994, and lasted for four days. After twenty-four witnesses testified, Sonoma County Municipal Court Judge Robert P. Dale ruled that Davis would be tried for the abduction and murder of Klaas.[5] Members of Davis's defense team filed a change of venue motion on December 5, 1994, arguing that Davis could not get a fair trial in Sonoma County. On July 11, 1995, after two trial date postponements, jury selection in Sonoma County began. On September 18 it was decided that the intense media attention to the case would force the trial to convene in Santa Clara County rather than Sonoma County. The trial against Davis began on February 5, 1996, before Santa Clara Superior Court Judge Thomas Hastings.

Numerous questions still remain about what exactly happened to Klaas after her abduction. One of the most elusive questions is whether Klaas was still alive when sheriff's deputies helped Davis out of the ditch on Pythian Road. According to Davis, he had carried Klaas to the embankment to wait for him as he attempted to ward off Jaffe and the deputies and get his car out of the ditch. Davis maintained that Klaas was indeed alive, not gagged, and was capable of calling for help as the deputies assisted him in dislodging his Pinto from the ditch. Early reports (Dougan, Ginsburg, and Fernandez, 1993) indicated that Klaas was so frightened that she was unable to scream for help. According to Davis's attorney and Sonoma County Chief Public Defender Marteen Miller, Davis "was absolutely amazed that she didn't scream" (Dougan et al., 1993, p. A1). Klaas's grandfather, Joe Klaas, argued that if his granddaughter had the opportunity to scream, she would have, and therefore, if she was alive at the time the deputies helped Davis on his way, she must have been gagged (Dougan et al., 1993). Davis claimed that after being helped along by the deputies, he returned to the embankment for Klaas and found her curled up asleep. Davis stated that when he returned Klaas said that she had thought Davis was not going to come back for her—a claim vehemently debated by most of those involved in the case.

At the trial, the prosecutor, Greg Jacobs, officially made the argument that Klaas was dead on the embankment at the time sheriff's deputies helped Davis out of the ditch. To support his claim that Klaas was dead on the embankment, Jacobs used the testimony of Anthony Maxwell of the FBI evidence recovery team that had responded to the scene where Klaas's body was found and testimony of Jay Chapman, a forensic pathologist. According to Maxwell, Klaas's badly decomposed body was found with her legs spread outward, bent at the knees. In the two months Klaas's body was exposed to the elements, the hair had separated from the skull and was found a distance from the body, likely due to animal activity. There was no clothing on her body from the waist down, except the remnants of her panties, with her skirt. The flannel nightgown she wore over her clothes was pulled up under her arms. It was this positioning of the body along with the unrolled condom found on the embankment off of Pythian Road that gave prosecutors the foundation for the sexual molestation charge. Chapman testified that if Klaas was indeed killed on the embankment rigor mortis could have set in, stiffening her body in the position in which she had died, even though her body was moved to the spot near Cloverdale. Because of the ambiguity of the physical evidence, the only person who will ever know if Klaas was still alive when Davis was being helped out of the ditch by the sheriff's deputies is Davis. Because her body was found in a largely skeletal state with some mummification and only some flesh present on the legs, buttocks, and thighs—no semen could be detected to prove that sexual assault had taken place, which is why Davis was instead charged with an attempted lewd act on a minor. The state of the body could not produce a conclusive cause of death, but the characteristics of the cloth and rope found in Klaas's hair, according to Chapman, were consistent with strangulation.

While the defense attempted to paint the incidents on the night that Klaas was abducted and murdered as a burglary gone wrong, the prosecution relied on witness accounts placing Davis in Petaluma and near Klaas's home in the weeks leading up to her death to demonstrate that the crime was not as spontaneous as Davis had tried to portray. Furthermore, the prosecution's case was strengthened by the fact that Davis did not remove any valuables from the home the night he took Klaas. Finally, the prosecution relied on the testimony of Howard, who questioned Davis regarding the trespassing call to demonstrate that the sheriff's deputies who encountered Davis found him sober when they questioned him that night. The prosecution also argued that it would have been difficult for Davis to sneak into Klaas's home, with Nichol sleeping one room away, if he had not been in control of his facilities.

The defense never questioned that Davis was guilty of kidnapping and murdering Klaas but did try to undermine the prosecution's charge of an attempted lewd act with a minor. The real issue at the trial was whether Davis would receive the death penalty or life without parole, and sexual molestation was a factor that gave support for a sentence to death, although it was necessary for the prosecution to prove that Klaas was molested for the jury to impose the death penalty. The prosecution also tried to prove that Davis had stalked Klaas prior to October 1, 1993, producing several witnesses who placed Davis in the area of Klaas's home in the weeks prior to the kidnapping and murder. Some witnesses also described a tall, thin man, never located by authorities, who was seen with Davis. One witness indicated that she saw Davis in the area talking to the tall, thin man who gestured toward Klaas's home.

THE FINAL RESOLUTION OF THE CASE AGAINST DAVIS

The jury found Davis guilty of kidnapping and murdering Klaas on June 18, 1996. As the verdict was read, Davis turned to the television cameras, pursed his lips, and raised the middle fingers on both of his hands. It was an image that was broadcast across the country and graced the next day's front-page news, shocking a public that already saw Davis as a monster. Because the defense never denied that Davis did in fact kidnap and murder Klaas, a guilty verdict was essentially a foregone conclusion. The real issue was what sentence the conviction would bring.

During the sentencing phase of Davis' trial, defense attorneys attempted to humanize Davis, contextualizing his actions as a product of his upbringing. Davis's maternal grandmother, Norma Johnny, who was ninety-one years old at the time, testified to the loveless environment in which Davis was raised. Johnny did defend her daughter, Davis's mother, in some parts of her testimony. Davis's aunt by marriage, Irene Davis, also testified that she looked after Davis and his siblings for a while in 1958, and she reinforced the portrait of Davis's mother as an affectionless alcoholic. When Davis's mother and father divorced, his father, who was dead at the time of Klaas's kidnapping and murder, obtained custody of the children after proving his mother unfit, but as a longshoreman, he spent little time with the children. His father married three times, and Davis's tumultuous relationship with his three stepmothers as well as his mother has been described as a contributing factor to his anger toward women.

The defense's efforts to humanize Davis fell short. On August 5, 1996, the San Jose jury, after twenty-one hours of deliberations, decided to sentence Davis to death. The jury foreman, Brian Bianco, told reporters that it was not an easy decision, with as many as seven jurors at one time leaning toward a sentence of life in prison. Bianco was quoted as saying, "We tried to come up with the other [life in prison] decision. That is what most people wanted. But we just couldn't" (Hoover, 1996a, p. A1). The judge officially handed down the sentence of death to Davis on September 26, 1996. Before his sentence was read, Davis was allowed to address the court, and he reiterated his denial of sexually assaulting Klaas. Then, Davis shocked the court again with what some termed his "final outrage." Davis said that he remembered that he did not sexually assault Klaas because she had said to him, "Just don't do me like my dad" (Locke, 1996c). Chaos befell the courtroom as Marc Klaas lunged for Davis and had to be restrained. The lead paragraph of an Associated Press account of the incident noted that, "Other defendants have erupted in court, shouted obscenities at judges, and even turned on their attorneys. But rarely, if ever, has one uttered the kind of malevolent insult Richard Allen Davis spewed before being sentenced to die" (Locke, 1996c). Davis awaits execution on San Quinten State prison's death row.

CALIFORNIA RESPONDS WITH "THREE STRIKES AND YOU'RE OUT"

The impact of the kidnapping and murder of Klaas was still strong a decade after her death. One legacy was the fuel that Klaas's death gave to California's "Three Strikes and You're Out" initiative. On March 5, 2003, the U.S. Supreme Court ruled five to four, in *Ewing v. California*, that the sentence of twenty-five years to life handed down to Gary Albert Ewing under California's third-strike provision for stealing three golf clubs was not a disproportionate punishment in violation of the Eight Amendment's prohibition against cruel and unusual punishment. Ewing, who had previous felony and misdemeanor convictions for theft, battery, weapons charges, robbery, and burglary was sentenced under the law that does not require a third strike to be violent or even particularly serious. Justice Sandra Day O'Connor, in presenting the opinion of the Court, began with a discussion of Davis, nearly a decade after Klaas's murder. O'Connor wrote,

On October 1, 1993, while Proposition 184 was circulating, [twelve]-year-old Polly Klaas was kidnapped from her home in Petaluma, California. Her admitted killer, Richard Allen Davis, had a long criminal history that included two prior kidnapping convictions. Davis had served only half of his most recent sentence ([sixteen] years for kidnapping, assault, and burglary). Had Davis served his entire sentence, he would still have been in prison on the day that Polly Klaas was kidnapped. (*Ewing v. California*, p. 1182)

Although Davis's criminal history illuminated turnstile justice created a salient symbol for keeping dangerous criminals behind bars, how Davis returned to the streets is usually left out of discussions. In fact, Davis's release from prison was more complicated than the "justice system gone soft" argument might indicate. During the 1970s in the United States, indeterminate sentencing schemes came under attack. Indeterminate sentences are those in which a judge sets a minimum and maximum sentence for an offender to serve, and parole boards decide when an offender is actually released from prison. Judges and parole boards were criticized for their expansive discretion; they were charged with being lenient, arbitrary, and unfair. At the same time, there was a trend away from rehabilitation and toward retribution, leading critics to challenge parole and its goal of reintegrating offenders back into freedom.

As the "get tough" era of crime control took hold, determinant sentencing schemes, where offenders serve a specified amount of time, which can be reduced by good time or earned time credits, flourished. One of the movements in this "get tough" era was the abolition of discretionary parole (prisoner release decided by parole boards), as the public had lost faith in parole board decisions. In 1977 California abolished discretionary parole for most offenses; parole boards no longer reviewed the readiness of an offender to be released from prison, and instead release dates are calculated by computer so that when offenders have served the portion of their sentence specified by law, they are released from prison automatically whether or not they are considered dangerous. In fact, California parole officials were well aware that Davis was dangerous. He had been denied parole six times until California abolished parole. It was then determined that Davis had served the amount of time in prison mandated by the new law, and he was released automatically (Petersilia, 2002). If Davis's case had been examined by a paroling authority, and he was still found to be too dangerous to be released as he had been six times before, rather than being released automatically, he would have still been in prison the night he kidnapped and murdered Klaas.

Even though Davis's release from prison was precisely a result of politicized "get tough" policies seeking to eliminate discretionary parole, politicians and the public sought remedy with yet another "get tough" policy. In 1994 California became the second state to adopt a "Three Strikes and You're Out" approach. California's three-strikes law was passed by the California State Legislature and signed into law by then Governor Pete Wilson in March of 1994. Seventy-two percent of California voters embraced the law later that year. Under the three-strikes policy, offenders with a previous felony conviction face a doubled sentence for a second felony conviction (a second strike) and a sentence of twenty-five years to life in prison for a third felony conviction. Although many states and the federal government have adopted three-strike provisions since 1994, the extent of its use in California is striking. By the end of September 2003, over 42,000 inmates were serving time on a second or third strike. However, questions remain about whether California's measures actually focus criminal justice resources on the most dangerous offenders such as Davis. Of the 7,234 inmates serving time for a third strike in 2003, just over 42 percent were serving time for a third strike related to a crime against persons, and 49 percent of third strike inmates were serving time for property and drug crimes (California Department of Corrections, 2003).

Although the murder of Klaas galvanized the "Three Strikes and You're Out" initiative in California, it was actually presented to the California lawmakers a year before by Mike Reynolds, whose daughter, eighteen-year-old Kimber Reynolds, was killed in June 1992. Reynolds was shot in the head after trying to protect her purse from two men who drove by and snatched her purse while on a motorcycle: the two men were out on parole.

Kimber Reynolds died two days later, and Mike Reynolds unsuccessfully pushed lawmakers to consider a three-strikes measure. Disillusioned with lawmakers, Reynolds began taking his push for a three-strikes law to the public, seeking a state initiative that would bypass lawmakers. The murder of Klaas, combined with Davis's long criminal record, was exactly the kind of impetus that was needed. Not only was the three-strikes initiative the hottest topic in California, but lawmakers responded themselves, drafting "get tough" measure after "get tough" measure. Although an initial supporter of Reynolds, Marc Klaas became critical of the three-strikes push when he realized that nonviolent offenders would also be caught in the net. He preferred another version that focused more on violent and sex crimes for the harshest punishments (Bortnick, 1995). The impact of the Klaas case on the three-strikes issue in California was discussed in the 1999 film, *The Legacy: Murder and Media, Politics and Prisons,* by Michael J. Moore.

MARC KLAAS: AN INSPIRED ADVOCATE

After the death of his daughter, Marc Klaas went from a rental car businessman and father to a nationally recognized advocate for missing children and legislative reform. At first he held a leadership position in the Polly Klaas Foundation, but he was removed by the board over an ideological clash concerning the direction of the organization (Martin, 1994). Klaas had created his own organization called Klaaskids (originally the Marc Klaas Foundation), and he turned attention largely toward legislative issues. Klaaskids is an organization dedicated to promoting education about child protection issues and promoting legislation seeking to protect children. More recently, Klaas developed Beyond Missing, which is a program that allows law enforcement across the nation to log on to a secure website and develop and distribute fliers of missing children.

Klaas was a central figure in debates over the 1994 Crime Bill. Klaas stood with other crime victims as President Clinton signed the 1994 Crime Bill. Clinton invoked the memory of Klaas's daughter and other victims, as he signed the bill dedicating the measure to their memory. Clinton used several ceremonial pens—the first of which he presented to Klaas. Klaas further raised his profile in the political realm when—after criticizing three Republican candidates in California for using his daughter's death in political ads—he appeared in an ad for Clinton in late October 1996 as the 1996 presidential election began to crest (Doyle, 1996). Klaas was featured in the ad that began with a home video of Polly, as Klaas praised Clinton's 1994 Crime Bill, and his "courage" in being tough on crime (Kurtz, 1996).

RESPONSE TO MISSING CHILDREN ENTERS A NEW ERA OF "ALERT"

The murder of Klaas began a fundamental shift in how law enforcement responds to missing children. Klaas's father kept a journal during the trial and titled the March 24, 1996, entry as the "Laurel and Hardy of Tragedy." This entry discusses the two Sonoma County sheriff's deputies' encounter with Davis less than two hours after Polly Klaas was reported missing as "a textbook example of how not to recover a kidnapped child." While an all points bulletin (APB) had been issued alerting local authorities to the disappearance of Klaas, the APB was stipulated as "not for press release." Because the press monitored police radio channels, Howard and Rankin— the two sheriff's deputies who helped Davis along his way the night of the kidnapping—did not know Klaas was missing because the alert had not been transmitted across their radio frequency to prevent media interception. During the trial, Klaas's father wrote, "If it were not for the fact that Polly's tragedy was rapidly unraveling, this scenario would be worthy of the Keystone Cops. Unfortunately, nobody's laughing" (Klaas and Klaas, 1996, p. 14).

The death of Klaas—along with that of nine-year-old Amber Hagerman who was abducted on January 13, 1996, from the parking lot of a Texas supermarket and whose body was found three days later—solidified new ways of approaching missing children's cases. After the death of Hagerman, local law enforcement and the Dallas Broadcaster's Alliance formed an informal partnership that they called "Amber Alert." Since then, the Amber Alert model has spread across the United States in regard to regional, state, and local alert systems. California even disseminates Amber Alerts via electronic highway signs that provide information about a missing child incident in which an Amber alert had been issued. Although the measures are named for Hagerman, those involved in the Klaas murder were instrumental in promoting the law. The Polly Klaas Foundation launched a campaign called Amber Alert Now in August 2002 to raise awareness about the system. Marc Klaas testified on Capitol Hill in an effort to gain federal support for the Amber Alert model, and on April 30, 2003, President George W. Bush signed the National Amber Alert Network into law.

THE LEGACY OF POLLY KLAAS

The impact of the kidnapping and murder of Klaas still resonates, not only in the town of Petaluma and not only in the state of California, but across the United States. The ten-year anniversary of her kidnapping on October 1, 2003, was remembered by numerous media across the nation. The *San Francisco Chronicle* remembered Klaas under the apt headline, "Polly Klaas' Legacy Looms Large" (Podger, 2003). Marc Klaas was featured on CBS's *The Early Show*, and an interview with Eve and Annie Nichol aired on NBC's *Today Show* to mark the passing of a decade since Polly Klaas's abduction. The memory of Klaas still haunts many debates over the "Three Strikes and You're Out" policy, as illustrated in the example where Klaas's memory was invoked by Supreme Court Justice O'Connor in *Ewing v. California*. Marc Klaas is a familiar face in the media, as he was called on to discuss various cases of missing children, such as the abduction of fourteen-year-old Elizabeth Smart from her Salt Lake City, Utah, home in June 2002. In fact, Klaas has been called "one of the most haunting images associated with the victims' rights movement" (Dubber, 2002, p. 180). The infatuation with Klaas's kidnapping and murder was both due to the shocking and terrifying incident and a broader trend—a trend in which victims become symbols, and what is done about children in regard to crime policy is dependent on these types of highly publicized cases.

However, the cases of crimes against children that receive the most media attention, and therefore, the greatest amount of political and public response are the cases that involve the rarest forms of victimization. In 2002, several cases of child abduction—including those of seven-year-old Danielle van Dam who was abducted from her San Diego home and murdered by a neighbor in February, Elizabeth Smart, and five-year-old Samantha Runnion who was abducted near her Stanton, California, home and found murdered a day later—dominated all forms of the media. If one were to form an impression about missing children in the United States by way of these media images, it would have been easy to assume that there was an epidemic of child abductions. There was no increase in abductions in 2002; however, there was increased attention to stranger-child abductions.

Jack Lule, a professor of journalism and communication at Lehigh University, explained that stories that are associated with abductions of especially young girls are deeply embedded in the lore of human storytelling:

We can find the essential narrative in numerous fairy tales and myths. For example, Rapunzel was snatched by a witch and kept in a tower where her long golden hair grew. Little Red Riding Hood fell into the clutches of the big, bad wolf. In Greek myth, Andromeda was chained to a rock and Hades abducted Persephone, earning the wrath of Demeter. (Chronicle of Higher Education, 2002, p. B4)

According to Lule, it would be a mistake to assume that the role of the media is to portray reality. Rather, the media can sometimes fulfill the kind of deeper role that speaks to the same fears and values latent in the aforementioned fairy tales and myths.

Fess (1997, p. 257) notes that "well-publicized child abductions often become a means for defining the critical social issues of a particular time." Fess's observation is pertinent to the Klaas case. By the time of Klaas's death, the United States had already waged its "war on crime" for over two decades, and support for "tough on crime" measures was increasing. The term "missing children" began to roll off the popular tongue in 1981 (Best, 1990). In 1981 the murder of Adam Walsh gripped the heart of the nation and propelled his father, John Walsh, host of the popular television show *America's Most Wanted*, in a crusade against crime.

Throughout the 1980s, the missing children debate raged as various estimates surged concerning the numbers of missing children; even milk cartons were a vehicle to express fear and concern. The "Satanic panic" and the furor surrounding purported ritual abuse also primed the public for fears about child abduction. Fingerprinting and identification kits flourished. By the early 1990s, the wave of panic over missing children that was felt throughout the 1980s had largely subsided. However, several high-profile incidents, including the murders of Klaas in 1993 and Megan Kanka in 1994, recharged those fears. Furthermore, concern over crime was growing along with media attention to the problem. In fact, according to Gallup polls, 1994 was the first year in which crime was the top concern of Americans, and the upsurge in concern over crime was dramatic. In January 1993, only 9 percent of those surveyed named crime as the most important problem facing the United States, and in January 1994, 37 percent of those surveyed named crime and violence as the top concern (Bureau of Justice Statistics, 2001).

Child abduction and murder, especially by strangers, while rare, is a parent's worst nightmare. Statistical perspective is an ineffective salve for the tragic stories—stories like that of Polly Klaas—that deeply move a nation. Rational analysis of the probability of a stereotypical kidnapping would lead parents to accept that the rare and extremely unpredictable incidents of such crimes leave protection against them out of their control. Rational analysis would indicate that efforts to keep children safe would be more efficiently disseminated toward harms that can be controlled. However, fear of crime is an emotional response, and it is precisely the unpredictable nature of stranger abduction and murder that makes that fear so visceral. When those crimes invade the bedrooms of little girls during slumber parties in "Anytown USA," there is a very real feeling that anyone could be a victim, and those fears are far more complex than a statistical remedy or rational analysis can address.

Furthermore, the kidnapping and murder of Klaas did not only generate fear; it also fueled anger. That anger was directed toward what seemed like a failed criminal justice system. That anger fed off the frustration that a violent and dangerous criminal such as Davis—who had been within the clutches of the justice system—would be allowed back on the streets, and a frustration with law enforcement for not being able to protect the innocent from him. Although Washington was the first state to enact community notification measures, the rape and murder of Megan Kanka in 1994, as the public still grieved Klaas, created a national awareness of community notification procedures. New Jersey was the first state to establish "Megan's Law" in 1994. In 1995, Klaas's father stood alongside Kanka's mother as New York's Megan's Law, which required sex offenders to register with police and that the community be notified, was signed into law (Dubber, 2002). In 1996, Megan's Law became a federal policy, and all states are required to have some type of notification procedures concerning released sex offenders. Megan's Law has become one of the most popular "across the board" policies in the realm of public safety (Proctor, Badzinski, and Johnson, 2002).

The legacy of the Klaas case continues to endure along with other victims whose symbolism transcends tragedy. Fueled by media attention and notorious cases, those victims—usually of very atypical crimes—and their families who receive notoriety become central to political debates about crime, as they are transformed by tragedy into media celebrity and political activists. Garland commented that "we have become used to seeing crime victims or their families accompany American politicians as they announce new mandatory sentencing laws, or declare measures that will alert communities to the dangers that released offenders represent" (Garland, 2001, p. 143). Klaas is one of the original symbols that heralded the dawn of this new era of victim symbolism.

NOTES

1. Figures in the report do sum to greater than 100 percent because children with multiple episodes are counted in each applicable category.

2. The examination of the Klaas abduction and murder is drawn generally from Bortnick (1995) and the following articles retrieved from LEXIS-NEXIS Academic database: Spolar, C. (1993a, October 15) Small California town pleads for child abducted at knifepoint, *Washington Post*; Ginsburg, M. and Herron Zamora, J. (1993, November 20) Klaas search leader resigns: Printer charged in 1970 molest case, friends shocked but supportive, *San Francisco Examiner*; Dougan, M., and Kornblum, J. (1993, November 24) Klaas 'hero' tried in '68 molest case: Jury in peninsula case acquitted Bill Rhodes: He organized Petaluma search for Polly, *San Francisco Examiner*; Woman sues leader of effort to find kidnap victim alleging

child abuse, *St. Louis Post-Dispatch*; Spolar, C., and Vobejda, B. (1994, March 10) Grass roots crusaders embrace a mission to find the missing, *Washington Post*; Dougan, M. (1994, May 12) Testimony details Polly's abduction: Eight claim seeing suspect that night, *San Francisco Examiner.*

3. The discussion of Richard Allen Davis is drawn generally from Bortnick (1995) and the following articles: Martin, G., and Hoover, K. (1993, December 9) Review of death of Davis's friend '73 case was called suicide, *San Francisco Chronicle*; Richard Allen Davis (1993, December 10) How suspect became "quintessential convict," *San Francisco Chronicle*; Richard Allen Davis's life of crime (1996, August 6) *San Francisco Chronicle.*

4. The discussion of the actions of law enforcement in this case are drawn generally from Bortnick (1995) and the following articles retrieved from LEXIS-NEXIS Academic database: Taylor, M. (1993, December 6) The Polly case: Two months of crossed paths and missed opportunities, *San Francisco Chronicle*; Fagan, K. (1993, December 7) Quick thinking led to arrest: Woman on a walk and diligent deputy followed their instincts, *San Francisco Chronicle.*

5. The examination of the trial of Richard Allen Davis is drawn from the following articles retrieved from LEXIS-NEXIS Academic database: Locke, M. (1996b, June 10) Prosecutor: Davis killed "in cold blood," *Associated Press*; Locke, M. (1996a, April 24) Deputy: Klaas killing suspect didn't seem to be on drugs, alcohol, *Associated Press*; Hoover, K. (1996b, May 7) Klaas jury hears gory testimony, family members leave courtroom, *San Francisco Chronicle*; Ken Hoover, K. (1996c, July 11) Davis's Grandmother, 91, tells jury about killer's boyhood, *San Francisco Chronicle*; Dougan, M. (1996, July 16) Trauma's of Davis childhood recounted: Polly Klaas's killer was physically abused, abandoned, *San Francisco Chronicle*; Hoover, K. (1996e, September 27) Davis provokes Polly's dad at Sentencing as death penalty affirmed, murderer claims Polly molest, *San Francisco Chronicle.*

REFERENCES

Best, J. (1990). *Threatened children: Rhetoric and concern about child-victims.* Chicago: University of Chicago Press.

Bortnick, B. (1995). *Polly Klaas: The murder of America's child.* New York: Kensington Publishing.

Bureau of Justice Statistics. (2001). *Sourcebook of criminal justice statistics.* Washington, DC: U.S. Department of Justice.

California Department of Corrections. (2003, November). *Second and third strikers in the institution population as of September 30.* Retrieved November 20, 2003, from http://www.corr.ca.gov

Chermak, S. M. (2002). *Searching for a demon: The media's construction of the militia movement.* Boston: Northeastern University Press.

Dougan, M. (1994, May 12). Testimony details Polly's abduction: Eight claim seeing suspect that night. *San Francisco Examiner*, p. A1. Retrieved September 29, 2003, from LEXIS-NEXIS Academic Database.

Dougan, M. (1996, July 16). Traumas of Davis' childhood recounted. *San Francisco Examiner.* Retrieved September 20, 2003, from LEXIS-NEXIS Academic Database.

Dougan, M., Ginsburg, M., and Fernandez, E. (1993, December 8). Polly's quiet terror: Suspect 'amazed she didn't scream.' *San Francisco Examiner*, p. A1. Retrieved September 22, 2003, from LEXIS-NEXIS Academic Database.

Dougan, M., and Kornblum, J. (1993, November 24). Klaas 'hero' tried in '68 molest case. *San Francisco Examiner.* Retrieved September 22, 2003, from LEXIS-NEXIS Academic Database.

Doyle, J. (1996, October 9). Klaas criticizes Riggs for TV ad: Polly's dad says politicians shouldn't exploit her case. *San Francisco Chronicle.* p. A13.

Dubber, M. D. (2002). *Victims in the war on crime: The use and abuse of victims' rights.* New York: New York University Press.

Enders, J. (1993, December 13). Police revisit student's 1973 suicide after Polly Klaas murder. *Associated Press.* Retrieved December 9, 2003, from LEXIS-NEXIS Academic Database.

Epidemic of child abductions. (2002, September 13). *Chronicle of Higher Education, 49*(3), B4.

Ewing v. California, 538 U.S. 11 (2003).

Fagan, K. (1993, December 7). Quick thinking led to arrest: Woman on a walk and diligent deputy followed their instincts. *San Francisco Chronicle*, p. A1. Retrieved September 22, 2003, from LEXIS-NEXIS Academic Database.

Fagan, K. (1998, October 4). A look back: Polly's killer was an outcast even on the fringe. *San Francisco Chronicle*, p. 5. Retrieved September 29, 2003, from LEXIS-NEXIS Academic Database.

Fess, P. S. (1997). *Kidnapped: Child abduction in America.* New York: Oxford University Press.

Finkelhor, D., Hammer, H., and Sedlak, A. J. (2002) *National incidence studies of missing, abducted, runaway, and thrownaway children nonfamily abducted children: National estimates and characteristics.* Washington, DC: U.S. Department of Justice, Office of Justice Programs, Office of Juvenile Justice and Delinquency Prevention.

Finkelhor, D., Hotaling, G. T., and Sedlak, A. J. (1990). *Missing, abducted, runaway, and thrownaway children in America. First report: Numbers and characteristics, national incidence studies.* Washington, DC: U.S. Department of Justice, Office of Justice Programs, Office of Juvenile Justice and Delinquency Prevention.

Garland, D. (2001). *The culture of control: Crime and social order in contemporary society.* Chicago: University of Chicago Press.

Hoover, K. (1996a, April 24). Davis's cold confession released: Polly 'never knew what hit her,' defendant says. *San Francisco Chronicle*, p. A1.

Hoover, K. (1996b, May 7). Klaas jury hears gory testimony, family members leave courtroom. *San Francisco Chronicle*, p. A13. Retrieved September 22, 2003, from LEXIS-NEXIS Academic Database.

Hoover, K. (1996c, July 11). Davis's grandmother, 91, tells jury about killer's boyhood. *San Francisco Chronicle*, p. A13. Retrieved September 22, 2003, from LEXIS-NEXIS Academic Database.

Hoover, K. (1996d, August 6). Death penalty for Polly's killer. *San Francisco Chronicle*, p. A1.

Hoover, K. (1996e, September 27). Davis provokes Polly's dad at sentencing as death penalty affirmed, murderer claims Polly molest. *San Francisco Chronicle*, p. A1. Retrieved September 22, 2003, from LEXIS-NEXIS Academic Database.

Klaas, M., and Klaas, J. (1996). *Polly Klaas daily trial journal.* Retrieved September 8, 2003, from http://www.klaaskids.org/pg-trialjournal.htm

Kurtz, H. (October 22, 1996). An emotional pitch for Clinton; TV spot features father of murder victim; Dole aid call it "cynical." *Washington Post*, p. A11.

Locke, M. (1996a, April 24). Deputy: Klaas killing suspect didn't seem to be on drugs, alcohol. *Associated Press*. Retrieved September 30, 2003, from LEXIS-NEXIS Academic Database.

Locke, M. (1996b, June 10). Prosecutor: Davis killed "in cold blood." *Associated Press*. Retrieved September 23, 2003, from LEXIS-NEXIS Academic Database.

Locke, M. (1996c, September 18). Davis insult to father prompts shockwaves. *Associated Press*. Retrieved September 30, 2003, from LEXIS-NEXIS Academic Database.

Martin, G. (1994, December 5). Polly volunteers protest Marc Klaas's ouster. *San Francisco Chronicle*, p. A15.

Martin, G., and Hoover, K. (1993, December 9). Review of death of Davis's friend: '73 case was called a suicide. *San Francisco Chronicle*, p. A25.

Petersilia, J. (2002). *Reforming probation and parole in the 21st century.* Lanham, MD: American Correctional Association.

Podger, P. (2003, September 28). Polly Klaas's legacy looms large. *San Francisco Chronicle*, p. A27.

Proctor, J. L., Badzinski, D. M., and Johnson, M. (2002). The impact of media on knowledge and perceptions of Megan's Law. *Criminal Justice Policy Review*, 13(4), 356–379.

Richard Allen Davis: How suspect became "quintessential convict" (1993, December 10). *San Francisco Chronicle*, p. A1. Retrieved September 29, 2003, from LEXIS-NEXIS Academic Database.

Richard Allen Davis's life of crime. (1996, August 6). *San Francisco Chronicle*, p. A11. Retrieved December 9, 2003, from LEXIS-NEXIS Academic Database.

Sedlak, A., Finkelhor, D., Hammer, H., and Schulz, D. (2002). *National incidence studies of missing, abducted, runaway, and thrownaway children national estimates of missing children: An overview.* Washington, DC: U.S. Department of Justice, Office of Justice Programs, Office of Juvenile Justice and Delinquency Prevention.

Smolowe, J., and Lafferty, E. (1993, November 1). A high-tech dragnet. *Time*, 18, 43.

Spolar, C. (1993a, October 15). Small California town pleads for child abducted at knifepoint. *Washington Post*, p. A18. Retrieved September 20, 2003, from LEXIS-NEXIS Academic Database.

Spolar, C. (1993b, December 2). Suspect queried in kidnapping of California girl. *Washington Post*, p. A3. Retrieved September 22, 2003, from LEXIS-NEXIS Academic Database.

Spolar, C., and Vobejda, B. (1994, March 10). Grass roots crusaders embrace a mission to find the missing. *Washington Post*, p. A23. Retrieved September 20, 2003, from LEXIS-NEXIS Academic Database.

Taylor, M. (1993, December 6). The Polly case: Two months of crossed paths and missed opportunities. *San Francisco Chronicle*, p. A6. Retrieved September 22, 2003, from LEXIS-NEXIS Academic Database.

Woman sues leader of effort to find kidnap victim alleging child abuse. *St. Louis Post-Dispatch*, p. 16A. Retrieved September 18, 2003, from LEXIS-NEXIS Academic Database.

11

Representing O.J.: The Trial of the Twentieth Century

Gregg Barak

Ten years after Orenthal James Simpson was accused of and charged with the June 12, 1994, double homicide of Nicole Brown Simpson and Ronald Lyle Goldman, he is found living in an affluent suburb of Miami as a single parent with his and Nicole's teenage kids, eighteen-year-old daughter Sydney and fifteen-year-old son Justin. Living very comfortably off his NFL pension and retired from any other noticeable income (because of legal obligations to pay monetary damages to various surviving family members), O.J. claims that he has essentially become a full-time father. When he is not engaged in parental activities, he can be found on one of the nearby public golf courses playing a round of eighteen or more with his buddies. Between these two very ordinary behaviors, Simpson also maintains that he has little time or interest in pursuing any serious long-term relationships with women.

In October 1995, O. J. Simpson was found criminally not guilty by a nonrepresentative jury of his peers. In February 1997, he was found civilly liable for the wrongful deaths of both Nicole Brown Simpson and Ronald Goldman, and he was ordered by another jury—not of his peers—to pay the victims' survivors $33.5 million. Nevertheless, O.J. has thus far avoided making any payments to the victims' survivors, as he often, but not always, avers when asked about the killings: "I didn't commit the crime, and I don't think these people deserve anything. I'm not putting myself in a position of having to give them anything" (Deutsch, 2003, p. 2). However, in a 1998 *Esquire* magazine cover story with a flattering picture of O.J., he was quoted as saying, "Let's say I committed this crime . . . even if I did this, it would have been because I loved her very much, right?" (Leibovich, 1998, p. 2). At other times, Simpson seemed to be in a state of denial about the Brown and Goldman affair or in a defensive mode that justified his anger or rage against a changed Nicole that was no longer the person that he had once loved (French, 1996).

Despite the fact that there were polls that showed a black and white racial polarity with respect to guilt and innocence, the majority of people—black, white, yellow, and brown—thought Simpson was guilty of the brutal slayings before and after the trial. Meanwhile, O.J. has continued to retain his celebrity status, tabloid popularity, and commercial appeal. In April 2003, for example, in response to what the BBC News referred to as a "row" over a proposed new reality show (thirteen episodes) based on the everyday life of O. J. Simpson, he was quoted from his Miami home in a telephoned interview with the Associated Press as saying: "I have no plans in any way to do a reality show even though people have approached me about it. There are no plans in the Simpson family to have any cameras coming in our house" ("Simpson Show," 2003, p. 2). During that same interview, Simpson also stated that he was considering the possibility of becoming a news commentator on actor Robert Blake's trial for murdering his wife, Bonny Lee Bakley, in Los Angeles in May 2001. Though declining to specifically identify any of the television outlets that he had contacted him, O.J. did have this to say: "I'd love to do it. I think I have a lot of insight. I don't know if he's guilty or not but I know there's no such thing anymore as innocent until proven guilty" ("Simpson Show," 2003, p. 1).

Notwithstanding his infamous reputation in ethical and cultural circles alike, as exemplified by the persistent telling of O.J. jokes on and off camera and by the ongoing sketches of the narcissistic and indefatigable Simpson some ten years after the live broadcast of the "low speed" chase of the white Ford Bronco by the Los Angeles Police Department (LAPD) on Interstate 405, he remains a newsworthy story. In part, this mediated reality is a result of Simpson's continued run-ins with the law, involving incidents of both domestic and community conflict, if not necessarily aggravated acts of violence. For example, between the time that Simpson and his two kids moved to Florida in early 2000 and January 2002, the police had responded three times to reported disturbances between O.J. and his on-and-off girlfriend, Christie Prody, and on at least one other occasion to a call from daughter

Sydney who asked the police to assist her in what she termed "an abuse thing" ("Daughter Calls Police," 2002, p. 1). In 2001, O.J. also made news when he was arrested—he had turned himself in and was immediately released on bail—for an alleged "road rage" incident that involved a relatively brief up-close and personal dispute with another driver outside their vehicles while Simpson's kids sat in the car urging their dad to "let it go" ("Out of Proportion," 2001).

In part, the mediated consumption of O.J. as a football and motion picture star and as a disgraced iconic celebrity results from his resilient personality and to a popular appeal that has born him numerous witnesses and fans alike. In 2001 and 2002, for example, there were Simpson's successful public appearances at a series of hip-hop concerts with such stars as Wyclef Jean, Lil' Mo, Noreaga, and Foxy Brown. The appearances were staged and promoted for both personal and commercial reasons. Commenting on the crowds' reactions to the appearance of O.J. at these concerts, Spiderboy founder Norman Pardo said, "When O.J. stepped on stage it was unbelievable, the crowd went crazy chanting his name 'O.J. O.J. O.J.'" ("Simpson Show," 2003, p. 1). While Simpson works on the restoration of his public image, his marketability still seems to exist, as evidenced on Ebay, the online marketplace.

All along, the story of O. J. Simpson has been much more than simply a story of two trials—one criminal and one civil—for the murder and wrongful deaths of two people. It was also before, during, and after the contested media and legal battles that a mass-mediated public trial required popular verdicts on the historical and contemporary practices of criminal justice, especially as these pertain to relations of race, class, and gender in the United States. In short, the images associated with the murders and trials of O. J. Simpson were represented not only by cameras in the courtroom and by the legal maneuvers of attorneys for the state and the defense, but those images were (and still are) representative of the larger legal, social, and economic representations of a deconstructed criminal justice system and the ongoing struggle for justice for all in America.

From another vantage point, the infatuation and captivation of the O.J. phenomena—past and present—has had as much to do with society as it has with him. As Patt Morrison, a *Los Angeles Times* columnist, wrote in a commentary reflecting on the Simpson matter five years after the murders: "Future social historians will be engrossed not by the case, but by how we were mesmerized by it. When they write it, perhaps for the 50th anniversary, we won't be the audience any more; we'll be just another ring in the circus" (1999, p. 2). Morrison's conclusions may help to prove the point that in the "present" of the postmodern future, the hyperreality of mass communications has been, for some time, busy bridging the real and the imaginary systems of justice where those in society find themselves assuming multiple roles or becoming simultaneously perpetrators and victims, prosecutors and defenders, judges and juries, and witnesses and spectators.

MASS-MEDIATED APPEAL

Assessing the "mass appeal" or the popularity and unpopularity of O.J. is more art than science. Nevertheless, the lasting but fading fascination with O. J. Simpson stems from many sources. During the summer of 2003, an internet search for Simpson and other celebrities—famous and infamous— yielded the following results: First, O.J. was the fourth most notorious case with 210,000 hits. Cases with more hits included Osama Bin Laden, which received 919,000 hits; Michael Jackson, the pop music icon and alleged child molester, received 2,690,000 hits; and Mike Tyson received 263,000 hits. Second—with number of hits in parentheses—in fifth, sixth, seventh, eighth, and ninth place, respectively, were Charlie Manson (82,700), Timothy McVeigh (81,900), Richard Speck (51,700), Adolf Hitler (65,800), and Jeffrey Dahmer (24,000). Third, for a bit more perspective, Mahatma Gandhi received 23,400 hits and Martin Luther King Jr. received 1,040,000.

Another indicator of Simpson's mass appeal was on February 4, 1997, the evening in which the verdict in the civil trial was being announced, and when MSNBC chose to broadcast the verdict live over President Clinton's State of the Union Address to the nation. As Nate Gehl, community producer at MSNBC, pointed out the next day in defense of MSNBC's decision, the traffic at the Simpson chat room was four times higher than that of the presidential speech (CNET News, 1997). A similar kind of ratings decision was made back in June 1994; the coverage of a live NBA championship final game broke away to go live to the Ford Bronco chase that involved O.J. and the LAPD. More generally, Morrison of the *Los Angeles Times* noted:

For two years, we binged and purged, gorging on O.J. and deploring ourselves for it. Websites and chat rooms talked of nothing else. It came up at birthday parties, in airport bars and doctors' waiting rooms. What with coffee-cart chats and wall-to-wall break-room TV coverage, employers figure O.J. cost them $40 billion in lost productivity. Even the Oscars couldn't draw a media crowd like this did: Every news agency short of Guns & Ammo wanted a piece of it, and if it had been a gun instead of a knife, they'd have been there too. (Morrison, 1999, p. 1)

The O. J. Simpson case was certainly not the first famous trial involving lethal or nonlethal violence that had garnished public preoccupation.

Similarly, descriptions of other famous trials found in this five-volume set have also been referred to with the phrase "trial of the century." However, the coverage of all the other famous trials of the twentieth century—alone or combined—pales in comparison with the coverage afforded the Simpson trials, especially the criminal trial with its nine months of live broadcasts from the courthouse. In short, for any trial to refer to itself as the trial of century, after the trial of O.J., is a hyperbole at least and wishful thinking at best. After all, nothing about the O.J. case was too trivial to address or to elevate to the realm of high culture: "People who would never dream of opening a tabloid could step clear of the trial's noisome tawdriness by speaking loftily of the semiotics of Marcia Clark's hair and Johnnie Cochran's ties, of Kato Kaelin as the echt Angelino, of the Brown sisters, in their morning-black Lycra and crucifix jewelry and artificially perfect California breasts, as a modern-day Greek chorus" (Morrison, 1999, p. 1).

When people characterize the O.J. criminal trial as the trial of the century, they do so less in terms of hyperbole and more in terms of spectacle. That is, it was no exaggeration to say that the morality plays surrounding the case were exhibited for the entire world to view as an object of wonderment. Court TV, with some 24 million subscribers at the time of the first (criminal) trial, provided gavel-to-gavel coverage. CNN provided more than 600 hours of trial coverage, attracting an audience about five times the size of its normal viewership. At the moment that the jury verdict of not guilty was read out loud in a court of law, there were an estimated 150 million Americans watching it live, breaking all previous television viewing records. From the very beginning of the trial, not only did newspapers and magazines feature daily and weekly updates on the legal procedures and anything else associated with O. J. Simpson, but radio and television talk shows did the same, some even converting their programs to full-time Simpson analysis such as *Rivera Live* on CNBC (Barak, 1996). Publishing houses were also not out of the loop, as more than fifty books were printed between the time of Simpson's arrest for the double murder in 1994 and the jury verdict in the civil case in 1997. A play, a couple of docudramas, and at least two made-for-television movies, not to mention books on tape, also appeared over the course of the next seven years.

In addition, there were hundreds of attorneys taking to the television and radio airwaves as part of an exploding cottage industry of mediated trial experts. In exchange for their legal knowledge, these attorneys received, if not large monetary compensation in most instances, exposure and fame that they would hopefully cash in on at some later date. During the first trial, networks such as ABC, NBC, and CBS were paying their legal experts as much as $3,000 and $4,000 per day; meanwhile, local television stations were paying no more than $500 a day. Many of these legal commentators offered their insights free of charge (Prodis, 1995). There were also several legal pundits who carved out ongoing careers as full-time network commentators. Some of those who became familiar faces as armchair analysts at the time and still serve the networks and Court TV in such capacities—to name but a few, Greta Van Susteren, Leslie Abramson, Dan Abrams, James Curtis, and Victoria Toensing.

All this mass-mediated appeal was not some kind of conspiracy in the making. On the contrary, the O.J. phenomenon was not only a product of a synergistically coming together of certain noteworthy and newsworthy elements that provided both a "shelf life" and "dramatic appeal," but it was also a technological coming together of real-time simultaneous live broadcasts. Propelled by television cameras in the courtroom and the internet outside of the courtroom, multiple voices and attitudes were expressed of both "pro" and "anti" establishment views on everyday aspects of the U.S. criminal justice system. Voices of conformity and voices of dissent could be heard as people expressed their views on issues of class, race, gender, sexuality, domestic violence, and social, if not cultural, control.

These issues were each represented in the relationships of both the double homicide of Nicole Simpson and Ronald Goldman and in the privileged treatment of Orenthal James Simpson throughout his ordeal and adjudication by the state. The circumstances of the case combined with Simpson's long history as a media star and celebrity—first, as a running back at the University of Southern California (USC) and winner of the highly coveted Heisman Trophy for college football player of the year 1968 and later, as an all-pro running back for the Buffalo Bills and an NFL Hall of Fame inductee in 1985. During his years as a professional football player, O.J. became a pitchman for various companies, most notably for Hertz car rental agency with its successful television ad campaign, starring O.J. dressed in a business suit running through airports and leaping over chairs and luggage as he dashes to make his connecting flight. Toward the end of his professional football career, O.J. started making films. After retiring from the NFL, he worked for two major networks as a sports commentator, and there were several more motion pictures, including the highly successful *Naked Gun* spoofs, where Simpson played a victimized and bumbling but sympathetic cop. Finally, there are the double murders of a white man and woman, with the accused as her ex-husband—a black celebrity—who was caught stalking his former wife and secretly watching her perform oral sex on other men in her condominium, while their kids were assumed to be upstairs fast asleep.

What transpired over time, directly and indirectly, and long before there were the double homicides, was the construction by the mass media and by

O.J. of a public persona of iconic proportions that flew in the face of the usual "criminal menace" that haunts U.S. society. Thus, when these contrasting images converged and wrapped themselves around Orenthal James Simpson, Nicole Brown Simpson, and Ronald Lyle Goldman, it was the American people's fascination with this contradiction rather than the media, per se, that drove (and continues to drive) our mass appeal. There was a negative photo on the cover of *Newsweek* that had darkened in O.J.'s lighter natural color. Never before and not since were so many people caught up in a mass-mediated criminal trial. Inquiring minds did want to know if O.J.—a kid from a poor and humble background who had grown into a rich, handsome, popular, and successful public figure—was guilty of the brutal murders, or if he was he being framed for them by the LAPD.

THE CRIMINAL TRIAL

In the end, what hooked a mass audience on the O. J. Simpson criminal trial was that people wanted to judge for themselves; they wanted to evaluate the circumstantial evidence, ponder what did not make sense to them or did not quite fit, and ultimately decide the question of guilt or innocence. Of course, people do not ordinarily wait for the presentation of all the evidence before "rushing to judgment." Typically, most of society—including those jurors selected in any criminal case—will have initial conclusions about the guilt or innocence of the accused. The conclusions are drawn from whatever information is at hand, no matter how complete or incomplete. So, from the time O.J. was first arrested to the time he did not turn himself in—as previously agreed—but chose, instead, to flee on the San Diego Freeway, people began to interpret these actions and arrive at their own assessments.

When people either become aware of or involved in a criminal trial, they bring to that adjudication a particular history, culture, and social experience of the administration of justice, reflected in part—at least—by their class, race, ethnicity, gender, and sexuality. Accordingly, the social realities of crime and justice in the United States—past and present—vary according to the perceptions and experiences of different socioeconomic and subcultural groupings and to the associated prejudices, biases, and stereotypes that they bring as part of their biographical baggage (Barak, Flavin, and Leighton, 2001). As a professor of criminology and criminal justice, as an author of two books on the criminal justice system, and as the editor of *Representing O.J.: Murder, Criminal Justice, and Mass Culture* (1996), I bring my own criminological baggage that includes—among other things—knowledge that there are significant gaps between scientific knowledge and legal knowledge and that legal and social justice are often illusive commodities.

In addition, as a layperson, I concluded both before and after the evidence was presented that Simpson was guilty of the crimes as charged. I had judged the circumstantial evidence based not on my knowledge of substantive and procedural criminal law but rather on common sense. Common sense helps attorneys for either side of a criminal controversy fill the gaps between scientific and legal truisms that they might persuade the jury to believe their theory, version, or story of the events. So, before presenting an overview of the facts of the Simpson case and of the respective theories of the prosecution and the defense, allow me to briefly explain my commonsense reasoning as to why I thought O.J. was guilty as charged. Let me also address that these conclusions need not influence or cloud my objective treatment of the case. In fact, throughout the nine-month criminal trial, I was the expert commentator for a radio station in Ann Arbor, Michigan, without ever letting the listening audience know what I had actually thought about Simpson's guilt or innocence.

Ironically and long before I heard or saw the "mountains of evidence" presented against the defendant in a court of law, including the blood, the fibers, the DNA, and other physical evidence, there was an array of other factual evidence that was never introduced by the prosecution. These excluded facts from the trial, including O.J.'s suicide note, that was read on national television by his former friend and attorney, Robert Kardashian; not to mention the Bronco "get away" with his life-long friend Al Cowlings at the driver's wheel and O.J. with his passport, a disguise, $8,750 in cash, and a pistol to his head. Of course, there were many other people who concluded that O.J. realized that he was about to be framed by the LAPD for the double homicide and that he had better leave Los Angeles quickly.

The Facts

The "facts" of the murders of Nicole Brown Simpson and Ronald Lyle Goldman, or the facts of any other criminal homicide, are reconstructions of what transpired, unless there is some fluke where the killings were deliberately or inadvertently caught on audio or video. In a typical criminal homicide, however, the reconstruction begins when the police are called to the scene of the crime by a witness or, more likely, by the person who discovers the body. With respect to the double homicide that occurred on the evening of June 12, 1994, at 875 South Bundy Drive in the genteel neighborhood of Brentwood in Los Angeles, a bloody body of a woman was first discovered by Sukru Boztepe and Bettina Rasmussen who were out for a midnight stroll. While out walking, they came across an agitated stray dog that led them to the front of Nicole Brown Simpson's condominium.

Officer Robert Riske was the first police officer to arrive on the scene. It was so dark when he arrived that it took a little time before he discovered the second body. The woman was identified as Nicole Brown Simpson, resident of the Bundy address. Hours would pass before the second victim was identified as Ronald Lyle Goldman, a friend of Nicole's. Both victims had bled to death following multiple stab wounds. Nicole's throat had been deeply slashed; Ronald had stab wounds all over his body, and there was evidence indicating some kind of physical struggle before he had died.

Mark Fuhrman—who would later be accused by the defense of planting the infamous glove at 360 North Rockingham Avenue that appeared "not to fit" during the course of the trial—was one of the first two detectives from the local police station assigned to the double homicide. The two local detectives were immediately aided by two other detectives from the Central Robbery and Homicide Division of the LAPD. One of these detectives, Philip Vannatter, would subsequently be accused by Simpson's lawyers of planting blood evidence. A few minutes after reinforcements had arrived at the scene, all four detectives were ordered by a superior to notify the ex-husband that his former wife had been murdered and that their children were safe and sound. The four men then left the murder scene and headed to Simpson's upscale Rockingham address a few miles away.

In the immediate hours following the discovery of the murdered bodies, police and criminalists would identify important evidence at both the scene of the crime and at O.J.'s house. At the scene of the crime there were bloody shoe impressions leading away from the bodies toward the back alley; several drops of blood appearing to the left of those footprints; the door to Nicole's condominium was ajar, but there was no evidence of any ransacking or blood inside her home; drops of blood were also found by several officers on the back gate leading to the alley; and a glove and knit hat were found on the ground near the bodies. Meanwhile, at Simpson's Rockingham address, blood was found inside and outside O.J.'s white Ford Bronco, including what appeared to be a bloody shoe impression in the carpet; blood was also found in O.J.'s driveway, foyer to his house, and in his bathroom; and a blood-drenched glove that matched the single glove found at the murder scene was found in an obscure and out of the way location on the estate grounds (Rantala, 1996).

One other fact of importance, of course, was not found at either the scene of the crime or at the accused home. There was a deep cut on one of O.J.'s left fingers that was acknowledged during his interview with the LAPD at their downtown office some fifteen hours after the murders. Simpson did not have an explanation for his fresh wound. In fact, at the time he could not recall how he had come to have that cut on his finger. Subsequently, O.J. and his attorneys came up with less than satisfactory explanations for the multiple cuts to his left hand. A doctor hired by the defense to examine Simpson less than seventy-two hours after the murders found multiple cuts and abrasions on his left hand.

The Prosecution's Case

The prosecution built its case on a mountain of evidence, including, but not limited to, the following:

DNA matched Simpson's blood to the blood drops at the murder scene that were to the left of the bloody footprints.

The shoes leaving the bloody footprints were identified as Bruno Magli's—expensive and rare Italian-made shoes—sold in only forty stores across the United States, including Bloomingdale's, where Simpson regularly purchased size twelve shoes— the same size as the footprints by the body.

The hat found at the murder scene had hairs in it consistent with O.J.'s hair.

Simpson's Ford Bronco had blood on the center console from both victims. On the driver's side carpet was an impression with Nicole's blood, which was consistent with the Bruno Magli shoe pattern left at the murder scene.

A trail of Simpson's own blood led from his Bronco into his house and in his bedroom socks were found that contained his and Nicole's blood.

The two gloves found, one at the Bundy crime scene and the other at Simpson's Rockingham estate, were a matched pair. The gloves were Simpson's size and they were rare and expensive and sold at only one store that the prosecution argued Nicole bought for O.J. the week before Christmas in 1990. Several photographs and videos reveal Simpson wearing gloves of the same make and model.

When the limo driver arrived at Simpson's home on the night of June 12 to take O.J. to the airport, there was no reply for 20 minutes and no white Ford Bronco. The limo driver's buzzes on the doorbell were only answered after he saw a tall, 200-pound black person enter the house.

On the night of the murder, at the same time that O.J. was scheduled to leave for the airport, Brian "Kato" Kaelin, living in Simpson's guesthouse, heard three thumps behind his room. When Kato left his room to investigate, he arrived at the front of the house from one direction, as Simpson was approaching his own door from a different direction. It turned out that is precisely where the Rockingham glove was found. And despite Kato's concern and the presence of O.J.'s eldest daughter from his first marriage residing in her own quarters on the premises, O.J. did not investigate or alert his private security service. Uncharacteristically, he also forgot to turn on the security system before he left for the airport.

Loading up the limousine, Kato offered to carry one of Simpson's bags from the pavement, however, Simpson insisted on carrying the bag himself. By the next morning, the bag had disappeared and has not been seen since, nor have the clothes that Simpson was allegedly wearing on the night of June 12.

The night after the murder, Simpson told an old friend and retired cop, Ron Shipp, that he had had dreams of killing Nicole. He also inquired about how long it took to get DNA results back.

In addition to the evidence presented, Simpson had no alibi to exclude him from consideration. It would also be argued, if not proven, that O.J. had the time, opportunity, and motive to commit the murder. As for the latter, the prosecution made the case that the murder of Nicole was a premeditated act born out of Simpson's obsession with her and his final realization that he could no longer have her. Goldman, the second victim, had the misfortune of showing up at the wrong place at the wrong time to return a pair of eyeglasses, and he was killed so that the murderer could escape without a witness. The prosecution argued that O.J. abused Nicole during the span of their seventeen-year relationship. Prosecutors disclosed a history of brutal beatings, verbal assaults, humiliation, and financial control. Consistent with classic abusive and battering cycles or scenarios, the worst episodes of domestic violence were followed by periods of contrition and attempts by both of them to try again. In sum, the prosecution advanced the theory that O.J. killed Nicole because of his need to possess and control her, because of his realization that he had lost Nicole once and for all, and because of his parallel rationalization that if he could not have her, then nobody could.

The Defense Case

The case for the defense centered on a conspiracy against O. J. Simpson orchestrated by the LAPD:

Some officers, like Vannatter and Fuhrman, were accused of actively participating in evidence planting and tampering. Others, both officers and members of the LAPD Scientific Investigation Division, were accused of a more passive role. Some of these passive participants knew that something was wrong, Simpson's lawyers argued, but refused to tell anyone about it, even when testifying under oath. The defense dubbed this latter aspect of their theory the "conspiracy of silence." (Rantala, 1996, p. 25)

Even before Johnnie Cochran's opening statement informing the jury that the evidence against Simpson was "contaminated, compromised, and ultimately corrupted," the multi-million-dollar "Dream Team" defense had been fueling ideas in the tabloid and mainstream news alike about evidence tampering and an O.J. frame-up by dirty cops who wanted to convict Simpson at any cost.[1] From the beginning, O.J.'s defense team was trying to put the police, the state, and the prosecution's case on trial and present the adjudication of Simpson as a miscarriage of justice.

Simpson's lawyers argued that the investigation was so botched that conclusions about the physical evidence could not be trusted. For example, the defense argued that the DNA evidence implicating O.J. was contaminated with the blood that Simpson voluntarily gave to the police. They further argued that the bloody glove found at Simpson's estate, as well as other blood droplets, were planted at the scene, at O.J.'s house on Rockingham, and in his Ford Bronco. They specifically charged Mark Fuhrman with planting the bloody glove at Rockingham and smearing some of the blood off of the glove and onto the Bronco, and they similarly accused Philip Vannatter of planting the blood that Simpson had voluntarily given to the police.

To buttress their argument against Vannatter, the defense argued that blood on the back gate and on the socks in Simpson's bedroom contained a preservative, so it must have been in one of the test tubes used by the jail nurse who drew blood from O.J. the day after the murders.

In short, whenever the defense could critique the LAPD's investigative process in relationship to any damaging evidence, they did so. When the defense could not offer any type of rebuttal, they simply chose to remain quiet, leaving the incriminating evidence alone. When there were uncertain or unknown aspects in the case that could be speculated about— like the time of the murders—the defense made a case for the murders happening later than the prosecution had surmised, hoping to show that O.J. could not have had the time to commit the murders and catch the early bird flight from LAX to Chicago. The defense alleged that Simpson was too infirm from his arthritis to have committed the double homicide. Similarly, they argued that Nicole had not bought the gloves as a Christmas present for Simpson in 1990, nor did the gloves have any connection to Simpson whatsoever. Finally, as for Simpson not responding for twenty minutes to the calls from the limousine driver at his Rockingham address at the approximate time of the murders, his lawyers maintained that O.J. had simply overslept.

As for the issue of motive, the defense upheld that Simpson was a happy man. Despite that the police had responded on several occasions to domestic violence calls from Nicole involving O.J., his defense attorneys argued that he regretted the lone incident in which he was officially adjudicated for battery in 1989. Simpson's attorneys further claimed that there had been no ensuing physical violence between O.J. and Nicole. They also claimed that he was not upset or agitated between the time when the murders were committed and when he learned of the deaths early the next day in Chicago. Furthermore, Simpson's family members denied that a private conversation had occurred between O.J. and Ron Shipp the evening after the murders.

Although the defense need not offer an explanation for the murders, they did come up with a "theory" for the crime; the defense suggested that the brutal killings were carried out by two men rather than one. They further speculated that the double homicide had something to do with cocaine used by Nicole's friend Fay Resnick and debts Resnick allegedly owed to some unidentified drug dealers.

Jury Selection and the Verdict of Not Guilty

Jury consultants were used by both the prosecution and defense in the Simpson criminal trial. Interestingly, Jo-Ellan Dimitris of Litigation Science, who was retained by the defense, and Donald Vinson of Decision Quest, who worked pro bono for the prosecution, came essentially to the same conclusions about the type of jury that would be more or less likely to convict Simpson. Not surprisingly, both Dimitris and Vinson thought white jurors would be more likely to convict Simpson than black jurors would. More significantly, both consultants thought that black men would be some three times more likely than black women to convict O.J.

Vinson, who conducted several fifteen-person focus group sessions, provided extensive research and data, created elaborate displays and exhibits, and stressed the importance of keeping black women away from the jury box. For example, he noted that his data revealed that 23 percent of black men thought O.J. was guilty, while only 7 percent of black women thought him guilty (Barak, 1996).

From the focus groups, Vinson learned not only what type of jurors to select, but he also gained insight into who should or should not prosecute the case against Simpson. It was clear that black women were more vocal in their support of O.J. than black men were. Black women were also ready to dismiss the importance of Simpson having beaten Nicole, rationalizing that "every relationship has these kinds of problems" (Bugliosi, 1996, p. 82). Finally, Vinson learned of the intense dislike and extreme negativity that these black women from the focus groups had for the white female prosecutor Marcia Clark; some went so far as to vocalize their hate and contempt by referring to Clark as that "bitch." As it turned out, however, the Los Angeles district attorney at the time, John Garcetti, and the lead prosecutor, Marcia Clark, both ignored what turned out to be sage advice from Vinson. In other words, not only did the district attorney's office not substitute another lead prosecutor in place of Clark, but they concluded that they knew best and that gender was a trump card over race. White or black women alike would convict Simpson, so Clark believed. As it would turn out, it was not a question of gender over race or vice versa, but rather it was a case of gender and race.

Meanwhile, Dimitris and the defense team had reached the same conclusions as Vinson. When the prosecution rejected essentially the same advice, but reversed, as the defense had accepted, they both were, in effect, selecting the same type of jury that turned out, as predicted by Litigation Science and Decision Quest, to be the least likely jury (e.g., the one with the most black women) in terms of demographics to convict O.J. of the double homicides. Simpson's jury of twelve consisted of two white women, nine black women, and one black man. Again, as jury consultant Vinson told Clark and Garcetti, "black females were the worst conceivable jurors for the prosecution" (Bugliosi, 1996, p. 82).

According to research by Russell, although black women have tended to be more physically assertive in their abusive and battering relations than white women, they have also been protective of black males in terms of the dominant white society (Russell, 1996). Moreover, the institutional suppression of the problem of domestic violence in the black community was underscored by Michael Eric Dyson—a syndicated columnist for the *Chicago Sun Times* and a distinguished professor of African American and religious studies, and the Avalon Foundation Professor of Humanities at the University of Pennsylvania—when he wrote:

The truth is that black male violence against black women is a mainstay of relations between the two. The oppressive silence black women have observed in deference to race loyalty, or had imposed on them out of fear, remains a tragically underexplored issue in black life. Domestic violence against women is a concealed epidemic in black communities. It needs to be exposed. (Dyson, 1996, p. 51)

What Marcia Clark and the prosecution failed to take into account was the emotional and psychological history of domestic violence in the black community. Not only the prevalence of such behavior but the fact that those who have experienced such violence as a victim, or who have encountered it in their families, tend to be forgiving, emphasize recovery, and do not conclude that domestic violence necessarily leads to homicide. Attitudes or rationalizations of this kind work on two levels: First, there are the more overt tendencies to identify with and to displace the blame of O.J. onto the victim Nicole with whom identification is blocked. Second, at a more latent or unconscious level, if O.J.—who had everything in the world going for himself with few of the everyday hassles and frustrations of many black men—could resort to escalating this domestic violence into murder, how safe were these black women (jurors) from the men in their lives?

When the trial was finished, the sequestered jury, who had spent nine months listening to one of the longest and most contentious trials in courtroom history, took only four hours to reach a decision of not guilty. It was "obvious" that they had bought the defense team's argument that evidence against O.J. was tainted, planted, and contaminated. To subordinate the uncontested evidence against O.J. to the contested evidence was to accept the defense team's assertion that the state had set out to frame O.J. for the double homicide. In effect, some have argued that, in a way, the jury's decision of a not guilty verdict was an act of unconscious "jury nullification."

On the other hand, not all jurors were as "unconscious" of the decision that they were making. The lone male juror, a black man, raised his right fist in a black power salute when the jury stepped down after the verdict was read. Gender and race came into play quite clearly. For example, the jury did not reach a unanimous verdict of not guilty on the first vote. The initial polling had ten jurors voting not guilty and two voting guilty. The two jurors who voted for the guilty verdict on the first vote and then subsequently changed their minds on the second vote were the only whites on the jury. The two white jurors were women who quickly decided to capitulate or acknowledge defeat rather than stage a racial contest with the other ten emotionally united blacks who had concluded that O.J. was not guilty.

SIDELINE PUNDITS AND POSTADJUDICATION AUTOPSIES

Both during and after the Simpson trials, sideline pundits consisted overwhelmingly of attorneys. Nearly every one of these lawyers had courtroom experience as a prosecutor or as a defense attorney or both. Out of the hundreds, if not thousands of hours of Simpson programming, scant minutes at most were allocated to contributions from those who were not lawyers, including forensic scientists, social and behavioral scientists, and other experts on culture and society. As a result, the mass-mediated discourse on the representation of O. J. Simpson was rarely about law and society in general. In particular, it was not about race and social control or about gender relations inside or outside the courtroom. For the most part, the coverage was restricted to the courtroom dynamics of the legal actors in this American tragedy and to how well they were playing to the jury and to the public.

Those legal pundits who had managed to capture a place at the Simpson trough did so because they were able to display emotions and connect themselves to the media frenzy. Their popularity was not their legal expertise per se, but rather their courtroom experience and viewpoints for what would and would not work in a court of law. Most of the time, those legal pundits were engaged in "evaluating" how well the judge, the defense, the prosecution, and the witnesses were doing on any given day. In other words, it was a "who's up, who's down" type of coverage. Much of their infotainment consisted of supplying endless praise and criticism for the way the attorneys had performed with respect to opening arguments, direct examinations, cross-examinations, re-directs, closing arguments, and so on. Occasionally these pundits ventured outside of the procedurally construed legal commentary and into the allied cultural issues of the wider society and the administration of social justice.

Defensive of the legal status quo and the U.S. criminal justice system as a whole, most of these "legal experts" acknowledged that, because of his fame and fortune, O.J. was afforded very special and privileged treatment by the state during his arrest, investigation, and prosecution. For example, in a reversal of how the criminal justice system normally works in a capital crime before the actual trial begins, the Los Angeles District Attorney's Office stipulated that the prosecution would not seek the death penalty if the verdict resulted in a guilty conviction. This was a calculated concession to O.J.'s popularity and the belief that his conviction would be even less likely if he was facing the death penalty. From the beginning, Garcetti and the prosecution were skeptical of their chances of winning despite their evidence against Simpson.

Most legal pundits in their postadjudicative autopsies—daily or at the climax of each one of Simpson's trials—were able to point out the differences in treatment afforded to Orenthal James Simpson and the treatment experienced by other black men who have been similarly charged with criminal homicide. Seldom, however, did these pundits discuss the differential impact of institutionalized racism, sexism, or classism on the administration of justice. Even more remote were the few discussions that tried to connect the larger social, political, and economic arrangements of inequality to the way in which these forces shape or influence the perceptions and attitudes that people have about crime and justice in the United States.

As for the average viewers, most pundits thought that they had received a worthwhile crash course—O.J. 101—in criminal law and procedural due process. Some believe that beyond the mediated spectacle there was not nearly as much valuable information communicated about crime and justice as there should have been, especially given all the airtime. For the most part, the lessons were superficial or they were so basic that they should have been known in the first place. For example, it was repeatedly pointed out how the public had learned the difference in the burdens of proof involved in criminal and civil litigations. That is to say, most laypeople who tuned into the legal proceedings came to realize that the state or prosecution in the criminal case had a tougher burden to prove than the plaintiff in a civil case. Regarding Simpson and the criminal case, the public understood that the prosecution had not proved its case against Simpson "beyond a reasonable doubt." In the latter civil case, people also understood that O.J. had been found guilty of the wrongful deaths of Nicole Brown Simpson and Ronald Lyle Goldman based on a "preponderance of the evidence."

MEDIA, DISCOURSE, AND THE O. J. SIMPSON CASE: A FINAL COMMENT

In the postmodern and contemporary worlds of telecommunications, there has been a blurring of the news and entertainment media. The blurring has been technological and thematic. Thematically, the blurring is exemplified by the public discourse surrounding the representation of crime and justice in America. When it comes to high-profile criminal trials in particular, especially since O.J., there is usually a flurry of activity to gain access to such media sites as CNN, Court TV, Hard Copy, Entertainment Tonight, CNBC, the major network news stations, and all the other entertainment news shows that are produced regularly. Those prime-time show formats like *Larry King Live* or the discontinued *Rivera Live* allow those immerged in high-profile criminal trials to try their case in the "court of public opinion"—free as much as possible from law.

Beyond the particulars of these high-profile criminal trials, those pundits or whoever attach themselves to the mass-mediated discussions of these cases possess the opportunity to assist and/or resist the reconstruction of a fairly solidified agenda of "law and order." During their encounter with the inequities, for example, involved in the administration of crime and justice in the United States, these pundits may choose to explore or ignore these social realities. For in the end, when it comes to reporting on the administration of justice there is much more involved than merely reporting "just the facts" as television detective Jack Webb used to say. Interestingly, for all the to-do, all the fuss, and all the debate about the Orenthal James Simpson double murder of Nicole Brown Simpson and Ronald Lyle Goldman, the influence of those trials on the practice of criminal and civil justice in the United States has been virtually nil.

NOTE

1. For more information, see Trial Transcripts, 1995, available at http://www.cnn.com/US/OJ/trial/jan/

REFERENCES

Barak, G. (ed.). (1996). *Representing O.J.: Murder, criminal justice, and mass culture.* Guilderland, NY: Harrow and Heston.

Barak, G., Flavin, J., and Leighton, P. (2001). *Class, race, gender, and crime: Social realities of justice in America.* Los Angeles: Roxbury.

BBC News. (2003). Row over O.J. Simpson show [Electronic version]. Retrieved July 25, 2003, from http://news.bbc.co.uk

Bugliosi, V. (1996, July). Outrage: The reasons O.J. Simpson got away with murder. *Playboy.*

CNET News. (1997). Chat rooms on O.J. case jam-packed [Electronic version]. Retrieved July 26, 2003, from http://news.com.com/Chat+rooms+on+O.J.+case+jam-packed/2100-1023_3-268291.html

Deutsch, L. (2003). OJ Simpson says not to reality show, but might comment on Robert Blake case. Associated Press. Retrieved from: http://www.cbsnews.com/stories/2002/04/18/entertainment/main506527.shtml

Dyson, M. E. (1996). Obsessed with O.J. In J. Abramson (Ed.), *Postmortem: The O.J. Simpson case* (pp. 46–56). New York: Basic Books.

French, L. (1996). Juror reciprocal antagonism and the intermittent explosive disorder: A plausible clinical diagnosis of the O.J. case. In G. Barak (Ed.), *Representing O.J.: Murder, criminal justice, and mass culture* (pp. 29–35). Guilderland, NY: Harrow and Heston.

Leibovich, L. (1998). The mystery of O.J. Simpson. Retrieved July 25, 2003, from http://www.salon.com/media

Morrison, P. (1999). Five years since the 'Simpson matter.' Retrieved July, 26, 2003, from http://www.juneauempire.com

O.J. Simpson says case blown out of proportion [Electronic version]. (2001). *CNN News.* Retrieved July 25, 2003, from http://www.cnn.com/2001/LAW/02/09/simpson.altercation.02/

O.J. Simpson's daughter calls police after fight with father [Electronic version]. (2002, January 20) *Associated Press.* Retrieved on July 25, 2003, from http://abcnews.go.com/sections/us/DailyNews/simpson_daughter030130.html

O.J. Simpson says no to reality show [Electronic version]. (2003, April 24) *Associated Press.* Retrieved July 25, 2003, from http://cbs2.chicago.com/entertainmentnews

Prodis, J. (1995, April 17). TV gives lawyers 15 minutes of fame and more as "O.J. experts." *Ann Arbor News*, p. A2.

Rantala, M. L. (1996). *O.J. unmasked: The trial, the truth, and the media.* Chicago: Catfeet.

Russell, K. K. (1996). Reality bites: Black protectionism, white denial and O.J. In G. Barak (Ed.), *Representing O.J.: Murder, criminal justice, and mass culture* (pp. 160–165). Guilderland, NY: Harrow and Heston.

12

The Susan Smith Case:
From Victim to Child Murderer
in Nine Days

Kevin Buckler

At around 9 p.m. on October 25, 1995, Shirley McCloud, a resident of Union, South Carolina, was just finishing reading the *Union Daily Times* when she heard a woman screaming from just outside her residence. Upon investigation, McCloud observed a young woman in her early- to mid-twenties haphazardly calling out for someone to help her. The young woman informed McCloud that a man had abducted her children. More specifically, the young, visibly shaken women exclaimed, "A black man has got my kids and my car!" McCloud and her husband, Rick, quickly told their son to call 911 emergency, and within minutes of the call one of the most complex, disturbing, and memorable cases in recent U.S. history was set in motion.

The woman that the McClouds assisted was Susan Smith, a twenty-three-year-old executive assistant of a local corporation and mother of two boys: three-year-old Michael and one-year-old Alex. Susan, in her first interview with police, asserted that she was at a stop light at Monarch Mills intersection, when a black man jumped in her car and told her to drive. Susan claimed that when she asked the man why he was abducting her and her children he told her to shut up and drive or he would kill her. She told the police that she drove northeast of Union for about four miles until the man requested that she stop the car next to a sign that advertised John D. Long

Susan Smith is escorted from the Union County Courthouse on Friday, July 28, 1995, after the jury delivered a verdict of life in prison. (AP/Wide World Photos)

Lake, which was located several hundred yards from the McCloud residence. Susan asserted that the man made her stop in the middle of the road and then told her to get out of the car. After asking the man why she could not take her children with her, the man told her that there was not enough time. He then pushed her out of the car while pointing a gun at her side. According to Susan's statement made to the police, the man then told Susan not to worry, he was not going to harm her children, and then he drove away. However, after a flurry of media attention and after several marked inconsistencies in her statements were noted by police investigators, Susan Smith confessed to murdering her children by driving them into John D. Long Lake where they drowned.

This chapter uses the Susan Smith case to examine the intersection of crime, justice, and media. First, the chapter provides a detailed description of the offense, the context of the offense, the participants in the case, the actions taken by the agents of the criminal justice system, and an account of the trial and the final resolution of the case. Second, the chapter explores the influence of the media on the outcome of the trial, the decision-making process of the key participants leading up to the trial, and how involvement in this high-profile case has likely impacted the lives of some of the key participants in the case. Finally, the chapter discusses the relevant social and legal issues in the Susan Smith case and how these issues have influenced popular and legal culture.

BACKGROUND AND DESCRIPTION OF THE CRIME

The title of one of the several books that was published about the Susan Smith case asks a very provocative question: *Susan Smith: Victim or Murderer?* (Rekers, 1996). It is a question that is intricately woven into one of the most intensely debated questions in philosophy, psychology, sociology, and other fields in the humanities. Have the individuals who commit horrific crimes such as these exercised free will in their actions, or are psychological, biological, and/or sociological and environmental factors at work that serve to compel behavior? To what degree do unfortunate and personally damaging incidents occurring in the life of an individual, especially a young person, affect his or her future behavior? Do these factors—if in fact they do determine future behavior—excuse behavior? The following section high- lights the personal, family, and behavioral background of Susan Smith and her family. Susan's defense team would eventually argue that these personal and familial factors explain her behavior that led to the deaths of her sons, Michael and Alex, on the night of October 25, 1994.

The Childhood of Susan Smith

Susan was born on September 26, 1971 in the small, rural town of Union, South Carolina, to Linda Smith, a homemaker, and Harry Smith, a local firefighter and textile worker. Susan's childhood home life was marred by conflict, dysfunction, and tragedy. The marriage of Linda and Harry Smith was a rocky one that was characterized by conflict and violent confrontation. On several occasions, Harry Smith had threatened to murder his wife and then commit suicide. Before Susan had entered elementary school, her half- brother, Michael Smith, had tried to commit suicide by hanging himself.

When Susan was six or seven years old, her parents ended their tumultuous marriage. Within five weeks of the final divorce decree, Susan's father commit- ted suicide. Harry's suicide occurred shortly after an argument had ensued between Linda and him that led Linda to call the police. The police, upon arrival at the scene of the incident, witnessed Harry strike his ex-wife; the police determined that Harry had gained access to his ex-wife's home by breaking and entering. Shortly thereafter, Harry placed a gun between his legs and fired one shot into his abdomen. He was later pronounced dead after emergency surgery was performed.

Within two weeks of her divorce from Harry, Linda Smith married Beverly (Bev) Russell. Russell, a businessman, was a member of the South Carolina State Republican Committee and of the advisory board of the Christian Coalition. After their marriage, the couple moved their family into Russell's exclusive Mount Vernon Estates section of Union. If the divorce of her biological parents, the suicide of her father, and the subsequent remarriage of her mother to Russell had an effect on Susan, the effects were not immediate and were initially concealed. She performed exceptionally well in elementary school, junior high school, and high school. She was a member of several clubs in school, maintained a B average or higher, and worked as a volunteer with the elderly and the Special Olympics.

Despite the apparent stability evidenced by Susan's life at school and in her extracurricular activities, reports maintain that her home life was filled with internal conflict and turmoil. At the age of thirteen, Susan attempted suicide by overdosing on aspirin. The most glaring example of this internal conflict was manifested in Susan's relationship with Russell. There are several documented reports of inappropriate behavior and sexual contact that had occurred between Susan and Russell. One such report occurred around Susan's sixteenth birthday when she had crawled into the lap of Russell and began to fall asleep. During this encounter, Russell, as his stepdaughter was falling asleep, moved his hand from her shoulder to her breasts. Reports also maintain that during this encounter, Russell moved one of Susan's hands directly on his genitals. Susan pretended to be asleep while the molestation occurred (Pergament, n.d.).

Susan filed a complaint against Russell with the Union County Sheriff's Office and the South Carolina Department of Social Services that resulted in Susan and her mother attending several family counseling sessions. During this time period, Russell temporarily moved out of the residence. However, Susan and her mother would eventually terminate the family counseling sessions, and Russell eventually returned to the family residence. At several points in the eventual murder trial of Susan Smith, it was revealed that the inappropriate sexual contact that had occurred between stepfather and stepdaughter did not end with the initial report that was filed after Susan's sixteenth birthday. In fact, the defense counsel's psychiatric expert testified that the family appeared to place the blame for the inappropriate acts on Susan as much as on Russell.

Moreover, in March 1988, official county and state records indicate that Susan, then seventeen years old, reported an incident of sexual molestation by Russell to a high-school guidance counselor who, under state law, was required to report the incident to the proper authorities. During Susan's eventual murder trial, the state caseworker who was assigned the case testified that she had learned that Russell, on repeated occasions, had fondled Susan's breasts, French-kissed her, and placed her hand on his genitals. No charges were brought against Russell for this second set of alleged inappropriate sexual contact because Susan had agreed not to press any charges. The caseworker attempted to convince Jack Flynn, assistant court solicitor at the time, to file aggravated assault and battery charges against Russell, but an agreement was reached between Russell's attorney and the assistant court solicitor not to file the charges. The agreement was accepted and sealed by an appropriate judicial authority.

The Adulthood Family and Intimate Relationships of Susan Smith

During her junior and senior years of high school, Susan Smith worked at a local Winn Dixie supermarket in Union as a cashier and bookkeeper. During her stint at the supermarket, she dated several coworkers and eventually married coworker David Smith. Susan's first relationship involved a married man and led to an eventual pregnancy and subsequent abortion. Following the abortion, the married man broke off his relationship with Smith. She became depressed and ultimately attempted a second suicide with an overdose of Tylenol and aspirin. She eventually met and married David Smith, the father of Michael and Alex.

Early in their relationship, Susan and David learned that Susan was pregnant, and they married in March 1991 before the birth of their first son, Michael. Right away, the marriage was characterized by conflict and difficulty, much centered on financial issues and on the different backgrounds of Susan and David. David grew up in relatively simple surroundings, and he envisioned a simple, country-style life for him and his family. Susan desired a grand and more financially expensive life than David had envisioned. As a result of their very different visions, the couple began to experience a great deal of stress and tension very early in their marriage.

Other sources of tension and stress in their marriage include Susan's mother's controlling and domineering attitude, and the fact that both Susan and David worked at the same company, Winn Dixie, with David as Susan's boss. Susan and David's marriage was marred by several extramarital affairs. By the couple's third wedding anniversary, they had separated on several occasions. In the winter of 1993, David and Susan attempted again to reconcile their chaotic marriage, and the couple purchased a small home in Union. Susan and David's second child, Alex, resulted from this attempt at marital resolution. Within three weeks of the birth of Alex, the couple mutually agreed that their relationship was over and split for a second time.

Following the end of their relationship, Susan realized that she could no longer work at the supermarket with her estranged husband as her supervisor and with David's new and reoccurring girlfriend, Tiffany Moss, employed at the store as well. Susan was eventually hired as a bookkeeper at Conso Products, and she served as the assistant to the executive secretary for J. Carney Findlay, the president and chief executive officer (CEO) of Conso. It was at Conso that Susan met Tom Findlay, the son of the company's CEO, and began a relationship with him. The initial relationship between Susan and Findlay was shortlived. Susan and David, in the spring and summer of 1994, attempted to resolve their relationship one final time; however, Susan, after realizing that the marriage was a failure, sought a divorce in July 1994.

Susan began to date Findlay again in September 1994. Accounts of her case suggest that Susan was beginning to feel that she finally had found some degree of stability in her life in her relationship with Findlay. Findlay— under obviously different views of the relationship—had decided to end their relationship, because he perceived Smith as being overly possessive and needy. In a letter to Susan, informing her of his decision, Findlay wrote, "You will, without a doubt, make some lucky man a great wife. But unfortunately, it won't be me . . . Susan, I could really fall for you. You have some endearing qualities about you, and I think that you are a terrific person. But, like I have told you before, there are some things about you that aren't suited for me, and yes, I am speaking about your children" (Pergament, n.d.).

The letter went on to explain that Findlay did not want the responsibility of caring for another man's children and that he had been upset by several aspects of Susan's behavior—including her behavior at a recent party the two had in which Susan and the husband of one of her friends had kissed and fondled each other in Findlay's hot tub. Concerning the incident, Findlay wrote, "If you want to catch a nice guy like me one day, you have to act like a nice girl. And you know, nice girls don't sleep with married men" (Pergament, n.d.).

Around the same time that Susan received this letter, her divorce with David Smith was becoming finalized. In September 1994, David Smith was served with divorce papers, and in October 1994, the divorce papers were filed at the Union courthouse. By most accounts, Susan was both angered and devastated by the end of her relationship with Findlay. On several occasions, Smith sought out Findlay at both his personal residence and at his work in attempt to reconcile the relationship.

The Drowning at John D. Long Lake

On October 25, 1994, the day of the eventual drowning of her two children, sometime in the early part of the afternoon, Susan requested that her supervisor allow her to leave work for the day, because she was feeling very distraught over the situation with Findlay. Susan further confided in her supervisor that she was in love with a man who does not love her and that the reason the relationship did not work out was because of her children.

Later that afternoon, on three separate occasions between 2:30 p.m. and 6 p.m., Susan initiated contact with Findlay, apparently in a desperate attempt to reconcile the relationship. On the first of these meetings, Susan concocted a story that her ex-husband, David, had threatened to go public with news of an affair between Susan and Findlay's father and expose Susan for cheating the IRS out of funds. After several attempts at salvaging the relationship with Findlay, Susan telephoned a coworker who was having dinner with Findlay to ask if he had mentioned her at all during the dinner. These repeated attempts to make contact with Findlay serve as strong indicators that Susan was having a difficult time accepting the end of their relationship.

At around 8 p.m., Smith dressed her two sons, placed them in their car seats, and began the fateful drive that ended with her rolling her car into John D. Long Lake with her children strapped into car seats inside. According to Smith's eventual confession, she had driven to the lake because she wanted to commit suicide. She wrote that she believed that her children would be better off with her and with God than if they were left without a mother. She indicated that her plan was that she, Michael, and Alex would die together. Smith wrote that on three separate instances, she had put the car in neutral, and as her car was starting to roll into the lake, she pulled the parking brake to stop it.

After the final attempt at suicide, Susan indicated that she got out of the car and stood for a brief moment until she returned to the car and released the parking brake, sending her car and two sons into the lake. After releasing the parking break and watching the car go into the lake, Susan ran to the McCloud residence and began to concoct the story of a black man who had abducted her and her two sons. The story would captivate and fascinate the nation throughout the investigation and subsequent trial.

THE INVESTIGATION

During the initial questioning of Smith that had occurred shortly after the 911 call was placed from the McCloud residence, the representatives from the sheriff's office simply documented the story as relayed by the dispatcher and then again by Smith herself. At this point in the investigation, the police were concerned only with collecting information as it was made available to them and following up on any leads as they developed. It was not until the police began a critical examination and assessment of Smith's statement that they began to suspect she knew something more about the disappearance of her two children.

In the initial stages of the investigation, the sheriff of Union County contacted representatives of the South Carolina Law Enforcement Division (SLED) for assistance in the investigation. The sheriff coordinated collaborative efforts with SLED to have divers search John D. Long Lake and helicopters with heat sensors fly over the area of the incident. A police artist met with Smith to construct a composite drawing of the suspect. Susan described a black man who was around the age of forty, wearing a dark shirt, jeans, a plaid jacket, and a dark knit shirt.

During these initial stages of the investigation, several recently emerging special interest groups and associated figures became involved in, or attempted to become involved in, the investigation process. The Adam Walsh Center[1]—a center developed in the honor of Adam Walsh, a six-year-old who was abducted from a Florida shopping mall and murdered—sent representatives from the regional office in Columbia, South Carolina, to Union to speak with Susan and David. These representatives met with Susan and David and explained the services that they could offer, and the representatives proposed that the organization serve as media liaison for the family. Also, within the first week of the investigation process, Marc Klaas and Jeanne Boyton, a cognitive graphic artist affiliated with the Polly Klaas Foundation and the Marc Klaas Foundation,[2] had attempted to become involved in the investigation, but Susan and David refused to meet with them.

A representative from the Adam Walsh Foundation and the sheriff of Union County convinced David to make a public plea for the safe return of his children. He made the following public statement: "To whoever has our boys, we ask that you please don't hurt them and bring them back. We love them very much . . . I plead to the guy please return our children to us safe and unharmed. Everywhere I look, I see their play toys and pictures. They are both wonderful children. I don't know how else to put it. And I can't imagine life without them" (Pergament, n.d.).

Once the standard protocol in cases of missing and abducted children—sketches of the suspect, photos of the missing children, and pleas for the safe return of the children—had been set in motion to ensure that if the boys were still alive and still in the area they had the greatest possible likelihood of being returned, police attention began to shift to the statement provided by Susan Smith. The sheriff of Union County contacted David Caldwell, director of the forensic sciences laboratory for SLED and requested that he come to Union to interview Susan. Two days after the alleged abduction had taken place, Susan and David were both administered a polygraph examination. The results of David's polygraph suggested that he knew nothing about the disappearance of his sons, whereas the polygraph of Susan Smith was inconclusive. A major point of contention that the sheriff's department and SLED investigators had with Susan's polygraph examination concerned her answer to the question "Do you know where your children are?"

Consequentially, over the course of the investigation, Susan would be constantly interviewed and reinterviewed, and in some instances she was interviewed multiple times a day. Subsequent interviews with Susan revealed several inconsistencies and questionable claims in her initial statement and in the statements that followed. First, during an interview with Caldwell, the SLED investigator, Susan had told him that around 7:30 p.m. on the night of the alleged abduction, her son, Michael, had told her that he wanted to go to the local Wal-Mart. Second, Susan had also told Caldwell that while they were out, Michael had also asked if they could go and visit Mitchell Sinclair, the fiancé of Susan's friend Donna Garner. When Caldwell pressed her on this issue, Susan recanted her statements and admitted that it was her idea to initially go to Wal-Mart.

Third, Susan had initially maintained that she had visited the Wal-Mart as planned. Caldwell informed Susan that investigators had spoken to several employees at Wal-Mart and individuals who were at Wal-Mart at the time and that no one remembered seeing her or her children. Moreover, Caldwell revealed that investigators had spoken with Sinclair and that Sinclair had told investigators that he was not home at the time and that he was not expecting Susan. After being confronted about these inconsistencies, Susan amended her story and claimed that she had actually been driving around for hours with her children in the backseat. She claimed to have lied because she was afraid that her behavior would have sounded suspicious.

Fourth, in the initial statement that Susan made to the police, she had claimed that she was at a stoplight at the Monarch Mills intersection when the black man had approached the car and abducted her and her two children. Susan further asserted that there were no other vehicles in the area, thus, there were no other persons in the area to offer assistance or to substantiate her story. However, Caldwell and the SLED investigators had determined that this claim could not be accurate because the light at the Monarch Mills intersection is permanently green unless a car on the cross street triggers the signal to switch. Therefore, if there were no other cars in the area, the light would not have been red at the intersection in question.

Sheriff Wells and the SLED investigators began to seriously doubt the validity of Susan Smith's statements. When she was confronted with each of the aforementioned inconsistencies during the lengthy and ongoing interrogation process, Smith modified her statements. When it became obvious to investigators that it would not be easy to obtain a confession from Smith, the investigators formulated a plan that called for the use of the media as an important tool in making her crack. The plan called for a buildup of the media frenzy that surrounded the case. The investigators held press conferences to inform the public that they were making little headway in the investigation, invited the producers of *America's Most Wanted* to Union to tape a show concerning the abductions, and encouraged local ministries to hold press conferences requesting the safe return of the children. The ultimate objective of the plan was to place intense pressure on Smith in an effort to get her to break down and confess to the murders.

The strategy worked. On November 3, 1994, Smith confessed to the murders of her children, Michael and Alex, by drowning the two boys in her car, a 1990 Mazda Protégé, in John D. Long Lake.[3] In Smith's confession, she told the investigators of her desperate mental state on the night of the murders, her difficult relationship with David, and the letter from Findlay. She told the investigators that she had driven to the lake with the intention of committing suicide and simultaneously ending her life and the lives of her sons. The confession further detailed three instances in which she allegedly attempted to roll the car into the lake, but at the last minute applied the parking break. Eventually, Susan claimed that she stood outside of the car, went back into the car, released the parking break, and then watched the car slowly descend into the lake. Susan was arrested and charged with double murder.

Smith's family hired David Bruck, a defense attorney from Columbia, South Carolina, who specialized in death-penalty cases to represent Susan. Before accepting Susan's case to defend, Bruck had represented clients in fifty capital cases and only three clients were given the death penalty. Bruck hired Judith Clarke—federal public defender from Washington State and an expert in death penalty cases—to assist in Smith's case. State Solicitor Thomas Pope would represent the state in the case.

THE TRIAL

While awaiting her trial, Smith was detained in the Women's Correctional Facility in Columbia, South Carolina. She was given immediate psychological and physical examinations by the staff. Smith was also placed on a twenty-four-hour suicide watch, which entailed, among other things, closed-circuit monitoring and consistent checks by the correctional facility staff in fifteen-minute increments.

The pretrial proceedings in the case generally followed those that occur in typical cases. On November 5, 1994, a bail hearing was held in the courtroom of Judge Larry Patterson at the request of solicitor Pope. Smith waived her right to be present, and through her attorney, Bruck, she waived her right to bail. On November 18, 1994, at Pope's request, a hearing was held in the courtroom of circuit court Judge John Hayes. At this hearing, the state motioned to have Smith undergo psychological examination by an impartial physician to evaluate her mental capacity in terms of determining her criminal responsibility for her behavior and to determine if she was mentally competent to stand trial. The judge ruled in favor of the defense team, noting that psychological examination was premature, since the defense had not decided whether it would enter an insanity plea on the behalf of Susan.

On January 16, 1995, Pope announced the intention of the state to seek the death penalty against Smith in the deaths of her two sons. The state maintained that there were two aggravating factors that were present that qualified the case for the death penalty. First, Smith had killed two different people in one act. Second, Smith's actions had taken the life of a child or, in this case, the lives of two children who were under the age of eleven. With the announcement of the state's intention to seek the death penalty, the public and media's interest in the Smith case became even more pronounced. On January 27, 1995, Judge William Howard issued a gag order, which prevented the defense and prosecution from releasing any prejudicial evidence or statements to the media that had not been released in court. Judge Howard would also eventually decide, prior to the start of the trial, in favor of a defense motion that banned cameras from the courtroom.

Before the trial began, defense attorney Bruck attempted to strike a deal with the prosecution that would have eliminated the need for a trial. The defense attorney offered thirty years in prison, without the possibility of parole. Pope rejected the offer. The pretrial activities were not without their surprises. Among the surprises was Bruck's decision not to request a change of venue for the trial. According to accounts of the context of Bruck's decision, Bruck had assessed the mood in Union as one that was becoming more appropriately characterized as sympathetic to Smith's condition and situation. A second controversial decision by the defense raised questions and criticisms by experts and media commentators. Just days before the start of the trial, with the defense counsel's consent, Smith's pastor, Mark Long, held a press conference in which he announced that Smith had undergone a Christian conversion and baptism while in prison. To many, the press conference gave the appearance of a ploy that was designed to garner sympathy for the accused.

The trial of Susan Smith began on July 10, 1995, with the selection of a jury that was composed initially[4] of five white men, two white women, four black men and one black women[5]. In the opening statements by the prosecution and the defense, the strategies of the opposing sides became readily apparent. The prosecution's theory maintained that Smith had drowned her two children in John D. Long Lake for reasons of rational self-interest. The prosecution depicted Smith as an egocentric, manipulative, and unremorseful mother who had drowned her children because she wanted to maintain a romantic relationship with Findlay—her ex-boyfriend who was opposed to a relationship with a woman that involved children from a previous relationship. The defense's strategy, on the other hand, was to depict Smith as a child-like individual who had suffered through a difficult and tragic life that had included her father's suicide, molestation, and her own attempts at ending her life. The defense presented these situations as an explanation of Smith's erratic and tragic behavior that led to the death of her children.

To make its case, the prosecution relied on the testimony of McCloud to place Susan at the scene of the crime on October 25, 1994, and to detail the events of the night that led to the 911 call reporting the alleged abduction of Smith's two children by a black man. Union County Sheriff Howard Wells and SLED interrogator Pete Logan offered testimony concerning the specific details that led to Smith's confession, including the lie that Sheriff Wells told Susan that triggered her confession. In an effort to depict Smith's state of mind as cold, calculated, and remorseless—following the alleged abduction and subsequent confession—other investigators and SLED representatives who had contact with Smith testified concerning her perceived (by the particular witness) lack of remorse and that she had seemed not to care about finding her children. Roy Paschal (SLED sketch artist) and David Espie (SLED polygraph examiner) testified about the vague description of the black abductor given by Smith and the insincere methods of sobbing employed by Smith during the polygraph examinations, respectively. Steve Morrow (SLED diving expert) and Dr. Sandra Condari (pathologist) offered testimony regarding the evidence that was retrieved from the lake. Morrow testified about finding the boys' bodies and Findlay's letter to Smith in the vehicle recovered from the lake. Dr. Condari provided limited expert testimony concerning the nature of the bodies recovered from the lake.[6]

The prosecution called Findlay and three of Smith's coworkers to testify as part of a general strategy to link the necessary removal of her children to the "ideal" life that Smith allegedly envisioned. Findlay testified that he had written the letter to Smith ending their relationship and had implicated Smith's children as a primary reason for the break. However, in testimony that supported the defense's overall position, Findlay asserted that Smith was a kind and caring person and not the monstrous individual that the prosecution was attempting to manufacture. The three coworkers of Susan testified that they had heard Smith speaking of what her life could have been like if she had she not married and had children at such a young age.

The Defense Witnesses

The defense presentation of their evidence was consistent with two overriding objectives. First, the defense, consistent with its theory of causation in the case, offered Smith's personal background and family background as explanations of her tragic behavior. Second, the defense had to address the prosecution's contention that the crime was a cold, calculated, and rational decision with the objective being the removal of Smith's children to clear the way for her to continue her relationship with Findlay.

To meet the first objective, the defense team recalled SLED investigators Pete Logan and Carol Allison—both witnesses for the prosecution—who were very sympathetic to Smith during their previous testimonies. Dr. Arlene Andrews, a professor of social work at University of South Carolina, offered testimony concerning the potential role of depression in Smith's family tree as being causally connected to Smith's behavior. More specifically, Andrews's testimony suggested that because depression and suicidal occurrences were relatively common in her family, Smith was biologically predisposed to depression and suicidal tendencies. To further advance this line of reasoning, the defense team called several witnesses who testified about Smith's past depression and suicidal tendencies that had begun to appear when she was ten years old.

To attack the credibility of the prosecution's assertion of motive in the case, the defense relied on the expert testimony of Dr. Seymour Halleck, a professor of psychiatry and law at the University of North Carolina. Based on his interviews with Smith, Halleck testified that Smith had been suffering from depression and suicidal thoughts leading up to the night of October 25, 1995. Moreover, Halleck testified that Smith coped with her depression through having sexual encounters with different men in her life, including David, Findlay, and Russell, in the six-week period that preceded the crimes.

The testimony further contended that Smith had intended to kill herself when she drove to the lake, but at the last moment her self-preservation instincts took over and prevented her from doing so.

The Verdict

After the prosecution and the defense had presented their witnesses and their closing arguments, Judge Howard ruled in favor of the defense on a motion to allow the jury to consider involuntary manslaughter as a potential lesser charge, even though the prosecution had not presented it as an alternative.[7] The jury, however, rejected the opportunity to find Susan guilty of the lesser offense and, after deliberating for two and one-half hours of deliberations, the jury returned with a verdict of guilty on two counts of first-degree murder.

THE PENALTY PHASE

The Prosecution's Evidence

During the penalty phase of the proceedings, the prosecution began by presenting the video evidence of Smith continually lying about the disappearance of her children, which was followed by witness testimony. During the first day of the penalty proceedings, three witnesses offered testimony that spoke to the manner in which Smith had initially responded to the disappearance of her children. The state attempted to demonstrate that Smith's responses to the alleged abduction were uncharacteristic of a mother that was grieving the loss of her children. Margaret Frierson, the executive director of the Adam Walsh Center, testified that Smith had appeared unusually calm during their initial interaction. Eddie Harris, a SLED agent who had transported Smith during her interrogations, testified that she seemed disinterested and calm in terms of finding her children. Margaret Gregory, Smith's cousin, testified about the number of times that Smith had appeared on television and lied about an alleged "black man" who had abducted her and her children.

The prosecution's presentation of the evidence culminated with the testimony of David Smith and with evidence of a video reenactment of Smith's vehicle being submerged by water and a display of the photos of the bodies of Michael and Alex upon removal from the lake—the photos showed the decomposing arms and legs of the children. David testified about how the actions of his ex-wife had affected him personally. Several times during his testimony, David cried, often uncontrollably. The defense, on Susan's request, did not cross-examine David.

The Defense's Evidence

The prosecution rested its case, and the defense team mounted its case by calling three witnesses to testify. Dr. Andrews—a professor of social work at University of South Carolina who had also testified during the trial—testified about the extremely strained nature of the intimate relationship between Susan and David, and how Susan's overall mental health began to deteriorate after the final attempt at reconciliation with David had failed. Andrews also noted that the tragic event in question had occurred just five days after David had confronted Susan about her relationship with Findlay and how a once amicable split with David turned hostile.

Scotty Vaughn, Smith's brother, testified and suggested that Smith's greatest pain is living and not in the fear of dying. Finally, Russell testified that he accepted part of the blame in the drowning deaths of Michael and Alex. Russell further testified that he had molested Smith when she was a teenager and that he had had consensual sex with her on multiple occasions after she became an adult. In the closing statements of the penalty proceedings, the prosecution strongly reasserted its position that the offense was committed by Smith as a rational choice and that she had murdered her two children because they stood in the way of her romantic relationship with Findlay. The defense team, in their closing examination, reemphasized Smith's difficult life history and the deleterious effects that her life experiences had on her mental capacity.

The Sentence

The jury—after again deliberating for about two and one-half hours—sentenced Susan Smith to imprisonment and not the death penalty, as desired by the prosecution. Judge Howard would eventually sentence Smith to serve thirty years to life. In 2025, Smith would be eligible for parole in South Carolina. When she will be eligible for parole, Smith will be fifty-three years old.

ANALYSIS OF MEDIA COVERAGE OF THE CASE

The media's coverage of the Susan Smith case contributed to the fame that has been accorded to the case in popular, social, and legal culture for a variety of reasons. First, the social context in which the case occurred must be taken into consideration when analyzing the popularity of the case. The Susan Smith case occurred during the O. J. Simpson case investigation and the subsequent televised trial. The general public, to a large degree, became fixated on the investigation and criminal trial of the former NFL superstar. Thus, the public's demand for coverage of crime and criminal trials and the willingness of networks to provide such extensive coverage that followed may have been at an all-time high. It was no coincidence that coverage of criminal trials by such networks as Court TV has increased dramatically since the O. J. Simpson trial. Simpson's trial either helped generate an intense demand for criminal trials, or at the very least, it tweaked a demand that had previously existed.

Second, media coverage of the initial alleged abduction propelled the Smith case from a local issue to a regional news topic and finally to national news prominence. Several major regional newspapers, including the *Atlanta Journal and Constitution* and the *Miami Herald*, provided coverage of the Smith case through its various stages. The majority of the news coverage of the case was on Court TV and the three major news networks. Over a two-year period beginning on October 26, 1994, the day after the murders, and extending through October 26, 1996, the three major networks aired 109 news segments during their national news telecasts that focused on some aspect of the case (Vanderbilt Network News Archive).[8] Collectively, these three networks combined to show 199 minutes of total coverage of the Smith case.[9] These figures do not include any of the time that was devoted to the Smith case by local network affiliates, or any "Special Episodes" that were generated during coverage of the case. For instance, each of the three major networks aired a twenty-one minute special program (total airtime) that focused on interviews with Susan and David Smith. ABC's *Nightline* also aired a special program on November 3, 1994, that lasted for forty-one minutes of total airtime.

Impact on the Potential Jury Pool

Despite local, regional, and national prominence of the Susan Smith case, the effects of the media coverage on the outcome of the case is rather difficult to assess. First, any potential influences on the case's outcome—after the case had been brought to trial—would have occurred through news media influence on the jury pool in terms of pretrial publicity and the release to prejudicial information to the public. In the Susan Smith case, Judge Howard—in contrast to Judge Ito in the O. J. Simpson case—took steps to ensure that pretrial publicity would not have maximum potential effects on the potential jury pool. Early in the case, Howard issued a gag order, which restricted the release of prejudicial information by the prosecution and the defense, and he subsequently banned cameras from the courtroom during the trial. It would be incorrect to suggest that there were no effects that emanated from pretrial publicity; however, measures had been put in place to ensure that such effects would have been minimal.

Furthermore, unlike the O. J. Simpson case and other high-profile criminal trials, the Susan Smith case, from beginning to end, played itself out in an entirely different setting and context. In the Susan Smith case, the potential jury pool for the case consisted of members from a small and rural community, and there was a greater potential for jurors to have had personal ties to Susan Smith, her family, or David Smith's family. Thus, to a certain extent, any prejudicial statements or circumstances that may have occurred in the case may have occurred regardless of the media presence, especially given the nature of the case. Moreover, once a case has reached the trial stage, the court has the ability to exclude prejudicial evidence, declare a mistrial on a show of prejudicial evidence, and sanction participants in the process who informally release unauthorized prejudicial evidence.

Potential Impacts on Events Leading to Trial

Although the impact of the media frenzy that surrounded the Smith case is difficult to assess in terms of the effects on the outcome of the trial, the potential effects of the media are more pronounced and easier to detect in terms of influence on the investigation and the events that led up to the trial. In this regard, there are many interesting points of debate. For example, how did the media presence influence the behaviors of Susan and David after the initial allegation of abduction—in terms of David's efforts to get his children back and Susan's effort to keep her secret concealed? Did the media's presence prolong the subsequent confession of Susan Smith? Did the media's presence affect the manner in which the case was investigated, charged, and prosecuted? Without the media pressure in the Smith case, would the case have even made it to trial or would a pretrial agreement likely have been reached?

These are the influences of media coverage on criminal trials that are missed frequently in analyses of the effects of the media on high-coverage crime news events. These influences can have a dramatic impact, not only on the trial but more importantly on the decision making of key players in the process, including the accused, the police, prosecutors, and judges. The Susan Smith case provides one such example of how the presence of media can affect the actions of criminal justice decision makers. As previously mentioned, investigators used the media to elicit Smith's confession by placing tremendous pressure on her and her family. Although the effects of the media pressure on Smith's subsequent confession are difficult to gauge (because of the direct role of the lie told by Sheriff Wells), the potential exists that investigators were able to use the media to fulfill their organizational objectives of obtaining a confession.

THE SOCIAL AND LEGAL IMPLICATIONS

Throughout the Susan Smith case, there was evidence of important social and legal issues. These important social and legal issues were not necessarily novel in terms of the issues being generated by the case itself; rather, these issues represented ongoing themes that were occurring in the social and legal culture of the United States at the time. For example, one of the first social issues that presented itself in the Smith case was the issue of the alleged abduction by a "black man." Initially, the assertion that Smith's children were abducted by a black man went largely unchallenged by the media. The depiction of the alleged offender fit the stereotypical vision of crime that was generally presented by certain elements of the media, despite evidence to the contrary, which suggests that, in typical abduction cases, most child abductions are perpetrated by someone close to the child like a relative (Dixon and Linz, 2000; Kappeler, Blumberg, and Potter, 1996). The tactic of blaming black men is not new in criminal cases in American culture.[10] One surprising—and somewhat welcomed—aspect of the Smith case was the degree to which investigators aggressively questioned Smith's initial claims.

Second, following Smith's confession, the case—much like the O. J. Simpson case—came to represent an instance of domestic crime that emanated within intimate family and social contexts. The coverage of the Smith case brought a relatively rare phenomenon (female homicide offenders) to the national stage and placed the occurrence within its proper social context; that is, crimes committed against one's own family members. In the 1990s, domestic forms of violence, while tragically remaining at the periphery in terms of important social concerns, received more attention from state officials, the media, and the general public.

A final potential social and legal implication of the Smith case concerns the increasing tendency in the 1990s and onward of countries and states extending more rights to children as a means of protecting them from potential dangers as part of a slowly evolving movement toward children's rights. Much of the activity, in this regard, has focused on nation-states and bringing various nation-states in line with democratic principles relating to the treatment of human beings generally and juveniles specifically (i.e., the United Nations Convention on the Rights of Children, 1989). The movement has also has garnered changes in the United States (i.e., the work of the Children's Rights Council that was formed in 1985). Further examples of the trend of children's rights are the increasing numbers of states in the 1990s—and into the twenty-first century—that allow for the termination of parental rights following a conviction of a felony-level offense by parents to the children and the development of several special interests groups such as the Jacob

Wetterling Foundation and the Polly Klass Foundation, which are devoted to protecting the interests of children in instances of abduction (Buckler and Travis 2003; Olivares, Burton, and Cullen, 1996). The Susan Smith case, although it did not directly involve ongoing domestic child abuse, communicated to a nationwide audience a clear need to protect children—sometimes even from their own parents.

NOTES

1. The Adam Walsh Center is a special-interest organization that was instrumental in the passage of the 1984 Missing Children's Act, which organized a computerized system for the sharing of information relating to missing children in the United States.

2. The Polly Klaas Foundation and the Marc Klaas Foundation are special-interest foundations that were developed to honor the memory of Polly Klaas, a twelve-year-old girl who was abducted from her home in Petaluma, California, and was murdered by her abductor. These two organizations actively lobby for stronger laws to protect children and keep violent and repeat offenders in prison for longer periods of time.

3. The confession of Susan Smith was obtained when Susan, in an attempt to change her statement to fit the information that the police investigators had given her, stated that she had not stopped at Monarch Mills intersection, but instead had stopped at a different intersection. Sheriff Wells, in response, lied and told Susan that he knew she was lying because the police had units stationed at the intersection and the police would have observed the incident as it occurred.

4. The jury that would eventually decide the case was partially comprised of two alternate jury members, as two of the initial members of the jury were excused; one for failure to disclose previous charges of credit card fraud, and the other as a result of a family tie to the case.

5. The gender and ethnic composition of the jury resulted in defense attorney Bruck challenging the jury on the basis that the composition of the jury was not truly representative of the community. This argument, outlined in a motion filed with the court, was rejected by the judge.

6. The judge strictly limited the testimony of Dr. Condari concerning the nature of the boys' decayed physical features due to the potentially prejudicial nature of the physical evidence.

7. Involuntary manslaughter does not place strict restrictions on the jury in terms of determining that the accused intentionally committed the homicide with malice aforethought. Under South Carolina law, if convicted of involuntary manslaughter, the accused faces three to ten years imprisonment. A conviction of murder for Susan Smith would have meant the potential for life imprisonment or a sentence of death.

8. The Vanderbilt University Television News Archive was searched for news segments that were aired on the national news networks ABC, CBS, and NBC. ABC aired thirty segments, CBS aired forty segments, and NBC aired thirty segments

during their regular news telecasts. This archive is available at http://tvnews. vanderbilt.edu/.

9. ABC accounted for forty-six minutes, CBS accounted for seventy-seven minutes, and NBC accounted for seventy-six minutes of the 199 total minutes of national network news coverage during its national news telecasts.

10. In Boston, in 1989, Charles Stuart shot and killed his pregnant wife in their car and then made allegations to the police that he and has wife had been attacked by a black man. The 911 call to authorities was repeatedly broadcast by the media, and during the investigation the police aggressively questioned a number of black men in Boston.

REFERENCES

Buckler, K. G., and Travis, L. F. (2003). Reanalyzing the prevalence and social context of collateral consequence statutes. *Journal of Criminal Justice, 31*(5), 435–453.

Dixon, T. L., and Linz, D. (2000). Race and the misrepresentation of victimization on television news. *Communication Research, 27*(5), 547–573.

Kappeler, V. E., Blumberg, M., and Potter, G. W. (1996). *The mythology of crime and criminal justice.* Prospect Heights, IL: Waveland Press.

Olivares, K., Burton, V. S., and Cullen, F. T. (1996). The collateral consequences of a felony conviction: A national study of state legal codes ten years later. *Federal Probation, 60,* 10–17.

Pergament, R. (n.d.) Women who kill: Susan Smith. Retrieved October 23, 2003, from http://www.crimelibrary.com/notorious_murders/famous/smith

Rekers, G. (1996). *Susan Smith: Victim or murderer?* Lakewood, CO: Glenbridge Publishing, Ltd.

Smith, D., and Calef, C. (1996). *Beyond all reason: My life with Susan Smith.* New York: Kensington Books.

13

1993 World Trade Center Attack: The Forgotten Bombing

Kelly R. Damphousse, Jason Lawson, and Brent L. Smith

The World Trade Center will forever be remembered as the site of a tragic 1993 terrorist bombing. . . . A small memorial on the sidewalk marks the tragedy in memory of the six people who were killed and the hundreds more who were injured in the senseless, horrifying blast that shook the city and the world.

(Mintzer, 2000)

My debate judge deducted points from my final score because I kept mentioning the World Trade Center bombings. She seemed to have forgotten that the WTC had been attacked prior to 9/11.

(Smith, 2003)[1]

The September 11, 2001, terrorist attacks that took place in New York City, Washington, and Pennsylvania were seen by some as the United States' introduction into the brutal world of international terrorism. As a result of the national trauma on "9/11," the significance of the events that occurred at

Table 1
Chronology of Events Associated with the World Trade Center Bombing of 1993

1991	1992	1993	1994	1995	1996	1997	1998
November –Nosair trial begins for the killing of Meir Kahane, a pro-Israel activist. –Nosair is found to be a follower of Omar Abdel-Rahman. –Nosair eventually sentenced on weapons charges and sentenced to seven years.	**September** –Ajaj and Yousef attempt to enter the United States. –Ajaj is detained and Yousef is allowed to enter. –Yousef moves in with Musab and Abdul Yasin. –Salameh, Ayyad, Abouhalima, and Abdul Yasin buy bomb-making chemicals.	**February** –Salameh rents a Ryder truck. –Bomb explodes in World Trade Center (WTC) garage. **March** –*NY Times* receives letter written by Ayyad claiming credit for the bombing. –Salameh, Ayyad, and Abouhalima are arrested. –Yousef is indicted (*in absentia*). Abdel-Rahman denies involvement.	**March** –Salameh, Ajaj, Abouhalima, and Ayyad convicted on all charges. **May** –Salameh, Ajaj, Abouhalima, and Ayyad each sentenced to 240 years in prison. The sentences were essentially cut in half in a 1999 resentencing.	**January** –Yousef, Murad, and Khan are in Philippines planning bombing attacks on U.S. airliners when their apartment catches fire; they flee. –Trial of Abdel-Rahman and nine codefendants begins. They are charged with plotting to blow up the United Nations and other NYC landmarks. **February** –Yousef arrested in Pakistan.	**May** –Trial starts for Yousef, Murad, and Khan on charges of plotting to blow up U.S. airliners. **September** –Yousef, Murad, and Khan are convicted for plotting to blow up U.S. airliners.	**July** –Two terrorists are captured with bombs and plans to destroy NYC subways (four days before start of Yousef trial for WTC attack). **August** –Trial of Yousef and Ismoil begins for the WTC attack. **November** –Yousef and Ismoil are convicted of WTC attack.	**January** –Yousef is sentenced to 240 years. –Ismoil is sentenced to 240 years. –Abdul Yasin remain at large.

October	June	October	August
–Salameh and Yousef build the bomb in a garage apartment.	–Abdel-Rahman and nine followers are indicted for plotting additional NYC attacks. **August** –First WTC trial begins.	–Abdel-Rahman and codefendants (Nosair, El-Gabrowny, Hampton-El, Alvarez, Elhassan, Saleh, F. Abdelgani, A. Abdelgani, and Khallafalla) are found guilty of most charges.	–Ismoil is arrested in Jordan.

the World Trade Center on February 26, 1993, has been mostly eclipsed, which is unfortunate because the 1993 World Trade Center bombing was indeed a watershed event in U.S. history. It was in 1993 that the United States learned, for the first time, that its unseen enemies halfway across the world were prepared and able to bring terror to the United States. Never had the violence that was so pervasive in Eastern Europe and the Middle East spread across the Atlantic Ocean. The United States had suffered casualties at the hands of Islamic extremists before, but never to this extent at home. The 1993 World Trade Center bombing forever changed how the federal government dealt with terrorism in the United States—moving from a reactive model of justice to a proactive "prevention" model of justice.

After February 26 (a date that seems much less remarkable than the ubiquitous 9/11), the United States was no longer insulated from the hate that existed in other parts of the world. International issues that Americans were once able to ignore were pushed directly on them. Instantly, the United States' relationships with Israel, Saudi Arabia, Iran, Iraq, Egypt, and other Middle Eastern countries became much more complex and delicate. Correspondingly, attitudes among U.S. citizens had changed. The 1993 bombing of the World Trade Center tested the celebrated American tolerance. The long-term impact of the 1993 World Trade Center bombing was obvious; for example, in the hours following the 1995 bombing of the Murrah Federal Building in Oklahoma City, Oklahoma, the first suspects of the attack were Middle Eastern terrorists.

As a result of the 1993 World Trade Center bombing, many important issues and questions were raised. Who was responsible for the bombing? Where did the motivation for the attack originate? How does the government respond in the face of a terrorist attack? What is the relationship between the media and terrorism (and counterterrorism)? This chapter addresses each of these questions. The information was drawn primarily from data located in the American Terrorism Study (ATS) database, which is composed of court-related documents associated with federal terrorism trials in the United States (Smith, Damphousse, Jackson, and Sellers, 2002).[2] The chapter uses information found in newspaper accounts written during the investigation and the trials and from case studies written about the 1993 World Trade Center bombing.

THE SETTING

The World Trade Center was owned and operated by the New York and New Jersey Port Authority. Located in lower Manhattan on a sixteen-acre site, the World Trade Center served as the headquarters for international trade on the east coast and symbolized the seat of American capitalism. Several buildings composed the "center." There were two 110-story office towers, a hotel, three smaller office buildings, and the U.S. Customs House. The World Trade Center also included the largest enclosed shopping mall in lower Manhattan and a subway entrance. The entire complex contained more than 12 million square feet of office space. In 1993, more than 50,000 people worked at the World Trade Center, and almost 100,000 people visited the complex each day.

THE CRIME

On February 26, 1993, at 12:18 p.m., New York City's World Trade Center was rocked at its foundation by a massive explosion that left a hole that was 200- by 100-foot wide in the bottom five levels of the complex (Shields, 2002). The epicenter of the blast was actually in the parking garage under the northeast corner of the hotel at the World Trade Center. The effects of the blast were dramatic. Three levels above the explosion, a 100-square-foot section of concrete was cracked and buckled. Two levels above the explosion, a 400-square-foot hole formed, and windows in the hotel's partition were blown out. The broken windows allowed smoke to enter one of the World Trade Center towers. One level above the explosion, an area the size of a football field was heavily damaged. On the B-2 Level (where the bomb was detonated), a 20,000-square-foot crater was formed, heavily damaging structural columns and collapsing many walls. Five people were killed on the B-2 Level. In the levels below the explosion, refrigeration equipment and water supply lines were damaged, and the ceiling of the train station collapsed (Manning, 1994).

The purpose of the explosion was simple: to topple one tower into the other, killing everyone inside instantly. The result of the plan could have been the deaths of an estimated 50,000 people. Fortunately, the construction of the World Trade Center was advanced enough to withstand the force of the bomb that was estimated to weigh 1,500 pounds. Still, six people (one was a pregnant woman) were killed in the blast, and over 1,000 were injured. For the planners of the attack, however, the bombing on February 26 was seen as a failure. The terrorists had underestimated the construction of the World Trade Center, and they would soon learn that they underestimated the resolve of the law enforcement and legal system that quickly began the hunt for their identities.

THE PARTICIPANTS

The case of the 1993 World Trade Center bombing is extremely complex because of the large number of conspirators, the numerous trials, and the length of time from the incident to the end of the trials. Because of the complexity of the case, a case chronology is provided in Table 1 (pp. 230–231).

Ultimately, the story of the 1993 World Trade Center attack can be traced back to a blind Muslim cleric named Sheik Omar Abdel-Rahman, a man who was bitterly opposed to American policies in the Middle East and the westernization of Muslim countries. In Egypt in 1984, Abdel-Rahman was acquitted of organizing the plot that resulted in the 1981 assassination of Egyptian President Anwar el-Sadat. Abdel-Rahman entered the United States in 1990 on a tourist visa and settled in the New York City area. While Abdel-Rahman was living in the United States, the Egyptian government unsuccessfully sought to extradite him on charges of inciting a riot that took place in Egypt in 1989 (Tabor, 1993). Abdel-Rahman spoke regularly at mosques in New York and in New Jersey. Following the murder of the local Muslim leader at the time, Mustafa Shalabi, Abdel-Rahman ascended into a leadership position.

One of Abdel-Rahman's faithful followers was an Egyptian named El Sayyid Nosair. Following the 1990 assassination of an anti-Arab rabbi named Meir Kahane in New York, Nosair was charged with Kahane's murder. While the evidence of his guilt seemed clear to court watchers, he was only found guilty of weapons charges and sentenced to seven years in prison. While Nosair was in prison, he began to plan acts of terrorism against the United States. Followers of Abdel-Rahman visited Nosair and a plan was hatched to plant several bombs around the New York City area. The leader of the attacks was to be Ibrahim El-Gabrowny—Nosair's cousin and another of Abdel-Rahman's followers. Emad Salem was to assist in the bombings. Unfortunately for El-Gabrowny, Salem was an FBI informant who had been placed into the organization that was planning these bombings during the Nosair murder trial. However, about the time these new plans were being made, the FBI broke off contact with Salem because they had feared that he was also working for the Egyptian government.

Eventually, the bombing plot evolved into an attack on the World Trade Center. The purpose of the World Trade Center bombing was to kill a large number of Americans by having one tower collapse onto the other (Parachini, 2000). The rationale was that the United States was to be punished for supporting Israel. The group believed that the U.S. government punishes other countries by punishing their citizens, for example, through embargoes. Thus, American citizens also needed to be punished. According to this logic, it was necessary to kill innocent Americans so that the United States would appreciate what was happening to the Palestinians.

One of El-Gabrowny's cousins, Mohammed A. Salameh, was a Palestinian who had migrated illegally to the United States from Jordan in 1987 (Miller, 1993). Salameh asked to be involved in the bombing as well. After the plans for the bombing were made, Salameh began to place several calls to his terrorist uncle in Baghdad for advice. In one of these calls, he requested assistance with building the bomb. Soon, two individuals traveling under assumed names arrived in New York City's JFK airport in September 1992 to help Salameh build the bombs.

The first person through the customs gate was explosives expert Ahmad Ajaj. U.S. Customs officials discovered that Ajaj's credentials were phony, and they detained him. When they searched his belongings, they found bomb-making instructions. Upon seeing Ajaj being led away, the second person changed his strategy of using fake identification and requested political immunity instead. The U.S. immigration officials fingerprinted him and asked him to file the appropriate forms. Ramzi Yousef was allowed to walk out of JFK airport and into an apartment that Salameh shared with Musab Yasin in Jersey City, New Jersey.

Days later, Abdul Yasin arrived from Baghdad and moved into the Jersey City apartment as well. Yousef and Salameh then moved into their own apartment in Jersey City. Eventually, the group of conspirators was joined by Nidal Ayyad (a U.S. citizen from Kuwait) and Mahmud Abouhalima (a permanent resident of the United States and Abdel-Rahman's driver). Ayyad was a chemical engineer whose skills would be useful during the creation of the bomb. Abouhalima was to act as the outside contact for the group.

The men began raising money from unknown sources to purchase the supplies needed to build the bomb. In a Jersey City apartment, Yousef (with the assistance of Salameh and Abouhalima) built an explosive device with urea nitrate (using half a ton of urea and over 100 gallons of nitric acid). Nitrourea is about as powerful as TNT. The bombers later added sulfuric acid and hydrogen gas cylinders—at Ayyad's suggestion—to intensify the blast. Hydrogen is an easily ignited and odorless gas that burns with an almost invisible flame. Thus, it converts all of its energy into heat energy; hydrogen burns at $3,700°$ F. Gunpowder was to be used to detonate the explosive device.

In February 1993, the completed bomb was moved to a storage shed until a vehicle could be rented for its transportation. Salameh rented a van from Ryder Truck Rental Company in his own name on February 23, and the bomb was loaded in the van on February 25. On February 26, Eyyad Ismoil drove the van containing Yousef and the bomb to the World Trade Center. They ignited the bomb on the B-2 Level of the World Trade Center and left the premises before the explosion.

In the confusion following the World Trade Center bombing, the terrorists were able to quickly flee the United States. Salameh drove Ismoil and Yousef to the airport the day of the bombing. Yousef left the United States for

Pakistan, and Ismoil traveled to Jordan. Abouhalima fled to Sudan four days later. Yousef had handed Salameh a ticket for a later flight to Amsterdam. Salameh later discovered that it was not useable because it was a child's ticket. Some scholars suspect that Yousef purposely left Salameh and Ayyad behind as patsies to be captured by the U.S. authorities. The only source of money that Salameh had remaining was the deposit on the van that he had rented for the bombing. His efforts to retrieve the deposit would eventually prove disastrous to each of the bombing participants.

Three days following the bombing, Ayyad sent a letter to the *New York Times* on behalf of a group calling itself the Fifth Battalion of the Liberation Army. The letter claimed responsibility for the bombing and demanded that the United States end aid to Israel and interference in Middle East affairs.

THE INVESTIGATION

Before law enforcement agencies were able to begin their investigation, emergency response teams from New York first had to deal with extinguishing the fire and rescuing victims. The Fire Department of New York eventually responded with nearly half of the on-duty staff, which included 144 engine and truck companies and thirty-seven battalion and deputy chiefs and thirty-one other special units. The FDNY would eventually stay on the scene for four weeks (Manning, 1994).

As is customary in large terrorism cases, the federal government assumed control of the 1993 World Trade Center bombing investigation and prosecution. In this case, the investigation was coordinated by the Joint Terrorism Task Force (JTTF). The JTTF is an amalgamation of local, state, and federal law enforcement agencies that is housed in federal districts throughout the United States. The aim of the JTTF is to combat terrorism in a unified manner. The lead agency of the JTTF is the FBI.

Within hours of the February 26 explosion, agents from the FBI, the Federal Bureau of Alcohol, Tobacco, and Firearms (ATF), the New York Port Authority, and the New York City Police Department began their investigation. Explosive experts soon concluded that the bomb used in the World Trade Center attack was homemade and not the result of manufactured explosives such as TNT or plastic explosives. Investigators of the damaged building suspected that the bomb's base comprised Nitrourea. Based on this assumption, investigators calculated how large the bomb had to be based on the damage created. The investigators estimated that the bomb was between 1,000 and 2,000 pounds. Based on this estimation, the investigators then concluded that only a large van or moving truck could have carried that much explosives without being noticed.

Their initial conclusions perfectly predicted the first main piece of evidence that investigators found two days after the blast. An ATF agent and an NYPD detective unearthed a piece of contorted metal that turned out to contain the vehicle identification number (VIN) of the truck that carried the bomb into the building (Shields, 2002). Using the VIN, investigators learned that the vehicle was a van owned by the Ryder Truck Rental Company (Bernstein, 1993a). This discovery resulted in the first major break in the case. Ryder reported that the van had been rented by a man named Mohammad Salameh in New Jersey three days before the attack (Bernstein, 1993b).

The investigators learned that Salameh had claimed that the van had been stolen the night before the attack. He claimed that when he attempted to report the van stolen, he was told by the police that he could only report a stolen vehicle if he knew the correct license plate number, which he did not know. The license plate number that Salameh provided to the police was incorrect. Later, when Salameh attempted to recover the $400 deposit, he was told by the Ryder rental agency that they would only give back his deposit if he provided a report from the police stating that the van had been stolen. Salameh made continuous requests to get his deposit back, even unknowingly calling the business while several FBI agents were interviewing the employees at Ryder (Shields, 2002). The FBI agents instructed the rental agency employees to tell Salameh that he would get his deposit back if he came in. This trap led to the arrest of the first suspect in the 1993 bombing case. The arrest of Mohammad Salameh would eventually lead to the arrest of many other bombing conspirators.

Even though Salameh did not have an official criminal history, the FBI had been aware of him because of his ties to Abdel-Rahman. The fact that Salameh had connections to individuals like Abdel-Rahman, and the fact that he had rented the van that was used in the explosion convinced the FBI of his active involvement in the attack. The FBI had originally planned to follow Salameh after he left the rental agency with his refund. The hope was that he would lead them to his coconspirators. Foreshadowing the extent of media involvement in the case, however, the FBI was forced to alter their plans when a local news crew, which was acting on a tip, showed up at the rental agency while Salameh was there. The FBI agents were forced to arrest Salameh immediately, possibly losing any information that may have been gained through surveillance (Shields, 2002).

After the arrest of Salameh, investigators went to the apartment that he had listed on the van rental form and found Abdul Yasin. Yasin voluntarily told the FBI where the bomb had been built along with other information. Seemingly satisfied that Yasin was not involved with the plot, the FBI released the Iraqi citizen from custody, and Yasin immediately left for Baghdad.

On March 5, the FBI discovered the shed where the explosives had been stored. They also went to the address listed on Salameh's driver's license (different from where he was living). There, they found and arrested Ibrahim El-Gabrowny on weapons charges and because of other suspicious material found in the residence.

During Salameh's arrest, the FBI also found the business card of Nidal Ayyad (Caram, 2001). Ayyad did not seem to fit the profile of a terrorist, because he was a naturalized U.S. citizen and he worked as a chemist at Allied Signal Corporation. Investigators discovered, however, that Ayyad and Salameh shared a bank account. The FBI tracked the account and discovered incoming wire transfers totaling over $8,000. Based on Ayyad's chemistry background and his business card that was found on Salameh during his arrest, investigators believed that Ayyad was also involved in the World Trade Center bombing. On March 10, the FBI searched Ayyad's home and arrested him for being involved in the bombing. On March 13, Egyptian police arrested Abouhalima based on a request by the FBI, and Abouhalima was returned to the United States on March 31 for trial.

Less than one month after the bombing, investigators had identified many of the key participants in the World Trade Center bombing. Salameh, Abouhalima, Ayyad, and Ajaj (along with a minor participant named Bilal Alkaisi, who had turned himself in) were ready to stand trial—Yousef, Ismoil, and Yasin remained at large. Although Abdel-Rahman was suspected of being involved in the plot, he publicly denied knowing any of the men arrested in the bombing conspiracy.

THE FIRST TRIAL

The prosecution in the trial against the four main accused terrorists was led by U.S. Attorney Mary Jo White. The lead prosecutors were J. Gilmore Childers, Henry J. De Pippo, and David Kelly. Childers had a very challenging task to complete. His argument was built largely on pieces of evidence that were not individually conclusive as to the guilt of any of the accused on their own. Once all the evidence was tied together, he hoped to form a convincing story. Adding further burden to trying the case was that the prosecution was given a complex case for which the media and the American people demanded success. Someone had to be held responsible for the attack that killed six innocent victims, injured a thousand more, and cost an estimated $550 million in damages ("Bombing Trial," 1994). Throughout the investigation and subsequent trial, the entire world watched how the U.S. government would respond to the attack.

Starting in September 1993, Childers began to argue before a worldwide audience that those indicted—Salameh, Abouhalima, Ayyad, and Ajaj with the help of others—were responsible for the 1993 World Trade Center attack. Even though the prosecution was unable to produce a "smoking gun," the U.S. government needed to provide enough evidence for a jury to convict the men in their involvement in the attack. As a result of the media coverage of the trials, the prosecution also had the task of proving their case to the public as well.

The prosecution demonstrated that Salameh had rented the van that carried the bomb. He was also seen at the shed where the bomb was stored and at the apartment where it was built. Finally, he was Ramzi Yousef's roommate. Invoices showed that Ayyad had purchased the chemicals used for the bomb. One of the most damaging pieces of evidence against Ayyad was his own personal computer. The FBI discovered the original messages on his computer that had been sent to the *New York Times* claiming responsibility for the attack on behalf of the Fifth Battalion of the Liberation Army (Bernstein, 1994a). A DNA test showed that his saliva was on the envelope in which the letter arrived. The fingerprints of Ayyad and Salameh were also found on some of the bomb materials.

Besides his connection to Abdel-Rahman, most of the prosecution's case against Abouhalima was based on his frequent associations with the rest of the defendants. Abouhalima was identified as having been at Salameh's apartment with Yousef during when the bomb was made (Bernstein, 1994d). Evidence also included numerous phone calls between Abouhalima and Salameh at his apartment. Prosecutor De Pippo also offered into evidence a witness's account of observing Abouhalima with Salameh and Yousef putting gas into the yellow Ryder van the morning of the explosion. The prosecution also showed that Abouhalima had purchased gunpowder before the bombing. The only piece of physical evidence that the prosecution provided against Abouhalima was a pair of shoes that were found in a closet in the basement of Abouhalima's apartment. One of the shoes contained an acid burn, which the prosecution argued occurred during the bomb-making process (Bernstein 1994d).

Along with the bomb-making plans that were taken from Ajaj when he was arrested coming into the United States with Yousef in September 1992, the prosecution provided the jury with Ajaj's record of phone activity while he was incarcerated following his arrest at JFK airport (Bernstein 1994b). The phone records show that Ajaj made several calls to a friend in Texas who redirected the calls to a phone in New Jersey at a residence where Yousef was known to have stayed.

Salameh, Ayyad, Abouhalima, and Ajaj had each pleaded innocent, and all faced life sentences without the possibility of parole if found guilty of the attack. The defense teams for the four defendants each used a separate defense strategy during the trial. Except for Salameh (whose attorney was appointed by the court), each of the defendants changed defense attorneys at least one time before the trial started.

Robert E. Precht, the court-appointed lawyer for Salameh, did not mount a formal defense but told the jury that the prosecution had Salameh's relationship to Yousef incorrect. Precht contended that Yousef manipulated Salameh and that Salameh never knew his actions were part of a plan to bomb the World Trade Center. Precht argued that Salameh was not a coconspirator but rather a dupe to the real criminal involved. He argued to the jury that the real criminals and perpetrators of the attack were still at large (Bernstein, 1994e).

Precht also argued that the van Salameh rented had in fact been stolen, and that he was not trying to simply offer an alibi for the missing van. Precht also claimed that a real terrorist would have to be a fool to seek the van deposit from Ryder after the bombing. He also argued that the money that had been wired into Salameh's account was for a "totally innocent purpose" (Bernstein, 1994a, p. 1). Finally, Precht brought up Salameh's driving record, which showed him to be a very reckless and dangerous driver. Precht summed up his client's poor driving record by saying that it was unlikely that Ramzi Yousef would trust him to rent and then drive the important van.

Abouhalima tried to hire William Kunstler, the flamboyant attorney who had successfully defended Nosair in the Kahane murder trial. Kunstler declined but recommended that he hire Jesse Berman, an attorney who had successfully defended individuals charged in a previous domestic terrorism case. Because Abouhalima could not afford to pay his fees, Berman was eventually replaced by Hassan Ibn Abdellah and assisted by Clarence Faines. In the time between Berman's departure and Abdellah's arrival, Abouhalima began negotiating with the prosecution team. He offered to testify against the other indictees in exchange for a lighter sentence and some money. When Abdellah discovered the negotiation, he ended it because he thought that what the prosecution would have offered would not be reduced enough to make it worthwhile. Instead, his defense team presumed that the government did not have enough evidence to bring about a conviction; however, Abdelleh could not have been more wrong. Abdellah argued that the witnesses who had observed Abouhalima at Salameh's apartment and getting gas the morning of the bombing were not reliable (Bernstein, 1994e). He also argued that the chemical-laden shoe that had been entered into evidence did not prove that Abouhalima had mixed any chemicals, especially chemicals that could be used to make a bomb (Bernstein, 1994c).

Ayyad originally hired Leonard Weinglass (a former partner of Kunstler). Later, also because of a fee problem, Weinglass was replaced by Atiq Ahmed.

Ahmed did not offer a formal defense but stated only that the chemicals Ayyad had ordered were not for a bomb but were instead for some friends who were setting up a legitimate business. The only other line of defense that was offered to the jury on behalf of Ayyad was that the entire prosecution of Ayyad was fabricated and twisted by a government that was only interested in oppressing him and convicting him of the attack (Bernstein, 1994e).

Finally, Ajaj hired a female attorney named Lynne Stewart who had worked with Kunstler in the past. She was later replaced by Austin Campriello, the only attorney to mount a vigorous defense. Ajaj's defense rested on the fact that he had been incarcerated in early September 1992, so there was no way that he could have participated in the attack. Also, the explosives' manuals that were in his possession when he was arrested at the airport were legitimate, because he had been a soldier in Afghanistan. Finally, Campriello argued that because Ajaj called Yousef does not mean he was involved in the attack on the World Trade Center.

The six-month trial of the four defendants began on September 13, 1993, with over 1,000 pieces of evidence and more than 200 witnesses presented. The four defendants were convicted by the jury on March 4, 1994, on all thirty-eight counts in the indictment, including conspiracy to build a bomb, explosive destruction of property, and assaulting a federal officer. By the time of their sentencing hearing on May 24, 1994, each defendant had dismissed his lawyer and represented himself. They were each sentenced to 240 years in prison and a $250,000 fine.

When they appealed their conviction and sentences, the federal appeals court granted new sentencing on grounds that the defendants did not have adequate counsel at sentencing. In October 1999, Salameh was resentenced to one month shy of 117 years in prison. Ayyad was resentenced to 117 years and one month in prison. Abouhalima was resentenced to a prison term of 108 years and four months. Ajaj was resentenced to a term of 114 years and ten months. Each man was fined $250,000 and ordered to pay $250 million in restitution.

THE SECOND TRIAL

In a bold move, the government indicted Omar Abdel-Rahman and several of his associates for seditious conspiracy in June 1993. Seditious conspiracy has generally been reserved for those plotting to overthrow the government, and it had seldom been used successfully in terrorism trials. Seditious conspiracy was a risky venture because it is difficult to prove in court. Also indicted with Abdel-Rahman were El Sayyid Nosair (the person who had originally planned the bombing), Ibrahim El-Gabrowny (one of the original leaders of the conspiracy), and seven other associates (Clement Hampton-El, Fares, Khallafalla, Amir Abdelgani, Fadil Abdelgani, Tarig Elhassan, and Victor Alvarez). The indictment listed specific targets including several New York City landmarks—bridges, tunnels, and the Statue of Liberty—and individuals (Hosni Mubarak and Richard Nixon).

This second trial began in January 1995. Most of the evidence in the case came from a former associate of the conspirators named Siddig Ibrahim Siddig Ali, who became a government informant in exchange for his freedom. The government also used secret tape recordings of Abdel-Rahman made by Emad Salem (also an FBI informant). In October 1995, Abdel-Rahman and his associates were found guilty of seditious conspiracy. Abdel-Rahman was sentenced to life in prison without parole. Nosair, who was also found guilty for conspiring to kill Meir Kahane in this second trial, also received a life sentence. The other defendants received sentences ranging from twenty-five to fifty-seven years in prison.

THE HUNT FOR YOUSEF AND ISMOIL

The trial of Ramzi Yousef (the builder of the bomb) and Eyad Ismoil (who drove the van to the World Trade Center and ignited it with Yousef) would have to wait until they were captured and returned to the United States. A worldwide manhunt for Yousef and his associate Ismoil began soon after the bombing. To aid in his capture, the U.S. government offered a $2 million reward.

After leaving the scene of the World Trade Center blast, Yousef flew to a remote area of Pakistan to visit his wife and child. Incidentally, the exact identity of Yousef is unknown. Some scholars believe that he is really an Iraqi undercover operative that had taken the identity of a dead Kuwaiti citizen (e.g., Mylroie, 2001). Some also suspect that Yousef's uncle was a close associate of Osama bin Laden (the mastermind of the World Trade Center attack on September 11, 2001).

Being on the run did not slow down Yousef's terrorist activities. While in Pakistan, for example, Yousef became involved in other terrorism plots that include an assassination attempt on Benazir Bhutto and an attack the Israeli Embassy in Thailand. Neither attack was successful. Eventually, Yousef traveled to the Philippines where he plotted attacks on U.S. airliners. The plan was to plant bombs on several planes and to detonate them at the same time over the Pacific Ocean. He tested the effectiveness of his new bomb on a plane bound for Tokyo. The successful detonation killed a passenger and severely damaged the plane. Subsequent investigation of the bombing led the Philippine police to Yousef's home in Manila, but he had already returned to Pakistan.

While in Islamabad, Pakistan, one of Yousef's associates agreed to tell authorities where he was hiding in exchange for the $2 million reward. On February 8, 1995, Ramzi Yousef was arrested by Pakistani police. On February 26, 1995, exactly two years after the World Trade Center bombing, Yousef was arraigned in U.S. District Court in New York City for the attack. He was also indicted (along with Abdel Murad and Wali Khan) for conspiracy to detonate bombs on U.S. airliners in Asia. Just six months later, Eyad Ismoil was arrested in Jordan and returned to the United States for trial in the World Trade Center bombing.

THE THIRD AND FOURTH TRIALS

The prosecution team decided to try Yousef and his associates—Murad and Khan—for conspiracy to bomb U.S. airliners before trying Yousef and Ismoil for the World Trade Center bombing. The evidence for this case was so solid that the trial ended quickly; plans for the attacks had been found on Murad's laptop. On September 5, 1996, each of the defendants was convicted of conspiracy to bomb U.S. airliners. Murad and Khan received life sentences, while Yousef's sentence was suspended until his World Trade Center bombing trial had ended. He and Ismoil were to be tried together starting in August 1997.

Prosecutors might have worried that the delay between the 1993 World Trade Center bombing and the 1997 trial of Yousef and Ismoil might have caused public concern about terrorism to wane in New York City. Fortunately for the prosecution, another group of terrorists—Gazi Mezer and Lafi Khalil—who had plans to bomb the New York City subway system were arrested on July 31, 1997, just days before the trial of Yousef and Ismoil was to begin. Heightened media coverage of the Mezer and Khalil arrests brought attention to the latest World Trade Center bombing trial.

The final World Trade Center bombing trial started on August 4, 1997. Ismoil was defended by Louis Aidala, and Yousef's attorney was Roy Kulcsar. The government was represented by U.S. Attorney David Kelly. The government showed that Yousef had entered the United States illegally on the same flight as Ahmad Ajaj in September, 1992. In addition, the military manuals for the construction of explosive devices that had been found on Ajaj also had Yousef's fingerprints on them. Yousef's fingerprints were also found at the storage shed where the bomb materials were stored. Yousef did not offer a vigorous defense, but Ismoil tried to claim that he thought that he was driving a load of soap and shampoo into the World Trade Center and that he was not aware of the conspiracy.

On November 9, 1997, the jury found the pair guilty of participating in the World Trade Center bombing. Ismoil was guilty of driving the van into the

WTC and igniting the fuse, and Yousef was found guilty of planning the attack and building the bomb. In January 1998, both men were sentenced to 240 years in prison. That sentencing marked the end of one of the most complex terrorism cases in the history of the U.S. justice system.

THE MEDIA COVERAGE

The impact of the media on this case is intriguing. A major development of a lead was almost destroyed because a news crew arrived on the scene, while the FBI was awaiting the arrival of Salameh at the Ryder truck rental store. The media also gave both the terrorists and the federal government a voice as the investigation and the trials ensued.

The mass media (especially television news and newspapers) are always interested in crime. The relationship is easy to understand: crime is interesting to people, so the media "sells" its coverage of the criminal event and its consequences to consumers. The more interesting the criminal event—either because of the notoriety of the victim or the offender or the "uniqueness" of the event—the more likely the event is to be covered by the media. Terrorism, as a subtype of criminal events, has an even more interesting relationship with the mass media because of the motivation behind the terrorist attack. It has been said that the media provides oxygen to terrorist organizations (Nacos, 2002).

Terrorist groups can be defined as entities that attempt to change how society is organized through nonlegitimate and usually violent methods. Change can only come about by attracting attention to the "cause" for which the terrorist group is fighting. As a result, terrorist groups have commonly contacted the media (through the use of a *communiqué*) after an attack to air their grievances to the public. In the case of this terrorist bombing, Nidal Ayyad sent a letter to the *New York Times* to inform the world of the motivation behind the attack. Thus, the media, which is already predisposed to cover terrorist attacks, was also used by the terrorists. The 1993 World Trade Center bombing is a perfect example of the relationship between mass media and terrorism.

It is important to remember that, in 1993, there was really only one national "all news channel," which was CNN. In addition, the internet existed but was not yet used by many people, and very few relied on it as a news source. Thus, much of the national electronic coverage of the World Trade Center bombing was limited to short-term "break-ins" by the major television networks and then nightly news broadcasts. Of course, local New York television stations covered the immediate events following the bombing for longer periods of time, and CNN provided nearly twenty-four-hour coverage of the first few days of the attack. Within a week, however, national television coverage reverted back to "normal," where reports were presented about the ongoing criminal investigation and the subsequent trials.

One issue that the 1993 World Trade Center bombing raised for the electronic media was whether or not television is appropriate in times of stress. Television is immediate; the pictures and sound that television conveys is sometimes delivered without the comfort of time and context. Increasingly, scholars and media experts began to worry about the media's representation of the Muslim world in the aftermath of the bombing. These issues would be revisited in 2001 when video clips of Arabs celebrating the collapse of the World Trade Center were instantly beamed around the world. The electronic media are now forced by their power of the "instantaneous" to balance the freedom of the press and the inciting of violence against groups of people (Goodman, 1994).

Newspaper coverage of the terrorist attack was far more detailed and long lasting. The newspaper media was also able to provide context for its reports. Many stories written in the days following the bombing, for example, described earlier attacks by Muslim extremists around the world. At the same time, many stories were presented about the Muslim faith and the problems Arab Americans faced following the bombing.

In the weeks after the 1993 bombing, the newspaper media were consumed with reporting about the investigation and the damage that resulted from the bombing. Every new detail and turn in the investigation was reported daily in the newspapers. Interested Americans were easily able to keep up with the progress of the investigation.

The first court case lasted nearly five months. The national and local media covered the daily activities and events that took place inside the courtroom. While television cameras were not allowed inside of the courtroom, spectators (including reporters) were allowed to attend. As with most trials, much of the courtroom activity was mundane, but at times the evidence that was presented was both fascinating and painful. Newspaper coverage of the trial, especially that of the New York papers, was very detailed. After the sentencing phase of the first trial, however, the media's attention slowly faded away from the World Trade Center bombing and instead started covering other stories that were occurring in the world. The story of the World Trade Center bombing, it seemed, had run dry, and new stories were appearing elsewhere in the world. The subsequent trials were covered in great detail by the local press, but national interest waned. Much had happened between the bombing and the trial (including the 1995 bombing of the Murrah Federal Building in Oklahoma City), and the public had turned its attention to a new terrorism threat: the domestic terrorist.

The media coverage of the 1993 World Trade Center bombing and its subsequent trials played three key roles in helping the American public come to understand the attack. The most important role of the media was in detailing how the bombing took place. The chapter presents information that was gleaned from newspaper reporting. A second role of the media was to chronicle the trial, showing how the federal government responded to the attack. To the extent that the trials were perceived as successful, the legitimacy of the U.S. government would be restored. The third role of the media was to raise questions about the bombing. Why was the United States attacked? How safe was the public from future acts of terrorism? How could the bombing have occurred, and why was more protection not given to the World Trade Center? Many hard lessons were learned by the organizations whose responsibility it was to protect the World Trade Center and its occupants. The weaknesses that were exposed at the World Trade Center became a wake-up call to local and federal law enforcement, immigration officials, and the security industry. Unfortunately, the warnings issued to these agencies were not enough to avoid the second attack on the World Trade Center in 2001.

DISCUSSION

Following the conviction of the original four conspirators, then Mayor Rudolph Giuliani confidently stated that the outcome "demonstrates that New Yorkers won't meet violence with violence, but with a far greater weapon . . . the law" (Kleinfeld, 1994, p. 29). Not everyone, however, was pleased with the outcome. Some Islamic groups saw the trial outcome as a "miscarriage of the American justice system" (p. 29). An Egyptian cab driver in New York stated that he saw the verdict as unjust. "The jurors don't know Muslims. How can they be fair? They see people in beards praying and they get scared" (p. 29).

Until the bombing in 1993, the United States had rarely suffered attacks from Islamic terrorists at home and never to this extent. The social, political, and legal ramifications that resulted from the attack were almost as powerful as the bomb itself. Both the U.S. government and public had been thrust into unknown territory by a handful of men. Following the attack, the federal government changed how it dealt with terrorists by taking a more proactive role in identifying terrorists and countering their activities. The terrorists also vowed to continue their struggle. Grimly foreshadowing the attacks that would take place 2001, one of the terrorists convicted of the 1993 bombings, Nidal Ayyad, wrote on his personal computer that the first bombing was a failure and that "next time it will be very precise" (Pellowski, 2003, p. 8).

As a result of the bombing, the United States became more ingrained in world affairs and began to create new laws that were designed to strengthen the nation's security. Calls were made by politicians and the public for the government to work to prevent future acts of terrorism. But, as Bruce Hoffman of the RAND Corporation explained, most Americans understood that prevention is probably impossible: "Four 'amateurs' with readily available, commercially produced materials, can build a bomb for under $400 that kills six people, causes untold millions of dollars in losses and generates endless publicity. Hitting a high-profile target shows that anybody can be a terrorist" (Goodman, 1994, p. 39).

NOTES

1. K. Smith (personal communication, February 28, 2003).
2. More information about the American Terrorism Study is available at www.mipt.org

REFERENCES

Bernstein, R. (1993a, October 7). Yellow van at center of trial's first confrontation. *New York Times*, p. B3.

Bernstein, R. (1993b, October 27). Process of linking blast debris begins. *New York Times*, p. B4.

Bernstein, R. (1994a, January 4). Bombing suspect's boss tells of van request. *New York Times*, p. B3.

Bernstein, R. (1994b, January 14). Trail left by phone calls may link bomb suspects. *New York Times*, p. B3.

Bernstein, R. (1994c, January 25). Nitroglycerin and shoe at center of blast trial testimony. *New York Times*, p. B3.

Bernstein, R. (1994d, February 8). Bombing trial witness sums up evidence. *New York Times*, p. B3.

Bernstein, R. (1994e, February 17). Lawyer in trade center blast case contends that client was a dupe. *New York Times*, p. A1.

Caram, P. (2001). *The 1993 World Trade Center bombing: Foresight and warning.* London: Janus Publishing.

Goodman, W. (1994, March 6). Television view; can a trial be too hot for TV? *New York Times*, p. B39.

Jurors given day off in the bombing trial. (1994, March 4). *New York Times*, p. B6.

Kleinfeld, N. R. (1994, March 5). Explosion at the Twin Towers: The reaction; convictions greeted with jubilation and big sighs. *New York Times*, p. A29.

Manning, W. (1994). *The World Trade Center bombing: Report and analysis.* Washington, DC: Federal Emergency Management Agency.

Miller, J. (1993, March 14). Arrests begin, questions remain. *New York Times*, p. D4.

Mintzer, R. (2000). *The everything guide to New York City.* Holbrook, MA: Adams Media.

Mylroie, L. (2001). *The war against America: Saddam Hussein and the World Trade Center attacks: A study of revenge.* Washington, DC: American Enterprise Institute for Public Policy Research.

Nacos, B. (2002). *Mass-mediated terrorism.* Lanham, MD: Rowman and Littlefield.

Parachini, J. V. (2000). The World Trade Center bombers. In J. B. Tucker, (Ed.), *Toxic terror: Assessing terrorist use of chemical and biological weapons* (pp. 185–206). Cambridge, MA: MIT Press.

Pellowski, M. J. (2003). *The terrorist trial of the 1993 bombing of the World Trade Center: A headline court case.* Berkeley Heights, NJ: Enslow Publishers.

Shields, C. J. (2002). *Great disasters, reforms, and ramifications: The 1993 World Trade Center bombing.* Philadelphia: Chelsea House Publishers.

Smith, B., Damphousse, K., Jackson, F., and Sellers, A. (2002). The prosecution and punishment of international terrorists in federal courts: 1980–1998. *Criminology and Public Policy, 1*(3), 311–338.

Smith, K. 2003. Personal correspondence.

Tabor, M. B. W. (1993, March 22). Witnesses report seeing suspects on eve of blast. *New York Times,* p. B4.

14

Timothy McVeigh:
The Oklahoma City Bombing

Jeffrey A. Gruenewald

OKLAHOMA CITY, 9:02 A.M.

Shortly before 9 a.m. on April 19, 1995, Timothy McVeigh carefully pulled a rented Ryder moving truck to the side of 5th Street. He leaned over the front seat to light a long fuse that ran from the cab of the truck to the storage bed; McVeigh expected the fuse to burn for five minutes before reaching fifty large, plastic barrels of ammonium nitrate and diesel fuel he and his accomplice, Terry Nichols, had mixed the previous morning. McVeigh returned the truck to 5th Street, as it filled with smoke from the burning fuse. Rolling down the windows of the truck, McVeigh lit a second shorter fuse as he quickly arrived at his target, the Alfred P. Murrah Federal Building in Oklahoma City, Oklahoma. Directly below the America's Kids Daycare Center located on the second floor of the federal building, McVeigh purposively backed the truck up to the front entrance of the building to maximize the impact of the blast. With the fuses burning, McVeigh exited the truck, locked the doors, and quickly walked toward his beat-up Mercury getaway car. At 9:02 a.m., the two-and-a-half-ton truck bomb exploded, killing 168 people and injuring over 500 more. As police, medics, firefighters, and heroic citizens frantically searched for signs of life from the rubble,

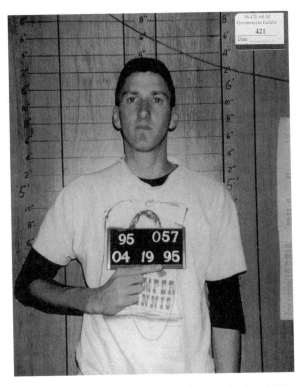

Timothy McVeigh is shown in this April 19, 1995, booking photo taken at the Noble County Jail in Perry, Oklahoma, just hours after the Oklahoma City bombing. (AP/Wide World Photos)

McVeigh felt the satisfaction of an accomplished mission. For him, the bombing was a defensive tactic in a war initiated by the U.S. federal government, and those killed were simply collateral damage. To the rest of Americans, the bombing in Oklahoma City was not only an attack on the federal government but on the freedom for which the United States prides itself on. On April 19, Timothy McVeigh's bomb ripped a hole in the social fabric of America.

THE ROLE OF THE MEDIA

This chapter retells the celebrated story of the Oklahoma City bombing by capturing the dynamic relationship among three of its main characters: Timothy McVeigh, the U.S. criminal justice system, and the news media. First, this chapter provides a contextual background of the life of Timothy McVeigh by examining the radical right-wing extremist culture and how McVeigh's political views were greatly influenced by this culture. Second, this chapter relies heavily on the insights found in Lou Michel and Dan Herbeck's book *American Terrorist*, which goes through a sequence of events capturing McVeigh's life before and after the Oklahoma City bombing.[1] Throughout this chapter, I have selected pieces of Michel and Herbeck's detailed work to retell the story of McVeigh's life and Oklahoma City bombing based on McVeigh's own words. Third, this chapter discusses the criminal justice system, which had the responsibility of bringing the most notorious American-born terrorist to justice. Finally, this chapter reviews the role of the news media, as it was weaved into the story of Timothy McVeigh and his experience with the criminal justice system, with an emphasis on the media's work to package and deliver the Oklahoma City bombing in an acceptable format to the American public. McVeigh's case was one of the most important media crime events in the 1990s, spurring an in-depth examination of relevant political issues and intense scrutiny of how McVeigh's criminal trial was processed by the U.S. criminal justice system. From the first news images of heroic firefighters carrying injured children out of the dilapidated daycare center to media images of McVeigh's emotionless courtroom demeanor, the media played an important role in defining how the public, political authorities, and the criminal justice system would react to the Oklahoma City bombing. In this account of the Oklahoma City bombing, the chapter attempts to capture how Timothy McVeigh, the criminal justice system, and the news media—all with their own agenda—interrelated to make one of the most phenomenal criminal cases of the twentieth century.

THE RADICAL RIGHT: CHRISTIAN IDENTITY AND *THE TURNER DIARIES*

A good place to begin any account of the Oklahoma City bombing is an examination of the religious and political ideologies of the radical right. The modern right-wing extremist movement, born in the early 1980s, has been loosely held together by the racist beliefs of the Christian Identity religion. McVeigh surrounded himself with Christian Identity followers. Christian Identity followers believe that Jews are the descendents of Satan and that white Aryans are the true Israelites—or God's chosen people. Followers also believe the world is entering an apocalyptic struggle between the Aryan race and the participants of a Jewish plot to combine all governments into a global dictatorship, known as the Zionist Occupied Government (ZOG). Active followers believe they are chosen by Yahweh, or God, to overthrow the evil U.S. government to create a single, united "Aryan Nation." Although McVeigh denied being a Christian Identity follower, he did admit to adopting many of their secular beliefs concerning an inevitable battle against a "tyrannous" U.S. government.

These beliefs held by McVeigh and Christian Identity followers are conceptualized in *The Turner Diaries*, which is a science fiction novel written by a neo-Nazi and former physics professor, William L. Pierce. In the fictitious book written in 1978, the federal government outlaws gun ownership and forces all races to integrate. To combat the evil government, protagonist Earl Turner forms a white supremacist group known as "The Order." The group wages a mortar attack against the U.S. Capital, assassinates gun control activists, and bombs the FBI headquarters in Washington, DC, with a truck full of ammonium nitrate and diesel fuel. Christian Identity followers do not consider *The Turner Diaries* as fiction but as a prophetic message. The book has served as a roadmap for radical right terrorist cells such as The Order, whose name is taken directly from *The Turner Diaries*.[2] The book has also served as an instruction manual for individual neo-Nazi terrorists and for Oklahoma City conspirators Timothy McVeigh and Terry Nichols.

GUN CONTROL, RUBY RIDGE, AND WACO

For McVeigh and other right-wing constituents, political discussion hinged on the issue of gun control. Although claiming that any one event led McVeigh to commit the Oklahoma City bombing would be simplistic, it is clear that McVeigh viewed three celebrated gun-related events as proof supporting his conspiracy theories of a corrupt government. The parallels McVeigh saw between *The Turner Diaries* and the political environment of the United States led McVeigh to take the advice of Pierce, the author of *The Turner Diaries,* and become proactive against what he saw to be a tyrannous government.

First, in 1992, a political catastrophe for the right-wing community occurred. In what is known as the standoff at Ruby Ridge, on August 21, 1992, U.S. federal agents raided the rural property of Randy Weaver, a white supremacist accused of selling a sawed-off shotgun to an undercover ATF agent. A gun battle ensued between agents from the U.S. Marshals and the Weaver family. After two days of gunfire, one U.S. Marshal lay dead along with Randy Weaver's pregnant wife and adolescent son. To McVeigh, the standoff at Ruby Ridge was further proof that the federal government was cracking down on the American right to freely own and sell guns. Second, McVeigh viewed the increasingly strict regulations set on the purchasing of guns as a wake-up call for right-wing extremists. In 1993, President Bill Clinton signed The Brady Handgun Violence Prevention Act, which dictated how long individuals had to wait before purchasing a gun. McVeigh saw gun control as the attempt by the federal government to get one step closer to a complete disarmament of U.S. citizens. Finally, McVeigh and other radical right advocates saw the federal siege and subsequent burning of David Koresh's Branch Davidian compound as another testament to the federal government's war against U.S. gun owners. On February 28, 1993, ninety ATF agents issued a search-and-arrest warrant on the Branch Davidian compound based on allegations that cult members were converting semi-automatic firearms into machine guns. At approximately 9 a.m., agents barged into the compound, while three National Guard helicopters flew overhead. A gun battle ensued and left four ATF agents and six Davidians dead. A siege lasting weeks followed, eventually causing 668 FBI personnel to be called into Waco, Texas. After weeks of watching the standoff on his television, McVeigh traveled to Waco to hand out anti-government pamphlets and bumper stickers.[1] Over a month later, on April 19, the siege ended when four armored vehicles punched holes in the compound and fired dozens of canisters filled with O-chlorobenzylidene malononitrite—a substance more potent than tear gas—into the building. After approximately three hours, the compound was engulfed in flames, leaving sixty-seven more Davidians dead and the source of the fire's ignition a controversy. In McVeigh's mind, Randy Weaver and David Koresh were not criminals but innocent gun owners that were bullied by the federal government. Instead of just waiting for the federal government to attack him, McVeigh would decide to attack them first. At some point shortly after the burning at Waco, McVeigh decided that bombing a federal building, as in *The Turner Diaries*, would wake up the American people to the atrocities committed by the federal government and avenge the events at Ruby Ridge and in Waco (Hamm, 1997).

Although it is clear that *The Turner Diaries*, Ruby Ridge, and Waco had a significant impact on McVeigh, these events do not completely explain how he evolved from an American boy to a decorated Gulf War veteran and finally to the most notorious U.S. domestic terrorist. Two days after the bombing in Oklahoma City, two *Buffalo News* reporters, Lou Michel and Dan Herbeck, began a quest to uncover the story behind the bombing. Despite McVeigh's apprehension of the media, Michel gradually earned McVeigh's trust and maintained a dialogue with McVeigh. Upset by false stories written about him by other media outlets, McVeigh eventually consented to tell his entire, unedited biography to Michel and Herbeck. It would be his chance to tell his side of the story. In *American Terrorist*, the authors offer a detailed biography of the most notorious domestic terrorist by incorporating McVeigh's own perspective of his life before and after the bombing. What follows is a brief summary of McVeigh's life with insights into McVeigh's own thoughts and motivations for the Oklahoma City bombing captured by Michel and Herbeck.

TIMOTHY JAMES McVEIGH: BEFORE THE BOMBING

Timothy McVeigh was born on April 23, 1968, to Bill and Mildred "Mickey" McVeigh in Lockport, New York. Bill, a shy blue-collar worker, had always been dedicated to the benefits of hard work, whether it was in the factory or in his garden. McVeigh's mother, Mickey, a boisterous, quick-witted woman, always enjoyed the excitement and adventure of travel. McVeigh had two sisters: Patty is two years younger than McVeigh, and his other sister, Jennifer, is six years younger. Bill and Mickey separated numerous times during McVeigh's childhood, forcing him and his sisters into two house-holds. Each time, McVeigh felt sorry for his father and chose to stay with him, and his sisters opted to leave their Lockport home to be with their mother. The differences in Bill and Mickey's personalities would eventually prove incurable and led to divorce in 1984. After they divorced, Bill sold their home to build a smaller one for him and his son. By this time, McVeigh had matured significantly and spent most of his time alone, nurturing his love for the out-doors. Detached from his feuding parents, McVeigh found refuge in his grand-father, Ed McVeigh, who introduced and fostered McVeigh's love for guns.

A PERFECT SOLDIER

After high school, McVeigh worked odd jobs as a security guard. He found the work unimportant, and he spent most of his free time indulging in radical right extremist literature and gun magazines. In 1988 a restless and searching McVeigh enlisted in the U.S. Army. Because he did so well on his military vocational aptitude test, McVeigh's options were somewhat open to which branch of the military he would enlist. He chose the army to acquire more survival skills, and he dreamed of being a Rambo-type soldier that he saw in the movie *First Blood*.[3] McVeigh had a purpose in the military, and he felt at home for the first time. He described boot camp as the finest period in his life, and he excelled in the army to become what some would consider a perfect soldier. He loved the physical challenges of all-night marches and found comfort in the detailed order and routine of army life. McVeigh quickly advanced to top gunner on the Fort Riley base and was selected to test for an Army Special Forces unit in 1999. McVeigh told Michel and Herbeck, the authors of *American Terrorist*, that while others went out on the weekends, McVeigh chose to stay behind and indulge in gun magazines and extremist literature (2001). Although he was reprimanded for distributing the extremist literature on the base, such as *The Turner Diaries*, he continued on, not phased. His words usually fell on deaf ears, but he continued to talk with other soldiers about his negative views of the federal government. Two people interested in what he had to say were Terry Nichols and Michael Fortier. Both held extreme antigun control views and a hatred for the federal government. They would become McVeigh's closest friends, and Nichols and Fortier would play an integral part in the rest of McVeigh's free life.

Before McVeigh could test for an Army Special Forces unit, he found himself in Saudi Arabia battling a gruesome dictator, Saddam Hussein, in Operation Desert Storm. McVeigh thought that the United States should not bully other countries; however, he also thought that Hussein was a ruthless dictator that should be taught a lesson. Despite his apprehension, McVeigh thought it was his duty to serve his country. During the war, he witnessed events that supported his negative feelings toward the government. Using McVeigh's own words, Michel and Herbeck describe how the soldier was negatively affected by the needless killing of women and children (2001, p. 69). He witnessed army officials lying to media about the number of innocent Iraqi villages destroyed. Although he had shot guns all his life, he had never imagined killing anyone that was not in self-defense, and he did not consider these killings to be self-defense. McVeigh thought that he had become the bully he so much hated. Nevertheless, he moved forward, and he was promoted to sergeant during a brief break in combat.

After returning from the war with new medals pinned on his military fatigues, McVeigh finally received his chance to test for Army Special Forces. Unfortunately, he had lost his endurance sitting idle for so long in the Gulf, and he removed himself from the grueling testing process. This was the last of McVeigh's military career, and he subsequently returned home to New York.

Disheartened, McVeigh planned to use his new military credentials to get a job that interested him. Unfortunately, the slow economy did not allow it, and he was forced to settle for the same security work that drove him to seek out the excitement and sense of purpose of the military. Discontent in New York, McVeigh had lost faith in his beloved army and in his country. Feeling guilty about the killing he had done in Iraq, his hatred for the government was growing. Unable to get suitable work, he left New York in search for something bigger. He first landed in Florida, where his brother-in-law found him a construction job, but for the most part he spent his days bouncing back and forth from Arizona to Michigan where his two army buddies—Michael Fortier and Terry Nichols—lived. Delving deeper into the gun-show circuit, he supported himself by selling illegal firearms and explosives.

THE BEGINNING OF THE END: PLANNING THE BOMBING

Driving back and forth to Fortier's Arizona home and the Nichols' farm in Michigan, McVeigh became increasingly angry with the federal government.

After witnessing the demolishment of the Branch Davidian compound in Waco, McVeigh vowed to seek revenge for the atrocities at Waco by blowing up a federal building with the help of his closest friends. McVeigh and Nichols began storing blasting caps and large amounts of ammonium nitrate in an Arizona storage unit near Fortier's house. McVeigh soon became frustrated at Fortier's lack of interest in his plot to explode a federal building. Despite his hatred for the federal government, Fortier was being passive aggressive, and according to McVeigh, he was just like all of the other radical right sympathizers. Nevertheless, McVeigh and Nichols continued with McVeigh's plan. Shortly thereafter, McVeigh took Fortier to his recently selected target, the Alfred P. Murrah Federal Building. They were both impressed with the seemingly endless amount of dark glass surrounding the hundreds of federal workers. It is still a debate if McVeigh and Fortier were aware of the daycare center on the second floor of the massive Murrah building. Although McVeigh claimed he could not have seen the children through the tinted glass, others argue that it would have been unlikely for McVeigh and Fortier not to notice the children. After returning home, Fortier, along with his wife, hoped McVeigh's plan would eventually fail when no one would agree to help him. They were wrong.

For months McVeigh and Nichols prepared for the bombing by purchasing and storing explosive materials and, in some cases, illegally acquiring bomb-making materials. In one instance, McVeigh and Nichols together burglarized a rock quarry near the ranch where Nichols had recently begun working. After drilling the locks on the quarry's storage units, they were able to steal explosives and store them in their storage unit near Herington, Kansas. On April 18, Nichols and McVeigh unloaded the Herington storage explosives into the rented Ryder truck. They then drove a short distance north to the mixing site—Geary Lake, Kansas—which McVeigh had chosen because it was right off the highway; a moving truck would not look too suspicious right off the highway. McVeigh mixed the nitromethane fluid with ammonium nitrite fertilizer, while Nichols measured the diesel fuel into twenty-pound increments. In the end, each barrel weighed nearly 500 pounds. Nichols and McVeigh left Geary Lake after washing up in the lake and leaving their soiled clothes and all other potential evidence in the back of the truck where they would be destroyed by the blast. It was the last time they would see each other as free men. On April 19, 1995, McVeigh detonated the bomb that he and Nichols carefully constructed.

THE RESPONSE OF THE CRIMINAL JUSTICE SYSTEM

Nearly sixty miles north of the dilapidated Murrah building, State Trooper Charles J. Hanger pulled McVeigh over for a missing license plate as he drove northbound from Oklahoma City. Both men were on edge; McVeigh knew from the sound of the blast that the Murrah building had been destroyed, and although Hanger was carrying out business as usual, his thoughts were on Oklahoma City. McVeigh contemplated killing Hanger, but he opted against it. He had respect for a state trooper doing his job (Michel and Herbeck, 2001). As McVeigh reached for his license, Hanger noticed a bulge in his jacket. McVeigh willingly informed Hanger that he was carrying a gun. As they stood beside McVeigh's car, Hanger helped McVeigh remove his jacket. On his black sweatshirt read a quote from Thomas Jefferson: "The tree of liberty must be refreshed from time to time by the blood of tyrants and patriots" (Michel and Herbeck, 2001, p. 226). Concerned, Hanger aimed his revolver at McVeigh's head and demanded he put his hands on the trunk of his car. He removed McVeigh's .45-caliber Glock revolver, along with an extra clip and a six-inch straight edge knife. McVeigh was arrested for driving without a license plate, carrying concealed weapons, and other minor traffic violations. He was then taken to Noble County Jail in Perry, Oklahoma. Soon after McVeigh arrived in Perry, Noble County Assistant District Attorney Mark Gibson met with McVeigh and took inventory of his belongings. McVeigh was issued an orange jumpsuit that would shortly be shown on the nightly news and in newspapers all over the United States. As McVeigh waited in his fourth-floor cell, Hanger took inventory of the items found in McVeigh's car. Found in the car were a pair of gloves, a large envelope, a toolbox, ear plugs, a cardboard sign he had placed on his windshield to keep his car from being towed, and a stack of papers. Included in the stack of papers was the Declaration of Independence and handwritten quotes from political philosophers. One such quote was from John Locke and spoke of the lawfulness of killing those who would take away your liberty. Although Hanger may have found the items out of the ordinary, it would be days before the significance of his arrest would be clear.

THE HUNT: THE NEWS MEDIA AND FBI

After the blast, FBI officials developed three possible profiles of the Oklahoma City bomber(s). They suspected the bombing could have been done by one of the following: an international terrorist, South American drug gang, or a radical right-wing extremist group (Hamm, 1997). By the evening hours, investigators were tracking Ibraham Ahmad, an Oklahoma Arabic teacher and naturalized American of Palestinian descent. Ahmad fit the description faxed to airport authorities by witnesses who saw three Middle Eastern men driving away minutes before the blast. By this time, the news media were already predicting the number of casualties and speculating on who was responsible. The most popular explanation after the bombing involved some type of militant Islamic group or Arabic terrorist, similar to those that had bombed the New York World Trade Center in 1993. This time, however, the terrorists had struck in America's heartland. Television news reported that Ahmad had been apprehended by U.S. Customs officials and was being questioned by the FBI. Ahmad was released only to fly to Europe and be apprehended again by British immigration authorities. He was then forced to return to Washington and was questioned further. During his interrogation, trash was thrown on his lawn in Oklahoma, and his wife was spat on as she left her work. Also during this time, reports of militant Islamic cells embedded in Oklahoma City were being circulated by the media, which caused the nation to be on the look out for Arabs who may look "suspicious." Muslim groups in Oklahoma and throughout the nation pleaded for the media not to fan the flames of violence (Hamm, 1997).

Other FBI agents were following a different lead. A security camera had spotted a Ryder truck slowly moving towards the Murrah building. The vehicle information number (VIN) from the axle found at the blast was traced to Elliott's Body Shop in Junction City, Kansas, where McVeigh had rented the truck. After agents traveled to the body shop, they discovered the truck had been rented to a Robert Kling of Redfield, South Dakota. As agents looked more closely at McVeigh's faulty license, they realized that his date of birth and the date the license was issued were both April 19— the infamous day that most recently had symbolized the demolishment of the Branch Davidian in Waco, Texas. Evidence was now pointing in the direction of the radical right.

By April 20, FBI agents were scowling the rural streets of Junction City. A salesman at an army surplus store told the agents he had sold two men a bomb-making book like the one found in McVeigh's getaway car. More incriminating evidence came from Lea McGown, owner of the Dreamland Motel. She told the authorities that she remembered a man driving a Ryder moving truck had checked into her motel on April 14. The man was registered as Timothy McVeigh from Decker, Michigan. In addition, a clerk at Elliot's Body Shop was able to provide an FBI sketch artist enough information to make a composite drawing of McVeigh and Nichols; the men in the sketch would become known as John Doe Number 1 and John Doe Number 2. On the evening of April 20, Waldon Kennedy, the FBI agent in charge of the investigation, called a press conference in Oklahoma City. Kennedy oversaw approximately 900 federal, state, and local law enforcement agents. During the press conference, Kennedy revealed the composite sketches to the world. He described the two fugitives as white males, thus slightly shifting public attention away from the Islamic groups.

As strong evidence pointed to the radical right, news reports were made about the possibility of the Oklahoma City bomber being involved in some type of right-wing militia group. Although all of the radical right militia groups despised the federal government, most were appalled at the needless mass killings in Oklahoma City (Chermak, 2002). Many radical groups publicly condemned McVeigh's act of terror via news media and organizational websites. Some consider the Oklahoma City bombing to be the downfall of the militia movement, causing some paramilitary groups to adopt more secretive cell-structured organizations.

BUILDING A CASE

Approximately forty-eight hours after the bombing, a former coworker of McVeigh's in the security business called a hotline that had been set up by investigators to intake the large number of possible leads being phoned in by concerned citizens. The man accused McVeigh of being an angry army veteran who hated the federal government and who might have something to do with the bombing. This information, in addition to the evidence found in Junction City, led an ATF agent to request that McVeigh remain at the Noble County Jail on charges related to the Oklahoma City bombing.

Meanwhile, a swarm of FBI and ATF agents were searching the farm of Terry Nichols's brother, James Nichols, in Decker, Michigan. There they found ammonium nitrate and diesel fuel similar to that used in the bombing, along with blasting caps and other firearms. James Nichols denied that he or his brother had anything to do with the bombing. James Nichols was arrested by federal authorities at a roadblock near his Michigan farm. Terry Nichols, after seeing that he was wanted as a material witness in the case, turned himself into Herington police. Federal agents followed Nichols into the police station and questioned him. He denied that he had any knowledge of the bombing and suspected McVeigh of being the perpetrator. Despite his claims, Terry Nichols was arrested for being a material witness until more substantial charges could be filed. Inside Terry Nichols's Kansas house, federal authorities found the fifty-five gallon plastic barrels, the extra fertilizer, detonator cord, and other bombing equipment. Radical right literature was found in both James and Terry Nichols's homes. Investigators also searched the spring break residence McVeigh's sister was visiting in Florida. Jennifer McVeigh was burning papers as the agents arrived, and in her truck they found militant documents and a copy of *The Turner Diaries*. In addition, a search of Bill McVeigh's home in Pendleton turned up more incriminating letters written by McVeigh to Jennifer. Substantial evidence was mounting against McVeigh.

Later that afternoon, four ATF and FBI agents met with McVeigh, and he was read his rights. He was then flown under tight security to a makeshift courtroom at the Tinker Air Force Base where he was assigned two federal attorneys, Susan Otto, a federal public defender, and John Coyle, a criminal lawyer from Oklahoma. He was charged with "malicious danger and destroying by means of an explosive," to which the death penalty could be applied (Michel and Herbeck, 2001, p. 259).

Building a Defense

In a secretary's room on the military base, McVeigh confessed to his lawyers that he was the sole Oklahoma City bomber. On the morning of Friday, April 21, 1995, prosecutors brought the charges made against McVeigh to U.S. Magistrate Judge Ronald Howland. After the brief court appearance, the SWAT team escorted McVeigh to his own wing of the medium security federal prison in El Reno, Oklahoma, where he was held without bail.

Weeks later, Otto and Coyle stepped down from McVeigh's case. They thought that because they had been personally affected by the bombing it was not in the best interest of the case to continue as McVeigh's representatives. After a long search for someone to lead the defense team, Stephen Jones, from Enid, Oklahoma, accepted the position. Jones had a long history of defending notorious cases as well as celebrated death penalty cases. McVeigh hoped Jones would be able to present a "necessity defense," claiming his actions were a response to the tyranny of Ruby Ridge and Waco. Despite McVeigh's wishes, Jones would reject McVeigh's "necessity defense," claiming that the jury simply would not buy it (Michel and Herbeck, 2001). Instead Jones wanted to poke holes in the prosecutors' claims of McVeigh acting alone. Against McVeigh's wishes, Jones began pursuing his own conspiracy theories. He would travel to the Philippines to look for international terrorists whom Terry Nichols may have communicated with on his trips there to visit his wife. Jones subsequently hired an international terrorist expert hoping to crack a bigger conspiracy.

Leaks to the Media

McVeigh became increasingly upset on March 1, 1997, when the *Dallas Morning News* reported that he had confessed to the bombing while incarcerated. Although prior reports had been made about his jailhouse confessions, the report in the *Dallas Morning News* described how McVeigh admitted to deliberately bombing the Murrah building during the day to increase casualties. The story was reprinted in a number of other media outlets across the United States. Jones reported to the media that the confession was a hoax, but McVeigh thought otherwise. All of the information was an accurate account given to his defense team by McVeigh at some point during the investigation. Someone was selling his story. Although it is unclear how the internal information was leaked to the media, McVeigh was convinced that any chance of a fair trial had been nullified (Michel and Herbeck, 2001). Jones asked federal Judge Richard Matsch—a judge for nearly three decades known for keeping tight reigns on his courtroom—to delay the trial in light of the leaked confession. Matsch's refusal to delay the trial convinced McVeigh that the leaked confession had also convinced Judge Matsch of his undoubted guilt.

McVeigh became frustrated as he realized his "necessity defense" would not be used by Jones, and that his case had already been tainted by leaked information. On top of that, Michel and Herbeck write that McVeigh believed the recent acquittal of accused murderer and football star O. J. Simpson influenced his case. The Simpson trial had been broadcasted daily to American living rooms allowing the public to become a part of the celebrated case. When Simpson was acquitted of criminal charges, many Americans felt as if justice had not been served. The U.S. criminal justice system had lost credibility in the public eye after Simpson's acquittal and finding McVeigh guilty was a good way to rebuild public confidence in the law. It became a question of whether the criminal justice system could effectively handle rare cases that reach the pinnacle of publicity. McVeigh was confident he would be found guilty and sentenced to death, but he wanted a fair trial, nevertheless (Michel and Herbeck, 2001).

Four months after the bombing, a federal grand jury handed the judge a fifteen-page indictment, claiming Timothy McVeigh and Terry Nichols used a truck bomb to kill and injure innocent persons and to damage U.S. property. Judge Matsch had learned valuable lessons from observing the O. J. Simpson media circus. Before the trial, he decided to keep cameras from having access to every part of the trial. Instead, the public would have to rely heavily on media sound-bite summaries for their information on the trial. During pretrial motions, the defense convinced court officials to move the case outside of Oklahoma City to Denver, Colorado. Matsch thought that it had been a mistake to keep the Simpson case in Los Angeles. He thought the case should be moved to Denver, which would make it easier to find jurors who were not personally connected to the Oklahoma City bombing. Although the defense had much going against them, they could count these as small victories. Nichols and McVeigh were moved to a federal prison in Colorado in March 1996, where pretrial motions proceeded for the next year.

The Trial

The eleven-week trial began on April 24, 1997. The prosecution was led by Joseph Hartzler, a dynamic attorney from Illinois. Hartzler began the trial with a story of one of the youngest victims. He described how the young boy cried when his mother left him at the daycare and walked across the street to her office. He described the other children and how their lives were tragically ended that morning. A stone-faced McVeigh sat through this and other testimonies from the witnesses and victims' family members. According to the ex-soldier, dying was a part of life and they needed to get over it. Most damaging to McVeigh's cases was the testimony of Mike and Lori Fortier and McVeigh's sister, Jennifer. Lori Fortier would describe how McVeigh revealed his bomb configuration to her by stacking soup cans on the kitchen counter. Her testimony came freely, as she was granted immunity from prosecution. Jennifer's testimony was also damaging. She described how her brother wrote her letters about how "something big" was about to happen, and he gave her instructions on what to do if the government came after her. However, of all the testimony, Mike Fortier's was the most damaging to McVeigh's case. He described how angry McVeigh felt after Waco, and the process McVeigh went through as he planned his revenge for the Branch Davidian disaster. He explained how McVeigh thought the government had declared war on the American people, and, as a result, how they together looked into creating a militia group to protect themselves from the government. Most destructive was his admission that McVeigh told him he was going to bomb the Murrah building and even what type of bomb he planned on using. What McVeigh hoped would surface in Fortier's testimony was the fact that neither Fortier or McVeigh were aware of the daycare center on the second floor when they visited the Murrah building prior to the bombing. McVeigh thought if the jury knew he did not intend to kill the children, it would be harder for the prosecution and news media to label him a heartless baby killer. The topic was never discussed.

The jury comprised five men and seven women, and all were willing to vote for the death penalty. He was hoping for more blue-collar people who might understand his political position. Instead he got what he viewed as wealthy conservatives. On top of that, three had heard leaks of McVeigh's confession to his lawyers. McVeigh was not happy with the jury selection. Stephen Jones's defense of McVeigh lasted only four days, and only twenty-five witnesses were called. Although Jones had spent millions of tax dollars sending lawyers to multiple foreign countries in search for evidence of his international terrorist conspiracy theory, Matsch ruled Jones's theory unsubstantiated. Also, Jones's strategy to discredit the FBI crime scene analysis was foiled when Matsch ruled the Justice Department's report, which indicated that the FBI's crime scene investigation was botched, irrelevant. In addition, the prosecution avoided calling to the stand those agents criticized in the report. McVeigh was disturbed by the more than fifty lawyers working on his case, and at how they all seemed to be going in different directions (Michel and Herbeck, 2001).

Guilty Verdict

Matsch worked hard to keep the trial moving to avoid the long, drawn-out trial illustrated by the Simpson case. Nevertheless, at various points in the trial McVeigh became annoyed at the long, tedious processes he saw as a judicial charade and waste of tax dollars. He viewed the trial as a media event, but he hoped the media attention would work to his advantage. He believed the media attention would give him the opportunity to share his views about the tyrannous federal government.

The jury convicted McVeigh after deliberating for four days. McVeigh was fully aware that the he would be found guilty and sentenced to death even before the jury handed him the verdict (Michel and Herbeck, 2001, p. 307). When the guilty verdict came, it received a large amount of media attention. Images of the dilapidated Murrah building, a rehashing of the initial investigation, and the damaging evidence against McVeigh filled the nightly news and newspapers. Reporters wrote that the verdict would give the public a sense of closure and send a message to potential terrorists.

The sentencing phase lasted eight days, and on June 13, 1997, the jury recommended McVeigh receive the death penalty. The jurors felt that none of the mitigating factors were worthy of sentencing McVeigh to a life in prison, and according to McVeigh, death was a more preferable sentence than life in prison. Stephen Jones argued that the media had produced the verdict and the sentence. He blamed the media for publishing false stories about the case and preventing McVeigh from receiving a fair trial. He thought the media had helped create public acceptance of McVeigh's fate. When prompted by Judge Matsch, McVeigh spoke the words of U.S. Supreme Court Justice Louis D. Brandeis, an advocate of individual rights: "Our government is the potent, the omnipresent teacher. For good or ill, it teaches the whole people by its example." McVeigh concluded with, "that's all I have" (Thomas, 1997).

THE CASE OF TERRY NICHOLS

Terry Nichols has been in federal custody since he turned himself in to police in Herington, Kansas, after hearing he was a suspect in the bombing.

It was during that initial nine-hour interview with the FBI that Nichols first admitted to associating with McVeigh, but he denied knowing anything about the Oklahoma City bombing. Nichols maintained that he was at his Kansas home at the time of the bombing and that McVeigh, along with an unidentified John Doe Number 2, are responsible for the bombing. Nichols's defense team, headed by Michael Tigar, claimed that McVeigh used Nichols only to attain bombing supplies, and that even if Nichols was aware of the plan, he had backed out of it long before the bombing. Nichols's story was backed up by Michael Fortier, an army buddy of Nichols and McVeigh who had served as a star witness in both cases in exchange for a twelve-year sentence.

Although Nichols and McVeigh received separate trials, in many respects the courtrooms were similar during the trials. Both trials took place in Judge Matsch's courtroom in Denver, Colorado. Larry Mackey, who worked for the prosecution team against McVeigh, headed the prosecution team against Nichols. Mackey's prosecution team resorted to the same emotional testimony of victims' family members, just as they had against McVeigh. After deliberating for forty-one hours, a jury was not convinced Nichols had "intent to kill" and could not convict Nichols of the murder charges brought against him. On December 23, 1997, he was found guilty of involuntary manslaughter and conspiracy, thus escaping the death penalty. Six months later, Judge Matsch sentenced Nichols to life in prison.

DEATH ROW

Along with McVeigh, Nichols was sent to the "Alcatraz of the Southwest," a federal prison in Florence, Colorado. The facility was considered the most secure federal prison in the United States. McVeigh shared his unit with three men: Theodore Kaczynski, Ramzi Ahmed Yousef, and Louis Felipe.

The four prisoners spent twenty-three isolated hours in their cells; one hour each day was designated for recreation. Both Kaczynski, known as the Unabomber, and McVeigh shared a hatred for the federal government, and they became good friends. Yousef, the mastermind behind the first World Trade Center bombing in 1993, was sentenced to 240 years in prison. Felipe, a Cuban native, was sentenced to life in prison plus forty more years.

Although they did not share the same unit, Nichols and McVeigh resided within the same prison walls of the federal prison until McVeigh was abruptly moved to the U.S. Penitentiary in Terre Haute, Indiana, in July 1999. Although the federal death row facility in Indiana was constructed in 1995, the government chose to not make it operational until there were twenty federal death row inmates. In 1999, the government had enough federal death row inmates for the facility to be cost-effective. McVeigh would be the fourteenth man to be federally executed since the federal death penalty was reenacted in 1988. McVeigh was convinced the government was in a hurry to put him to death (Michel and Herbeck, 2001, p. 374). In 2000 the federal courts denied McVeigh's appeal to have his conviction overturned in light of Jones's poor defense tactics. McVeigh did not plan to pursue an overturned sentence any further, especially with the inauguration of President George W. Bush (the person who would ultimately be deciding his fate). The State of Texas had a reputation for a high number of death penalty cases, and McVeigh thought that there was little chance he would be granted clemency by the incoming president.

Nichols also left the federal prison in Florence, Colorado, only to travel to Oklahoma in 2000 to face 160 murder charges that were filed against him by the State of Oklahoma. The Supreme Court had previously rejected Nichols's appeal to overturn his conviction, as Nichols claimed a key witness was excluded from his trial. The Supreme Court also ruled against Nichols, stating that the murder charges brought against him by the State of Oklahoma would not be classified as double jeopardy. Oklahoma would be permitted to bring 160 murder charges against Nichols that were not brought against him in his federal case. As a result, Oklahoma sought the death penalty against Nichols in the controversial case, but the jury deadlocked over his sentence.

McVEIGH'S MANIPULATION OF THE MEDIA

Millions of Americans had watched the horrible aftermath of the Oklahoma City bombing and the news coverage of Timothy McVeigh's trial. After the trial, many of these same Americans then witnessed Ed Bradley engage Timothy McVeigh in conversation on the news program *60 Minutes*. Beforehand, McVeigh set conditions of what could be discussed in the interview, thus barring his guilt and motivations for the bombing of the Murrah building from discussion. Instead, Bradley allowed McVeigh to compare the violence used in the Oklahoma City bombing to government actions in Sudan or Afghanistan and to the U.S.'s policies on the death penalty. McVeigh had no apology for the victims' families and expressed no regret. One could argue that the interview was a chance for McVeigh to justify his actions and finally explain to Americans his political reasoning behind the bombing. Although McVeigh felt that the news media had worked hard to demonize him, this was his chance to use the celebrated nature of his case to his advantage. Until his death, McVeigh claimed his actions were needed to fight the wrongs of a corrupted U.S. government. Some may see his actions as vengeance, but McVeigh believed he acted for larger good. He considered himself a true patriot and wanted to use his celebrity status to make sure America knew it.

McVeigh's relationship with the news media did not stop with the *60 Minutes* interview. From death row, McVeigh contacted major news networks, offering to have his execution nationally televised. He believed that televising the execution would be a way to show the public how his death was being made into a spectacle, especially those victims' family members pushing for a closed-circuit viewing of his execution. His requests were denied but not until after his outlandish offer received significant media attention (Michel and Herbeck, 2001). One could argue that McVeigh's point may have been expressed, despite the rejection of his request for a nationally televised execution.

FBI FILES, MEDIA CIRCUS, AND DEATH

Approximately one week before McVeigh's execution, which was scheduled for May 16, 2001, the FBI turned over more than 3,000 pages of witness testimony and other evidence not available to McVeigh's attorneys during the trial. The uncovered evidence consisted of FBI reports of investigation, photographs, letters, and tapes. In light of the recovered FBI files, McVeigh's execution date was postponed until June 11, 2001, by Attorney General John Ashcroft. Along with the controversial files, the Justice Department sent a statement to McVeigh's lawyers stating that the Justice Department thought the uncovered files contained no new evidence that would cast any doubt over McVeigh's guilt.[4] Although McVeigh had confessed to the bombing and had a history of waiving appeals, he thought the FBI's withholding of evidence was unfair and damaging to his case. The uncovered files were more fuel for his suspicion and hatred toward the federal government. The FBI mishap tarnished what many considered to be a near perfectly handled case by the U.S. criminal justice system. The mistake leaves much doubt to the issue of whether the criminal justice system is able to properly process a celebrated case such as the Oklahoma City bombing.

Due to the passing of the Antiterrorism and Effective Death Penalty Act in 1996, the court can only allow an appeal if new evidence showed that McVeigh would not have been convicted if the defense had the evidence during the trial. After the prosecution, defense, and judge read through the files, there was disagreement about whether the files substantiated enough reason for an appeal; nevertheless, most legal analysts agreed that McVeigh's execution would again be postponed by Judge Matsch. On June 6, to the surprise of most legal analysts, the defense's request to again extend McVeigh's execution date was denied by Judge Matsch. Although the judge made it clear that he was furious at the FBI for their mistakes, he was certain that the evidence did not leave any lingering doubts over the guilt of either McVeigh or Terry Nichols.

It is easy to understand how the execution of the man responsible for the worst terrorist act on American soil would be an important media event. Although many other celebrated cases receive extensive media attention, the amount of media attention McVeigh's execution received is especially noteworthy. It is estimated that over 1,400 journalists traveled to Terre-Haute, Indiana, to cover McVeigh's execution. On Sunday, June 10, news media outlets set up tents hundreds of yards away from the death chamber. Because the majority of animated death penalty advocates and protestors were kept at distant parks where they could be monitored, the news media personnel spent most of their time socializing with one another outside the prison walls. The news coverage of the execution lasted for hours on that notorious Monday morning, despite the fact that other than the ten reporters randomly selected to witness the execution in person, the media could only guess what was going on inside the prison. On June 11 at 7:14 a.m., federal authorities pronounced McVeigh dead by lethal injection. The stories of the ten reporters who witnessed the execution and the other family members of victims filled the airways with descriptions of McVeigh's final minutes of life. While some witnesses felt relieved, others stated that McVeigh's execution brought no closure to the death of their loved one. Interestingly, McVeigh's execution also became an international media event as foreign governments and protestors around the world rallied against the United States' continuance of their "barbaric" capital punishment. Despite the outcry by foreign nations and the extended news coverage that Monday morning, the celebrated story of Timothy McVeigh quickly became less newsworthy after that fateful morning.

SOCIAL SIGNIFICANCE OF THE OKLAHOMA CITY BOMBING

The social significance of the Oklahoma City bombing was tremendous. On April 19, 1995, U.S. citizens were faced with the most devastating terrorist act ever on American soil. Other than the New York World Trade Center bombing in 1993, terrorism was something that other countries experienced. After the Oklahoma City bombing, the American public felt vulnerable to future attacks from within their own borders and now by their fellow Americans. The bombing affected the trust developed between Americans who before did not feel they had to look at neighbors as potential threats. Before it was known that the Alfred P. Murrah Federal Building was destroyed by a homegrown terrorist, many Americans were quick to blame the popular scapegoats: Middle Eastern terrorists. When it was discovered that the bomber was actually an American, U.S. citizens were forced to adapt their social definitions of terrorism. Chermak (2002) suggested that the news media played an essential role in framing this new domestic terrorism as a larger threat coming from the right-wing militia movement. He argued that when the news media linked McVeigh to the militia movement, the public created new social perceptions and stereotypes of militia groups. In essence, the media were able to reshape public consciousness in a way similar to how they have influenced the public's shared understanding of international terrorist threats after the September 11 attacks (Chermak, 2002).

The Oklahoma City bombing also forced the government to adapt to the new social definition of terrorism. As a result of the Oklahoma City bombing, President Clinton signed the Antiterrorism and Effective Death Penalty Act.[5] The bill became law with Clinton's signature on April 24, 1996, approximately one year after the bombing. The bill gives federal authorities the ability to better monitor individuals thought to be terrorists or suspected of conspiring to commit a terrorist act. It also clarifies less concretely defined acts, such as funding a terrorist group, as unlawful. Although many claim that the passing of the legislation will aid in the prevention of terrorism, others believe it restricts individual civil liberties and restricts personal freedoms.

McVeigh perceived the political effects of the bombing differently. For example, McVeigh believed that—as a result of the Oklahoma City bombing—federal agents began to use more peaceful negotiation tactics instead of the violence used in Ruby Ridge and Waco. He also believed that the U.S. federal government was beginning to compensate for its mistakes in previous years (Michel and Herbeck, 2001). In a settlement four months after the bombing, the federal government awarded Randy Weaver and his remaining children $3.1 million. Despite a Texas jury finding the federal government not responsible for the deaths in Waco, McVeigh was pleased to hear that President Clinton considered his decision to allow federal agents to invade the Branch Davidian a mistake, and that Clinton felt personally responsible for the incident.

One could argue that the Oklahoma City bombing laid the groundwork for how the news media, government, and public would respond to the attacks on New York City and Washington, DC, on September 11, 2001. Subsequent legislation—the USA Patriot Act—has been passed since the recent terrorist acts on September 11. In addition to the liberties granted to federal authorities under the Antiterrorism and Effective Death Penalty Act, the USA Patriot Act gives federal authorities freer access to monitor the communication between suspected terrorists and those thought to be associating with them, as well as further outlining the penalties for terrorist activities. Because news media attention has shifted to the more recent terrorist attacks of September 11, the Oklahoma City bombing has taken a backseat in the public consciousness. Our primary public enemy now comes from the militant Muslims. Talk of neo-Nazis, *The Turner Diaries*, and truck bombs has settled, and, unfortunately, it will only be with another act of domestic terrorism from within U.S. boundaries that the media will speak again of the radical right threat.

RATIONALIZING THE TERROR

Although news media and government policymakers worked diligently to bring back social stability after the Oklahoma City bombing, the question of *why* still lingered for many Americans. An examination of McVeigh's life provides no simple conclusions. It is known that he hated bullies, and that he viewed the federal government as the worst of them. It is also known that he loved guns and feared that gun control legislation would strip gun ownership rights away from U.S. citizens. For McVeigh, a decorated Gulf War veteran, the standoffs at Ruby Ridge and at Waco were enough proof that the government had waged war against gun owners, and they are considered crucial to the understanding of *why* he thought it necessary to destroy a federal building that housed many federal employees. He thought that he was not on the offensive but on the defensive side of the battle. The Oklahoma City bombing was vengeance; revenge for Ruby Ridge and Waco. It was also a political statement and a call to arms for fellow gun owners. Pierce's *The Turner Diaries* made the battle between the "evil" government and American gun owners clear in McVeigh's mind, and the book ultimately served as inspiration and a roadmap to the Murrah building. For McVeigh, the Oklahoma City bombing was just the beginning: more bombs and more warfare were sure to follow.

McVeigh knew the bombing would become a celebrated media event, and even before that notorious day he had imagined how the dilapidated Murrah building would look on the nightly news. He believed the bombing would be a call to arms to the radical right watching the bombing coverage on television. Instead, many right-wing groups scurried underground for the fear of being connected to McVeigh's actions. During his trial, McVeigh hoped the media would be an avenue for his political ideologies, and Americans would realize that he did this for the good of the country. Instead, the media demonized him by calling him a "baby killer" and a "neo-Nazi." There is evidence that the media even bought stories from people close to McVeigh, reporting his jail cell confessions and crippling his chances for an unbiased trial. McVeigh believed that in addition to the leaked confessions, the intense media coverage of the O. J. Simpson trial and O.J.'s subsequent acquittal had embarrassed the U.S. criminal justice system and caused a loss of legitimacy in the public eye. As a result, McVeigh feared there would be increased pressure for the criminal justice system to convict him quickly to regain credibility. After his conviction and death sentence, McVeigh and his defense team blamed the media for an unfair trial. Although the media played an important role in the Oklahoma City bombing, it was not in the way McVeigh had hoped.

THE MEMORIAL

There is no doubt that the Oklahoma City bombing caused trauma and significant grief for citizens of Oklahoma City. Interestingly, the news media was instrumental in allowing the rest of the nation to share in the grief felt by residents of Oklahoma City. From April 19 through May, the public experienced the anguish of search and rescue efforts; public memorial services, including the opening of the Oklahoma City National Memorial on the fifth anniversary of the bombing; and televised funerals of the victims. Although the news media allowed millions to experience the pain and anguish of the bombing, they were also intent on finding closure for the American public. Whether it was after the death of Timothy McVeigh, the conviction of Terry Nichols, or the completion of the Oklahoma City National Memorial, the news media consistently hounded survivors and members of the victims' families, asking them if they had found closure since the bombing (Linenthal, 2001). Although many were pleased by the convictions and the memorial, nothing could bring their loved ones back. For them, closure was not just being able to go on with life.

In the wake of the disaster, Oklahoma City residents found a symbol of hope in a tree that survived the blast that had leveled the Murrah building. One hundred and fifty feet away from the bomb site, and amidst the fiery debris, stood a hardy tree protruding from the asphalt, today known as the "Survivor Tree." The Survivor Tree now stands on an overlook gazing onto the Oklahoma City National Memorial. Carved into the stone wall that curves around the outlook are the following words: "The spirit of this city and this nation will not be defeated; our deeply rooted faith sustains us." Visitors standing beneath the "Survivor Tree" can look onto the "Field of Empty Chairs," 168 bronze and stone chairs placed in rows where the Murrah building once sat. Whether the news media's simplistic attempts at finding national closure after the bombing were successful, many people have used the Oklahoma City National Memorial, if for nothing else, as a way to remember those that perished. As for closure, that may never be found by some. They just go on with life, surviving.

NOTES

1. In *American Terrorist* (2001), Lou Michel and Dan Herbeck, two Buffalo News reporters, tell the story of Timothy McVeigh and the Oklahoma City bombing after conducting over seventy-five hours of interviews with Timothy McVeigh, and also interviews with Timothy McVeigh's family, friends, coworkers, army buddies, the legal actors involved in his case, among many others.

2. For two years, the Order, a white supremacist, anti-Semite organization acting out the fictitious story of *The Turner Diaries* went on a two-year terrorist rampage killing a Jew, Odinist (Mormon), and police officers. The group, led by Christian Identity follower, Robert Mathews, also committed armed robbery, stealing millions and donating the money to various white-supremacist organizations. By 1985, all Order members had been killed or imprisoned. Mathews died in a shootout with police in which the house he was in burned down.

3. *First Blood* (1982), starring Sylvester Stallone, is a movie about a Green Beret Vietnam veteran who drifts from town to town searching for war buddies and food. After being arrested by a corrupt, abusive sheriff, Stallone escapes jail to start a one-man war by arming himself in the Oregon Mountains.

4. The statement by the Department of Justice Spokesperson, Mindy Tucker, can be found at http://govinfo.about.com/blagencyrelease06.htm

5. The Antiterrorism and Effective Death Penalty Act can be located under Pub. L. No.104-32 TitleVII 110 Stat.1216 (1996).

REFERENCES

Bispkupic, J. (1999, March 9). Supreme Court rebuffs McVeigh's appeal; convicted Oklahoma City bomber claimed trial was tainted by publicity, juror prejudice. *The Washington Post*, p. 2.

Chermak, S. M. (2002). *Searching for a demon: The media construction of the militia movement*. Boston: Northeastern University Press.

Davis, R. T. (1995, April 24). Capturing McVeigh: Key lead, lots of luck. *USA Today*, p. 2.

Ezzard, M. (1997, June 2). Judge deserves credit; McVeigh trial conduct restores faith in justice. *The Atlanta Journal and Constitution*, p. 8.

Hamm, M. S. (1997). *Apocalypse in Oklahoma: Waco and Ruby Ridge revenged*. Boston: Northeastern University Press.

Levins, H. (1997, May 30). McVeigh's quiet trial avoided what fueled the Simpson circus. *St. Louis Post-Dispatch*, p. 1.

Lewis, N. (2001, May 13). Nichols, citing FBI papers, files new appeal. *The New York Times*, p. 17.

Linenthal, E. T. (2001). *The unfinished bombing: Oklahoma City in American memory*. New York: Oxford University Press.

Locy, T., and O'Driscoll, P. (2001, June 1). McVeigh lawyers: FBI guilty of fraud. Bomber files for execution delay. *USA Today*, p. 1.

Michel, L., and Herbeck, D. (2001). *American terrorist: Timothy McVeigh and the Oklahoma City bombing.* New York: HarperCollins.

Neiwert, D. A. (1999). *In God's country: The patriot movement and the Pacific Northwest.* Pullman, WA: Washington State University Press.

Romano, L. (2001a, May 13). McVeigh lawyers study FBI papers; three options available to defense in seeking new trial or sentence. *The Washington Post*, p. 7.

Romano, L. (2001b, June 7). Judge refuses to delay execution of McVeigh. *The Washington Post*, p. 1.

Thomas, J. (1997, August 14). McVeigh speaks at last, fleetingly and obscurely. *New York Times*, p. 14.

Torry, S. (1995, May 8). Finding counsel for McVeigh a true test of legal system. *The Washington Post*, p. 7.

Index

About the Editors and
the Contributors

FRANKIE Y. BAILEY is Associate Professor at the State University of New York, Albany. With Steven Chermak, she is co-editor of *Media Representations of September 11* (Praeger, 2003) and *Popular Culture, Crime, and Justice* (1998). She is author of *Out of the Woodpile: Black Characters in Crime and Detective Fiction* (Greenwood, 1991), which was nominated for the Mystery Writers of America 1992 Edgar Award for Criticism and Biography, and *"Law Never Here": A Social History of African American Responses to Issues of Crime and Justice* (Praeger, 1999).

STEVEN CHERMAK is Associate Professor and Director of Graduate Affairs in the Department of Criminal Justice at Indiana University. He is the author of *Searching for a Demon: The Media Construction of the Militia Movement* (2002) and *Victims in the News: Crime and the American News Media* (1995).

HEIDI AHL-QUANBECK is a Ph.D. student at the Department of Criminal Justice and Political Science, North Dakota State University.

GREGG BARAK is Professor of criminology and criminal justice at Eastern Michigan University and visiting distinguished professor at the College of Justice and Safety, Eastern Kentucky University. He is the author or editor of eleven books, including the award-winning *Gimme Shelter: A Social*

History of Homelessness in Contemporary America and his most recent *Violence and Nonviolence: Pathways to Understanding*.

LEE BERNSTEIN is Assistant Professor of History at the University at New Paltz (SUNY). He is the author of *The Greatest Menace: Organized Crime in Cold War America*.

KEVIN BUCKLER is Assistant Professor in the College of Liberal Arts, Department of Criminal Justice, University of Texas at Brownsville and Texas Southmost College. He has published research in the *Journal of Criminal Justice* that examines the collateral consequences of felony convictions, and he has recently completed research examining the historical context and current state practices with regard to rape shield protections.

GRAY CAVENDER is Professor in the School of Justice and Social Inquiry, Arizona State University. His publications include *Corporate Crime Under Attack: The Ford Pinto Case and Beyond* (coauthored by Francis Cullen and William Maakestad) and *Entertaining Crime: Television Reality Programs* (coauthored by Mark Fishman and Aldine de Gruyter).

FRANCIS T. CULLEN is Distinguished Research Professor at the University of Cincinnati and President of the American Society of Criminology. His publications include *Criminological Theory: Context and Consequences, 3rd ed.* (coauthored by Lilly J. Robert and Richard A. Ball); *Combating Corporate Crime: Local Prosecutors at Work* (coauthored by Michael L. Benson); *Criminology, 2nd ed.* (coauthored by Gresham M. Sykes); *Corporate Crime Under Attack: The Ford Pinto Case and Beyond* (coauthored by William J. Maakestad and Gray Cavender); *Rethinking Crime and Deviance Theory: The Emergence of a Structuring Tradition*; and *Reaffirming Rehabilitation* (coauthored by Karen E. Gilbert).

KELLY R. DAMPHOUSSE is Associate Professor in the Department of Sociology, University of Oklahoma. Damphousse has published numerous scholarly articles and is involved in several research projects, including the American Terrorism Study.

T. DAVID EVANS is Professor in the Department of Sociology and Criminal Justice, University of North Carolina at Wilmington. He has published articles with colleagues in *Criminology, Justice Quarterly, American Sociological Review* and other sociology, criminology, and criminal justice journals.

LAURA L. FINLEY is Adjunct Professor of Sociology at the University of Northern Colorado. She is currently working on a book titled *Piss Off! How Privacy Violations in Public Schools are Alienating America's Youth*. Other publications include "Using Content Analysis Projects in the Introduction to Criminal Justice Classroom" (in the journal *Teaching Sociology*); and "Teachers' Perceptions of School Violence Issues: A Case Study" (*Journal of School Violence*).

BENJAMIN FLEURY-STEINER is Assistant Professor in the Department of Sociology and Criminal Justice, University of Delaware. His publications include *Jurors' Stories of Death: How America's Death Penalty Invests in Inequality*; *Limestone: A Sociolegal Autopsy of Preventable Deaths in One Alabama Prison*; *The New Civil Rights Research: A Constitutive Perspective* (edited collection with Laura Beth Nielsen and Idit Kostiner).

JEFFREY A. GRUENEWALD is a Ph.D. student at the Department of Criminal Justice, Indiana University–Bloomington.

TOMAS GUILLEN is Associate Professor in the Communication Department at Seattle University. He often is asked to discuss law enforcement and criminal justice issues on CNN, FOX, and other national broadcast news programs. Before joining Seattle University, Guillen worked as a reporter for 20 years at several daily newspapers, including the *Seattle Times, Omaha World-Herald*, and the *Tucson Citizen*. In 1988 he and a colleague were Pulitzer Prize finalists for their articles on a serial killer, and in 1995 his stories on crime laboratories won the Silver Gavel in the American Bar Association investigative reporting competition. In 1990 he coauthored *The Search for the Green River Killer*. The book was a *New York Times* bestseller. In 1995 he authored the book *Toxic Love*, which is based on a poisoning case in Omaha.

AMY KEARNS is a Ph.D. student at the Department of Criminal Justice, Indiana University–Bloomington.

SARA L. KNOX is Senior Lecturer in the School of Humanities, University of Western Sydney. Her publications include a book titled *Murder: a Tale of Modern American Life* and many essays on violence and contemporary culture. The most recent of these is "Crime, Law and Symbolic Order" (*Theory and Event*).

JASON LAWSON is a graduate student in the Department of Sociology, University of Oklahoma.

WILLIAM J. MAAKESTAD is Professor of Management and Co-director of the Program for the Study of Ethics, Western Illinois University. His publications include *Corporate Crime Under Attack: The Ford Pinto Case and Beyond*; "Corporate Homicide" (*New Law Journal*); and "*State v. Ford Motor*

Co.: Constitutional, Utilitarian and Moral Perspectives" (*Saint. Louis University Law Journal*).

SHELLEY L. SCHLIEF is a Ph.D. Student at the School of Criminal Justice, University at Albany (SUNY).

BRENT L. SMITH is Professor in the Department of Sociology, University of Arkansas. He is the author of *Pipe Bombs and Pipe Dreams: Terrorism in America*. He is involved in several major research projects, including the American Terrorism Study.